Andean Diaspora

New World Diasporas

UNIVERSITY PRESS OF FLORIDA / STATE UNIVERSITY SYSTEM

Florida A&M University, Tallahassee
Florida Atlantic University, Boca Raton
Florida Gulf Coast University, Ft. Myers
Florida International University, Miami
Florida State University, Tallahassee
University of Central Florida, Orlando
University of Florida, Gainesville
University of North Florida, Jacksonville
University of South Florida, Tampa
University of West Florida, Pensacola

New World Diasporas
Edited by Kevin A. Yelvington

This series seeks to stimulate critical perspectives on diaspora processes in the New World. Representations of "race" and ethnicity, the origins and consequences of nationalism, migratory streams and the advent of transnationalism, the dialectics of "homelands" and diasporas, trade networks, gender relations in immigrant communities, the politics of displacement and exile, and the utilization of the past to serve the present are among the phenomena addressed by original, provocative research in disciplines such as anthropology, history, political science, and sociology.

Andean Diaspora

The Tiwanaku Colonies and the Origins
of South American Empire

Paul S. Goldstein

University Press of Florida

Gainesville · Tallahassee · Tampa · Boca Raton
Pensacola · Orlando · Miami · Jacksonville · Ft. Myers

Copyright 2005 by Paul S. Goldstein
Printed in the United States of America on recycled, acid-free paper
All rights reserved

10 09 08 07 06 05 6 5 4 3 2 1

Library of Congress Cataloging-in-Publication Data
Goldstein, Paul S., 1959–
Andean diaspora: the Tiwanaku colonies and the origins
of South American empire / Paul S. Goldstein.
p. cm.—(New World diasporas)
Includes bibliographical references and index.
ISBN 0-8130-2774-8 (alk. paper)
1. Tiwanaku culture. 2. Indians of South America—Bolivia—Tiwanaku
River Valley—Migrations. 3. Indians of South America—Bolivia—Tiwanaku
River Valley—Politics and government. 4. Indians of South America—
Bolivia—Tiwanaku River Valley—Antiquities. 5. Tiwanaku River Valley
(Bolivia)—Antiquities. I. Title. II. New World diasporas series
F3319.1.T55G665   2005
984'.00498—dc22   2004061173

The University Press of Florida is the scholarly publishing agency
for the State University System of Florida, comprising Florida A&M
University, Florida Atlantic University, Florida Gulf Coast University,
Florida International University, Florida State University, University
of Central Florida, University of Florida, University of North Florida,
University of South Florida, and University of West Florida.

University Press of Florida
15 Northwest 15th Street
Gainesville, FL 32611-2079
http://www.upf.com

Contents

Figures and Maps

Tables

Series Editor's Foreword

An awareness of the role of the state and the international state system is certainly a central feature of contemporary research on diasporic processes. However, the particular and historical nature of the development of the specific states in question—and indeed the notion of state formation as a historical, multilayered process—often eludes those writers from divergent disciplines who work on modern and postmodern diasporas. And this is the case despite the lessons provided in much of the cutting-edge literature on the state over the past decade, such as the heralded and influential book *Everyday Forms of State Formation: Revolution and the Negotiation of Rule in Modern Mexico*, edited by Gilbert M. Joseph and Daniel Nugent (Durham: Duke University Press, 1994), where the emphasis is on the dialectic between state formation and expansion, and more "cultural" processes—under which could fall (although it is not a concern of the contributors to the Joseph and Nugent book) the development of diasporic identities. This blind spot on state formation leads to other problems when it comes to tracing diasporas. In some work, the state is not only assumed to exist as an apparatus of governance, influencing but ultimately separate from the identities we carry into civil society, but it is also assumed to antedate the dispersal of its subject peoples.

By contrast, in *Andean Diaspora* archaeologist Paul S. Goldstein is avowedly concerned to account for the nature of the state—a preoccupation of North American anthropological theorizing for many years now—and he is further concerned to relate the state formation process to the movement and settlement of people with some sense of a common cultural identity. In this closely argued book, Goldstein marshals extensive and detailed historical and archaeological evidence on the Tiwanaku polity that, from its highland core region in present-day Peru, colonized the lowland agricultural valleys around the years 500–1000 of the Common Era. Rather than conceive of the Tiwanaku state as already formed and consolidated before this colonization occurred, Goldstein places the movement across time and space of more or less loose assemblages of people who considered themselves somehow affiliated as central to the story of Tiwanaku state formation. This movement emanating from the Tiwanaku core region cannot be seen as being peripheral or as an afterthought, but is indeed exactly what Tiwanaku state formation entailed. At the same time, the complexities of multiple identities and the crosscutting allegiances demanded by membership in different *ayllus*, a kind of corporate group, meant that Tiwanaku colonization was a heterogeneous rather than homogeneous affair. Rather than a top-down, elite-directed, and centralized (and centralizing) process, a rather acephalous, decentralized, and segmented "structure" (if that is the proper word here) emerged. Rather than cultural uniformity, Tiwanaku colonists carried complex and often conflictive identities with them into diaspora. In developing his diasporic model of state formation and expansion, Goldstein, following ethnohistorian John V. Murra, refers to the result as "archipelagos" of colonial settlement.

Goldstein's book is remarkable for a number of reasons. These include the following: One is that it adds substantially to our knowledge of state formation. We now know that state formation is not just about the materiality of domination. Perhaps one reason this comes through is because of the case at hand. Goldstein argues that Tiwanaku state formation was not as coercive as that of other more famous Andean states, but meant, instead, the establishment of internally differentiated subjective frameworks that arose from cultural materialities, human ecologies, and purposive agency. Because of the time depth of Goldstein's process-oriented research, state formation in this mode is thrown into bold relief for the contemporary reader, and thus we can no longer take the formation and expansion of the state, and the basic uniformity of types of states, for granted. This leads to a second important contribution. Goldstein takes on what he calls the "globalist" view of state formation, a school of thought holding that state societies act as systems, increasing hierarchy, centralization, and specialization as they become more economically developed and politically complex. Goldstein presents a sustained, and successful, challenge to this view and thus contributes in important ways in setting the new agenda in Andeanist archaeology. A third is his understanding of diasporas as "ethnicity in motion," recognizing the difficulties of investigating these (by definition) mobile social forms through the archaeological record. He emphasizes the maintenance and development of identities through differing cultural practices between diasporic Tiwanaku and locals. This case takes us beyond the familiar concept of "trade diasporas" because diasporic communities of the Andes were involved in other kinds of economic activities. And finally, not only does Goldstein prove himself to be a meticulous scholar, patiently presenting a wealth of archaeological evidence, but he also shows himself to be a theorist intent on convincing the reader that the alternatives are not that attractive, one method of which includes self-reflexive and frank discussions of the use of archaeological analogies, their seductiveness and their dangers.

In the end, while caution is certainly called for in purporting to transform social science concepts by applying a set of empirical materials that challenges the established epistemological order, the wider importance of this book is that it will make us rethink many expansive states in the ancient world. It could, for example, provide a conceptual underpinning for what are now being seen as hybrid and interconnected social and cultural formations, the *logiques métisses* of precolonial Africa, as Jean-Loup Amselle calls them (see his "Anthropology and Historicity," *History and Theory* 32(4) [1993]: 12–31). Widening the lens a bit further, this book also provides lessons for those of us who see as the object of our study the creation and movement of diasporas in the modern and postmodern worlds. We need to rethink the development of states and diasporas as complementary and conterminous and begin to reevaluate the diaspora-state interface.

Kevin A. Yelvington
Series Editor

Acknowledgments

In late September of 1983, Robert Feldman and Michael Moseley hitched a ride in a mining company Cessna over the Moquegua Valley. As a graduate student in South America for the first time, I remember them returning to the field house shaking their heads at the size and scale of an archaeological site called Omo that we had somehow missed in our windshield survey. I could not predict how much this discovery was to change the course of my life. Over the next 17 years, the challenge of Omo and Tiwanaku expansion became a great constant in my research. That first season, I was privileged to participate in a loosely organized but amazingly productive research consortium known as Programa Contisuyo. Work in the 1983 and 1984 seasons was led by Moseley, Feldman, Garth Bawden, and Luis Watanabe, with a team that included Pat Essenpreis, Chip Stanish, Marc Bermann, Dave Jessup, Dan Rogers, Edmundo de la Vega, Antonio Oquiche, Nené Lozada, George Morse, and Don Rice. Those were exciting days.

I went back to Omo to direct dissertation research in 1986 and 1987 under a Fulbright-Hays Dissertation Fellowship. At this time, I had the opportunity to work with a special group of students from the Catholic University of Arequipa, many of whom have become fine archaeologists and friends for life. The Omo project also was fortunate to count on the assistance of topography students of the Instituto Técnico José Carlos Mariategui and logistical support from Southern Peru Copper Corporation. I must thank professors Don Rice, Jane Buikstra, and Alan Kolata at the University of Chicago and my spectacularly generous supervisors at American Museum of Natural History, Charles Spencer and Craig Morris, for their guidance and support on doctoral and postdoctoral writing.

Dissertation done, I could not stay away from revising my own work. First, I returned to work at the Omo temple in 1990, supported by a grant from the Wenner-Gren Foundation and counting on the skills and good humor of Adán Umire and Augusto Cardona. In 1991 and 1992 I followed the Tiwanaku south of the border with a survey of Chile's Azapa Valley. I am indebted to Ivan Muñoz for the invitation; to Raul Rocha and the staff and faculty of the Museo San Miguel de Azapa for their hospitality and support;

and to Guillermo Focacci, Percy Dauelsberg, Calogero Santoro, Mario Rivera, and Oscar Espoueys for their lively consultation. Most recently I have returned to the original scene of the crime, directing the Moquegua Archaeological Survey (MAS). This was supported by 1993–94 grants from the Wenner-Gren Foundation and the J. M. Kaplan Fund. My work on the habitation sectors of the Chen Chen site in 1995 was part of an emergency salvage effort codirected by Bruce Owen, Antonio Oquiche, Ryan Williams, and myself and involving a host of wonderful Peruvian and international volunteers. This bootstrap salvage project not only rescued invaluable data from a site that no longer exists but started a positive trend toward institutional support for saving archaeological resources endangered by development. The 1999 salvage investigations at Omo Alto M16 were supported by funds from INADE Proyecto Especial Pasto Grande.

In 1998 and 1999, a Department of Education Fulbright-Hays Fellowship, NSF Standard Grant Award 9809720, a Dartmouth College junior faculty fellowship, and an H. John Heinz III grant gave me the opportunity to devote a full year to Moquegua. It was a good year for grants, but be careful what you wish for. Moquegua in the late 1990s was a living model of folk migration, with implications for Tiwanaku in the seventh through tenth centuries that could not be ignored. My year of regional settlement pattern study radically changed many of my ideas about Tiwanaku colonies. These revelations made this a later book than planned but I hope a better one. Very special thanks are due to Mónika Barrionuevo and Frank Magilligan, my codirector and coauthors on the MAS project, and to my invaluable friends in Moquegua, Andrew Mitchell and Roberto and Betty de Olazabel.

These projects were conducted in agreement with the Instituto Nacional de Cultura under permits INC 003-94-CNTCICMA/INC, INC C/060-98 and 415/INC. I thank all of the dedicated civil servants who are doing their best to stem the tide of site destruction and looting in Peru. None of my recent research, nor future studies, would have been possible without the heroic efforts of the Asociación Contisuyo, and the Contisuyo Museum staff who have miraculously turned the detritus of all this fieldwork into a collections resource that, sadly, will probably outlive most of the Tiwanaku sites of Moquegua.

I am indebted to the scores of students, archaeologists, and friends who have assisted me in field research—far too many to name everyone. Some with whom I worked extensively were Matthew Bandy, Augusto Cardona, Sidney Carter, Tara Carter, Ruby Chan, Cecilia Chavez, Amanda Cohen, Allison Davis, Edmundo de la Vega, Christine DuRocher, Antonio Gamonal, Corina Kellner, Ernesto Lazaro, Timothy McAndrews, Antonio Oquiche, Patricia Palacios, Erika Simborth, Yamilex Tejeda, Kayoko Toshihara, Adán

Umire, and Brian Zentmyer. At home I counted on the work of research assistants and volunteers Matt Erie, Jessica Webster, Elise Berman, and Denis Rydjeski at Dartmouth and of Stacie Wilson, Pepe Aguilar, Adolfo Muñiz, Vanessa Van de Weg, Liz Monroe, and Emily Wick at University of California, San Diego.

Archaeology is a collaborative effort, and I must thank many experts who have consulted on the Moquegua Tiwanaku collections. Marc Bermann's inventory and initial aging and sexing of skeletal material was augmented in detailed analysis by Jane Buikstra and Lisa Hoshower in 1988. A preliminary analysis of the Omo M16 burials was undertaken by Deborah Blom in 1999. Kari Sandness's pioneering isotope analysis of Omo samples opened the door to future studies of Tiwanaku diet. Analysis by Amy Oakland Rodman at Omo in 1986 gave me an entirely new appreciation of our textile finds. William Conklin and Mary Frame have also generously consulted on Tiwanaku and Formative textiles. Jane Wheeler, Katerina Ditmar, and Susan de France have shared ideas on Tiwanaku faunal collections, David Goldstein has consulted on macrobotanical remains, Heather Lechtman has examined Tiwanaku bronze, and Richard Burger has sourced Tiwanaku obsidian.

This is an ambitious book, and I only hope its grasp does not exceed its reach. I have tried to keep up with a torrent of important recent research on Wari and Tiwanaku in other regions, but publishing deadlines always make this a difficult task. It seems that there is always one more new and exciting thing to read these days. My thanks go to John Janusek, Martin Giesso, Ryan Williams, and others who have shared advance versions of works that I have been able to cite, and my apologies to authors of works that came out just too late to be incorporated in my analysis (notably Chip Stanish's *Ancient Titicaca* and volume 2 of *Tiwanaku and Its Hinterland*, edited by Alan Kolata). Guillermo Algaze, Brian Bauer, Elise Berman, Deborah Blom, Allison Davis, Jana Fortier, Arthur Joyce, Tom Levy, Denis Rydjeski, Sloan Williams, and reviewers Michael Moseley and Helaine Silverman have shared their perspectives on sections of this manuscript. I also appreciate the constructive responses of numerous colleagues to papers I have presented at the Midwest Conference on Andean and Amazonian Archaeology and Ethnohistory, the Northeast Conference on Andean and Amazonian Archaeology and Ethnohistory, and meetings of the Society for American Archaeology.

This book is for my parents Bernard and Marilyn, and above all for Jana and Sarah, two fearless souls who help me daily to live with, learn, and love the joys and terrors of a two-career anthropological household. Today in Moquegua, next year in Kathmandu?

Finally, I thank the people of Moquegua, past and present, and especially the Tiwanaku who lived, worked, and died at Omo, Chen Chen, and Río Muerto. The Tiwanaku tolerated my attempts to understand them and always kept the work interesting by adding a new dimension to every facet, and a new facet to every dimension—usually just when I thought I had it all figured out. I hope this book is as true to them as it possibly can be and that learning about their lives and culture can teach us a little bit about ourselves.

|

State Expansion

This book explores Tiwanaku and the role of colonization in the expansion of ancient states. I argue that Pre-Columbian Andean states originated not through conquests led by charismatic warlords but as ethnicity in motion: a demographic process of colonization that was only later followed by political consolidation. I propose that the expansive Tiwanaku polity was not the coercive centralized state structure that is commonly assumed but a consensual confederation among peoples of distinctive ethnic and political identities who shared some common identities that we now call Tiwanaku culture. These nested identities—both the distinctive and the common—spread with Tiwanaku colonists across a wide diaspora of enclave communities. Too often, we assume that expansive states grew only from the top down at the behest of powerful ruling elites. The structural variability and internal diversity of the Tiwanaku diaspora indicate that the Tiwanaku polity was pluralistic and far less hierarchical than is commonly believed. My redefinition of Tiwanaku expansion as ethnicity in motion recasts ancient state growth in the bottom-up dynamics of identity. I infer that some early states in the Andes, and perhaps throughout the ancient world, were far more segmentary than has been presumed by neoevolutionist political economists and remained so even as they grew into expansive empires.

The seeds for this book were sown by research in the Department of Moquegua, Peru, in the late 1980s, when I documented the massive colonization of lowland agricultural valleys by highland Tiwanaku colonists in the seventh through tenth centuries A.D.. My studies of household archaeology at the Tiwanaku colonial sites of Omo and subsequent excavations of Omo's Tiwanaku-style temple in 1990 favored what I call a "globalist" interpretation of Tiwanaku—as a monolithic state "core" that dominated peripheral outliers. My discovery of large, well-organized enclaves of Tiwanaku peoples in distant regions supported a globalist model of Tiwanaku as a proto-imperial expansive state. The best available explanations for Tiwanaku lowland colonization, one of the earliest episodes of Andean state expansion, seemed to lie in a model of peripheral annexation under the central direction of a bureaucratic state.

This is not, however, the same book that I would have written ten or even five years ago. In the late 1990s, I chose to return to Moquegua to direct the Moquegua Archaeological Survey (MAS), a systematic settlement pattern study in this densest region of Tiwanaku colonization. My findings provide a critical regional counterpoint to the site-centered perspective of my earlier work at Omo. Reconnaissance results, now being supplemented by multisite surface investigations, excavations, and a growing series of dates, demand a new interpretation of the Tiwanaku occupation as a multiethnic landscape in the Pre-Columbian past. These new data alone would have led me to reexamine many of my own preconceptions about Tiwanaku colonization and the nature of the Tiwanaku polity.

The present reevaluation of Tiwanaku colonization goes deeper than the simple addition of new settlement pattern data, however. First, many things have changed in the archaeology of the south-central Andes since I first considered Tiwanaku expansion. In the 1980s, when Peru was a difficult and often risky place to work and Bolivia was closed to international archaeological projects, research programs on the Tiwanaku culture were few, and understanding of Tiwanaku as a political entity was in its infancy. By the late 1990s, however, an explosion of new research on Tiwanaku and its peripheries had greatly increased our knowledge of this neglected part of the ancient world. As a new generation of Tiwanaku specialists produces dozens of theses, dissertations, and articles, the debate over Tiwanaku as a social and political entity has entered a spirited adolescence that will eventually lead to a mature synthesis.

More important, the south-central Andean region is changing in ways that might not have been foreseen in the late 1980s. These changes have had a profound effect on rural society in southern Peru. Although Moquegua was one of Peru's wealthiest agricultural provinces in the colonial and republican eras, years of neglect left the region an economic backwater through most of the twentieth century, with its richest farmlands controlled by the descendants of old *hacendado* families—often absentee descendants. With the decline of the Shining Path and other terrorist insurgencies in the 1990s, Peru experienced rapid incorporation into the global economy and a long-delayed burst of internal development. The effects of these changes were felt even in rural regions like Moquegua, where both government and private sector investment spurred enormous irrigation projects, roads, power lines, and other infrastructural developments.

Figure 1.1. Highland Aymara woman from Carumas. PSG photo.

By the late 1990s, the complexion of agricultural wealth in the Moquegua Valley had changed dramatically. Arriving first as itinerant herders, hired hands, or tenants, Aymara-speaking highlanders from the upper reaches of the Department of Moquegua found that their hard labor at irrigation agriculture could make even the most marginal of the valley-bottom lands far more productive than their own homelands. The old families of Moquegua called all these newcomers Carumeños, after the highland town of Carumas, but this was only one of their many *sierra* home communities. From a trickle to a stream to a flood, the immigration of these twentieth-century highlanders transformed the valley as the most successful early immigrants claimed or bought the best land available and invited kinfolk to follow.

The new colonists both revitalized the land and created a new cultural landscape. As our archaeological survey crew walked the length and breadth of the Moquegua Valley, we everywhere saw the shantytowns, squatters' shacks, and cactus boundary markers of highland immigrants who laid claim to every square meter of potentially irrigable land. Both old and new immigrants returned frequently to their *sierra* communities and proudly wore the distinctive traditional dress of their highland Aymara towns, both in the

Figure 1.2. Carumeña woman in Moquegua. PSG photo.

countryside and in the town of Moquegua. The wealthiest and most influential figures in the valley were the earliest highland immigrants who had purchased or obtained title to vacant lands. A few of these more successful early arrivals could be seen making large bank deposits, driving new trucks, and building some of the largest homes in town.

I first met Doña Cecilia Mamani, one of these highland homesteaders or *invasores* at the Cerro Trapiche archaeological site in 1999.[1] Her story is typical of this new Andean diaspora. A single mother, she had arrived in Moquegua a decade earlier from the highland Aymara village of Muylaque, bringing two children and a determination to build a better life. During a drought a few years before, her father had passed through Moquegua, perhaps with his herds or to trade. He did not stay, but he noticed a few vacant locations just above the existing canals that he thought might be made green if water could be brought to them. He marked them with stone cairns just in case, because he had many children and only a small farm in Muylaque.

Doña Cecilia's father never returned to Moquegua, and being the eldest daughter, she seldom thought about his stories of opportunities in the lowlands as she married and began a family. It was not until her husband left her for another woman that she decided to become one of the first from her village to move to Moquegua. She began her life in diaspora in a small

Figure 1.3. Moquegua City. PSG photo.

chosita, a woven mat hut that she built to mark her place on the lands her father had scouted. Supporting herself with the backbreaking work of sorting river stones and gravel for construction, she gradually accrued the capital to legalize her land claim or *denuncia*, obtaining title from the state by proving it viable for farming.[2] With this modest success, she invited her younger siblings and cousins from Muylaque to help her farm, tend herds, and dig and maintain the canal that irrigates the sliver of land that the Mamanis carved out of the desert hillslope. Life was still hard, but the lower slopes of Cerro Trapiche were green for the first time in centuries, and the Mamanis were landholders in Moquegua. Far from assimilating to their new land, however, the Mamanis still speak of themselves as people of Muylaque, maintaining close contacts with their homeland relatives and frequently traveling there to visit and bring produce.

Hearing stories like Doña Cecilia's made it obvious to me that Moquegua's present-day Aymara migration was inextricably linked to enduring ties of community identity and had little to do with the kind of globalist-directed colonization I had described for Tiwanaku a thousand years before. True, unlike the Tiwanaku, the Carumeños live within the parameters of the modern Peruvian state and a global capitalist economy. In Moquegua, the state's massive Pasto Grande canal irrigation project, the creation of a Bolivian-Peruvian free trade zone, and the completion of the Ilo–La Paz highway all played some role in encouraging migration. However, state policies alone could not explain what was motivating and integrating these communities in motion. The central government's role in inducing migration seemed indirect, unforeseen, and usually unintended. Indeed, the Carumeño invasion has been the bane of Moquegua's Euro-American ruling elite, as the old political balance has been permanently upended. I began to wonder whether any centralized state, past or present, could motivate this kind of popular migration.

If we can imagine Moquegua without banks and trucks, the massive peasant migrations of highland Aymara farmers to this lowland valley uncannily evoke the diaspora of Tiwanaku colonization a millennium ago. Yet as I observed the Carumeño "invasion" of the middle Moquegua Valley firsthand, it became clear to me that a central authority need not instigate, guide, or direct popular colonization. This late twentieth-century diaspora of Carumeño colonists led me to suspect that the organizing fabric of their migrant communities was woven of complex webs of kinship and nested identities. If even a modern nation state cannot regulate migration through a centralized hierarchy, why should we assume that an ancient state like Tiwanaku could? Could something else explain the expansion of Tiwanaku peoples into the same region a millennium earlier?

This question has led me to reexamine the dynamics of ancient state expansion. In the present chapter I argue that globalist interpretations of expansive states, whether they focus on imperial conquest and territorial incorporation or hegemonic "world systems," all share a similarly limited centrist perspective. Although these regimes differ in their mechanisms of control, they all assume that the dynamics of core-periphery relations were primarily dictated by decision making from a single central source. I propose that in many cases early state expansion might best be considered from an agency-oriented perspective that takes into account the segmentary, heterogeneous, and internally conflictive nature of corporate groups within early states and on their peripheries.

In chapter 2 I review one such model for colonial state expansion in the south-central Andes. I base my reconstruction on ethnographic and ethnohistoric evidence for the social formations known as *ayllus* and suggest that Andean polities comprised a nested and crosscutting array of these often conflictive corporate groups. When Andean states expanded through colonization, migrants took with them this complex structure of identities. The implication of this diasporic model for state expansion is a form of nonterritorial and only partially centralized state control, which I describe as an "archipelago" of colonial settlement.

The applicability of a diasporic state expansion model to ancient Tiwanaku hinges upon data suggesting that the Tiwanaku state was an extraordinarily complex and heterogeneous amalgam of component entities and that it was far less politically centralized than is commonly believed. Chapters 3 and 4 consider this current debate over the political economy and cultural diversity of the Tiwanaku core region and its peripheries. In chapter 3, after reviewing the history of Tiwanaku studies, I consider research at the Tiwanaku site itself and other sites of its *altiplano* core region. Conflicting interpretations of the Tiwanaku core have sparked a lively controversy over the degree of state control over urban and rural production. Chapter 4 follows this debate into the Tiwanaku peripheries, introducing research on the relationship of the Tiwanaku culture and power to peripheral regions.

In chapters 5 through 8 I present the results of my own archaeological settlement pattern studies and household, mortuary, and monumental archaeology in the Moquegua Valley. The Moquegua case study informs on how Tiwanaku became an important prototype for later Andean empires. Finally, in chapter 9, I discuss how the diverse organization of colonial settlements, public rituals, and diasporic identities throughout Tiwanaku's peripheral territories suggest a very different kind of expansive state than the monolithic entity that many believe Tiwanaku to have been.

The Globalist View of Ancient State Expansion

Whether conquered, annexed, colonized, or more subtly incorporated into a socioeconomic sphere, peripheries bear witness to the ebb and flow of a state's fortunes over time. Unlike homeland areas, where political and cultural affiliation may be more persistent, peripheries remain highly sensitive to power shifts and fluctuations in central authority through conquest and consolidation (Schreiber 1992:38). An understanding of the integrative process in the peripheries of ancient states can help us view complex societies as dynamic interregional systems that integrate a variety of social, economic, and political subsystems. Studying peripheries can therefore help us discover how entire state systems were assembled and integrated.

Traditional discussions of the incorporation of peripheries by ancient states have followed what can be called globalist approaches to state expansion. Since the 1970s, a majority of archaeologists has emphasized systemic analysis in the formation and growth of state-level polities. Generally, these interpretations assume that complex societies add levels of hierarchical administration as social and economic complexity increases. Increasing complexity and scale are related to systemic processes of segregation (the internal differentiation and specialization of subsystems) and centralization (the linkage between the various subsystems and the highest order controls; Flannery 1972:409). Accepting that information flow and regulatory decision making are the essential features of state integration implies that complex societies should demonstrate a hierarchical distribution of settlements by population and size, with a minimally three-tiered hierarchy taken as the criterion of statehood (Wright 1977; Wright and Johnson 1975). To put it another way, the complexity of a society is directly related to the efficacy of its top-down organization.

These generalizations have served archaeology well and are supported by an enormous body of comparative empirical data from civilizations worldwide. Nonetheless the assumption that social complexity is invariably correlated with increasing social hierarchy may not be true in all cases. It has been pointed out that globalist views of ancient states tend to portray states as monolithic actors in these systemic analyses (Blanton et al. 1996; Blanton 1998:140; Brumfiel 1992, 1994:3). Nowhere is this more apparent than in archaeological approaches to state expansion. It is assumed that expansive states were integrated by and from powerful core societies that acted with a unified intent as they imposed their will on foreign communities.

Globalist views of state expansion thus share a "metrocentric" perspective on expansive states (Doyle 1986). Metrocentric conceptions assume "underdeveloped" and politically weak societies on the state's periphery with less complex forms of political, social, and economic organization (D'Altroy 1992:15; Doyle 1986:131). This is not to say that all globalist views of elite exchange ignore local conditions in the peripheries. Indeed, reconsiderations of empires and archaeological world systems acknowledge indigenous resistance to external domination and the diminution of power with distance-related costs of control (Stein 1999b:62). Even these critiques, however, fall back on a calculus that balances core interests against costs. Regardless of the terminology, metrocentric views of state expansion imply strategies of power that flow from the top down and from the center out.

States and Empires

The prevalent globalist conception of expansive states is that of territorial empires. Empires are "relationships of political control imposed by some political societies over the effective sovereignty of other political societies" (Doyle 1986:19). The behavior of empires, known as imperialism, consists of an expansionist policy abroad that maintains an expanding state political economy at home. Generally, large-scale states are considered empires when a strong center imposes some degree of centralized political control over "broad territorial contours" and a range of conquered peoples beyond the boundaries of their original core area (Eisenstadt 1968). At least implicitly, empires are presumed to dominate linguistically, ethnically, and culturally diverse peoples as subjects (Marcus and Flannery 1996:207). Imperial control usually has some material motivation and effect, and the relationship of empires to their peripheries is usually assumed to be an asymmetrical exploitation of territory as well as of natural and human resources. By encompassing and exploiting diversity, empires aspire to "the absorption or subordination of peoples with differing traditions and levels of socioeconomic integration into an overarching tribute-taxation structure and an ideological apparatus that seeks to legitimate class relations" (Patterson and Gailey 1987:8).

Because less information is available for the earliest expansive states, they are often reconstructed by analogy to later, better documented empires. Thus Protoliterate Uruk can be fruitfully compared to the Ur III Sumerian state (Yoffee 1988:60), the feudal Chola state to the Vijayanagara Empire (Stein 1980); Teotihuacán or the Zapotec to the Aztec (Kowalewski 1990:52; Marcus and Flannery 1996:197; Zeitlin and Joyce 1999:388), and Wari or Tiwanaku to the Inca (Schreiber 1992:41; 1999). Beyond analogies to late prehistoric or historic empires, our imagining of ancient state expansion cannot help but be influenced by the modern imperial experience. As with all archaeological analogy, the use of fully developed imperial systems as models for their antecedents carries with it the danger of confusing ultimate product with early process. The designation of any ancient expansive state as an empire carries with it a baggage list of expected features derived from observation of full-scale imperial systems, both ancient and modern. Because archaeologists are inconsistent on the use of the term "empire" for antecedent forms of state expansion, I use the term "expansive states" for prehistoric expansive episodes of less than imperial scale.

Conquest and Consolidation

Perhaps the most familiar model for empires and, by extension, for early expansive states, is military conquest. Most analysts define empires as states that expand by military conquest, or "polities that take over other polities" (Schreiber 1992:3). Coercive force is thus considered a necessary and inevitable element of imperial expansion, and many scholars also assume a key role for military force in pre-imperial state expansion. While examples of military conquest in the formation of historic and late prehistoric empires are too numerous to mention here, there is less direct evidence of military conquest in the earliest expansive states.

One convincing case for violent military expansion in a pre-imperial state is the absorption of territories by the Zapotec state society with its capital at Monte Albán, in the highland Mexican state of Oaxaca. In a uniquely documented case of expansionist propaganda, rulers in Monte Albán Phase II (100 B.C.–A.D. 100) adorned a ceremonial structure known as Building J with over 40 inscribed stones that are identified as place glyphs for conquered or colonized provinces (Marcus and Flannery 1996:195–201). In at least one such peripheral region, the Cuicatlán Cañada, the building of fortifications, the clearing of settlement to create a buffer zone with Monte Albán's northern neighbors, and the gruesome display of severed heads on a skull rack at the village site of La Coyotera suggest that external aggression and internal repression were integral to the extension of Zapotec (Redmond 1983; Spencer 1982; Spencer and Redmond 1997:603; 2001). This case in particular has led some to generalize Monte Albán as "an imperial capital, the full extent of which once encompassed 20,000 km² of subject territory" (Balkansky 1998:455).

Mutually supporting evidence like this is rare, however, and when there is no epigraphic record, military subjugation by ancient states can be virtually impossible to document through archaeological sources (Marcus and Flannery 1996:198). Indicators such as the presence of weapons and fortifications, episodes of site destruction, and skeletal trauma, while they may point to incidents of violence, cannot prove that coercion was part of imperialist behavior. Proxy data, such as the disruption of settlement patterns and the intrusions of new ceramic or architectural styles, are even more open to alternate explanation (Webster 1998:315).

Globalist views of empires and earlier expansive states typically consider phases of consolidation and integration to follow imperial conquest. However, in practice these are not entirely separable enterprises. The consolidation of empires is characterized by continuity in the state's monopoly on repressive force for internal control of conquered areas through coercive diplomacy, implied threat, and terror (Sinopoli 1994:167). Indeed, in situations of chronic resistance, revolt, and repression, the state's long-term reliance on repressive force in a province may be indistinguishable from the process of conquest. By extension, force is considered an important element of integration and administration, with state investment required to repress revolt, guarantee tribute flow, and maintain secure borders.

The dominant paradigm for imperial consolidation is that of territorial integration. Continuing in the same spirit as the conquest phase, territorial empires integrate lands and peoples with a heavy hand through direct political control, supported by heavy state investment in garrisons, administrative bureaucracies, physical state infrastructure, and imperial ideologies. The political economy of territorial empires was supported by surplus extracted from peripheries to underwrite elites and state personnel and provide sumptuary goods for political ends, ceremony, and status validation.

As state systems forged in military adventure, territorial empires typically are associated with charismatic individual leaders. Often, in cases where we have written or graphic evidence, deeds of imperial leadership were memorialized in megalomaniacal and gruesome detail, suggesting that emperors cultivated powerful cults of personality (Sinopoli 1994:163). Imperial royal families, like the rulers of lesser states, can be presumed to have enjoyed particularly lavish lifestyles. Opulent royal tombs and governmental and residential palaces of appropriate scale may thus be considered necessary components of empire (Flannery 1998).

Imperial Political Economies

According to the globalist perspective, there is a direct causal relationship between the development of state political economies and episodes of peripheral expansion. Foreign conquests allowed ancient state cores to fund expanding political economies by extracting tribute from new sources. Globalist reconstructions assume that the extractive policies of expansive states require the top-down reorganization of subject domestic economies to fund the state (Sinopoli 1994:171). In Marxist terms, peripheries are "forcibly interrelated" by more powerful cores through the "juxtaposition and articulation of peoples with different relations of production and social reproduction within a dominant state and political economy" (Patterson and Gailey 1989:78). In neoevolutionary terms, states are by nature predatory, and competitive selection requires successful states to institutionalize new efficiencies in hierarchy and central decision making (Spencer 1998:15).

Absorption of a periphery in an imperial political economy thus requires a reorganization of production to produce goods in amounts greater than required by the local community. This shift toward tributary production should be recognizable in changes in settlement pattern, alienation of lands or resources for state purposes, and shifts in the focus and location of agriculture (e.g., Bauer 1992:104; Hastorf 1990). Simultaneously, the intensification of household production for tribute should be evident in changes to household size, infrastructural features and assemblages of tools, and debitage (D'Altroy 1992:12; Johnson and Earle et al. 1987; Stanish 1992). The extraction of tribute from households is not a simple tithing and is often conjoined to larger patterns of accentuated household inequality, changing gender roles and family structure under state political economies (e.g., Brumfiel 1991; Hastorf 1991:150).

Territorial and Hegemonic Empires

Globalist views of expansive states need not assume military conquest and the imposition of state infrastructure. For some observers, empires comprise an elastic category in that they encompass "more than just formally annexed territories" but "less than the sum of all forms of international equality"

(Doyle 1986:19). For archaeologists this leads to something of a semantic quandary, in which one person's empire may be another's world system, "interaction sphere," or even trade network. The usual solution is to consider empires and expansive states along a descriptive continuum from territorial to hegemonic modes of state control. Paralleling the distinction between "direct rule" and "indirect rule" that is commonly invoked to describe the variation among nineteenth-century European imperial policies (Doyle 1986:361), the distinction of territorial and hegemonic integration has been applied to the integration of ancient empires like the Roman, Inca, and Aztec (e.g., Hassig 1988; D'Altroy 1992; Luttwak 1976; Santley and Alexander 1992; Sinopoli 1994:160; Smith 1987; Smith and Berdan 1992). On one end of this continuum, undeniably imperialistic states conquer and incorporate territory and impose costly institutions of direct control to maximize political security and surplus extraction in peripheries. Most analysts agree that this sort of militaristic expansion and territorial integration by expansive states represents true imperial behavior. At the other extreme, state metropoles may incorporate peripheries hegemonically, using indirect political, economic, and ideological mechanisms as a way to reduce the costs and risks of regulation. As shall be seen, the popularity of the world systems terminology suggests a hesitancy to describe the behavior of these hegemonic states as imperial. There is nonetheless concordance in viewing territorial and hegemonic states and empires from a metrocentric perspective, assuming that powerful core societies acted with a more or less unified intent.

Territorial states efficiently extract tribute from a given territory by—literally—eliminating the middleman, as local political leadership is replaced by an imposed administration. To regulate natural, agricultural, and human resources, territorial expansive states impose a hierarchical political system upon a territorially contiguous regional base. The authority of new leaders is received from the state core rather than affirmed in a social contract with the immediate community. Territorial integration relies on imposed institutions to manage unemployment, population stress, and elite population pressure with maximum efficiency (Santley and Alexander 1992).

Accepting the convention of a minimally three-tiered organization of "information flow and regulatory decision making" as the essential feature of state integration, archaeologists expect that such a hierarchy should be represented in the distribution of settlements by population and size (Wright 1977; Wright and Johnson 1975). In the Andes, settlement size hierarchy has been invoked to explain the "statehood" of Middle Horizon Wari (Isbell and Schreiber 1978; Schreiber 1992, 1999), and scholars have examined the Inca state's institution of similar hierarchical frameworks in its early incorporation of Cusco (Bauer 1992:104) and distant peripheries (e.g., D'Altroy 1981,

1992; Dillehay 1977; Julien 1982; Morris 1982, 1986; Morris and Thompson 1985).

Because they assume a one-sided flow of tribute from periphery to core, globalist views of expansive states and empires stress the physical infrastructure related to communication, administration, and above all military security and tribute extraction. The infrastructure of direct rule has a high economic and social cost in military and bureaucratic manpower and infrastructure, and territorial states may become bogged down in expensive displays of force in support of tribute extraction (Hassig 1988; Sinopoli 1994:167). Yet effective infrastructure can increase a state's extractive potential, and physical means of storage, transport, and force projection are hallmarks of most ancient empires. Infrastructure is given particular importance in archaeological interpretations of ancient expansive states because built facilities can be the most archaeologically visible aspect of state integration.

In the Inca Empire, the provinces were linked to Cuzco by 30,000 km of roads, along which were placed numerous storehouses, way stations known as *tambos*, messenger stations, religious centers and military posts. Larger imposed provincial centers such as Hatun Xauxa and Huanuco Pampa served as seats for provincial administration. Key aspects of these centers included residences for both permanent state service personnel and temporary labor levies known as *mita* (D'Altroy 1992; Morris 1982; Morris and Thompson 1985). An enormous network of storage facilities held surplus produce, elite goods, and paraphernalia. The Inca system stored vast quantities of foodstuffs to support garrisons and advancing armies, administrative officials, and labor for public works. However, Inca storehouses also held sumptuary items, maize beer, and foodstuffs that were distributed in ritualized gift giving and hospitality on a massive scale.

Hegemonic States and Empires

Hegemonic states project power through implication, intimidation, and the attraction of imposed values, rather than through brute force alone (Hassig 1988:11, 19). Globalist views assume that state cores select among hegemonic and territorial strategies according to a rational calculus of coercion. Hegemonic integration can extract tribute, distribute manufactured goods, and achieve a degree of regional security without the enormous expenses of training and maintaining bureaucracies and standing armies. Globalist views see hegemonic strategies as a pragmatic choice of state cores, made on the basis of a rational analysis of distance, importance of resources, and the strength and organization of indigenous resistance. By carefully balancing wealth extraction and political control against the costs of regulation, hegemonic strategies conserve states' limited resources for enforcement.

Hegemonic power, supported by the promulgation of a state ideology, could be largely psychological, building a perception of state control from implied force and intimidation. At the local level, hegemonic integration might entail manipulation of local ideologies and the identity and socio-political loyalties of subject populations. As in India under the British Raj, local rulers often are permitted to maintain their authority if they collaborate with the larger system. In this way, hegemonic power resorts to the use of direct force only in circumstances carefully chosen for maximum effect (Hassig 1988:11, 19). Hegemony thus could be far lower in cost than territo-rial control because distant peripheries could be exploited through elite ac-culturation and consent building rather than naked intimidation. Hegemonic cores are content to dominate peripheries by subverting, rather than replac-ing, local political hierarchies and ideologies, as regional leaders are seduced into the core culture's system of values.

Globalist Perspectives on Prestige Goods Exchange

Seduction often entails gift giving, and from the globalist perspective of the core, strings could be attached to gifts to peripheral elites. As political cur-rency, sumptuary objects have been described as one of the most efficacious ways to "materialize" ideology (Earle 1997:154). Craft items of exotic origin can have an almost talismanic role in structuring the political interactions among geographically distant elites. Because they are cherished for their rar-ity and for the labor, skill, or technological process in their manufacture and importation, sumptuary goods are convertible to prestige and power that surpass their use value (Brumfiel and Earle 1987; D'Altroy and Earle 1985; Earle 1987, 1994:445; Paynter 1989; Rowlands et al. 1987; Wolf 1982:82–83).

Globalist interpretations see the asymmetry of long-distance prestige goods exchange as an important component of hegemonic control. Gift giving is seen as a political act that reifies the core's dominance and the submission of peripheral elites. Exotic gifts could cement the ties between patron and client, assuring the cooperation of potentially disruptive frontier groups. Con-versely, the long-distance exchange of exotic sumptuary items and raw mate-rials provides an option for peripheral tribute where high transport costs limit tribute in bulk commodities (Brumfiel and Earle et al. 1987; D'Altroy and Earle 1985). The main advantage of wealth as a basis for finance is its high value to weight ratio: this of course minimizes the cost of transportation and permits movement across great distances. "The central control of wealth strengthens vertical ties of dependence and inhibits the growth of opposition coalitions" (Earle et al. 1987:69).

Especially where distance physically limits the movement of goods, good things could come in small packages. Exotica not only represent congealed labor and rare materials but are often associated with the supernatural and the cosmopolitan. Exotic gifts bear the imprimatur of the giver and transfer some of his prestige to the receiver. Unlike the extraction of agricultural tribute, which can be nakedly coerced by implied violence, the demand for sumptuary goods from the core must be carefully cultivated. In ancient societies, this was done by involving commodities in the ideological model promulgated by the core elite and through the subordination of peripheral societies to a hegemonic value system (Whitecotton 1992:54). The well-crafted power of exotic goods to sway peripheral elites can lead to the "emulation" of exotic materials, in which "a set of values and social procedures . . . are more readily adopted because of the sophistication of the source society's products and the prestige in which they are held" (Renfrew 1975:33).

The importance of prestige exchange to interregional interaction between precapitalist states can be traced to Polanyi's concepts of reciprocal diplomatic "gift trade" between empires: "The organization of trading is here usually ceremonial, involving mutual presentations; embassies; political dealings between chiefs or kings. The goods are treasure, objects of elite circulation" (Polanyi et al. 1957:262).

Thus exotic sumptuary goods metaphorically illustrate even scarcer commodities of knowledge and power. From the point of view of the dominant partner in such relationships, long-distance trade was thus inextricably linked to pragmatic statecraft through elite clientage. Prestige goods could serve as a sort of foreign aid or bribe to assure the co-option, if not pacification, of leaders of these potentially disruptive frontier groups. In the southwestern United States, Nelson (1994, 2000; Nelson et al. 1992) has noted that exotic Mesoamerican artifacts such as mirrors, bells, and parrot feathers found in Hohokam contexts displayed a strong correlation with high status contexts and individuals of high rank in mortuary contexts. He described such a status-selective long-distance exchange system as a "prestige sphere" that was qualitatively different from the subsistence exchange sphere and even local artifact exchange spheres. The correlation of high rank and access to exotic imports suggests an alliance or specialized relationship between Hohokam elites and groups in Mesoamerica." Although perhaps not a fully formed clientage, this description suggests an asymmetrical projection of power from more complex Mesoamerican centers to small-scale southwestern societies.

World Systems

In the 1970s, Emmanuel Wallerstein formulated the concept of World Systems Theory to describe the globalist relations of dependence that develop with capitalist expansion and industrialization in the modern world (Wallerstein 1974). The World System model postulates the systematic transfer of surplus from "satellites" to "metropoles" and implies inherently asymmetrical relations of dependence, known as "uneven development," between cores and peripheries (Doyle 1986:362; Frank 1993; Stern 1988:837). A core may be defined as an elite geographical area, segment of society, or institution that commands economic tribute, military respect, and political fealty. Cores institutionalize asymmetrical power relations to structure exploitative economic and political relationships with peripheries. Peripheries are areas, segments of society, or institutions that are brought into the orbit of a core to meet its demand for surplus "product" (Rowlands et al. 1987), broadly defined to include locational, strategic, or even ideological resources as well as tangible goods.

Because undeveloped transportation systems precluded the market exchange of bulk commodities, Wallerstein himself discounted the importance of core-periphery relations in determining the economies of the ancient world. Nonetheless, some anthropologists argued that even under precapitalist tributary regimes, surplus could be exchanged in the form of luxury goods or preciosities (Wolf 1982:82–83), an interpretation of the fungibility of sumptuary goods more recently termed "wealth finance" (Earle 1994). The high value and easy convertibility of prestige goods became the cornerstone of Schneider's (1977) seminal adaptation of Wallerstein's formulation to the ancient world. "Pitting some against others, gift giving promotes the co-optation of class enemies, making the patron-client relationship a forceful political adjunct to energy capture" (Schneider 1977:23).

Following Schneider, many archaeologists have explicitly considered interregional interaction under early states within a construct of precapitalist world systems (Abu-Lughod 1989; Algaze 1993a, 1993b; Chase-Dunn and Mann 1998; Kardulias 1999; Kohl 1987; Peregrine and Feinman 1996; Rowlands et al. 1987; Whitecotton 1992); "macroregional systems" (Wilcox 1999:137); or core-periphery systems (Paynter 1989:380). In contrast to Wallerstein's modern World System, most archaeological adaptations of world systems assume a variety of modes of production and peoples of diverse identities who interact across a larger social and spatial field.

The absorption of peripheries was more than a search for tributary wealth to support ruling elites. The high demographic potential of successful cores could be an asset to the aggrandizement of core societies, providing a large pool for frontier settlement (Stein 1999b:56). Developed cores also often needed frontiers to relieve social tensions caused by disenfranchised peasants, workers, or elites (Santley and Alexander 1992). Conversely, smaller societies on state peripheries could have difficulty maintaining their populations at viable levels and could be unable or unwilling to fend off immigrants from the core (Blanton 1983:227). With a frontier option, the core's disenfranchised could better their living standards through military exploits, grants of land, new administrative posts, and new categories of work. Peripheral expansion thus resolves tensions in the core by redistributing population and providing new options for social mobility (Boone 1986; Kopytoff 1987). Thus, if cores could be reliant on peripheries for demographic relief, peripheries could become dependent on cores for demographic replenishment and economic development. Expanding core political economies could bring entire new industries to peripheral regions of expansion.

The same Classic Zapotec polity that provided such clear evidence of coercive violence in its northern province has also been cited as an example of a world system approach to state expansion elsewhere in its orbit (Blanton and Feinman 1984; Feinman and Nicholas 1992; Feinman 1999). While not denying its coercive and terrorist extension of power elsewhere, Feinman describes the influence of Classic Monte Albán on the Ejutla Valley on its southern periphery as an example of hegemonic control over specialized labor-intensive industries introduced to peripheries. Under the sway of Monte Albán, Ejutla underwent a florescence of exotic craft production in shell, obsidian, and cotton textiles that surpassed the level of these enterprises in the core region of the central Oaxaca Valley. The development of these industries and the region's role as an "economic gateway" for imported raw materials brought about increases in population and social complexity, as demonstrated by site size hierarchy. The construction of an architecturally elaborate center marks Ejutla's conversion from a sparsely settled frontier to a dependent periphery (Feinman and Nicholas 1992:112). These indirect transformations of the periphery occurred in Monte Albán Phase II, well after the core state was established as an urban and agrarian power and simultaneous with its gruesome displays of conquest and coercion at Monte Albán and in the Cuicatlán Cañada.

The great contribution of world systems approaches is in the realization that the historical analysis of complex societies cannot be limited to bounded spatial concepts of state centers or regions and that long-distance trade cannot be considered epiphenomenal to state expansion. However, world systems approaches often tip the balance in the other direction by underplaying the role of local exchange and endogenous social change within regions. The application of archaeological world systems theory to ancient states rests on the assumptions that (1) ancient state cores were militarily, technologically, and organizationally superior to peripheral societies; (2) cores dominated asymmetrical long-distance exchange relationships with the periphery; and (3) core-dominated long-distance exchange structured all other aspects of political economy in the peripheries (Stein 1999b:154). These globalist assumptions of world systems approaches underestimate the roles of autono-

mous peripheral elites in structuring interregional exchange. Indigenous social complexity, resistance, and factional competition, if considered at all, are
considered as confounding rather than determinant factors in world systems relations of dominance and dependence. Because these assumptions
strip agency away from peripheral societies, world systems approaches are
every bit as globalist as imperial models for state expansion.

Agency-Oriented Perspectives on State Expansion

A growing minority of theorists questions the universal relationship of social
complexity to processes of segregation and differentiation in states. I collectively call these "agency-oriented" interpretations—which include segmentary states, theatre states, galactic polities, heterarchy, and corporate models—because they emphasize the presence of enduring corporate segments
who remain capable of independent action within complex societies. Agency
might be considered as the sum of actions, choices, and strategies for achieving the goals of individuals or groups within a society. Agential behavior may
be manifest through explicit actions or implicitly in the sum of the smaller
actions of daily practices (Bourdieu 1977, 1990; Giddens 1984). Agency-
oriented perspectives consider complex human social and political systems as
the sum of their parts, rather than as monolithic entities. As such, they
privilege the conflictive processes within state societies, rather than the systemic analysis of the state as an organic whole (Brumfiel 1992, 1994:3).
Unlike globalist perspectives, agency-oriented views see complex societies in
a more dynamic light, focusing on the parochial arenas in which chiefs, kings,
kin groups, sodalities, cults, guilds, and other corporate factions compete for
followers and forge coalitions.

There remains the problem of what to call polities that display many of the
Agency-oriented models have been successfully applied to societies at the
level of the chiefdom but only sporadically to larger-scale polities termed
states. In part, this may be attributed to a subtle sampling bias in the archaeological literature against less hierarchical states that do not fit the globalist
paradigm (Stahl 1999:39). A second reason for the scarcity of alternative
state models is conceptual rather than empirical. The survival of corporate
groups as autonomous actors within states violates the definitional distinctions between "chiefdom" and "state" in the comparativist paradigm (Marcus and Feinman 1998:7). To emphasize generalities of process, mainstream
neoevolutionist theory tends to package chiefdoms and states as discrete
products.

There remains the problem of what to call polities that display many of the
defining features of states but are less centralized than our traditional notion
of states and empires. One option is to expand the chiefdom designation to

include a category of complex chiefdoms for polities of greater scale and splendor (Earle 1987, 1997; Wright 1994:69). Some archaeologists avoid using chiefdom and state altogether when discussing problematic aspects of civilizations like the Indus Valley Harappa or the Maya (Possehl 1998; Webster 1998). An increasingly popular option is to apply evolutionarily neutral designations like "principality," "kingdom," or "polity" or local terms like *hesp, nome, altepetl, chchcabalob, cacicazgos, curacazcgo,* and so on (Marcus and Feinman 1998:9). While the use of these terms is not objectionable, their profusion suggests that we may be missing an opportunity to identify important comparative categories for intermediate-scale state societies (e.g., Nichols and Charlton 1997) or the component units within them (e.g., Yaeger and Canuto 2000).

Recent reappraisals of Maya social organization exemplify the need to reconsider the unitary nature of states. While accepting that the Classic Maya were a state society, McAnany has called for a "broadening of the playing field" to include a wider variety of organizational structures. McAnany notes that the neoevolutionist focus on nuclear households as the only atomistic units within state societies may impoverish the analysis of political economy, agricultural organization, and land tenure systems. She suggests that Maya society was organized according to corporate principles into "macrofamilies" defined by descent and ideologies of ancestor veneration (McAnany 1995:157, 159).

Joyce and Gillespie (2000) have expanded upon this model, substituting the term "house" to describe corporate groups within Maya society. Following Levi-Strauss, the house is defined as a recurring corporate entity with its own identity and responsibility. Although house membership was expressed in the language of kinship, the house could recruit members by marriage or affiliation, and houses also shared common ideologies acted out in ritual. The Classic Maya "noble and "royal" dynasties thus arose from houses that successfully competed for followers and retainers. If the Maya individual's primary allegiance and identity lay with his or her house, this calls into question the power and permanence of Maya kingship and other state institutions.

Relationships of nested and scaled sovereignty expressed in ritual are key elements in several differing but overlapping decentralist views of early states. These share the conception that complex societies of diverse scales can accommodate autonomous and nonhierarchical societal segmentation. Several of these decentralist state models focus on polities where central authority was limited to the sphere of religious practice. Geertz's concept of a Balinese "theatre state" (1980), for example, describes state centers as primarily loci of public rituals rather than administration, a position that is supported by the decentralized economic organization of irrigation farming (Lansing

1991; Kolata 1993:216). Similarly, Tambiah's interpretation of early Southeast Asian states as "Galactic Polities" maps the ritual responsibilities that could only be discharged by the royal family in the Thai state's "provinces." Despite this "galactic" responsibility, the kingdom was in fact decentralized politically and economically, with agricultural production fully controlled by local kin groups (Tambiah 1977).

Segmentary States

A survey of sub-Saharan African polities also suggests a wide array of intermediate-scale states where corporate groups retain autonomy and power, and political action is achieved through ritual, personal, or charismatic authority. In many of these, political action is articulated through horizontally arrayed assemblies or councils rather than a centralized hierarchy (McIntosh 1999:15, 77). One of the earliest and most controversial of these multiple-agent models was the "segmentary state," a term first applied by Aiden Southall to describe an intermediate political form between western states and societies considered "tribal" by agents of European imperial powers.

Southall conceived of segmentary states as large-scale polities in which diverse political and social entities are only partially subsumed under the central authority of a king. These were dynamic confederations, integrated by structured oppositions between similar segments. Southall termed these polities segmentary not because of any particular kinship structure but "because there is complementary opposition between their component parts, the boundaries of political jurisdiction are differently perceived from different points of the system, and a central focus of ritual suzerainty is recognized over a wider area than effective political sovereignty" (Southall 1974:156).

A key element of segmentary states is that the range of ritual suzerainty and political sovereignty do not coincide. The largely ceremonial authority of the centers of segmentary states could be contrasted to "unitary states" that enjoyed absolute central authority, that monopolized the use of force, and that instituted powerfully hierarchical power structures (Fox et al. 1996:797; Southall 1956:257; 1988; 1999).

As is often the case when archaeologists borrow theories from other fields, there is considerable confusion about Southall's model, most of it revolving around the word "segmentary" itself.[3] Nonetheless, the segmentary state continues to have utility for describing states characterized by nonhierarchical division into corporate segments (e.g., McIntosh 1999). The term has been particularly popular among "decentralist" archaeologists of the Pre-Columbian Maya, most of whom emphasize the importance of lineage-based corporate descent groups as the keystone suprahousehold units of Maya social organization (Ball 1994; Fox et al. 1996:798; Houston 1993; Potter and King 1995:22).

Segmentary descriptions have also been applied to polities of imperial scale and infrastructure. The Inca, for example, are described as a segmentary state by Gose, who suggests that the basis of state power in some contexts was "ritual suzerainty, expressed through symbolic manipulation and ritual" (Gose 1993). These applications of the term have been controversial on both empirical and theoretical grounds (Chase and Chase 1996; Marcus 1995; Marcus and Feinman 1998).

Segmentary States of South Asia

The segmentary state concept has been successfully applied to South Asian states by medieval historians (Stein 1980; Thapar 1984:163) and by archaeologists of some of the earliest complex societies of the Indus Valley (Possehl 1998:289). The historic Chola state of southern India is one example. Chola society was profoundly divided according to castelike societal categories known as *nadu* (Stein 1980:206). Nadu, unlike modern castes, were mainly horizontal rather than vertically defined divisions. Thus Stein describes a society composed of largely autonomous collectivities of peasants, "framed in the idiom of kinship, amounting to a sort of clanship. Dominant peasant groups in this region characteristically defined themselves with respect to ancestors who purportedly first settled their localities. These origin and charter explanations were usually expressed by a simple locality designation . . . and in lineage myths" (Stein 1985:76).

Stein describes the Chola state as segmentary in that royal power was exercised in constant negotiation and largely limited to the ritual field. Inscriptions describe the status of Chola kings among local chiefs as that of a king of kings (*rajadhiraja*), or first among equals. This relationship was expressed and reified through ceremonial patronage that Stein described as "ritual sovereignty" (Stein 1985:77). Although Chola society's segmental components could become vertical—hierarchical—during the reigns of the stronger Chola rulers, their natural propensity was to revert to a horizontal or heterarchical condition (Stein 1980:207, and see discussion later in this chapter). According to Stein, the Chola monarchs, and even kings of the later Vijayanagara Empire, were "states" only "as and to the extent that their claims to sovereignty over large parts of the southern peninsula were acknowledged by peasant chieftains in particular coded contexts such as Brahman villages and temples. South Indian political traditions preserve a notion of multiple and simultaneous kingships, large and small, of which one, at any time, was seen to enjoy a hegemonic status. The state as a state was not perceived as an administrative or coercive fact, as much as the expression of an idea of unity among many diverse peasant localities as actualized in ritual linkages between kings and chiefs" (Stein 1985:75).

Thus the Chola state was segmentary because its unification was situational and constantly being negotiated in complex idioms of caste, ritual, and kinship. Although the Chola did expand through conquest, the power held by its kings was far more ephemeral than that of rulers in either territorial-imperial or hegemonic–world systems models. Coercion, central administration, and economic dominance were less significant than other forms of royal suasion over the kingdom's autonomous factions. A similar emphasis on Brahmanic values and ideological manipulation also characterized royal legitimation in the Mauryan and Satavahana dynasties (Sinpoli 2001:177).

Heterarchy

Crumley first proposed the term "heterarchy" to describe settlement systems in complex societies that do not fit well into hierarchical assumptions of central place models (Crumley 1976, 1987, 1995). By implication, heterarchy indicates crosscutting categories of differentiated societal elements that cannot be fully explained by hierarchical ordering. Instead, following studies of artificial intelligence in cognitive psychology, Crumley suggests that in complex societies, functionally distinct sections of society arise to accomplish different tasks. Complex societies thus are formed of an intricate net of flexible and constantly negotiated relations among "counterpoised" elements. The interests of these different elite groups or other societal elements exist in dialectical social relationships with other corporate groups and may not coincide with the interests of the state at large. "Power relationships are predicated on systems of values that are ranked and reranked in their importance by individuals, groups, and organizations as conditions change" (Crumley 1995:4). Although heterarchical social groups can situationally become ranked, forming hierarchies, they can and most often do "unrank," returning to heterarchy. Crumley's view of the instability of hierarchy is consonant with neoevolutionist concepts of periodicity in the rise and fall of central state authority (Marcus 1998) and systems concepts of pathological hypercoherence leading to the downfall of centralized states (Flannery 1972). The difference is one of time scale. To Crumley, hierarchy is only a temporary and inherently unstable solution to the problem of maintaining order.

Corporate Strategies

Recently, Blanton has distinguished "corporate" strategies from "exclusionary" strategies as two polar types in ancient complex societies. Exclusionary strategies range from small-scale networks of personal dominance (patron-client or vassalage) to large-scale bureaucratic governments. In contrast, under corporate strategies "power is shared across different groups and sectors of society in such a way as to inhibit exclusionary strategies. . . . This does not mean a hierarchically flat society or a completely egalitarian one. . . . In corporate polities, the distribution of power is structured, determined, legitimated, and controlled within the limits set by the prevailing corporate cognitive code" (Blanton et al 1996:2).

Drawing on processualist studies in political anthropology, Blanton proposes a multiple-actor approach that emphasizes political behavior, viewing the state as "the major social arena within which the competition for power is played out in society" (Blanton 1998:139). Instead of as a monolithic entity, the state is perceived as a collection of political actors with varying aims:

> This approach leads the researcher to focus on political process, in other words, the competition among various individuals and groups attempting to exert power in such as way as to shape or control the state states are "consciously established, maintained, fought over and argued about rather than taken for granted." . . . Political actors with various aims, such as secondary elites (e.g., local patrimonial nobility or middle-level bureaucrats) versus central elites (who control the central institutions of the state), often employ diverse often conflictive, political strategies, frequently making use of differing material and symbolic resources to further their aims. . . . In this framework, the state is not necessarily the kind of highly integrated information processing subsystem the systems theorists would have us believe. Instead, the formal, functional and dynamic properties of the state are outcomes of the often conflictive interaction of social actors with separate agendas, both within and outside the official structure of the decision-making institution. (Blanton 1998:140)

Corporate groups within archaic states, Blanton argues, could exhibit "egalitarian behavior" through political actions that prevent exclusionary power strategies. Like Crumley's conception of value systems that foster enduring heterarchy over temporary hierarchy, Blanton's corporate strategy specifies a "corporate cognitive code" that serves to limit the exercise of power (Blanton 1998:152). While neither scheme denies the importance of centralized authority in the state, each asserts that central authority is negotiated in a complex dialectic with diverse interest groups.

Local Agency and Prestige Exchange

Agency-oriented interpretations of prestige goods exchange contrast sharply with globalist perceptions of projected power from state cores. From this perspective, the association of exotica with distant power centers is relevant not because of the power politics of core hegemony but only because of the high value of the exotic to local elites. "Effective competition at the community level requires aggrandizers to traffic outside their home communities and establish significant ties to individuals elsewhere, preferably other aggrandizers. . . . The physical and social resources and knowledge thus gained allow an aggrandizer to compete more effectively within his own community" (Clark and Blake 1994:19).

This is not to say that distance does not matter. Writing of early sixteenth-century Panamanian chiefs located midway between the complex political organizations of Mesoamerica and northern Andean South America, Helms (1993) has described how their exotic origins add an "aura of esoterica" to precious items imbued with aesthetic qualities closely associated with political ideology. Thus the exquisitely worked Quimbaya and Sinu gold artifacts, once accepted by Panamanian elites, were material symbols not only of wealth and power but of even scarcer commodities of esoteric knowledge and chiefly sanctity: "The geographically distant and the supernaturally distant were closely related . . . this association was succinctly stated by the acquisition from distant geographical regions of elite prestige items" (Helms 1979:110).

The importance of precious exotica thus resided in the possessor's ability to construct power out of an outside-inside dichotomy (Helms 1993). Even if some of the salient symbols of power came from outside, long-distance exchange relations were most significant for their role in constructing local preeminence. Local factions or individuals participated in extralocal networks because this gave them an "insider" status, as political and spiritual power could be reified through control of empowered and empowering exotic goods.

An instructive example of this agency-oriented approach may be found in an alternate interpretation of Mesoamerican exotic imports in Chaco Canyon. In contrast to Nelson's interpretation of Hohokam's participation in a Mesoamerican world system, for Chaco Canyon McGuire proposes a "prestige good economy" in which local elites sought political power through control of imported exotica (McGuire 1989). McGuire suggests that prestige goods were most significant locally in the competition of the heads of ranked lineages for status and legitimacy. Rather than dwelling on clientage relationships with a distant power, McGuire sees the source of exotica as largely incidental to its local symbolic role of attracting followers.

Thus pre-state prestige goods networks may not indicate dominance by foreign trade powers as much as they indicate factional competition and the emergence of local ranking. Ironically, even as elites used exotica to separate themselves from their own people, they created networks that joined them to fellow elites elsewhere. Elites could transcend political and social boundaries, building shared class identities by employing exotic prestige objects as "mutually reinforcing, visible symbols of identity membership uniting dispersed local rulers" (Schortman 1989:58; Schortman and Urban 1992, 1994). By creating a common symbolic vocabulary and an "international style" that crosscut cultural boundaries (Blanton et al. 1996:4), even distant elites could share recognizable identity, creating a "network of chiefdoms from a network of interacting chiefs" (Clark and Blake 1994:20).

Network theory states that certain kinds of exotica can travel in culturally transcendent elite exchange networks without transmitting the hegemony of a core society. This tenet is implicit in a long line of prestige goods exchange constructs ranging from "peer polity interaction" (Renfrew 1996) and "multinational cultures" (Willey 1973:158–159) to "interaction spheres" like the Hopewell burial cult of the Eastern Woodlands (Caldwell 1964). Nonetheless, by reminding us that sumptuary exchange networks can form from the bottom up without centralized intervention, network theory provides an agency-oriented alternative to hegemonic or world systems interpretations of prestige trade.

A third region-specific interpretation of Zapotec state expansion illustrates this agency-oriented prestige goods network approach. Archaeologists working in the Río Verde Valley and on the Pacific coast of Oaxaca describe a long-standing tradition of fancy ceramic imports from the Monte Albán center, dating to 200 B.C. (Joyce 1991; Joyce and Winter 1996; Zeitlin and Joyce 1999:384). This prestige exchange, which is followed by the stylistic emulation of Oaxaca ceramics by local potters, corresponds with the period of Zapotec militaristic imperialism in the Cuicatlán Cañada and Zapotec world system economic exploitation of the Ejutla Valley already described. It has been suggested that the identification of one of the Monte Albán conquest slabs with the site of Tututepec could represent the conquest of at least the upper Verde, while an increase of Monte Albán grayware pottery, obsidian, and marine shell among elites in the lower Verde must represent a Zapotec entrepreneurial presence on the coast (Marcus and Flannery 1996:202) and probably some element of coercive control by Zapotec trading posts (Balkansky 1998:472). Without evidence for Zapotec military conquest in the lower Verde, however, Zeitlin and Joyce discount the likelihood of any disruption in local sociopolitical organization there and prefer to conclude that some Monte Albán conquest slabs may have represented raids, alliances, idle propagandistic boasts, or a "wish list" of tempting neighbors (Zeitlin and Joyce 1999:389). Instead, despite its contemporaneity with Zapotec globalist action elsewhere, the Zapotec influence in the lower Río Verde is interpreted as an example of the independent agency of peripheral elites competing for prestige, rather than either imperial or world system extension of globalist imperial power from a state center.

Heterarchy in Expansive States?

Heterarchical, segmentary, or corporate models of polities composed of locally autonomous entities are more problematic when applied to expansive states as a whole. How, after all, could a collection of autonomous clans either conquer and consolidate an empire or build a world system by hegemonically dominating weaker trade partners?

Despite its consideration as an empire based on consideration of its scale, the Vijayanagara state of southern India "cannot be easily incorporated into traditional models of imperial structure" (Sinopoli and Morrison 1995:85). Focusing on the symbolic geometry of the Vijayanagara capital, Fritz (1988) followed Stein in describing it as the ceremonial and pilgrimage center of a segmentary state. Vijayanagara excelled in matters of military organization and directed a limited number of the massive public constructions and irrigation projects. Despite the grandeur and military prowess of the Vijayanagara capital and the spread of its architecture and artifact styles, centralized elite control over resources was limited, much as appears to have been the case in the earlier Mauryan and Satavahana states (Sinopoli 2001). In contrast to the expectations of territorial empires or world systems, Vijayanagara's rulers never assumed control over local relations of food or craft production in either core or periphery (Sinopoli and Morrison 1995:85). Even at the empire's height of expansion, these responsibilities remained firmly in the hands of locally based corporate groups such as craft and merchant castes. The ability of Vijayanagara rulers to project power and underwrite their political economy thus depended on constant negotiation with local chiefs and castes. If this is indeed the case, as Stein argues it was in the predecessor Chola state, Vijayanagara is difficult to explain under globalist models of coercive core-centered hierarchy.

Summary

In this chapter I have reviewed several very different archaeological paradigms for how ancient expansive states integrated peripheral territories. Taken as a single continuum, these range from globalist views of territorial and hegemonic control to agency-oriented perspectives on ancient state expansion. It should be kept in mind that all of these conceptions are heuristic constructs, rather than mutually exclusive types. Most expansive state cores, or at least dominant elements within them, chose among territorial and hegemonic strategies according to pragmatic considerations of peripheral resources, indigenous sociopolitical structure, and distance from the homeland nucleus. It is equally true that state expansion cannot be considered without taking into account agency—the dynamic interplay among myriad counterposed factions in both the core and periphery.

Both territorial and hegemonic models of early state expansion are globalist in that they tend to paint the agency of early state expansion with a wide brush and from the top down. Territorial models of state expansion, based on the observation of large-scale historic empires, focus on military conquest, territorial integration, direct governance through a bureaucratic provincial administration, and economic exploitation through a tributary economic structure. The model of direct territorial control fits well with traditional western models of imperial state expansion and suggests the incorporation of peripheries as contiguous administered provinces. Territorial interpretations emphasize the centralization of hierarchical political control through imposed provincial centers and administrative infrastructure and the reorganization of local relations of production to fund a tributary political economy.

Hegemonic globalist perspectives, particularly those influenced by world systems theory, focus on economic and ideological domination and indirect governance through networks of political clientage and asymmetrical exchange. According to these models, states create situations of demand and dependency to co-opt potentially troublesome peripheral groups as clients. State cores control interregional exchange of prestige goods that explicitly or implicitly convey state power and confer status to their receivers. As is explored in the next chapter, states may sponsor specialized classes of merchant-agents for this kind of work, and small enclaves of such agents distributed across a trade diaspora may be discernible in the archaeological record.

Recent critiques point out that the globalist nature of the territorial-hegemonic framework treats the cores of archaic states as if they were individual actors. In contrast, agency-oriented models stress the factional nature of complex societies and the analytical importance of corporate strategies, individual interests, and power aggrandizement by within state societies. Although many accept that archaic states could simultaneously encompass elements of factional heterarchy alongside hierarchy (Crumley 1995:4; Marcus and Feinman 1998:11; Zagarell 1995:97), agency-oriented constructs have been applied primarily to periods of chiefly and state formation rather than state expansion. If one accepts that some states were less hierarchical in structure than others, the question that remains is whether this kind of internal segmentation and heterarchy persisted as early states began to expand to new provinces. If powerful urban state cores could be confederacies of conflictive and disparate parts, could their interaction with distant peripheries be determined by the sum of diverse factional interests both at home and abroad?

Can agency-oriented models for early states be extended to the level of expansive states or empires?

In the next chapter, I propose that the earliest expansive states in the Andes may indeed have been far more decentralized than is commonly believed. A form of diasporic colonization, known in the Andes as an archipelago, provides an alternative to globalist state expansion models and suggests the possibility of far more segmentary and heterarchical expansive states than the monolithic empires that are so well known in the archaeological literature.

2

Ayllus, Diasporas, and Archipelagos

Ethnic boundaries in pluralistic contexts tend to persist when they are instrumental in securing access to some vital resource.

Spence (1992:79)

In this chapter, I propose that corporate groups within Andean states retained a structural diversity and a lively dynamic of political discourse among component ethnic groups, even as they expanded into new lands. In the first section I argue that the ethnographic and historic evidence concerning contact period Andean states supports a model of social organization and cohesion that is based on the Andean *ayllu*, a suprahousehold social, economic, and (at its maximal level) ethnic corporate unit. In the second section, I consider diasporas as a form of ethnicity in motion and examine comparative examples of diasporic colonization by ancient states. Drawing these two themes together, in the final section I consider an Andean variant of diasporic colonization known as the archipelago and consider criteria for describing *ayllus* and archipelagos as forms of identity-based colonization in the archaeological record.

Ayllus

The Andean *ayllu* is a corporate body of ascriptive identity held together by shared conceptions of behavior, history, and common ancestry. In ideal terms *ayllus* are endogamous corporations that trace ancestry from a common ancestor, and *ayllu* (pronounced "ay-yoo") is often translated from Quechua as "clan." In fact ayllus are likely to include lineages, but their composition is fluid and ayllu membership may be determined by literal and fictive descent, adoption, political negotiation, marriage, alliance, or other criteria (Abercrombie 1998:341; Albarracin-Jordan 1996a:185; Isbell 1997:99; Salomon 1991).

In its complexity, ayllu membership is comparable to the broader concept of ethnicity. An ayllu, like an ethnic group, may be viewed as any "kin-based identity larger than the family or lineage" (Emberling 1997:303). At the same time ayllu members, like members of an ethnic group, may also be defined by "a feeling of solidarity founded on shared patterns of behavior motivated by similar assumptions, values, and standards of evaluation which are, themselves, perceived as reflecting a common history of the group" (Schortman 1989:54).

In practice, ayllus have also been used in a broader form to describe a variety of corporate units within Andean societies. Functional definitions emphasize the ayllu as a land-holding collective (Brush 1977:41; Rowe 1946: 255), an economically autonomous kin collective (Moseley 1992:49), the proprietor of water rights (Sherbondy 1982), or the key unit of a "communal mode of production" for exchange and productive labor organization above the level of the nuclear family (Patterson 1987). Under the Spanish colonial legal system, many ayllus claimed ownership of territory and land since time immemorial (Albarracin-Jordan 1996a:186). However, the veracity of such claims made amid the chaos of newly imposed European terms of land tenure is controversial (Isbell 1997; Van Buren 1996). In the end, the most inclusive definition of the ayllu may be the most accurate. Urton defines ayllus as any "group or unit of social, political, economic, and ritual cohesion and action" (Urton 1990:22).

Structuralist definitions of the ayllu emphasize its tendency to fit into nested hierarchies of moieties and identify miniature ayllus at different levels of scale. This recursive tendency might be described as "fractal" because any part of the whole ayllu tends to have the same mathematical structure as the original. At many levels of subdivision, for example, ayllus typically exhibit binary oppositions, splitting in half by gender or moiety (Duviols 1974; Platt 1986). The symmetry and particularly the dualistic structure of this Andean system have led to the generalizations of ayllu structure as "recursive hierarchy" (Urton 1993), "nested hierarchy" (Albarracin Jordan 1996a,b), or a "Chinese box" arrangement of component parts (Astvaldsson 2000:148; Bouysse-Cassagne 1986:207). Because the term *ayllu* can be used to refer to units at any level of scale, the terms maximal, minor, and minimal ayllu are often used to distinguish different levels in the fractal set (Platt 1986).

Platt presents the present-day Macha of Potosí, Bolivia, as an example of a nested system of ayllu identities. First, the entire Macha population may be considered as one maximal ayllu. Maximal ayllus, the largest of these nested boxes, may be considered synonymous with ethnic groups. Below this maximal level of ethnic identity, the term *ayllu* is also used for specific community segments nested within the larger grouping of the maximal ayllu. The Macha ayllus are next segmented into two moiety divisions, known as Alasaya and Maasaya. Further, individuals identify with a total of ten minor ayllus, five for each moiety, and finally with minimal ayllus of family kin groups. In the case of the Macha, minor ayllus were arrayed like the ten fingers of two hands. While this elegant binary symmetry is unusual, similar recursive hierarchies have been noted for the Laymi and K'ulta Aymara (Abercrombie 1998:154–157; Harris 1986).

Other definitions of the ayllu accept the prevalence of nested structural oppositions but stress the metaphoric and symbolic activity that constitutes the recombinant nature of ayllus. Regularly, members of ayllus organize and sponsor cooperative labor parties, ritual battles, feasts, and drinking bouts. These diverse festive and symbolically rich ceremonies reinforce social relationships, member affiliation, and group solidarity. Bastien reminds us that "the ayllu is formed by a continual process of matching terms and constituting separate parts into wholes" (Bastien 1978:192). He associates the Aymara term *tinku* (meaning "coming together") with the tendency of the ayllu to reunite symbolically such complementary components as highland and lowland, and living and dead (Bastien 1978:121).

Among the Macha, the constant rejoining of opposites is expressed through the ethnosemantic term *yanantin*, which refers to a "completeness through duality" that is considered a cultural ideal. Platt perceives *yanantin* as an operative principle in virtually all ritual activity, ranging from house dedication ceremonies to village planning and the ordering of gender, moiety, and minimal ayllus in dance and in violent ritual battles also known in Aymara as *tinku* (Platt 1986). These ritual activities are important to the creation and affirmation of ayllu identity and further help determine political leadership. As in *cargo* festival systems elsewhere in the Americas, senior figures in ayllus can accrue power and prestige by sponsoring these ceremonial events (Abercrombie 1998).

Ayllu identities are also inextricably tied to landscape. Members of particular ayllus revere specific sacred places on the land such as mountains, stone outcrops, lakes, and springs. These revered "earth shrines" (Bastien 1978:191) are known as *huacas* in Quechua or *mallkus* in Aymara. These terms were also used historically for living lords, their mummified remains, people of unusual birth, high mountain peaks, or even unusual fruits or vegetables (Isbell 1997:52). In many historic ayllus, the most potent huacas were those related to real or mythic ancestors (Salomon 1995). Often, as was the case with the Inca royal ayllus (Bauer 1991) and with ethnographic ayllus (Abercrombie 1998; Allen 1988; Bastien 1978), each ayllu recounts its genesis from specific huacas or mallkus that mark ancestral origin places known as *pakarinas* or dawn places. The importance of these sacred places to ayllu identity was well understood even by the Spanish clerics assigned to their dismantling: "Every child who has learned to talk knows the name of the *huaca* of his clan. For every clan and faction has a principal *huaca* . . . and members of the clan take the name of the community *huaca*. Some *huacas* are thought [of] as the guardians and advocates" (Arriaga 1968 [1621]).

Although ayllu membership is tied to landscape, it is less connected to ideas of bounded territory. Aspects of ayllu identity that explicitly involve place refer not to spatial boundaries but to the points on the landscape that link the ayllu to its ancestors. Indeed, Andean mortuary practices are often interpreted as a means to connect the ancestral dead to landscape huacas, and to connect huacas to the ancestral dead. The excessive care afforded ancient Andean interments is typically seen as part of a larger process essential to the formation and maintenance of community identity (e.g., Dillehay 1995). Isbell explicitly links the history of ayllus with the appearance of mortuary monuments with "open sepulcher" burials that permitted an ongoing relationship with ancestral mummies (Isbell 1997).[1] This association of ancestor worship to group identity suggests that as a community form, if not a biological reality, the ayllu is more genealogical than territorial in nature. Ayllus, bounded by history rather than by borders, can thus operate within state societies, yet remain independent of hierarchical state structures.

Diasporas

Considering ayllus as forms of "ethnicity in motion," it becomes clear that they have much in common with other diasporic communities. Many discussions of transnationalism and migration in globalization studies have focused on a type of transnational community known as the diaspora. James Clifford has described diasporas as "expatriate minority communities (1) that are dispersed from an original center to at least two peripheral places; (2) that maintain a memory, vision or myth about their original homeland, (3) that believe they are not—and perhaps cannot be—fully accepted by their host country; (4) that see the ancestral home as a place of eventual return, when the time is right; (5) that are committed to the maintenance or restoration of this homeland and (6) of which the group's consciousness and solidarity are 'importantly defined' by this continuing relationship with the homeland" (Clifford 1994:304).

This definition represents only the latest evolution of the Greek term "diaspora" meaning scattering or dispersion. For most of its history, the term "diaspora" referred primarily to the scattered settlement of Jews outside Palestine following the Babylonian exile.[2] In the twentieth century, this term was applied to scattered migrations of communities driven by exile or overt oppression (e.g., England 1998; Ledgerwood 1998). The concept has been expanded to include guest workers, transnational economic migrants, and other historically displaced though perhaps not exiled communities (Hall

1990; Mortland 1998; Tambiah 2000:169), and a broader definition of "migration" has been added to most dictionaries. Nonetheless, as Clifford implies, the salient usage of the term "diaspora" is limited to transnational communities with strong shared identities, expectation of return, and unwillingness, difficulty or inability to assimilate in host societies. Using "diaspora" to refer to a specific form of identity-based community represents a general trend away from spatial definitions of community. Following Anderson's dictum that all human community above the level of the household is "imagined" (1987), many studies emphasize the historical dynamics of identity formation rather than static boundaries of group membership. Social, cultural, or ethnic groups are now better understood as complex and dynamic networks of relationships, interests, and identities (e.g., Cohen 2000). Inconveniently for archaeologists, collective identities are never "eternally fixed in some essentialized past" but are "subject to the continuous play of history, culture, and power" (Hall 1990:225).

Writing about transnational migration in the postmodern system, Stanley Tambiah suggests that diasporic migration contradicts some of our most cherished basic assumptions about territory and hierarchy in state societies: "In combination, these flows test and breach the autonomy, sovereignty, and territorial boundaries of nation-states that were formerly viewed as the main units of collective sociopolitical identity and existence. In addition, they intensify and sharpen sociocultural diversity in plural societies, posing for them the challenges of multicultural coexistence, tolerance, and accommodation. Multiethnicity and pluriculturalism—is the current idiom of that struggle" (Tambiah 2000:163).

This new understanding of the fluid nature of ascriptive groups within the state poses a significant challenge to anthropologists studying complex societies. If even modern diasporic communities escape clear spatial definition, how are ancient diaspora and colonial communities to be reconstructed from an archaeological record that is, after all, largely spatial in nature? While this challenge is daunting, archaeologists may assume that ancient diaspora communities, like those of the present day described by Clifford and Tambiah, defined themselves in opposition to others. Archaeologically, this fact might be marked by distinctions in practice and activities, and thus by stylistic and practice-based ethnic distinction as well as spatial segregation from other communities.

Trade Diasporas and Ethnic Enclaves

Some of the best-studied diaspora communities in antiquity are ethnic enclaves situated to facilitate trade, known as "trade diasporas." These trade communities of merchants living among aliens have been found on every continent since the origins of urban life (Curtin 1984:3). Unlike interpretations constructed of evidence of the exchange of commodities alone, the trade diaspora offers a contextual advantage for archaeologists in that it postulates a context for traders, diplomats, or foreign agents living abroad that is both ethnically and spatially distinct. Such diasporic enclaves should be recognizable archaeologically as precincts in which distinctive material culture and domestic traditions stand out in contrast to the predominant local majority settlement.

A growing body of examples suggests that trade diasporas can exhibit any of a broad range of relationships between enclaves and their host communities. Diaspora communities may be (1) of marginal or even pariah status, (2) autonomous, or (3) dominant over their hosts (Curtin 1984:5; Stein 1999b:49). The valence of diaspora-host relationship may depend on the relative social complexity of homeland and host, the availability and desirability of the goods or services in play, cultural mores or taboos concerning trade, and situational variables of relative power. One of the most important factors involves the diasporic community's distance from the homeland. Great distance both increases the costs of transport of goods (Drennan 1984; D'Altroy 1992, 2001) and makes a core's extension of power through the diaspora difficult. This phenomenon, described by Stein as "distance parity," suggests that even powerful states' ability to project hegemonic power decays with distance, leading to increasing symmetry in economic and political relations with increasingly distant peripheries (1999:62). The effect of distance parity would be to level the playing field between the trade diasporas of powerful complex societies and less powerful host communities.

Notably, our analysis of ancient trade diasporas may be overly influenced by the prevalent example of nineteenth-century European colonialism, with its globalist assumption of core dominance through greater political complexity and technological superiority (Curtin 1984:9; Stein 1998:14). This has led to an assumption of core dominance and consequently of peripheral dependence in models of archaic states. A less state-centered model of trade diasporas was described by Abner Cohen in his 1969 study of the present-day Hausa trader community living in the Sabo district of the Yoruba city of Ibadan (Cohen 1969). Instead of emphasizing the role of trade colonies in the exercise of a core polity's projection of power, Cohen focused on the colony itself as a field of play for corporate interest groups that crosscut state boundaries. Since the nineteenth century, the Hausa have established enclaves, called *zongos*, throughout West Africa to control trade in cattle and kola nuts. To this day, Hausa *zongos* survive throughout Ghana and Nigeria, both as isolated ethnic islands along the kola nut routes and as large, ethnically distinct wards in cities like Ibadan and Kumasi, the capital of the Asante kingdom (Curtin 1984:40; Schildkraut 1978). To Cohen, the colonies of the Hausa trade diaspora were not so much state outposts as economic interest groups operationalized through ethnicity: "No matter how long the Hausa broker has been living in the South he will always be anxious to preserve the symbols of his Hausaism, dressing like a Hausa, speaking and behaving like a Hausa. Hausaism is essential for his livelihood" (Cohen 1974:xxi).

While it might be argued that the trade colonies Cohen describes are a far cry from the transnational globalized diasporas Clifford describes, there is resemblance in structure, if not in scale. Indeed, the maintenance of ethnic distance from their host communities remains a hallmark of transnational Hausa trade networks that today include communities in most of the world's major cities (Steiner 1994).

If early states sanctioned trade activities for political ends, the long-distance traders themselves must have represented a specialist class in state societies. Trade diaspora colonies might be expected in states that had traditions leading to merchant-agent classes like the *dam-gar* of Mesopotamia (Adams 1966, 1974) or the *pochteca* of the Aztec Empire (Hassig 1988). Traders often functioned as agents of the state, on which they depended for military protection, maintenance of transportation facilities, and favorable regulation of market times and places (Hassig 1988). With these advantages, trader classes usually exploited the privileges of their state commission to engage in entrepreneurial trade. The very existence of such entrepreneurial classes depended on the existence of open markets and some mechanism to protect agents of the home society in distant resource zones. But what of trade colonies in civilizations that have not yet reached the level of conquest empires? Let us look at two examples.

Mesopotamian Enclaves: The Uruk Trade Diaspora

The extension of a trade diaspora has been seen as a critical component of the growth and expansion of Uruk, one of the world's earliest state societies and the antecedent of the Sumerian states and empires. Organized trade colonies were established on the periphery of Mesopotamia in Iran, Syria, and Anatolia during the Late Uruk Period (3400–3100 B.C.; Algaze 1989, 1993a, 1993b; Baines and Yoffee 1998:215; Oates 1993:417; Stein 1998, 1999). Weiss and Young (1978) suggested that small government-staffed trading posts were established by the developing city-state in preexisting towns of the Susiana Plain. For example, trade stations such as Godin Tepe in the Zagros Mountains of western Iran facilitated long-distance exchange of commodities such as lapis lazuli or copper. The walled entrepôt of Godin V was "a Susian trading post immediately supported by a local agricultural village or town . . . involved in long distance trade, in strictly local trade, or in both"

(Weiss and Young 1978:14). The spread of the Uruk enclaves appears to have been peacefully negotiated with their hosts rather than militarily imposed. Trading colonies like Godin V maintained a late Uruk artifact assemblage distinct from those of their surrounding host communities. The household preferences and practices implied suggest that enclaves of Uruk traders maintained their lowland cultural integrity despite their physical location within culturally distinct highland villages (Henrickson 1994:88).

Contrasting interpretations of these earliest Mesopotamian trade colonies exemplify the distinction of globalist world systems from local agency approaches. In his globalist interpretation of the Uruk colonization Algaze points out that these cultural outposts were located "efficiently . . . to control the flow of resources" (Algaze 1989:580), ultimately leading to a world system that comprised diverse and independent networks of trade entrepôt established by each of several independent Sumerian city states (1993b:115–118). Algaze characterizes the Uruk colonies as "an early instance of an 'informal empire' or 'world system' based on asymmetrical exchange and a hierarchically organized international division of labor that differs from modern examples only in degree" (Algaze 1989:571). In this view, Uruk's system of trade entrepôt was centrally directed and dedicated to resource extraction from the peripheries. Additionally, the Uruk world system might be read as a relief response to internal demographic growth, slavery, and debt in the Mesopotamian core and as an outlet for the growing crafts production of the Uruk metropole (Zagarell 1986). Uruk influence caused a restructuring in peripheral societies, instigating new institutions, technologies, and greater craft specialization (Algaze 1989:585). Sites that hosted Uruk enclaves were more likely to develop complex features such as defensive walls and a city grid (Algaze 1989:578).

Following an approach more attuned to local agency, Stein examined the economic and social relationship of a colony of the Uruk "trade diaspora" with its host community within the site of Hacinebi, Turkey, 1,300 km from the Mesopotamian homeland (Stein 1998, 1999). As at Godin, the Uruk enclave at Hacinebi was established as an enclosed compound of foreigners that coexisted with an indigenous local population. The enclave maintained a high degree of economic autonomy from its host community, pursuing a "parallel economy" that included all productive activities within their sector of the site (Stein 1999:153). As at Godin, the Uruk enclave at Hacinebi led lives largely separate from those of their hosts, retaining a recognizable cultural identity reflected in "ethnically specific contrasts in technological style" in ceramic, textile, and lithic assemblages and in administrative devices like commodity seals (Stein 1999:148–162). The economic independence of the enclave is reinforced by faunal data from Hacinebi. A full range of animal body parts was represented within the Uruk enclave, suggesting autonomous herding and butchering by the colonists, while a distinction in species consumption patterns suggests culinary preferences distinct from those of their native hosts (Stein 1998:235–236). All told, these data suggest that Mesopotamian trade diasporas lived as socially and economically autonomous enclaves, dealing with their host communities on a limited basis. Stein argues that the Anatolian receiver communities were probably more complex technologically than has previously been recognized, with advanced crafts industries. Under his reconstruction, any hegemonic effect of the more complex Uruk polities was negated by the distance parity phenomenon, which leveled the political playing field. In this view, the relationship of indigenous polities to Uruk's trade outposts was as equals in a symmetric exchange system (Stein 1998). Local societies were not substantially transformed by the Uruk presence and did not adopt Uruk forms of political complexity, agricultural intensification, or technological developments (Stein et al 1996:256). Host communities—particularly those located at great distances—tolerated their Uruk guests but did not change their way of life significantly to emulate cosmopolites from the world's first city.

Ethnic Enclaves in Classic Mesoamerica

Some of the most extensive interregional networks of ethnic enclaves in precontact Mesoamerica have been described in association with the Classic civilization of Teotihuacan (A.D. 300–750) in central Mexico. The Teotihuacan enclaves are particularly instructive because they suggest that colonial enclaves were exchanged on a reciprocal basis with neighboring complex societies. Teotihuacan enclaves reported at Kaminaljuyu, over 1,000 km away in the Guatemalan highlands, may have served as ports of trade to other Maya centers and as a source of exotic raw materials such as jadeite (Marcus 1998:72; Sanders and Michels 1977; Turner 1992:107). Kaminaljuyu, and an enclave at Matacapan on the southern coast of Vera Cruz, included temple platforms of Teotihuacan style and would appear to represent the long-term presence of Teotihuacan communities (Manzanilla 1992b: 331; Millon 1988:125, 1992:354; Santley et al. 1987).

Within the Teotihuacan metropolis, at least two districts or *barrios* suggest an enduring presence of foreign communities. The "merchants' barrio" included unusual circular architecture and a high frequency of thin orange ceramics that link the neighborhood to the Gulf Coast (Millon 1992:367; Rattray 1989, 1990). The "Oaxaca barrio" of Tlailotlacan has been described as an enclave of ethnic Zapotecs who arrived in Teotihuacan during the Monte Albán II–IIIA transition period (Spence 1992:76). Like the Uruk colonists at Hacinebi, the Tlailotlacanos demonstrated a certain amount of acculturation to their host community, adopting much of the Teotihuacan utilitarian ceramic assemblage, manufactured elsewhere in the city, and some items of ritual function. Nonetheless, inhabitants of the barrio expressed their distinct ethnicity in daily practices, rituals, and burial customs that set them apart from the rest of the city. Tlailotlacanos were buried in slab-lined chambers with typically Zapotec offerings, including anthropomorphic urns, instead of the simple primary burials prevalent in Teotihuacan. In domestic areas, about 3 percent of the ceramic assemblage consisted of vessels of Zapotec forms and styles, most made locally in reduced gray wares. These include utilitarian vessels, fine serving wares, and particularly ritual ceramics such as censers, figurines, and urns.

Andean Trade Diasporas

As compared to Classic Mesoamerica and Protoliterate Mesopotamia, the Pre-Columbian Andes are unusual because markets and market-based entrepreneurial activities were undeveloped, perhaps because of high transport costs in this mountainous region (Murra 1980; Stanish 1992). Without a stronger entrepreneurial tradition, Andean states may have relied more on reciprocity and redistribution for exchange with their peripheries. Although they may have enjoyed some entrepreneurial latitude, Andean traders usually operated in roles prescribed by the redistributive demands of elite patrons. In the coastal region of Chincha, Rostworowski describes an Inca occupational category of *mollo chasqui camayoc* (*Spondylus* messenger-worker) for merchants who traveled by raft along the northern Peruvian coast and inland by camelid caravan to trade spondylus shell and copper (1988:210). This Quechua term implies that they operated under an Inca-sanctioned status comparable to that of the *chasqui* (imperial messengers), their status directly dependent on and directly commanded by the state.

Salomon describes a professional trading class of "politically sponsored long- and medium-distance exchange specialists" in Ecuador known as *mindalae*. The mindalae trafficked in exotic prestige items such as cloth, gold, silver, salt, and coca leaf, forming "a unique corporate group, set aside from common noble, servile or foreign categories . . . responsible only to the apical chief of their home communities . . . [and] exempt from the usual political obligations such as corvée, owing only a special tribute in sumptuary goods" (Salomon 1986:101–102).

Some Andean traders may have established trade diaspora as enclaves in foreign communities. In the Quito region, mindalae traders concentrated at the "locally preeminent nexus point of transport and exchange." Salomon's description suggests that the mindalae fit many of the definitions of a trade diaspora, as "extraterritorial residents, dwelling at certain sites advantageously placed on the routes connecting the major ecological zones . . . also forming links in the more remote articulation of the various inter-Andean basins and of those with the remoter coast and the Amazonian regions" (Salomon 1986:112).

On the whole, these cases appear to be exceptions. Generally, the non-market nature of exchange in Andean states suggests a form of diasporic colonization that might be contrasted with Uruk and Teotihuacan. Because long-distance trade never became institutionalized as an entrepreneurial activity to the extent that it was in Mesopotamia and Mesoamerica, it is not surprising that trade diasporas were a rarity in the ancient Andes. Instead, a distinctive kind of diasporic enclave community developed in the south-central Andes to facilitate production and reciprocal exchange.

Archipelagos

Murra (1964, 1968, 1972, 1985) and others (Flores Ochoa 1972; Fonseca 1972; Pease 1980) document a specific type of colonization practiced by Inca-contemporary polities in the south-central Andes. According to this model, a core population, usually with its demographic center in the highlands, would establish colonial settlements in a variety of ecological and productive zones. Murra (1972) described such systems as "archipelagos" of colonies because they tended to consist of dispersed "islands" of settlement rather than being contiguous territories.

The Vertical Environment

Part of Murra's archipelago model suggests that nonmarket Andean social relations of production and reciprocity-based exchange developed in response to uniquely Andean ecological conditions of resource zonation. Like other mountainous areas, the Andes are marked by a dramatic ecological diversity caused by the interaction of tropical latitude, the radical relief of the mountains themselves, and proximity to the Pacific Ocean. Because the zonation of the Andean environment is largely determined by elevation, the human economic response to this phenomenon is often described as "vertical complementarity."

The interaction of the cold Peruvian coastal or Humboldt current and warm trade winds produces supersaturated westerly sea breezes that effectively prevent precipitation on the coast. Paradoxically, while nutrient upwelling from the ocean floor supports a rich coastal marine life, the current is also responsible for one of the world's driest deserts along the western slope of the southern Andes, where even xerophytic shrubs and cacti can only be found at higher elevations. The only relief to this vegetationless landscape is found in the fifty-two Pacific-flowing river valleys that are watered by mountain runoff. Only in the riverine oases is irrigation agriculture of temperate crops possible. The oasis valleys have been the scene of the most intensive prehistoric and historic human habitation in the region.

High in the *sierra* and especially in the *puna* or *altiplano* (high plain) region, snow and rain provide the moisture for a variety of microzones. A gross division may be made between the dry puna that borders the peaks of the Western *Cordillera* and the wet puna around and to the east of Lake Titicaca, where rainfall exceeds 700 mm annually. Conditions of the altiplano—thin air, great diurnal temperature variation with frequent nightly frosts, and high daily solar radiation—have given rise to specialized vegetation that might be described as herbaceous, perennial, and dwarf (Moran 1980) and a limited cultigen complex of frost-resistant tubers and chenopod grains (Kolata 1986; Towles 1961; Weberbauer 1936).

Beyond the peaks of the Eastern Cordillera, a rich well-watered transitional zone known as *montaña* gradually gives way to the tropical forests of the Amazon Basin. These regions are suitable for temperate and tropical fruits, vegetables, and coca, a leaf greatly valued by Andean peoples as a high-altitude stimulant and for ritual purposes.

The Andean environment also provides an element of risk in the form of periodic catastrophic reversals of normal patterns. The best known of these, known as El Niño because of its appearance in December, occurs in years when the Humboldt current is deflected by warm tropical currents. This reversal of fortune, occurring at irregular intervals, is accompanied by a devastating disruption of marine life, catastrophic heavy rains on the coast and western sierra, and drought in the highlands (Caviedes 2001; Waylen and Caviedes 1987).

It is logical that in regions where resource variability is defined by sharp gradients in altitude, securing access to a variety of altitude-defined ecological zones would be a fundamental goal for human groups. The central role of altitude in the vertical differentiation of high montane human ecosystems has been a topic of comparative research since the 1970s. Alpine Europe and the Himalayas, for example, have been compared as parallel adaptations of agropastoral transhumance through the "vertical oscillation of cultivators, herders and beasts" (Rhoades and Thompson 1975:539, cited in Goldstein and Messerschmidt 1980:119). Mixed mountain agriculture systems maximized seasonal procurement and served as risk-averaging mechanisms to minimize the effects of catastrophic climatic events in any one zone and provide for self-sufficiency through a variety of complementary resources.

The discussion of the Andean adaptation to altitude-defined resource zonation has concentrated on resource access via nonmarket exchange systems. At its most basic level, interzonal resource exchange among Andean ayllus has been described as "compressed" vertical complementarity. Brush (1977) describes how present-day ayllus of the Uchucmarca Valley of the central Andes send individual households of family members to different resource zones located within a few days' walk of their central settlement. For the same region, John Murra cited the sixteenth- century *visita* by the Spanish bureaucrat Ortiz de Zuñiga, who describes a similar compressed system among ayllus of the Chupaychu and Yacha. These communities routinely dispatched groups as small as a single household, individual couples, or widows from the communities' maize and potato-growing nuclear zone to "resource islands" such as *altiplano* salt licks and lowland timber, cotton, wheat, and particularly coca-producing areas: "Of the three Indians who are in the coca of Pichomachay, one (is sent) from the town of Pecta and another from Atcor and another from Guacas . . . and these are exchanged if their wives die or when they die they put others in their place" (Ortiz de Zuñiga [1562] 1967:44, translated in Murra 1968:142).

In compressed systems, reciprocal economic relationships were codified in the kinship bonds among community members. As colonial enclaves were small, and seldom more than a few days' walk from the homeland, these colonists retained their membership in their homeland communities despite their physical displacement. Especially if the stationing was temporary or rotating or involved marginalized members of the community, there was no reason to fear that these enclave households would cease identifying with their home community.

The idea of dispersed community members "away on business" becomes problematic if we extend it to groups that are farther away and not linked on a daily basis with their community of origin. In the seminal articles concerning this peculiarly Andean type of diaspora community, Murra (1972) described a larger scale version of vertical complementarity in which distant settlements were established by denser and more socially complex core populations. This paradigm, constructed to explain the persistence of altiplano colonists in lowland valleys of the south-central Andes, has become known as the archipelago model.

The Archipelago Model

The ethnohistoric prototype for the archipelago model is based on the sixteenth-century kingdom of the Lupaqa, an Aymara-speaking ethnic polity that had its capital on the western shore of Lake Titicaca, near the abandoned Tiwanaku site. Unlike other ethnic groups, who were assigned in *encomien-*

das (grants) to individual Spaniards, the Lupaqa enjoyed the unusual status of "royal Indians," belonging to the demesne of the Spanish king. Because of this accident of history, the Lupaqa were extensively examined by the royal *visitador* (inspector) Garci Diez de San Miguel in 1567, making them one of the best-documented complex polities of the contact period.

From their capital of Chucuito at an elevation of 3,800 m, the Lupaqa controlled an altiplano core region with a population of over 100,000. The Lupaqa also established colonies in the lowland oasis valleys of Lluta, Sama, and Moquegua, between 150 and 250 km or a minimum of ten days' walk from the Lake Titicaca core area (Murra 1968:143). Garci Diez's interviews of informants who interpreted Inca *quipus* (knotted strings used as recording devices) found that Lupaqa settlers were permanently assigned to collect *guano* (bird manure fertilizer) and to grow coca leaf, maize, hot peppers, and cotton in these and other *yungas*, or lowland regions. Craft specialists such as potters were also sent to "island" settlements situated at resource locations such as clay sources. Although these Lupaqa colonies maintained long-term occupations, they did not establish Lupaqa territorial sovereignty in these altitude-defined resource zones. Rather, the Lupaqa's "vertical archipelago" shared each productive zone with enclaves of other ethnic polities (Murra 1968, 1972; Rostworowski 1986).

It has become fashionable to debunk a vaguely defined concept of verticality as reductionist, determinist, and overly particular to the Andes. Indeed, the caricature of an essentialized verticality as "a functionalist perspective easily wedded to the ecological concept of adaptation" has become such a popular straw man that it even has been given a name: "Lo Andino" (Van Buren 1996:340). I argue that this caricature is incorrect and that the critics have missed the far more interesting structural implication of the extended nature of diasporic communities, not only in the Andes but worldwide. A stricter use of the term "archipelago" permits us to consider expatriate ayllu communities that disperse across geographical space, yet remain tightly knit by shared identity. In short, for the Andean region, archipelagos are ayllus in diaspora.

Viewed in archaeological perspective, the archipelago model involves several testable principles. According to the archipelago model, peripheral colonies should demonstrate several features in the archaeological record: (1) permanent or long-term *residence* in complementary resource zones, (2) explicit manifestation of a maintained *identity* with the homeland nucleus, (3) *structural reproduction* of the social structure of the homeland, and (4) *multiethnicity*—the distribution of immigrant colonies interspersed with colonies of other ethnic groups.

Residence and the Archipelago Model

Expatriate communities must demonstrate a long-term settlement that is distinguishable from seasonal transhumance or temporary contact such as trade, proselytizing, or elite clientage. Further, the scale of such settlements should be commensurate with the social and ideological reproduction of the expatriate community—minimally, enclaves of several hundred households.

The Lupaqa provide an example of the scale of resident colonial populations under the archipelago model. Through interviews with the local lords who interpreted Inca *quipus*, Garci Diez found that the Lupaqa *yungas* settlers lived in *mitmaquna* (colonies) of up to several hundred households. Indeed, Lupaqa colonies were considerably larger than the four to sixteen households reported for the Chupaychu and Yacha of Huanuco (Murra 1972:443). Although the Lupaqa colonies were located in rural rather than urban settings, they must have been of the same order of magnitude as the Hausa, Uruk, or Teotihuacan enclaves, or considerably larger.

Ethnic Identity and the Archipelago Model

Another feature of the archipelago model that is in keeping with trade diasporas might be described as the maintenance of identity, the "shared patterns of behavior motivated by similar assumptions, values, and standards of evaluation which are, themselves, perceived as reflecting a common history of the group" (Schortman 1989:54). Under Murra's model, archipelago colonists exclusively maintained their privileges and obligations as members of specific homeland communities. The maintenance of an ethnic identity among emigrants in an archipelago community should be apparent in both style and disposition of domestic and specialized artifact assemblages. For example, the village plan, architecture, activity areas, cuisine, and disposition and choice of tools and utensils should all reflect the lifestyles of the homeland community. Colonial identity with a homeland population, perhaps maintained by endogamous marriage patterns, should also be evident in skeletal biology in biological distance, common patterns of diet and pathology, and shared stylistic body practices like cranial deformation.

Cultural markers should define a diasporic colonial identity by setting colonists apart from indigenous populations. This accentuation of social identity through opposition is conveyed by a visible set of mutually understood cultural diacritics that signify separation as well as affiliation. These might include contrary settlement patterns, ritual practice, distinctive dress, marriage taboo, and maintenance of distinct languages. In historic Andean archipelagos, the maintenance of homeland allegiances and identities was so conscious and pervasive that census takers were easily able to distinguish colonists from local residents: "Today we inspected . . . in a town called Chinchao, 33 Indians who are coca camayos (cultivators) from all the different factions of the Chupaychus. Of these, twenty had already been inspected *in their own native towns*" (Ortiz de Zuñiga [1549] 1967:303–304, quoted in Murra 1972:431, emphasis added).[3]

The identity of colonists' homelands could be maintained in a variety of ways. The modern Macha of Bolivia, for example, signify ayllu ties between the altiplano homeland and the lowland valleys through interregional marriage between members of the same maximal ayllu. Ideally, a man from the puna and a woman from the valley marry, representing the joining of complementary opposites sanctioned in the concept of *yanantin* (Platt 1986). Similarly, the Kaata also emphasize complementarity between highland and lowland communities by idealizing maximal ayllu endogamy and minimal ayllu exogamy. Kaata wedding rituals symbolically associate the woman's access to lowlands and the man's claim to highlands by emphasizing the exchange of persons between the Kaata's minimal ayllu groups (Bastien refers to these as "lineages"; 1978:116). The identity of the maximal Kaata ayllu is thus solidified by "symbolizing the interdependency of the lineages within the context of the mountain metaphor" (Bastien 1978:125).

Structural Reproduction and the Archipelago Model

"Structural reproduction" refers to the tendency of diasporic archipelagos to reproduce the recursive social hierarchy of their homelands. If an archipelago model holds, colonies should structurally reproduce the homeland's segmentation into ethnic (maximal), moiety, and minimal ayllu units. Typically, as with the historic Lupaqa, a bipartite division of upper and lower moieties was replicated in historic Andean colonies in other ecological tiers. Lupaqa colonies were each directly aligned with one of the two homeland moieties, Aransaya and Urinsaya, and reported specific allegiance to their respective lords Martín Qari and Martín Kusi (Murra 1968:126). Other segmentary categories with ethnic, occupational, or status-related definitions, such as the Uru, were likewise represented in Lupaqa colonies.

Finer longitudinal social divisions are also reproduced in present-day Aymara colonies. Harris found that the tripartite subdivisions of the Laymi Aymara moieties are typically reproduced in outlier settlements: "As at the moiety level, the territory of each of the three subdivisions of Laymi in theory encompasses all the major ecological variation of the Laymi" (Harris 1986:264). Seen from the perspective of any one region, this would represent a reproduction of the homeland's tripartite social divisions in each area colonized by the Laymi Aymara. The recursive structure is thus reproduced in diaspora, with segments corresponding to each level of the ayllu subdivisions of the homeland.

For the Macha in the early historic period, Platt describes the reproduction of the entire nested minimal ayllu substructure in colonized regions. His discussion explicates how the recursive structural relations of Macha ayllus are repeated in lowland colonies: "In 1579 we find the Macha defending their right to maintain *uchucamayos* (hot pepper cultivators) in the warm valleys near Karasi . . .. Ten uchucamayos are involved, one for each of the ten ayllu constituting the Macha" (Platt 1986:230).

Within colonial communities, these segments may be evident archaeologically in one of several ways. First, ayllu segments may be distinguished through spatially discernible material distributions. Additionally, ayllu segments may display stylistic patterns that parallel their counterparts in the homeland. These similarities could be evident in micro-variations in costume, utensil use, ceremonial or mortuary practice, or other stylistic practices that leave a mark on material culture. Compared with markers for ethnic identity, however, the markers of the smaller ayllu segments (or other heterarchical subdivisions) may be more subtle. For example, intentional cranial deformation, a stylistic behavior that leaves a permanent and unchangeable record on the human body, may be a particularly telltale marker of a descent-based yet socially chosen identity (Blom 1999; Hoshower et al. 1995). Skeletal, dental, or molecular biological distance studies of significant human skeletal samples may all offer insight into how the genetic component of ayllus varied over time and across space (Blom et al. 1998; Blom 1999; Lozada 1998; Sutter 1996).

Multiethnicity and the Archipelago Model

What makes the archipelago a unique community formulation is the proposition that colonized regions consisted of multiethnic island colonies that were not contiguous with their homelands. This type of scattered settlement is in keeping with the mosaic character of resource zones that characterize the south-central Andes. However, the dispersed island arrangement of ayllu colonies contradicts the assumption of the globalist position that territorial control was a key factor in state expansion. In Murra's interpretation, each archipelago of colonial settlement could be spatially interdigitated with archipelagos of other affiliations, under an umbrella of "multiethnic coexistence," much as different ethnic communities coexist with one another and with indigenous populations in modern immigrant cities.

To reduce the political instability of such multiethnicity, a structurally prescribed multiethnic coexistence that minimized conflict must have been in operation. Indeed, such a system apparently was in operation in the sixteenth century on the altiplano. With surprise, Juan Polo de Ondegardo records the peaceful comings and goings of altiplano cultivators to and from lowland valleys: "In accounting for and distributing the things they bring, it is curious and difficult to believe, but no one is wronged" ([1571] 1872:137, translated in Julien 1985:193).

Historically, there is extensive evidence for the sharing of resource zones by different ethnic or political groups. For the Aymara colonists of Bolivia's *yungas* valleys of Larecaja, a similar multiethnic rubbing of shoulders was described in 1595 litigation that affirmed joint land ownership by various highland as well as valley ayllus, including "*indios lupacas, yungas, huarinas y achacaches*" (Saignes 1986:316). Similarly, the Lupaqa colonies in the western oasis valleys of Moquegua, Sama, Caplina, and Azapa were discontinuously distributed and interdigitated with less well documented colonies of other highland ethnic polities such as the Pacaxe (Hidalgo 1996; Murra 1972:439; Pease 1985:154), the Colla (Julien 1985:194; Stanish 1992:101; Van Buren 1996), and indigenous coastal fisherfolk known as Camanchacas (Hidalgo and Focacci 1986:138; Rostworowski 1986:129).[4]

In order for the archipelago model to be supported archaeologically, it requires evidence of peoples of distinct ethnic affiliations coexisting in close proximity. Enclaves of different ethnic groups or ayllus, distinguishable by distinctive material culture and lifeways, should share regional space in an interspersed manner, without evidence of territorial divisions or hostilities. Conversely, evidence that a spatially bounded territory contained homogeneous settlements of a single affiliation would contradict the multiethnic coexistence intrinsic to the archipelago model. Demonstrating multiethnicity in the archaeological record thus requires a research strategy that addresses regional settlement patterns as well as within-site household and mortuary studies.

The Archipelago and the Inca State

As the largest native empire ever to bestride the Americas, the Inca state is justly famous for building upon ancient Andean strategies of conquest and state rule with dramatic innovations in imperial administration. It has been suggested that the amplification of archipelago-style vertical complementarity to encompass much larger territories offered a competitive advantage that may have been important in the expansion of the Inca state (Isbell 1977; Paulsen 1976). The Inca Empire manipulated entire ethnic communities to its advantage by the forced establishment of permanent *mitmaquna* colonies throughout the empire (Cieza de León 1959 [1553]; Cobo 1984; Diez de San Miguel 1964 [1567]; Rowe 1982; Wachtel 1982). However, the *mitimae* of the Inca colonization program were part of a broader Inca *real-politik* that Salomon has described as "pseudo-conservatism" (1986:112). By this he means that Inca colonization was more often motivated by economic and strategic rather than ecological considerations. Cieza's description of the system, for example, makes no mention of complementary resources, instead emphasizing colonies as a mode of domination:

> Inasmuch as all this length of territory was inhabited by barbarous peoples, some of whom were very warlike, in order more easily to insure and keep their power and tranquility, the following policy had been put into force from the time of Inca Pachacuti [d. 1471], father of the great Topa Inca [d. 1492] and grandfather of Huayna Capac. As soon as one of these larger provinces was conquered, ten or twelve thousand of the men and their wives, or six thousand, or the number decided upon, were ordered to leave and remove themselves from it. . . . They were given land to work and sites on which to build their homes. And these *mitimaes* were ordered by the Incas to be always obedient to what their governors and captains ordered, so that if the natives should rebel, and they supported the governor, the natives would be punished and reduced to the service of the Incas. Likewise, if the *mitimaes* stirred up disorder, they were put down by the natives. In this way these rulers had their empire assured against revolts and the provinces well supplied with food, for most of the people, as I have said, had been moved from one land to another. (Cieza 1959 [1553]:56–57)

Tellingly, Cieza even states that colonists were most often moved to resource zones identical to their homelands, hardly a practical policy for increasing diversity from an ecological point of view: "These were transferred to another town or province of *the same climate and nature as that which they left*; if they came from a cold climate, they were taken to a cold climate, and if from a warm climate, to a warm, and these were called *mitimaes*, which means Indians come from one land to another" (Cieza 1959 [1553]: 57, emphasis added).

The geopolitical pragmatism of Inca resettlement policies is further illustrated by one description of state-directed settlement in the valleys of Larecaja:

> Since they could neither absorb the Aymara-speaking population within the empire nor deport all of them to the periphery, Inca policy attempted to infiltrate their territory in the Collao and its lower outliers. They were surrounded and watched by resettled state colonies brought from afar. Chinchaysuyu households from northern Peru were installed on both sides of the lake, facing each other; Charcas garrisons and some from Yampara were placed on the northern shore and Huanca colonies on the eastern. J. V. Murra has stressed this reutilization of an ancient Andean practice *whose very meaning was changed*,

since such long-distance resettlement makes it difficult if not impossible for the colonists to continue exercising their traditional rights at their ancestral homes. (Saignes 1986:317, emphasis added)

Rather than expanding their access to ecological zones, the Inca's *mitmaquna* represent the replacement of populations as a means of subjugation—removing suspect groups to secure parts of the empire, peopling key frontier areas with more loyal populations, and so on. The sophistication and widespread success of Inca period resettlement policy suggests that they were able to draw upon a preexisting repertoire of archipelago strategies and a popular acceptance of colonization that was conditioned by centuries of practice. The Inca exploitation of these ancient diasporic traditions for strategic ends surely indicates a coercive provincial control more in keeping with globalist constructions of state expansion. But what were the origins of Andean diaspora in state expansion? Was the deliberate globalist strategy of the Inca anticipated by a more ancient tradition of states in which each ayllu dispatched its own diaspora of colonies?

Summary: *Ayllus* as Diasporic Communities

An archipelago model of state expansion, seen in light of what we know about Andean ayllus, bears a strong resemblance to formulations of diaspora communities. First, members of an Andean archipelago of colonies, like diaspora communities, are true long-term residents in exile, or in Clifford's terminology "expatriate" communities. This attribute critically distinguishes colonists from traders, missionaries, or other travelers. Second, archipelago colonists carry and maintain an identity with a homeland community that "importantly defines" their consciousness and group solidarity. Like diasporic populations, archipelago colonists see the ancestral home as a place of eventual return. Third, colonists in an archipelago maintain finer-grained nested identities with their specific homeland communities. In the preceding discussion of Andean ayllus, I have described how individuals align with minor and minimal ayllus at levels nested within the larger universe of the maximal ayllu. Finally, what makes the archipelago unique is that colonized regions were multiethnic. This should be identifiable in the archaeological record through stylistic and material differences indicating the coexistence of enclaves of different polities.

Notably however, there remain several distinctions between trade diaspora communities and archipelagos. First, the diasporic enclaves of the Hausa, Uruk, and Teotihuacan existed to facilitate *trade*. In contrast, Andean archipelago colonies were dedicated to agricultural *production*. Second, goods in modern Africa and ancient Mesopotamia and Mesoamerica moved through market exchange systems. In contrast, archipelago exchange was orchestrated through nonmarket reciprocity. Third, classic trade diasporas were small business communities living within the multiethnic urban settings of imperial capitals, border cities, or towns along major trade routes. In contrast, because archipelago colonial enclaves were typically farming settlements, they shared rural rather than urban space with neighbors of other ethnicities.

Despite these differences, trade diasporas and the archipelagos have in common a salient central feature. Both require diversity and multiethnicity in colonized areas. For the south-central Andes, John Murra himself sketched out an archaeological hypothesis: "I wouldn't be surprised if we find in one single valley settlements of diverse antecedents without any temporal stratification between them. These would simply be peripheral colonies established in the lowlands by cores that were contemporary, but diverse in material culture" (Murra 1972:441).

In the chapters that follow I examine the Tiwanaku state and its colonies in the south-central Andes in light of what we know about ayllus, diasporas, and archipelagos. I propose that a diasporic archipelago model best explains the balance of hierarchical and heterarchical tendencies in Tiwanaku expansion and provides an agency-oriented alternative to globalist models of early expansion of multiethnic states.

3

The Tiwanaku Core Region

"Nosotros no somos de aquí, somos de la parte alta" (We are not from here, we are from the highlands).

Cecilia Mamani, squatter at Cerro Trapiche site, Moquegua, 1999

In the Moquegua Valley today, there is little mistaking the Carumeños. Like diasporas everywhere, these highlanders hang on to the myriad customs that tell of their villages, families, and lives back home in the high sierra. Their dress, their language, and their own recounting are constant reminders that they are "not from here" but from the highlands. Clearly, to understand either modern or ancient migrants, we must first understand something about the homelands that command this kind of enduring identity in diaspora. In this chapter I reconstruct what we know about the homeland of the Tiwanaku peoples who colonized the fertile oasis valleys of the southern Andes a millennium before their descendants, the Carumeños.

The Homeland

Before examining the Tiwanaku expansion into peripheral zones, we must understand the demographic, political, and social complexity of Tiwanaku's core region (fig. 3.1). The Tiwanaku culture dominated the south-central Andes between A.D. 500 and A.D. 1000. The Tiwanaku type site, 20 km south of the Bolivian shore of Lake Titicaca, is famous for its monumental public architecture, stone sculpture, and distinctive craft objects. The skills evident in Tiwanaku engineering and arts bespeak effective labor mobilization and demographic power. Yet Tiwanaku's homeland is in the harsh steppelike environment of Bolivia's altiplano, at an elevation of 3,800 m above sea level, making Tiwanaku the world's highest ancient urban center.

Although European scholars have been aware of the Tiwanaku site's vast and impressive ruins virtually since the Spanish conquest of Peru, the culture that built them remains the least understood of the New World civilizations. Most important, Tiwanaku left behind no written records, and several cycles of conquest and ethnic displacement between the site's abandonment and the

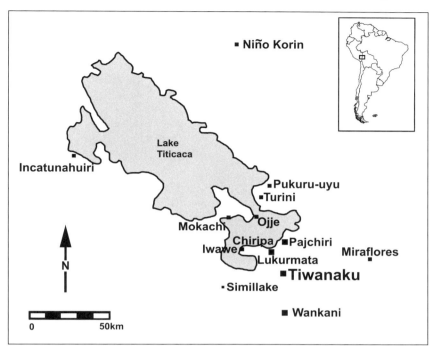

Figure 3.1. Map of the Tiwanaku core region.

arrival of Spanish chroniclers place Tiwanaku beyond the reach of direct historical sources. Studies of the Tiwanaku phenomenon were further limited by the inaccessibility of the Tiwanaku ruins, the depth of soil deposition on altiplano archaeological sites, and the shifting political fortunes of the three modern nations of Bolivia, Peru, and Chile in which Tiwanaku ruins are found.

Above all, the very improbability of a great civilization at 3,800 m contributed a powerful mystique to westerners' views of Tiwanaku. Because of its strangeness and inaccessibility, for the last five centuries Tiwanaku has been a culture more imagined than studied. The unique juxtaposition of scenic desolation and archaeological grandeur has long intrigued archaeologists, and it is not surprising that interpretations of the Tiwanaku culture have been a subject of contention. Reconstructions of the Tiwanaku site and its immediate hinterland have ranged from considering it a vacant religious shrine or the urbanized demographic heart of a centralized state to more nuanced interpretations of a segmentary political confederacy. Fortunately, new research in the late twentieth century has revitalized this discussion with some real data, and we can now debate the nature of Tiwanaku on something approaching its own terms. But first, we must understand the long and fascinating record of research in the Tiwanaku core region.

The First Western Explorers

Many of Peru's earliest Spanish chroniclers were awed by the Tiwanaku ruins and sought to explain their antiquity and grandeur. Foremost among these was Pedro de Cieza de León, a remarkable soldier who stands out as one of the few conquistadors who brought a true intellectual curiosity to the Andean world. As a teenager Cieza fought for the crown in the conquest of Colombia and in the 1547 civil war against Gonzalo Pizarro's rebellion. Unlike his contemporaries, who sought rewards for their services in *encomiendas* of land and labor, Cieza was awarded the title of *cronista* (chronicler) in 1549. This allowed him to continue his travels through the Andes, leading to the publication of his *Chronicle of Peru* in 1553.

In his all-too-brief account of Tiwanaku's monumental precinct, Cieza offered accurate descriptions of the great stone-faced pyramid mound of Akapana as "a man-made hill built on great stone foundations" (fig. 3.2; Cieza 1959 [1553]:283; 1984 [1553]:283). Other descriptions refer to the massive stone stela now known as the Bennett Monolith and its companion sculptures in the sunken court of Tiwanaku's Semisubterranean Temple (fig. 3.3),[1] the two sculptural figures that can now be found in front of the Tiwanaku church (fig. 3.4),[2] and the great rectangular cut-stone enclosure now known as the Kalasasaya (fig. 3.5).[3]

Perhaps Cieza's clearest description is of the massive stone temple complex of Pumapunku and its monolithic gateways (fig. 3.6): "In another spot further to the west there are other still greater antiquities, for there are many

Figure 3.2. Akapana Pyramid, Tiwanaku, January 1984. PSG photo.

Figure 3.3. (*above*) Templete Semisubterráneo
(Semisubterranean Temple), Tiwanaku, January 1984.
PSG photo.

Figure 3.4. (*left*) Turban figure.
PSG photo.

Figure 3.5. Kalasasaya, Tiwanaku. PSG photo.

Figure 3.6. Gateway of the Sun, Tiwanaku. PSG photo.

large gates with jambs, thresholds, and door, all of a single stone. What struck me most when I was observing these things was that from these huge gateways other still larger stones project on which they were set, some of which were as much as thirty feet wide, fifteen or more long, and six thick, and this and the door, jamb and threshold were one single stone, which was a tremendous thing" (Cieza 1959 [1553]:284).

Beyond describing the type site, Cieza conveys a surprising understanding of Tiwanaku as a larger cultural phenomenon. Struck by Tiwanaku's appearance of great antiquity and the differences in building plan and style between Tiwanaku and the familiar architecture of the Inca, Cieza was impressed that "before the Incas ruled, there were people of parts in these kingdoms" (Cieza 1959 [1553]:282–283; 1984 [1553]:284). With this realization, he is arguably the originator of the concept of pre-Inca cultural unification now known to Andean archaeologists as the Middle Horizon. Another correct assessment of Tiwanaku's antiquity was made during a 1610 visit by Bernabé Cobo, whose detailed descriptions of Tiwanaku named and supplied measurements for the Akapana and Pumapunku (Cobo 1990 [1653]:104).

Indigenous Perspectives on Tiwanaku

Who were the people we call the Tiwanaku? Due to the frequent conquests and population shifts during the past millennium, the ethnic identity of the ancient Tiwanaku culture remains a topic of considerable debate. The site was already in ruins when the Inca conquered the Titicaca basin in the fifteenth century, yet Tiwanaku looms large in the myth and folk traditions of subsequent cultures. This suggests that a high regard for the Tiwanaku ruins persisted many centuries after the city's abandonment. The more perceptive chroniclers afford us a view of Tiwanaku's place and meaning in the lore of its Aymara, Uru, Pukina, and Inca/Quechua successors in the altiplano. The often contradictory references to the ruins of Tiwanaku ascribed to each of these ethnolinguistic groups remind us how interpretation and reinterpretation of linguistic and ethnic identity have always been an inseparable part of political and social discourse in the Andes.

Aymara is the dominant language of the altiplano today and would appear to be the most likely candidate for the language of Tiwanaku as well. Browman (1984a:237) notes the archaeological correspondence of Tiwanaku expansion with the modern distribution of Aymara speakers in the Bolivian altiplano and regions of southern Peru and northern Chile. Dittmar also finds both linguistic and biological data to connect Tiwanaku with Aymara peoples (1994, 1996). Aymara memories of Tiwanaku as an ancestral capital could also account for one Aymara name for the site, Taypicala, which Cobo records as "the stone in the middle, because the Indians of the Collao were of the opinion that this town was in the middle of the world, and that the people who repopulated the world after the flood came out of this place" (Cobo 1990 [1653]:100). The chroniclers' descriptions of *chulpa* burial towers at Tiwanaku indicate the ongoing veneration of the site by ancestors of Inca-contemporary Aymara kings (Cieza 1959 [1553]:284).[4]

Others, notably Torero (1992) have used glotto-chronological linguistic analysis to suggest that Tiwanaku was more strongly affiliated with the now disappearing minority languages of Uru and Pukina. Torero argues that protouruquilla, a hypothesized ancestral language that later differentiated into modern Uru, was spoken by the agro-pastoralists of Tiwanaku and the pre-Tiwanaku Qaluyu, Chiripa, and Wankarani archaeological complexes of the southern Titicaca basin. At the same time, according to Torero, proto-puquina, the parent language of the Pukina language of contact times, was the tongue associated with the florescence of the Pukara site and its cultural tradition in the northern lake basin. Torero suggests that expansive policies of the Pukara state came to "Pukina-ize Tiwanaku" (puquinizar a Tiahua-naco), forging a new linguistic identity that combined Uru and a Pukina court language. According to this scenario, Tiwanaku later extended Pukina to the southern altiplano and the valleys of the western slopes. The Uru-Pukina position is also supported by ethnographically recorded traditions of Uru identity with peoples of a pre-Aymara period known as the *chulpa* (Wachtel 1997:686). One song of the Uru-Kjotsuni of Lake Titicaca recorded by ethnographer Weston LaBarre in the mid-twentieth century explicitly traced their ancestry to the Tiwanaku ruins: "We the Kjotsuni are the oldest on this earth. A long time we were here, before when the sun was hidden . . . Then our nation was large and happy . . . Then the Kollas (Aymara) came, despoiling us of our lands . . . Before Camak pacha (time of darkness) Tiahuanacu was built. We have built our houses where our ancestors lived. The broken pots of many colors and *topos* (copper pins) you find when plowing the ground belong to them" (LaBarre 1943:522).

These apparently contradictory claims to Tiwanaku ancestry could be explained by a complex multiethnic Tiwanaku that encompassed several distinct ethnolinguistic groups. The diverse ethnicities that comprised Tiwanaku may have been associated with discrete subsistence strategies. In this view, the present-day Uru and Pukina are perceived as water people, with an ethnic occupational specialization that stretches back in time through Tiwanaku to much earlier lacustrine cultures such as Chiripa. Similarly, the importance of herding in modern Aymara society is projected back in time to Jaqi or proto-Aymara origins in pre-Tiwanaku cultures like Wankarani, a Formative culture in the Oruro region (Kolata 1993:67–69). A multiethnic melding is proposed, in which proto-Aymara herders formed Tiwanaku's elite, incorporating lower status Uru and Pukina aquatic specialists (Kolata 1993: 101). Arguing by elimination that non-Aymara tendencies must be Pukina (1993:98), Kolata concludes that dualistic ethnic dynamics explain the division of ritual space between Tiwanaku's Akapana and Pumapunku temples.[5]

This specific interpretation of multiethnicity within the Tiwanaku state depends on both a literal reading of Aymara dualist categories of cosmos, landscape, and social organization and the projection of present-day occupational stereotypes to the distant past. The characterization of the Uru as water people, for example, may be a recent phenomenon of marginalization and Aymarization.[6] Melchior de Larcón, a sixteenth-century Spanish settler interviewed by Garci Diez de San Miguel (1964 [1567]), explicitly refutes the "water people" stereotype as an Aymara defamation and suggests that the Uru worked their own lands. Ethnographically, LaBarre (1941) described tuber and chenopod agriculture practiced by the Uru of Iru-Itu, and Metraux (1945) reported that the Chipaya Uru constructed complex raised fields that resembled those of ancient Tiwanaku. The Chipaya had their own term— *skxala*—for these plots, the likes of which were unknown to modern Aymara agriculturists. Twentieth-century Uru also herded llamas and alpacas. Metraux described the "amphibian" grazing of livestock by the Ancoaqui Uru, and Abercrombie (1986, 1998) notes that the words used by Andean herders to describe animal colors are in fact Uru names for water birds of corresponding colors. The ambiguities posed by the Uru example remind us how risky it is to link modern constructions of ethnicity to ancient political systems like Tiwanaku without archaeological evidence. Modern cultural identities may provide heuristic examples for comparative purposes but cannot be assumed to emulate historical conditions.

Tiwanaku in Inca Myth and Ideology

Perhaps the least likely Andean allusions to Tiwanaku are the claims of ancestry voiced by the Incas of Cusco. The Inca state, controlled by ethnic Incas who spoke the Quechua language, did not conquer the altiplano until well into the fifteenth century and seem unlikely to have descended directly from Tiwanaku forbears. As conquerors, however, the Inca became the final inheritors of the Andean imperial tradition started at Tiwanaku.

In swiftly rising empires like those of the Assyrians or the Aztec it is not unusual for leaders to seek legitimacy by adopting the royal titles, rituals, and iconographic traditions of earlier states (Adams 1988:59; Smith 1987). The Aztecs' Mesoamerican empire was arguably the culmination of three increasingly large cycles of coalescence and collapse in the Basin of Mexico (Marcus 1998). According to this "dynamic model," Teotihuacán, Toltec Tula, and finally Aztec Tenochtitlán each built upon the cultural context created by its predecessor. Thus the Aztecs built empire upon "the knowledge and memory of Teotihuacán" (Nichols and Charlton 1997:188).

It is not surprising that the Inca venerated the Tiwanaku ruins and mimicked surviving aspects of a Tiwanaku state tradition to legitimate their own rule. Even four centuries after the Tiwanaku collapse, the site's tradition as a political capital was sufficiently powerful to warrant its inclusion in the ideology of Inca expansion. It is useful to consider two aspects of this Inca reverence of the Tiwanaku ruins. First, Tiwanaku was idealized by the Inca as a mythical origin place. Second, Inca rulers considered the Tiwanaku monuments as a touchstone to legitimize their own dynastic and political tradition.

The first common thread in the chronicles is a reference to the creation of the world and humankind in the Lake Titicaca region. Inca traditions revered the Tiwanaku ruins themselves as an origin place. The Inca appear to have incorporated enthusiastically local tales citing the lake as the creation place: the creator deity Viracocha "made all things in Tiaguanaco, where they pretend that he resided, he ordered the Sun, Moon and Stars to go to the Island of Titicaca, which is located in the lake of this same name, and that from there they should go up to the sky" (Cobo 1984 [1653]:105).

Sixteenth-century chronicler Sarmiento de Gamboa offers a more detailed origin tale, in which the Tiwanaku site and its stone sculpture are incorporated into two separate creations. Viracocha created a dark world and peopled it with a race of giants. When their behavior displeased him, Viracocha and his subordinates destroyed this first world with a great flood, turning the giants to stone. Then:

> The flood being passed and the land dry, Viracocha determined to people it a second time, and, to make it more perfect, he decided upon creating luminaries to give it light. With this object he went, with his servants, to a great lake in the Collao, in which there is an island called Titicaca, the meaning being "the rock of lead". . . . Viracocha went to this island, and presently ordered that the sun, moon, and stars should come forth, and be set in the heavens to give light to the world, and it was so. . . . Viracocha gave various orders to his servants, but Taguapaca disobeyed the commands of Viracocha. So Viracocha was enraged against Taguapaca, and ordered the other two servants to take him, tie him hands and feet, and launch him in a balsa on the lake. . . . This done, Viracocha made a sacred idol in that place, as a place for worship and as a sign of what he had there created.

> Leaving the island, he passed by the lake to the main land, taking with him the two servants who survived. He went to a place now called Tiahuanacu in the province of Collasuyu, and in this place he sculp-

tured and designed on a great piece of stone, all the nations that he intended to create. This done, he ordered his two servants to charge their memories with the names of all tribes that he had depicted, and of the valleys and provinces where they were to come forth, which were those of the whole land. He ordered that each one should go by a different road, naming the tribes, and ordering them all to go forth and people the country. His servants, obeying the command of Viracocha, set out on their journey and work. One went by the mountain range or chain which they call the heights over the plains on the South Sea. The other went by the heights which overlook the wonderful mountain ranges which we call the Andes, situated to the east of the said sea. By these roads they went, saying with a loud voice "Oh you tribes and nations, hear and obey the order of Ticci Viracocha Pachayachachi, which commands you to go forth, and multiply and settle the land." Viracocha himself did the same along the road between those taken by his two servants, naming all the tribes and places by which he passed. At the sound of his voice every place obeyed, and people came forth, some from lakes, others from fountains, valleys, caves, trees, rocks and hills, spreading over the land and multiplying to form the nations which are to-day in Peru (Sarmiento 1908 [1571]).

It is unclear how deeply rooted the tale of a Lake Titicaca genesis was in Inca cosmology. Sarmiento's informants connect the Inca with this second creation, implying that the Inca progenitors of Cusco were among the peoples created by Viracocha at Tiwanaku. It is possible that this myth represents ancestral linkages between Cusco and the altiplano. Tiwanaku-derived pre-Inca ceremonial pottery styles in Cusco could suggest early participation in a Titicaca basin religious tradition many centuries before the rise of the Inca polity (Bauer 1999; Mohr Chávez 1985:152). Parssinen (1997) takes this linkage further, suggesting that the Inca myths reflect a real migration from the Titicaca basin. On the other hand, the connection of Inca origins to a world creation in the Titicaca basin may have arisen only after the Inca subdued the region in the fifteenth century and syncretized local beliefs. Furthermore, because many of these "Inca" beliefs were recorded by chroniclers in the altiplano, they could have been the myths of Titicaca basin natives.

The attempts to reference Inca state ideology to an earlier imperial tradition also involved conscious attempts to connect Inca rulers to the ruins of Tiwanaku. Referring to the Inca emperor Pachacuti's remodeling of Cusco on the grandeur of Tiwanaku, Cieza wrote that "the Incas built their great edifices of Cusco along the lines of the wall to be seen in this place" (Cieza 1959 [1553]:284). Cobo also refers to Pachacuti's enthusiastic adoption of the Tiwanaku architectural and stone carving tradition (Cobo 1984 [1653]:

141). Careful technical analysis of both architectural traditions suggests that this influence was indirect at best (Protzen 1993; Protzen and Nair 1997, 2000; chapter 8, this volume). Nonetheless, the oft-repeated tale of Pachacuti's borrowing reminds of us that Tiwanaku's hold on highland consciousness was powerful enough to help materialize Inca imperial ideology.

The Inca also patterned other media after Tiwanaku archetypes. During imperial Inca times, precise ceramic replicas of Tiwanaku drinking and storage vessels were made by Inca potters for ceremonial burial in some of the most sacred sites in Cusco, notably at the Inca fortress-temple of Sacsayuaman (fig. 3.7; Julien 1993; Valcárcel 1935). These copies of Tiwanaku *kero* drinking goblets and some storage jars of the Inca *urpu* or arybaloid form were carefully painted with Tiwanaku motifs, suggesting an intimate knowledge of a four-hundred-year-old style. This points not only to a strong interest among Cusco Inca elites in imitating the Titicaca basin tradition but to the incorporation of Tiwanaku symbols into some of the most sacred contexts of Inca ritual practice.

Figure 3.7. Inca copy of Tiwanaku *kero* found at Sacsayhuaman, Cusco. PSG photo.

Even as they absorbed elements of its architectural and artistic tradition for their own capital, the Inca elites also maintained a symbolic royal presence at the Tiwanaku ruins themselves. Cieza wrote that "the first Incas talked of setting up their court and capital in Tihuanacu" (Cieza 1959 [1553]: 284). Cobo suggests that this Inca court at Tiwanaku was actually established, with its principal palace adjacent to the Pumapunku:

> They considered the above-mentioned temple of Pumapuncu to be remarkable, and they enhanced it by increasing the amount of decoration as well as the number of attendants and sacrifices. Next to it they constructed royal palaces where they say Guayna Capac's son Manco Capac was born. The ruins of this place are seen today, and it was a very big building with many rooms and apartments. (Cobo 1990 [1653]: 105)

The building of an Inca palace at the Tiwanaku ruins is strong evidence for an Inca attempt to appropriate an ancient political legitimacy for Inca imperial ends. Such an Inca occupation has been confirmed by excavation of Inca ceramics in crude structures adjacent to Tiwanaku's Pumapunku temple (Vranich 1997; Yaeger 2000). While considerably less grand than the palace of Cobo's description, these Inca structures directly abutted the ruins of the Tiwanaku temple structure, sharing walls and reusing stone from what would still have been one of Tiwanaku's most impressive stone temples. Kolata even suggests that Manco's royal birth at this splendidly rebuilt Tiwanaku court was contrived as a "symbolic master stroke" linking Inca imperial design to Tiwanaku's "coveted legitimating power" as the seat of a deeply revered ancient dynasty (Kolata 1993:5). Manco was not a principal heir, so this would seem to be an overstatement. Taking the royal court to consolidate newly conquered territory was a standard policy in many monarchies, and the Inca's children were born throughout the empire. The last Inca emperor, Atahualpa, was born at Quito, for example.

It seems unlikely that the conquered peoples of the altiplano would long have been fooled by claims of Inca legitimacy arising from Tiwanaku ruins. Cieza, for one, noted the Aymara natives' accurate perception of the antiquity of the Tiwanaku ruins and their scorn for any Inca pretense to them: "I asked the native . . . if these buildings had been built in the time of the Incas, and they laughed at the question, repeating what I have said, that they were built before they reigned" (Cieza 1959 [1553]:284).

Nonetheless, it would have been both politic and reasonable for the Inca to hold court at the greatest ruin of their most populous conquered province. Cobo relates that Tiwanaku's inhabitants "adored it from time immemorial before they were conquered by the kings of Cuzco, and these [Inca] kings did the same thing after they became lords of this province" (Cobo 1990 [1653]:105). To conquer and rule the Titicaca basin, the Inca found it effective to appease the natives' veneration of the Tiwanaku site and to appropriate the symbols of Tiwanaku's power and splendor for the Inca Empire.

The Modern Era of Tiwanaku Archaeology

Considering the biases of ethnographic sources on Tiwanaku, our primary source for its interpretation must be in the scientific study of the archaeological record. Because the site was well-known from the Spanish colonial period, it attracted considerable interest among early adventurers, who were drawn to the romantic visage of its ruined stone architecture. The wonders of the site's monumental core were portrayed by travel reports of nineteenth-century visitors to Tiwanaku like Efraim George Squier. Squier's hyperbole is exemplified by his exaggerated line drawing of a horseman riding through a gargantuan Gateway of the Sun (fig. 3.8; Squier 1877). This kind of exaggerated publicity whetted public curiosity about the mysterious site. Most enigmatic of all was the contrast between the lost magnificence of the ruins and the surrounding desolation:

> We can hardly conceive of remains so extensive as those of Tiahua-
> nuco, except as indications of a large population, and as evidences of
> the previous existence on or near the spot of a considerable city. But we
> find nowhere in the vicinity any decided traces of ancient habitations
> such as abound elsewhere in Peru in connection with most public edi-
> fices. Again, the region around is cold, and for the most part arid and
> barren. Elevated nearly thirteen thousand feet above the sea, no cereals
> grow except barley, which often fails to mature, and seldom, if ever, so
> perfects itself as to be available for seed. The maize is dwarf and scant,
> and uncertain in yield; and the bitter potato and quinoa constitute al-
> most the sole articles of food for the pinched and impoverished inhab-
> itants. This is not, prima facie, a region for nurturing or sustaining a
> large population, and certainly not one wherein we should expect to
> find a capital. . . . Tiahuanuco may have been a sacred spot or shrine,
> the position of which was determined by an accident, an augury, or a
> dream, but I can hardly believe that it was a seat of dominion. (Squier
> 1877:300)

Beyond inspiring scientifically minded investigators, early accounts like Squier's piqued the appetite for the mystical in the West, giving rise to a tradition of occult interpretations of Tiwanaku that continues to the present day. A typical interpretation appears in an encyclopedia of mythology that

Figure 3.8. Gateway of the Sun in (a) Squier's 1877 drawing and (b) rear view photo. MMA Archive photo.

remained in press into the 1960s: "sacred cites in remote sites were venerated by the Andeans. . . . Tiahuanaco and the islands represent, in part at least, the devotion of distant princes, who here maintained another Delphi or Lhassa" (Alexander 1964:233).

Even among scholars it became well established that altiplano Tiwanaku was far too isolated to have been a major population center in its own right. For most, the contrast of desolation and urban splendor cast Tiwanaku as a vacant pilgrimage center for visitors from more hospitable climes, rather than as a true urban center (Bennett and Bird 1960:185; Mason 1957:90).

Other interpretations attributed great antiquity to Tiwanaku in an effort to explain its Atlantean grandeur. A characterization of Tiwanaku as an antediluvian origin center for world civilization distinguishes one of Tiwanaku's most dogged and sincere early advocates, the German-Bolivian adventurer Arturo Posnansky (1945, 1957). Posnansky's work is particularly important because it documented some of the extensive but poorly recorded 1903 excavations of Georges Courty in the Kalasasaya, the Templete Semi-subterráneo, the walled "palace" compound now known as the Putuni, and elsewhere in the monumental site (Courty and Crequi-Montfort 1906). Posnansky defined three main periods for the site's construction, beginning with construction of the Akapana mound and the carving of naturalistic human heads in stone, progressing through the construction of the "sun and moon" temples of Kalasasaya and Pumapunku, and terminating with the unfinished carving of most of the stone monuments, including the famous Gateway of the Sun. Unfortunately, Posnansky's bizarre theories about Tiwanaku's great antiquity, its role as an origin center for the peopling of the New World, and the site's demise in a catastrophic flood invalidate his interpretive contribution. Nonetheless, his exhaustive recording of Tiwanaku's architecture and ceramic and lithic art still serves as an invaluable source.

Only a few early investigators were able to look beyond the enigmatic Tiwanaku site itself with a dawning appreciation of its centrality to a wider cultural phenomenon. German archaeologist Max Uhle became familiar with Tiwanaku material culture from museum collections and Squier's report. Uhle was among the first to recognize a Tiwanaku art style, co-authoring a description of Tiwanaku's architecture before even visiting South America (Stubel and Uhle 1892). Later, when Uhle visited the site, he described the Kalasasaya as the site's "stonehenge" and observed stylistic groups among the stone sculptures at the site and elsewhere in the Titicaca basin (Uhle 1912). Uhle's work in Peru permitted him to connect Tiwanaku to a larger "Tiahuanacoid" Horizon as the first period of pre-Inca cultural unification in the Andes.

Turn of the century Swiss-American scholar Adolph Bandelier also recognized Tiwanaku as a true urban center. A disciple of Lewis Henry Morgan, the autodidact Bandelier became the first U.S.-based scholar to conduct long-term field research in the altiplano and the first to map the ruins of the Tiwanaku's monumental core (fig. 3.9). Although Tiwanaku was one of his initial motivations to work in South America, Bandelier spent only nineteen days at the site in 1894. Bandelier's field notes suggest that tensions with Uhle may explain this short stay.[7] Unable or unwilling to excavate, Bandelier abandoned Tiwanaku to Uhle and he later deferred to the German's "learned and elaborate works" on the archaeology of the ruins (Bandelier 1911:218; Lange and Riley 1996:176). He instead concentrated on an ethnohistoric approach to the Titicaca origin myths and ethnography in the village of Tiwanaku, arriving at several perceptive early observations on the community's ayllus and other aspects of social structure (1911).

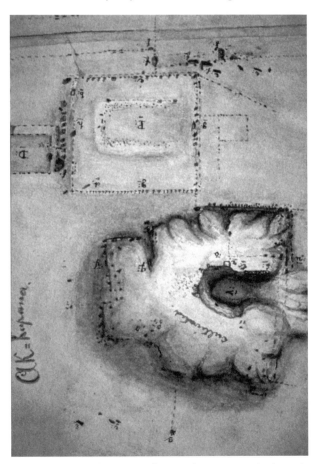

Figure 3.9. Bandelier's map of Tiwanaku. AMNH, Anthropology Folder X, Tiahuanaco. PSG photo.

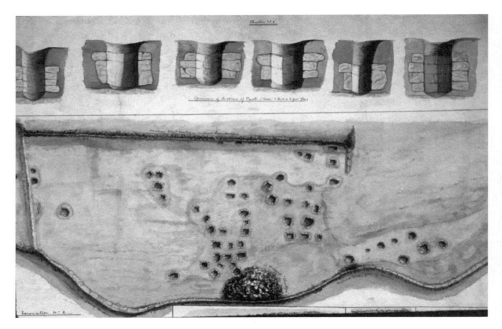

Figure 3.10. Bandelier's cemetery map, Challa 8 site, Ciriapata, Island of the Sun. AMNH Anthropology Folder XI, Island of Titicaca. PSG photo.

Abandoning the Tiwanaku site to Uhle, Bandelier turned in 1895 to Lake Titicaca's Islands of the Sun and Moon. Although his *Islands of Titicaca and Koati* (1910) concentrates on the Inca occupation, Bandelier also excavated a number of Tiwanaku cemetery sites on the islands (fig. 3.10). His reluctance to recognize the Tiwanaku culture by name in his book is odd and probably another outcome of his feud with Uhle (Bandelier 1910:180, 185). Bandelier's unpublished notes and papers on the Tiwanaku cemeteries on the island reflect that he, like Cieza de León, was keenly aware that the Tiwanaku cultural phenomenon extended beyond the boundaries of the type site: "The peninsula of Copacavana is very important. It is the bridge connecting the Islands geographically with *Tiahuanaco*. We have already some indications that the culture was the same in both places, only locally modified" (letter to John Winser, secretary of the American Museum of Natural History, July 22, 1895; emphasis original).

Although he never followed up on this interest in Tiwanaku expansion, Bandelier's largely unpublished collections from Tiwanaku sites had an enormous impact on subsequent scholarship. Examination at the American Museum of Natural History of ceramic vessels from Bandelier's excavation at the

Qeya Kollu Chico site, for example, later inspired Wendell Bennett's definition of the "Qeya" style.

Bennett, curator of South American archaeology at the American Museum, became the first North American to attempt scientific excavation in the altiplano (Bennett 1934). He excavated ten test pits at Tiwanaku, concentrating his effort on the monumental precinct. His test pit 7, in what is now known as the Semisubterranean Temple, exposed the colossal anthropomorphic stela today known as the Bennett Monolith. In 1934, Bennett returned to Bolivia to excavate at Lukurmata, Chiripa, Pariti, and several other Tiwanaku sites in the altiplano. He also identified the Formative Chiripa culture and, after some initial confusion caused by inverted stratigraphy, correctly recognized it as a pre-Tiwanaku phenomenon (Bennett 1936, 1948). Moving to Cochabamba in the eastern lowlands, Bennett recognized the diffusion of "Decadent" and "Derived" variants of Tiwanaku style at the Arani site (1936).

In 1939, the Swedish archaeologist Stig Rydén augmented Bennett's work with seven additional test pits at Tiwanaku (Rydén 1947) and the altiplano site of Khonko Wankani (Wankané, Wancane), before moving to Cochabamba and the Bolivian lowlands (Rydén 1957, 1959). Rydén's work, like Bennett's, focused on basic culture historical questions and is particularly useful because of his comprehensive sherd-by-sherd tabulation and illustration of ceramic forms.

A second era of scientific research at Tiwanaku began with excavations in the 1960s under the direction of Carlos Ponce Sanginés and other Bolivian archaeologists. These efforts concentrated on the exposure and reconstruction of the monumental precincts, notably in the Akapana pyramid, Putuni palace, Kalasasaya, Pumapunku, Kantatayita, and Semisubterranean Temple (Escalante 1994; Ponce 1969, 1970, 1972; Vranich 2001). The clearing and reconstruction of these monuments and the administration of Tiwanaku museums at the site and in La Paz made Tiwanaku a major tourist destination, a focus of national identity and pride for Bolivia, and even a central icon of its present-day political discourse. Unfortunately, considering the extent of the monuments that were cleared and restored, this era of research produced few comprehensive reports. In particular, although dates and general descriptions (Ponce 1972) and in some cases architectural plans (Ponce 1969) are available, little contextual analysis of ceramic lots from these excavations has been published. Additionally, with the exception of a single pioneering study, the focus on exposing monumental architecture precluded any attention being paid to the extent of Tiwanaku settlement patterns and habitation (Parsons 1968).

After a long period of near total inaccessibility to international scholars,

the third and most comprehensive era of scientific study of Bolivian Tiwanaku began in the late 1980s under the aegis of the Wila Jawira project,
directed by Alan Kolata. This phase of research began in the altiplano hinterland with a survey of the Pampa Koani in the southern Titicaca basin (Kolata
1986). Kolata and colleagues later moved on to study the major Tiwanaku
satellite of Lukurmata (Bermann et al. 1989; Bermann 1994, 1997; Janusek
1994; Kolata 1989; Rivera Sundt 1989) and additional settlement survey
areas (Albarracin-Jordan and Mathews 1990, Albarracin-Jordan 1996a,b;
Mathews 1997). Many of the earlier publications of the Wila Jawira researchers placed particular emphasis on long-neglected agro-ecological variables and the importance of climate change (Binford et al. 1997; Kolata 1996a,
2000; Kolata and Ortloff 1996). At the same time, some scholars in the
project strongly stressed ideological factors in sociopolitical development
(e.g., Kolata 1992, 1993, 1996b, 1997). By the 1990s, the fieldwork focus
returned to the monuments of the type site itself with new excavations in the
Akapana and Putuni (Alconini 1993; Kolata 1993; Manzanilla 1992a,b) and
independent architectural analyses of the Pumapunku and other major monuments (Conklin 1991; Protzen and Nair 1997, 2000; Vranich 1997, 2001).
Simultaneously, large exposures in the residential and industrial sectors of the
Tiwanaku site began to elucidate the households and neighborhoods of the
Tiwanaku capital (Janusek 1994, 1999, 2003; Rivera Casanovas 1994;
Webster 1993). As we shall see, participants in this new era of Bolivian
Tiwanaku research apply a broad spectrum of interdisciplinary research to
the project of reconstructing Tiwanaku as a cultural system and employ a
diversity of explanations for Tiwanaku's development.

Material Culture and Culture History

In the case of a state society that has generated as much interest and as many
interpretations as has Tiwanaku, it is surprising to learn that there is still no
comprehensive typology of Tiwanaku cultural material. One unfortunate
concomitant of this has been a tendency to conflate and confuse developmental stages with chronological phases. Unfortunately, Tiwanaku's material
culture has never gone through a period of rigorous explication and debate.
In fact, most Tiwanaku archaeologists do not conceptually distinguish ceramic *typologies* from ceramic *sequences* and use the terms interchangeably.
This has permitted some scholars of Tiwanaku the luxury of making their
interpretations of material culture fit predetermined reconstructions of culture history. Such divergence of goal from means has impeded comparative
studies of Tiwanaku.

Wendell Bennett's three-phase stylistic analysis of excavated material has provided the basis for all subsequent Tiwanaku chronologies (1934). Although John Rowe, the leading figure in Andean ceramic seriation and chronology at the time, criticized Bennett's original phase distinctions as purely typological, Rowe's student Dwight Wallace (1957) proposed an eight-phase stylistic seriation that generally supported Bennett's sequence. The most influential restatement of Bennett's sequence was proposed by Ponce in 1947 and modified in 1961 (Disselhoff 1968:213). Ponce (1972) charts a series of radiocarbon dates for five phases and designates several illustrated vessels by phase. However, the complete typology, which emphasized decorative motifs, was never adequately described, and as a result, different archaeologists developed very different concepts of each phase. Additionally, the excavation stratigraphy to support these phases was incompletely published. Only recently have ceramic typologies from the Tiwanaku core region begun to supply the necessary typological detail and tie it stratigraphically to suites of radiocarbon dates (Alconini 1993, 1995; Burkholder 1997, 2001; Janusek 2003). This late start toward basic standards of comparability has impeded discussions of variation of assemblages between sites or regions. Equally unfortunate was Ponce's choice to tie his sequence to developmental stages such as "mature urban," "expansive," and so on. Beyond glossing basic issues of culture history, this developmental terminology also implied that many of the most compelling questions driving Tiwanaku archaeology had already been answered.

The "Early Tiwanaku" Phases and the Establishment of Tiwanaku

The origins of Tiwanaku both as a metropolitan center and as a ceramic style are still obscure. Bennett defined an "Early or Pre-Tiahuanaco" period, described as having significantly fewer painted sherds, in some of his lower levels. Ponce identified three early phases in excavations in the site's monumental sector. The earliest pottery from the Tiwanaku site appeared in Ponce's excavations in the Kalasasaya precinct. Pottery of the Kalasasaya style, which Ponce called Tiwanaku Epoca I, includes a coarsely polished, deeply incised brown ware and a well burnished polychrome painted ware that Ponce dated at between 400 B.C. and A.D. 100 (Ponce 1972). Typical Tiwanaku I vessel forms include jars with globular or slightly flattened bodies, round-bottom bowls with one handle, and some modeled types (Ponce 1976). Unfortunately, no buildings or occupation levels have been securely tied to this complex at the Tiwanaku type site. Tiwanaku I vessels bear a resemblance to fine ceramics of Pukara (Pucara), a contemporary ceramic tradition centered at the monumental site of the same name at the north end of the Titicaca basin (Chávez 1992; Franquemont 1986; Kidder 1943; Mujica 1990; Steadman 1995). The resemblance of these and other styles of non-fiber-tempered, polychrome zoned incised ceramics has been ascribed to a pan-Titicaca tradition in the Upper Formative period between 100 B.C. and A.D. 100 (Stanish and Steadman 1994:55).

Ponce's contribution to the later parts of the Tiwanaku ceramic sequence exemplifies a tendency to assume cultural phases and attempt to fill them with ceramic series. Tiwanaku Epoca II is not described anywhere and appears to have been a postulated transitional phase—a placeholder that was never filled. Ponce applied the new name Tiwanaku Epoca III to Bennett's Qeya Early Tiwanaku style. Bennett first identified this style in Bandelier's collection from the cemetery of Qeya Collo Chico, on the Island of the Sun, and not in ceramics from the Tiwanaku site (fig. 3.11). In applying the name Tiwanaku III, Ponce overturned the type site precedent in favor of a developmental phase he described as *Tiwanaku urbano temprano* and dated to A.D. 100 to 375. Ponce (1972) describes vessels of this ceramic style with a friable light brown ceramic paste and forms such as libation bowls, bulbous-base vases with interlocking black and white triangle motifs, and specific *incensario* forms from the lower levels of his Kalasasaya excavations. However, Qeya pottery is relatively rare at the Tiwanaku site and the Qeya typology has been better described by archaeologists using collections from other sites (Burkholder 2001; Janusek 2003:49; Mujica 1978).

Ponce's renaming of these early styles to associate them with the Tiwanaku

Figure 3.11. Qeya (Tiwanaku III) style ceramic vessels from Qeya Collo Chico Collection. AMNH catalog B2421. PSG photo.

site led to the assumption that Tiwanaku was already a large urban center in the late Formative. Kolata, for example, suggests that "a critical mass of accelerating social complexity" in the Titicaca basin led to the "conversion of the emergent capital into a shared center of moral and cosmological authority, a place of pilgrimage and wonder," perhaps as early as 200 B.C. (Kolata 1993:83, 85). This reconstruction suggests that Tiwanaku III (Qeya) must have witnessed the planning and construction of the monuments of the Tiwanaku site's ceremonial core, including the retaining walls of the Akapana, the Kalasasaya, and the Semisubterranean Temple (Ponce 1972; Kolata 1993:132).

Despite these optimistic reconstructions of early urbanization at Tiwanaku, the search for Formative occupations at the type site has met with limited success. Qeya/Tiwanaku III ceramics are rarest in association with Tiwanaku's monumental architecture. Girault's detailed analysis of 6,976 fragments from excavations in the Semisubterranean Temple, a context Ponce believed was one of Tiwanaku's earliest monuments, found only three Qeya/Tiwanaku III sherds (Girault 1990:185). Vranich's reinterpretation of the construction and fill technique of the Akapana also implies a later date for that monument than was previously believed (2001:303). Tiwanaku domestic areas of Akapana East and Kk'araña have produced only minimal numbers of Late Formative (Tiwanaku I and Qeya) sherds (Janusek 1994; 2003:48). A settlement pattern survey of the Tiwanaku valley also found relatively few sherds of the Formative styles in surface collections or in test excavations at nearby sites (Albarracin 1996:190; Albarracin and Mathews 1990; Janusek 2003:49). These faint traces of early occupations at Tiwanaku pale in comparison to the massive urban construction and middens that follow and cannot represent much more than unconsolidated villages or towns. In contrast, there were substantial Qeya-related Formative occupations at many sites on the shores of Lake Titicaca (Bandelier 1910:173; Bennett 1948; Eisleb and Strelow 1980:11; Mohr Chávez 1985; Mujica 1978, 1985; Ponce 1972; Wallace 1957:19). Excavation of Formative house floors at Lukurmata (Bermann 1994) and Iwawe (Burkholder 1997; Stovel 1997a) produced significant occupations and quantities of Qeya-related ceramics, all stratigraphically below the red-slipped pottery of Tiwanaku IV and V.

Finally, the Qeya-style assemblage can now be dated to A.D. 300–500, considerably later than previous estimates of Tiwanaku's urban origins (Janusek 2003:53). Even at this late date, the Tiwanaku valley was sparsely populated, and the future city of Tiwanaku was at most a town of moderate importance, perhaps little more than a collection of hamlets. This stands in contrast to the bustling Formative lakeside settlement of Titicaca's south shore, where the people of the altiplano first experimented with urban living.

The most remarkable thing about Tiwanaku is not its antiquity but the suddenness of its rise.

The Rise of Urbanism and Tiwanaku's Corporate Style

Tiwanaku's great urban and monumental development coincides with the appearance of the Tiwanaku corporate ceramic style. Almost immediately, this style diffuses to Tiwanaku's altiplano satellite sites and beyond, suggesting rapid codevelopment of the Tiwanaku core and the culture's peripheral expansion. The Tiwanaku corporate style is usually represented by a characteristic red-slipped serving pottery and the appearance of the *kero* form, a flared drinking goblet (fig. 3.12). Considering the importance of drinking ceremony in Andean state integration, it is not surprising that the kero's ascendancy in the ceramic inventory coincides with the rise of Tiwanaku as a complex urban site and state center. Keros appear prominently in the hands of the massive anthropomorphic monoliths of the Tiwanaku site, strongly suggesting that they played a vital role in elite-sponsored ritual. Finally, as is discussed in the next chapter, the diffusion of keros and the Tiwanaku ceramic assemblage coincides with the first expansion of Tiwanaku control to maize-growing regions.

In addition to its serving wares, the Tiwanaku corporate style also brought mass production of a characteristic set of plain cooking and storage vessels. Unfortunately, these far more numerous domestic and industrial assemblages were never comprehensively studied. Little has changed since 1947, when Rydén noted that "only the artistic genre of pottery has been subjected to study . . . we know very little of this culture's plainer utility vessels (and) implements" (1947:11). Core region Tiwanaku utilitarian wares have only

Figure 3.12. *Kero* ceramic goblets, Island of the Sun, Bandelier Collection, AMNH. PSG photo.

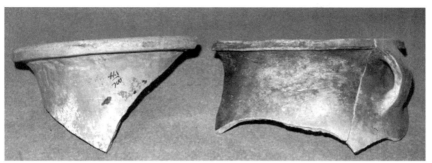

Figure 3.13. Tiwanaku *tinaja* and *olla* fragments, Tiwanaku, Bennett excavation collection, AMNH. PSG photo.

recently received any attention, and formal types like the *tinaja* water jug (fig. 3.13) are gradually being named and described (Alconini 1993; Bermann 1994; Janusek 1994, 2003; Janusek and Alconini 2000).

While discernible from earlier phases in the Tiwanaku core region, the Tiwanaku corporate style has resisted reliable temporal subdivision. Most attempts are largely intuitive and ultimately derive from Bennett's distinction of "Classic" and "Decadent" phases (Bennett 1934). In the absence of dating or stratigraphic confirmation, this selection of phase designations betrays certain assumptions about the development and degradation of art styles. The Classic period was defined by an even ratio of painted to unpainted sherds and the appearance of keros and other characteristic well-fired red-slipped decorated vessel forms (Alconini 1993:53). In the Decadent period, many of the classic forms continued, but background slip colors shifted from red to orange, and design motifs became more abstract as they suffered a "breakdown of Classic design" and a "general simplification of technique" (Bennett 1934:405, 456).

Unfortunately, neither Bennett's nor subsequent excavations offer convincing stratigraphic proof of this design decay. Moreover, the concentration of Bennett's sample on ceremonial or elite parts of the site could explain the high ratio of painted sherds in the Classic levels, supporting Rowe's objection that the distinction was "purely typological." Despite Bennett's failure to document a stylistic transition within the Tiwanaku corporate style, Ponce adopted his Classic phase as Tiwanaku Epoca IV, which he developmentally termed *Tiwanaku urbano maduro* (developed urban). Radiocarbon dates presented by Ponce suggested a duration of Tiwanaku Epoca IV from A.D. 375 to A.D. 725 (Browman 1980a; Kolata 1983), though others consider it to have begun as late as A.D. 500 (Isbell 1983).

Ponce's Tiwanaku Epoca V, or *Tiwanaku expansivo* (expansive), corresponded to Bennett's Decadent Tiahuanaco phase. Ceramically, Ponce retained the suspect concept of design decadence originally proposed by Bennett for the Tiwanaku IV/Tiwanaku V transition, describing a "greater simplicity of painted designs and the "disappearance of zoomorphic designs" (Ponce 1947). Other observations of assemblage shifts, including the "immense diffusion" of flaring-sided bowls shaped like half keros and now known as *tazones*, are more verifiable. As the name implies, this phase coincided with the period of Tiwanaku urbanism and territorial expansion into the western sierra (e.g., Browman 1984b:125, 130; 1985:66–67). Ponce's dating of Tiwanaku V ranged from A.D. 725 to the thirteenth century A.D. (Ponce 1972); however, recent dates for Tiwanaku V ceramic contexts at Tiwanaku and Lukurmata find few to date later than A.D. 1000 (Bermann 1994; Janusek 1999; Kolata 1993, 1996a).

Although the Tiwanaku IV–Tiwanaku V phase division has proven useful as an arbitrary temporal distinction, its vague material associations have vexed Tiwanaku archaeologists and prejudiced the interpretations of excavation and survey projects in the Tiwanaku core region. Only recently have quantitative ceramic analyses turned to associating some of the typological categories proposed by Bennett and Ponce with archaeological contexts. Most of these studies have focused on social and functional distinctions within the corporate Tiwanaku assemblage, rather than on its temporal seriation (Alconini 1993, 1995; Girault 1990, Rivera Casanovas 1994; Janusek 1994, 1999). Only two studies have proposed ceramic seriations that specify temporally sensitive attributes within the five-century span of the Tiwanaku corporate style (Burkholder 1998; Janusek and Alconini 2000).

Contemporary with the creation of the corporate style of Tiwanaku IV and V, Tiwanaku material culture is characterized by the adoption of a coherent iconographic corpus. Unfortunately for those interested in thematic or narrative interpretations, most Tiwanaku art is highly stylized, with few of the realistic depictions of human or supernatural figures, dress, or actions that characterize other styles such as Moche (Donnan 1978; Quilter 1997). Most attention has been paid to the more complex iconographic images of the Tiwanaku corpus and particularly to the rare figures of humans or deities. The Tiwanaku and Wari cultures shared imagery representing a state deity and supporting pantheon, best known from the low-relief carved stone figures of Tiwanaku's Gateway of the Sun. This Gateway or Front-Faced God has been identified with a generalized Andean celestial deity (Demarest 1981). Other analysts emphasize his specific association with political unification in both Tiwanaku and Wari symbolic systems, where "power elites attempted both internal and external integration through a common imagery reflective of relations of dominance" (Cook 1983:179). Versions of the state god and his supporters may be discerned in low-relief stone carvings at the

Tiwanaku site and in a wide range of portable media such as tapestry textiles, wooden snuff tablets, and bone implements. In pottery, the Front-Faced God appears in simplified masklike form on ceramic keros and other vessels.

The altiplano cultures are particularly famous for their stone sculpture tradition. Early styles of stone sculpture in the Titicaca basin emphasized animistic and natural images and geometric and other motifs similar to those on Pukara textiles (Browman 1978b; Chávez and Chávez 1976). Diverse examples of these earlier and foreign sculpture styles may have been collected or even captured for display within the Tiwanaku monumental precinct. In one celebrated case, matching fragments of the same Pukara-style stone sculpture have been found at Arapa, on the north shore of the lake, and at Tiwanaku (Chávez and Chávez 1976:66; Chávez 1976:12; Chávez 1981). The remarkable capture, transport, and curation of this presumably sacred object might represent a Pukara "root" transplanted at Tiwanaku. Lesser Classic Tiwanaku sculptural types may represent fantastic beings, kneeling captives, or masked sacrificers (Kolata 1993:126).

However, it has been the massive human figures portraying ceremonialized leadership that have captured the imagination of generations of visitors to the Tiwanaku site. These Classic Tiwanaku stelae, which include the largest sculptures ever carved in the pre-Columbian Americas, were given central positions in Tiwanaku's sacred precincts. These stelae depict human figures modeled in an abstract planar style defined by the prismatic shape of the

Figure 3.14. Fraile, Ponce, and Bennett monoliths, Tiwanaku, holding *keros* and snuff tablets. PSG Photos.

carved stones themselves. Complex low-relief carving that represents face painting, tattooing, and highly elaborate tapestry shirts, headgear, and belts bear the images of the Gateway God ensemble. Examples of these figures, such as the Bennett, Ponce, and Fraile monoliths, appear to be performing rituals with keros and hallucinogenic drug tablets grasped in either hand (fig. 3.14).

The City of Tiwanaku

Although the Tiwanaku site's origins remain obscure, it is clear that an urban explosion was associated with the creation of the Tiwanaku corporate style. Investigations of the Tiwanaku site's urban core have embraced the city as both symbolic center and true metropolis during Tiwanaku IV and V. Some scholars have seen Tiwanaku as a city planned according to structural principles of cosmogonic representation and social control. Kolata argues that the site's monumental core was a sacred and ritually charged "island enciente" that "structurally recapitulated basic social formation and generated a perduring sense of participation among urban and rural populations" (Kolata 1993:87, 1996a). Interpretations of elite contexts excavated in the Akapana pyramid (Manzanilla 1992) and in the Palace of the Multicolored Rooms have contributed to a reading of the city's monumental core as "a kind of public, symbolic text" (Kolata 1993:106). Tiwanaku is painted as a huge but strangely primitive "company town" where the company business was attending to the symbolic and physical needs of controlling elites (Kolata 1993:173–179, 1997:254). In this planned and socially controlled "patrician city," urbanites and craftspeople are said to have enjoyed high status and living standards solely because of their attachment to ruling lineages. Indeed, urban residence was permitted only for those who serviced the aristocracy (Kolata 1997:253). In this vision, Tiwanaku was an extension of elite households, and the "true *raison d'être* of the city" was servicing the elites and their aristocratic lineages (Kolata 1991:174).

This hypothesis seems reasonable for practitioners of certain highly skilled or sumptuary crafts at Tiwanaku. Impressive concentrations of imported shell and precious stones have been associated with elite residence and palace burials at Tiwanaku (Kolata 1993:157), and lapidary and fine lithic production is known to have used exotic imported rare materials, such as obsidian from distant Arequipa (Brooks et al. 1997). Although textile preservation in the altiplano is poor, the depiction of tapestry textiles in stone sculpture suggests restricted access to garments made in this highly labor-intensive technique and could suggest workshop production similar to that described for the cloistered "chosen women" who wove for Inca nobility (Murra 1962). Highly skilled metalworkers at Tiwanaku and other core region sites like Lukurmata produced objects of gold, silver, copper, and an array of bronze alloys of copper-arsenic-nickel, copper-tin, and copper-arsenic (Lechtman 1997:158). Gold and silver were reserved for jewelry, headdresses, and ornamental items for the elites, and even bronze items such as pins, needles, small figures, and axes were cast, hammered, or repoussé decorated for ornamental rather than strictly utilitarian use.[8] The use of bronze T-shaped architectural cramps cast in situ at Tiwanaku's Pumapunku and other monumental buildings to join cut-stone architectural elements attests to the buildings' importance, and gold decorative elements may have been added to stonework in a similar fashion (Conklin 1991).

In sharp contrast to Kolata's "company town," a different picture of more organic and metropolitan residency and crafts production has begun to emerge with more extensive household archaeology in the urban districts of the Tiwanaku core region (Bermann 1994, 1997; Janusek 1994, 1999). Although we cannot discount attached specialists altogether, it now appears that the majority of Tiwanaku crafts were produced by independent households or larger co-resident collectives. Some production activities, notably food processing and the making of ordinary textiles, utilitarian hoes, and other stone tools, were universal and are represented by the presence of production tools in virtually all individual domestic contexts (Bermann 1994; Janusek 1999).

Other crafts were indeed made by specialists but apparently not by the kind of attached specialists hypothesized by Kolata. These corporate co-residential artisan groups lived in urban barrios or rural settlements and appear to have been largely autonomous in their social and exchange relationships. Typical of these was Chiji Jawira, a potters' barrio on the outskirts of Tiwanaku producing ceramics of a unique stylistic identity within the larger corporate Tiwanaku style (Rivera Casanovas 1994). Specialized workshops at Lukurmata produced bone tools, pan pipes, and ceramic whistles (Bermann 1994; Janusek 1999). It now appears that these craft-producing enterprises may have corresponded to descent-based or ethnically constituted ayllus living within the urban landscape. If this is the case, both urban residence and craft production were embedded in Tiwanaku's diverse and segmentary social substructure and not dictated by the demands of patrician sponsors (Albarracin-Jordan 1996a,b; Janusek 1999).

The *Altiplano* Subsistence Base

We have seen how the apparent barrenness of the Tiwanaku core region is a common theme in the early history of Tiwanaku studies. Ancient states depended on agriculture, and agriculture at high elevations would appear to be an impoverished and risky endeavor. In the altiplano, the primary barrier to agriculture is wide diurnal temperature variation of up to 15°C, with intense solar radiation by day and frequent frosts at night. The altiplano rainy season is from November through March, with a mean annual precipitation approaching 700 mm. With an annual mean temperature of 9°C, night frosts are a significant limiting factor.

Only in recent years have we learned how the seemingly barren altiplano was capable of supporting dense populations. Tiwanaku's core region depended on a resource triad based on the herding of camelids, lacustrine resources, and above all the cultivation of specialized frost-resistant crops through labor- intensive raised field systems. Excavations at altiplano Tiwanaku sites demonstrate extensive consumption of the domesticated llamas and alpacas, which would also have been crucial as beasts of burden and for wool production (Bermann 1994, 1997; Browman 1974, 1980b, 1984b, 1993; Lynch 1983; Webster 1993). The faunal evidence indicates that a fully integrated agro-pastoral system was in place throughout the Tiwanaku period. Wild resources including water birds, freshwater fish, and amphibians were pursued with small reed watercraft. Deer, the wild camelid species of vicuña and guanaco, and small mammals, hunted with snares, bow and arrow, darts, slings, and bolas, played a significant supplementary role in Tiwanaku diet.

Contrary to the prejudices voiced by Squier, Tiwanaku enjoyed a highly productive agricultural hinterland. Tiwanaku core region farmers cultivated a complex of potatoes, other tuber crops such as *oca*, *olluco*, and *mashua*, and chenopod grains such as *quinoa* (Browman 1984b; Towles 1961; Weberbauer 1936). Altitude, with its combination of intensive sunlight and nightly frosts, permitted the preparation of *chuño*, or dehydrated potatoes, through a uniquely Andean freeze-drying process. This would have been particularly important for the accumulation of agricultural surplus, as it permits the storage of tuber crops.

Agriculture in the Tiwanaku homeland depended upon a vast complex of over 120,000 hectares of raised fields and related canals and watercourses (fig. 3.15; Kolata 1986, 1989, 1993, 1996a; see also Denevan 1970, 1980; Erickson 1984, 1987, 1999; Graffam 1988; Kolata 1982, 1983, 1986; 1991; Lennon 1982; Mathews 1989). The raised fields, or more precisely the water-filled swales between them, absorbed and stored daily solar radiation and effectively raised mean soil temperatures after sunset (Kolata and Ortloff 1989). Experiments suggest that these advantages can dramatically decrease failure risk and can increase yield over flatland agriculture in the altiplano (Erickson 1985; Kolata and Ortloff 1996). The organic sediment that accumulated in the water-filled ditches also contributed to the biotic potential of the fields, fertilizing crops as organic material was dredged up in canal maintenance (Carney et al. 1993). Increased exploitation of lacustrine flora and fauna may have been a by-product of the extensive artificial wetlands created

Figure 3.15. Abandoned lakeside raised fields near Lukurmata. PSG photo.

by the raised field systems, which extended the Titicaca basin's fish, birds, and amphibians into the miniature ecosystem formed by drainage ditches and canals (Kolata 1993:221).

Considerable debate has focused on the effects of climate change on the agricultural systems of the Tiwanaku homeland. Long-term trends suggested by glacial ice cores correlate the Tiwanaku tradition with two relatively wet periods from A.D. 610–650 and 760–1040. Decreasing rainfall inferred after A.D. 1040, culminating in severe drought and low lake levels from A.D. 1245 to 1310, have been implicated in the Tiwanaku collapse (Ortloff and Kolata 1989:199–200; Kolata and Ortloff 1996:183–186). However, Erickson argues that most Tiwanaku site abandonment took place a hundred to two hundred years before the onset of this drought (Erickson 1999:635).

This discussion points to a more fundamental controversy over the extent to which Tiwanaku raised field agriculture depended on a hierarchical centralized administration of production and distribution. Kolata describes an administered agricultural system corresponding to state investment and labor control for surplus production (Kolata 1993, 1996a; Kolata and Ortloff 1996). This Wittfogelelian interpretation of Tiwanaku agriculture posits a highly intensified system where intensification was possible only with elite management of labor, engineering, and adjudication of water rights. In contrast, Erickson (1984, 1985, 1999) has pointed out the successful modern rehabilitation of raised fields by households and small kin-based communities. Erickson further suggests that raised field technology was practiced by individual small farmers in the altiplano for centuries before the rise of Tiwanaku, and that raised field agriculture persisted after the Tiwanaku state collapse, under much smaller-scale political systems (Graffam 1988, 1992). These views call into question the assumption that Tiwanaku raised field agriculture was necessarily associated with unitary agricultural policy under a centralized state.

Tiwanaku Core Region Settlement Patterns

Tiwanaku's level of hierarchical integration as a demographic and political system has only recently been the subject of systematic research. Unlike most early states, Tiwanaku left us little evidence of administrative structures and social status in texts, palaces, mortuary monuments, and sumptuary grave offerings. Although elite burials have been reported from Tiwanaku's palaces (Kolata 1993:156), no unambiguously royal tombs have been found, and there is no written record of Tiwanaku leaders' names or dates. This has left us the conundrum of a Tiwanaku state without any known statesmen and without a clearly understood state structure.

One entree to understanding Tiwanaku's political structure is study of settlement patterns in the Tiwanaku core region. Considering that Tiwanaku ceramic sherds are visible in road cuts, plowed fields, and even adobe bricks in modern buildings for many kilometers around the site's monumental precinct, it seems remarkable that many early researchers considered the altiplano to be too unforgiving a landscape to support dense settlement. Incredibly, Parsons's rudimentary two-day survey (1968) was the first to consider the population of the Tiwanaku site by surveying the spatial extent of its surface ceramic scatter. He estimated a contiguous occupation of 2.4 km^2 and an immediate urban population of up to 20,000.

Understanding the subsistence potential of the Tiwanaku core region opened a vista of the altiplano as both garden spot and demographic center. Subsequent estimates have placed the Tiwanaku site's occupied area at closer to 4 km^2, with a population of 25,000 to 40,000 (Browman 1978, 1984b: 124; Kolata 1993:30; Ponce 1972), and one survey suggests an extended urban area as large as 8–9 km^2, with a population that may have exceeded 40,000 (Mathews 1989). Kolata estimates the urbanized population of a "Tiwanaku metropolitan district," including settlements of the Catari, Tiwanaku, and Machaca-Desaguadero drainages, at 115,000, with a supporting rural population of 250,000 available to farm 19,000 hectares of raised fields (Kolata 1993:205).

Outside the Tiwanaku site, the size and administrative functions of Tiwanaku's secondary centers in the Titicaca basin have become key research questions. Bennett's excavations at Lukurmata, Chiripa, and Pajchiri (1936) were a first step toward demonstrating the Tiwanaku cultural affiliation of those sites through their ceramic assemblages and the presence of Tiwanaku-style stone sculpture and temple architecture. Though some centers, such as the lakeside port facilities of Iwawe (Burkholder 1997; Ponce 1972), may have had specific functions, most were probably built to extend state political authority to the vast system of agricultural works that dominated the landscape in the Tiwanaku period. David Browman (1978:342) and others (Tschopik 1946; Kidder 1943, 1956) cited the presence of semisubterranean temple architecture in defining some twelve "secondary temple centers" in the southern Titicaca basin. In a descriptive sense, Ponce (1972) characterized four of these as "urban," four as "habitations," one as a "rural habitation," and three as temples only. However, only with Kolata's surveys of the Pampa Koani between the "satellite centers" of Pajchiri and Lukurmata and subsequent settlement pattern surveys of the Tiwanaku valley, the Juli-Pomata region, and the Island of the Sun has the true population density of Tiwanaku's altiplano hinterlands come to light (Albarracin-Jordan 1996a, 1996b; Albarracin-Jordan and Mathews 1990; Bauer and Stanish 2001; Kolata 1982, 1985, 1986, 1989; Mathews 1997; Stanish 1999; Stanish et al. 1996).

The first order site of Tiwanaku, with its extensive monumental center of cut-stone temples, enclosures, and platform pyramids, and at least 420 hectares in urban area, dominates the Tiwanaku core region settlement pattern. The Tiwanaku site's ceremonial, administrative, and residential palace precincts were laid out on a cardinal orientation and surrounded by a moat to separate them from the rest of the city (Kolata 1993:90). Elite residential complexes have been identified on the summit of the massive Akapana pyramid (Manzanilla 1992) and in the Putuni palace, implying that the monumental center was reserved for royal or high status residents. The 4 km^2 of surrounding non-elite residential sectors at Tiwanaku maintained the same cardinal orientation as the monumental center. Residential groups were bounded by perimeter walls into socially or functionally differentiated barrios, which in turn were subdivided into patio groups. These are believed to represent segmentary social units corresponding to ayllus or kin groups within the city (Janusek 1999).

Interpretations differ on the systemic integration of second order sites like

Lukurmata, Pajchiri, Khonko Wankani, Chiripa, and Iwawe, all of which have extensive domestic areas and temple structures or some other form of public cut-stone architecture. Ponce (1989) and Kolata (1993, 1996a) describe a highly hierarchical four-level Tiwanaku settlement system corresponding to state agricultural investment and a quadripartite division of administrative and production functions. In this view, Tiwanaku's agricultural hinterlands, were characterized by: "(1) massive public reclamation and construction projects . . . which required a large and coordinated labor force; (2) a consistent distinction between an elite, luxury-oriented material culture and a subsistence-oriented proletarian material culture implying some form of class stratification; and (3) a contemporaneous hierarchical settlement network marked by unambiguous distinctions in size, status and function. This settlement hierarchy implies minimally a nested quadripartite division of administrative and primary production responsibilities" (Kolata 1986:760).

Kolata thus considers the secondary temple centers as little more than the local apices of an efficient constructed landscape of agricultural production, where elites co-opted land and managed labor on state or elite corporate estates (1993:230). Tiwanaku core region settlement indeed corresponds closely to raised field systems, and the Tiwanaku incorporation of the Titicaca basin often meant the abandonment of Late Formative sites as new political centers were established to control them. The fact that the Tiwanaku secondary centers are seldom fortified (Stanish et al. 1994:10) would appear to support centralized coordination of agricultural activity rather than autonomous local control. These interpretations of settlement patterns, together with a view that a powerful social hierarchy dictated the spatial layout of the site's monumental core, support Kolata's view of the Tiwanaku site as the centripetal capital of a bureaucratic and strongly centralized Tiwanaku state (Kolata 1982, 1985, 1986, 1993, 1997).

In contrast to this classic model of a highly centralized state, however, systematic settlement pattern data for the Tiwanaku core region reveal a very different picture (Albarracin-Jordan 1996; Mathews 1997). Rank-size and cluster analyses of these more extensive data from the upper and lower Tiwanaku valley suggest autonomous "sub-system settlement enclaves," focused at each of the Titicaca basin regional centers (McAndrews et al. 1997). These authors specifically negate Kolata's reconstructions of the Tiwanaku polity as a highly centralized state organized in a "pyramidal" fashion. Instead, they suggest a society that was "segmentary in nature and organized into a nested hierarchy . . . consistent with ethnohistorically-derived constructs of indigenous Andean sociopolitical structure" (McAndrews et al. 1997:81).

Similar segmentation at the community level appears to be the case within core region settlements like Lukurmata (Janusek 1999). This more autonomous view of regional settlement clusters fits with an emerging "local perspective" that finds a long history of autonomous development to the "secondary centers" before and after the period of Tiwanaku influence or incorporation (Bermann 1994, 1997). For the Tiwanaku site itself, these interpretations suggest that within-site spatial variations of ceramic style and household organization represent diverse social segments subsumed within the Tiwanaku polity. A conception of "nested hierarchies," applying the segmentary ethnographic concept of the ayllu, is invoked to explain barrios within the urban Tiwanaku site (Janusek 1994, 1999). Similarly, researchers focusing on regional settlement patterns and local approaches to smaller sites of the Tiwanaku core region have emphasized more segmentary interpretations of Tiwanaku as a loose ethnic confederacy of politically autonomous communities who shared only cultural and ceremonial ties to the capital (Albarracin-Jordan 1996; Bermann 1994, 1997).

This interpretation of largely autonomous, interacting communities is supported by evidence from biological anthropology. A comprehensive study of nonmetric skeletal traits by Blom (1999; Blom et al. 1998) found no significant biological distance among burial populations from Tiwanaku, Lukurmata, and rural sites of the Tiwanaku valley and the Katari basin. This indicates open migration and mating among a fairly homogeneous core region majority population. Nonetheless, the same sample demonstrated heterogeneity in the cultural practice of cranial deformation among the Tiwanaku populations. Annular banding cranial modification types predominating in the Katari basin contrast with the fronto-occipital cradleboarding that dominated in the Moquegua subtradition, for example. These different Tiwanaku cranial modification styles may have correlated with regional, ethnic, or clan affiliations. As might be expected for a cosmopolitan city, populations from the Tiwanaku site displayed the greatest heterogeneity of styles, and small groups from sectors at Tiwanaku who exhibit different mortuary practices and cranial deformation styles could represent foreign populations within the city (Blom et al. 1998:250).

Despite the controversy over the coordinating role of central political authority, it is now clear that the Tiwanaku-period Titicaca basin, although culturally unified, encompassed diverse communities that were intricately subdivided structurally at several levels. And despite this peculiarly segmentary nature, or perhaps because of it, Tiwanaku's cultural florescence in the core region coincided with the expansion of Tiwanaku peoples out of their altiplano homeland into new regions with very different physical, economic, and sociopolitical landscapes. This phenomenon of Tiwanaku expansion is discussed in the next chapter.

4

The Tiwanaku Periphery

I have detected that Tiahuanaco is *not* an isolated fact, that it stands in relation with a whole section of ruins including those on the islands of the Lake. The only thing that distinguishes Tiahuanaco from the other vestiges is the number of great Monoliths.

Adolph Bandelier, field notes for September 22, 1894, emphasis original

Examining some of the current reconstructions of Tiwanaku expansion allows us to trace the evidence for the diffusion of Tiwanaku dominion outside the core region. While the evidence for an extension of Tiwanaku material culture is convincing and well documented, our understanding of how Tiwanaku and indigenous interests came together in these regions is still in its infancy. My primary goal in this chapter is to consider cases where Tiwanaku colonization did or did not occur and to consider whether distinctive patterns of colonization are evident in regional cultural, sociopolitical, and ecological settings.

Since the turn of the twentieth century, various models have been proposed to explain the widespread diffusion of the Tiwanaku style throughout the south-central Andes. While there was little question that Tiwanaku extended some kind of cultural authority beyond the altiplano to the eastern Andean lowlands, the deserts of Atacama, and the river valleys of the Pacific coast, problem-oriented archaeological research was rare until recently, and most interpretations were based on object-oriented studies of artifacts and iconography. Only recently have archaeologists and biological anthropologists begun to evaluate interaction models through sustained archaeological projects in the Tiwanaku periphery. However, research on the nature of Tiwanaku dominion has been slow to coalesce and is still far from the point of final synthesis. Partly because the Tiwanaku periphery is distributed across the borders of four modern nations, most research has taken place in the context of independent projects, testing independently derived models, in widely disparate and isolated regions. Further bias may be injected by differential preservation of sites and artifact categories between regions. More insidiously, the particular methodologies chosen for each of these projects, ranging from mortuary archaeology to household archaeology to settlement

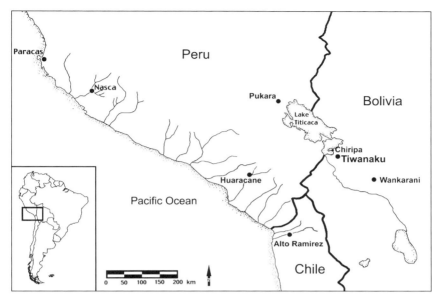

Figure 4.1. Map of Formative cultures of the south-central Andes and south coast of Peru.

pattern survey, may produce results that are not directly comparable or even contradictory.

Thus, while a growing and diverse body of research has clarified the geographic extent of Tiwanaku's influence in the south-central Andes, there is still debate over the nature and intensity of Tiwanaku dominion. Interpretations for Tiwanaku interaction range from conquest to colonization, indirect trade through prestige networks, and "status quo" models of little change to local communities. Because methods and interpretations vary so widely from archaeologist to archaeologist, and from region to region, our search for diasporic colonization during the Tiwanaku period must evaluate these specific regional examples on a case by case basis.

The Formative: Pre-Tiwanaku Colonies?

The altiplano was the cradle of a series of complex polities centuries before Tiwanaku and the Aymara kingdoms (fig. 4.1). Migration or colonization by altiplano populations may have brought agriculture and village life to the Pacific coastal valleys as early as the Wankarani and Chiripa complexes of Bolivia in the first millennium B.C. (Dauelsberg 1972a,b; Feldman 1989; Muñoz 1983a,b; Nuñez 1972; M. Rivera 1976, 1991). Kolata argues that "substantial quantities of early *altiplano* ceramic materials" demonstrate an "ethnic *altiplano* occupation" (Kolata 1993:268). It is often assumed that there was a very ancient "continual pattern" of colonization of lowland zones by the Formative cultures of Wankarani, Chiripa, and Pukara as early as 1000 B.C. (Stanish 1992:52). The presence of "Chiripa-like" ceramics is seen to suggest complex exchange or colonial relationships between the altiplano and the western valleys (Feldman 1989; Stanish 1992:67, 71). Unfortunately the wide distribution of vegetable fiber temper and the neckless *olla* vessel form among coastal and highland Formative populations calls into question the precision of this correspondence, as these generic attributes were shared across a wide geographical and temporal range.[1]

More compelling evidence of altiplano interaction with the western valleys exists for Pukara, a late Formative polity of the northwest Lake Titicaca basin. The Pukara culture (250 B.C.–A.D. 380) was centered at the eponymous type site near the village of Pucará in the Ayaviri-Pucará valley of the Peruvian altiplano at an elevation of 3,950 m above sea level. The Pukara site's monumental pyramidal platforms indicate an advanced degree of planning and labor organization, and with an area of 6 km² Pukara can also be described as one of the altiplano's first urban sites (Chávez 1992; Kidder 1943; Mujica 1990:162). Regionally the Pukara site has been seen as the apex of a three-level site size hierarchy with populous secondary centers at nearby Taraco, Maravillas, and Incatunuhuire supported by raised field intensive agriculture (Erickson 1987; Mujica 1990:171).

Considering the sociopolitical complexity of the Pukara core region, there has been considerable interest in Pukara expansion. Pukara was the source for the diffusion of a style in ceramics and stone sculpture that enjoyed a wide influence in the highlands (Browman 1980a,b; Chávez 1976, 1981, 1992; Conklin 1983; Cook 1983). Affinities with pottery and early ceramics from the Vilcanota and Apurimac valleys suggest Pukara contact with Cusco at a very early date (Mujica 1990:176). The "zoned incised" Pukara ceramic style of the Pucará site dates roughly between 100 B.C. and A.D. 100 (Chávez 1992; Franquemont 1986:2). Similar traits appear subsequently in highland traditions to the south, notably the Kalasasaya/Tiwanaku I style of Tiwanaku (Lumbreras 1974b:88; Ponce 1976) and the Sillumocco style of the Juli region (Steadman 1995). This suggests that Pukara decorative techniques and vessel forms were emulated throughout the altiplano as a "pan-Titicaca tradition" of polychrome incised ceramics during the Upper Formative (Stanish and Steadman 1994:55).

Pukara contact with the Nasca and Paracas traditions of the Peruvian south coast is also suggested by the ceramic similarities. The traditions share the zoned incised ceramic technique and depictions of geometric figures, staff-bearing deities, trophy heads, and felines with the body shown in profile and the face turned toward the viewer (Goldstein 2000b; Lumbreras 1974b:88; Menzel et al. 1964).[2] A Pukara tapestry found in the Ica Valley suggests that coastal Peruvian weavers in late Paracas and Early Nasca times emulated stone carving styles of the Lake Titicaca basin (Chávez and Chávez 1976:66; Chávez 1981; Conklin 1983; Silverman 1996:125–126).

The outward transfer of these stylistic ideas could reflect the projection of political power by Pukara as a state core. It has been suggested that Pukara polities might have colonized coastal valleys to access lowland ecological resources (Mujica 1990; Mujica et al. 1983; Rivera 1985). However, Pukara colonies are not supported by the evidence. In the Azapa Valley of northern Chile, Pukara-style textiles found in *túmulo* tombs of the Alto Ramírez Phase suggest contact with the north Titicaca basin between 500 B.C. and A.D. 200. The altiplano-associated textiles of the Alto Ramírez Phase include tapestry bags, shirts and head deformers depicting trophy heads, zoomorphic figures, stair-steps, crosses, and other geometric figures resembling those of altiplano stone sculpture and ceramic iconography (Focacci and Erices 1971:50, 59; Mujica 1985:111; Muñoz 1986:305; 1987: 124; Rivera 1985:42; Ulloa 1982). Because Alto Ramírez saw for the first time the fusion of camelid pastoralism, lower valley agriculture, and marine exploitation in a single social and subsistence system, it has been suggested that Pukara colonists brought new lifeways and sociopolitical complexity to the region (Muñoz 1987:93) along with motifs affiliated with the transmission of politico-religious authority (M. Rivera 1976, 1985). However, no Pukara pottery has been found in Azapa. The small number of and high incidence of repair in imported textiles suggest that they were exotic imports rather than a colonial assemblage. This is supported by a bioarchaeological study of Alto Ramírez individuals that suggests strong genetic continuity with earlier indigenous occupations in Arica, rather than colonization (Sutter 2000:63).

As can be seen in the following chapter, a phase of Pukara colonization, named the Trapiche Phase, has also been proposed for the Moquegua Valley of southern Peru (Feldman 1989). Pukara- style zoned incised polychrome sherds were collected at the Chen Chen site and perhaps elsewhere in the Moquegua Valley in the early 1960s (Disselhoff 1968:215; Vescelius 1960). In 1984, Robert Feldman noted Pukara-style ceramics and paired warp tapestry fragments in an area of looted stone structures at Cerro Trapiche (M7; Feldman 1989:215). Feldman judged the sherds to represent "a permanently resident population that was in contact with the altiplano center" and suggested that the "Trapiche Phase represents an occupation in Moquegua by people making variants of Pukara pottery and textiles" (1989:213).

Do Pukara-related finds in the western valleys meet the criteria I established earlier for diasporic colonies, or do they represent forms of interaction short of colonization? The small number and sumptuary nature of Pukara imports recovered in Ica, Azapa, or Moquegua suggests minority trade components within predominantly local assemblages. Moreover, the mortuary context of these exotic imports reinforces this association with elite long-distance trade (Browman 1985:64) or "mortuary offerings associated with local elements" (Mujica 1985:111). No Pukara residential occupation or Pukara utilitarian plainware ceramic assemblages has been found in any region outside the altiplano. Without households that can be ascribed to Pukara settlers, the Pukara-related finds instead suggest an exchange of luxury goods with indigenous local elites, rather than colonization.

Despite hard evidence of elite trade and stylistic and cultural affinities, the network connecting the coastal and altiplano regions during the Formative period is not yet evident in the archaeological record. The oasis river valleys of the south-central Andes may have seen the comings and goings of traders of both altiplano and coastal cultural traditions. The elites of less complex agrarian societies in contact with early states like Pukara profited from this trade by accruing and redistributing exotic valuables to recruit local followers (Goldstein 2000b).

There is no evidence that Tiwanaku played any role in the western valleys during its own period of initial Formative development. No finds pertaining to Tiwanaku's early phases have been reported in the western valleys. This indicates that early Tiwanaku, a contemporary of Pukara, did not project power or influence beyond the confines of the southern altiplano (Mujica 1985). This was to change dramatically with the explosive rise of the Tiwanaku site and the coalescence of a corporate material culture style in Tiwanaku IV.

"Coastal Tiahuanaco": A False Start

Even early scholars like Cieza de León and Cobo were aware that the ruins of Tiwanaku had once been a city with an influence throughout much of the Andes. Cieza de León also noted that the weathered ruins of Wari (Huari), on the Viñaque River in the Peruvian highlands, were of pre-Inca construction (Cieza 1959 [1553]:123; 1984 [1553]:249; Isbell 1977:2).[3] After interviewing local informants and noting the Wari buildings' non-Inca square plan and reports of "letters" inscribed on stones, Cieza explicitly linked the builders of the Viñaque ruins to those of Tiwanaku, concluding that both were built by a pre-Inca race of bearded white men (Cieza 1984 [1553]:284).

It was not until late the nineteenth century that long-term studies began to analyze Tiwanaku's broad regional significance in more scientific terms. German archaeologist Max Uhle, among the first to recognize the Tiwanaku art style, later noticed that it bore strong iconographic similarities to pottery and textile designs he found in the Pachacamac temple complex on the Peruvian coast near Lima.[4] Uhle concluded that Tiwanaku had a wide influence as a unified pre-Inca cultural phenomenon he called the "Tiahuanaco Style" (Uhle 1903:22, 47).

Uhle's characterization of a single Tiahuanaco Style that dominated the entire Andes triggered a cycle of confusion in Middle Horizon nomenclature that continues to affect research to this day. Unfortunately, Uhle was unaware of what is now known as the Wari culture and was unable to distinguish Tiwanaku from Wari styles in his "Tiahuanaco" horizon. Working on the Peruvian coast before the discovery of the Wari type sites, A. L. Kroeber compounded Uhle's error, coining the new term "Tiahuanacoid" for "painted pieces . . . having more or less Nazca resemblance . . . which in our poverty of knowledge of the highland, I would call Tiahuanacoid, if not Tiahuanaco" (Kroeber 1944:99). Nonetheless, by the late 1930s, it became

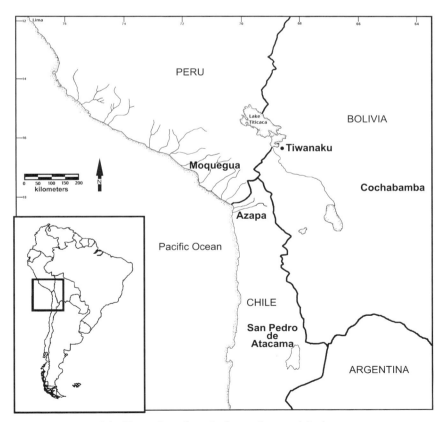

Figure 4.2. Map of the Tiwanaku culture in the south-central Andes.

clear that despite similarities in decorative motifs, great differences existed between the pottery of altiplano Tiwanaku and the Tiahuanaco-influenced styles that Uhle and Kroeber found on the Peruvian coast.

Only after the first investigations of the site of Wari in the highland Peruvian Department of Ayacucho by Julio C. Tello in the 1930s did it become apparent that these Tiahuanacoid ceramics were only indirectly related to the Tiwanaku site. Instead, with the publication of ceramics from the Wari (Huari) site, it became evident that the so-called Tiahuanacoid pottery of the coast, with its particular combination of Tiwanaku-related iconography and Nasca forms and technology, was of the same independent style that originated in the Peruvian sierra (Bennett 1953; Rowe et al. 1950). Unfortunately, by this time the terms "Coastal Tiahuanaco" and "Tiahuanacoid" had become so deeply ingrained in Peruvian archaeology that they continued to be used for the Wari style. Not until more extensive investigations at Wari sites (Isbell 1977; Lumbreras 1974b) and the development of the "Middle Horizon" sequence in the 1960s and 70s (Menzel 1964; Rowe et al. 1950) was the "Tiahuanacoid" terminology finally retired.[5] The effect of this semantic wrong turn has been to retard and confuse the investigation of altiplano Tiwanaku's genuine peripheral contact.

Max Uhle, who was responsible for the broad application of the "Tiahuanacoid" terminology to non-Tiwanaku cultures, was also one of the first to document true Tiwanaku materials on the coast of southern Peru and northern Chile (1918). Today finds of Tiwanaku materials in the eastern Andes, northern Chile, the river valleys of the Pacific Coast, and as far away as northern Argentina provide an opportunity to understand the relationships between Tiwanaku and peripheral regions and to evaluate the possibility of Tiwanaku colonization (fig. 4.2).

Hegemony or Prestige Networks?—The Altiplano Model

The wide extent of Tiwanaku material culture has become increasingly clear in the century since Uhle's first consideration of a "Tiahuanacoid" empire. Early interpretations of this stylistic diffusion ascribed Tiwanaku expansion to an entirely religious phenomenon (Menzel 1964:67). More recent interpretations of Tiwanaku peripheral integration presume a political economy that sought hegemony through indirect means. This brand of Tiwanaku hegemony has been characterized as a "Titicaca Interaction Sphere" acting through cultural or economic clients without political or ethnic domination or colonization (Moseley et al. 1991) and as a form of "indirect complementarity" (Mujica 1985). The term "clientism" is often used to describe Tiwanaku's integration of distant peripheries through asymmetrical elite-to-elite relationships. It is often assumed that these patron-client relation-ships were articulated through prestige exchange with preexisting peripheral chiefs. Kolata's view of Tiwanaku's long-distance trade with its distant pe-ripheries is typical: "In this exchange, which was structured along the lines of a clientage relationship, local elites of these distant lands maintained personal relationships with the lords of Tiwanaku and their agents, managing the production and long distance exchange of desired commodities and simulta-neously appropriating emblems of status and authority from their altiplano patrons" (Kolata 1992:83).

In explicating what he described as the "altiplano model" Browman (1980b) emphasized the low cost of hegemonic integration as compared to the "political difficulty and the high economic and social costs" of direct territorial exploitation by altiplano colonists. According to the altiplano model, Tiwanaku's broader sphere of influence was founded upon "mutual economic interchange" through a crafts exchange network maintained by markets and caravan trade (Browman 1985:63):

> The *altiplano* individual has found that in order to acquire access to resources from other ecological zones he must become either (1) a skilled trader, or (2) a skilled craftsman, with some sort of marketable skill. . . . Mercantile exchange was an important factor in both the maintenance of the Tiwanaku urban center, and the extension and ex-pansion of Tiwanaku influence in the Andean altiplano and adjacent coastal areas. Tiwanaku served as the industrial center, with guilds of craftsmen and artisans. It imported raw materials and exported fin-ished trade goods. Tiwanaku increased its political control because its developing industrial specializations made it mandatory to develop in-creasingly larger market areas for its specialized productions. (Brow-man 1980b:108–109)

Although they differ in their interpretation of the nature of the Tiwanaku state, both of these models imply the kind of core-centered hegemony through clientage that is often suggested by world systems approaches and other globalist perspectives. This model has been reinforced by archaeologi-cal data from San Pedro de Atacama, an obscure corner of the northern Chilean desert that has come to symbolize Tiwanaku as a merchant state whose hegemony depended on missionary activities and elite trade.

San Pedro de Atacama

The oasis of San Pedro de Atacama is perhaps the most enigmatic and in some ways the most glamorous area of Tiwanaku peripheral influence. Separated from Tiwanaku by 800 km of difficult terrain, San Pedro would seem an unlikely candidate for Tiwanaku settlement. San Pedro is situated at an altitude of 2,430 m above sea level in the Andean foothills of the Atacama Desert, 105 km northeast of the modern city of Calama, Chile. Irrigation from intermittent rivers has supported limited cultivation of grain crops since the late pre-Hispanic period (Orellana 1985:243; Hidalgo 1996), but it is unlikely that San Pedro's thirteen small agricultural oases, known locally as *ayllus*, could have supported dense populations, let alone produced a surplus worthy of Tiwanaku's interest. Because it is a three-month round trip from Tiwanaku to San Pedro, bulky commodities like foodstuffs or pottery would have been difficult cargo for llama caravans and presumably would not have merited transport (Browman 1985:64). This would appear to make Tiwanaku conquest or colonization for agricultural exploitation unlikely, and as we shall see, the highland state's influence is only manifest in a small number of Tiwanaku imports found in special contexts and in stylistic influences on the local San Pedro tradition. Yet San Pedro is situated at a key location controlling the northernmost Andean pass to the Salta region of Argentina and the fertile Quebrada de Humahuaca. The Atacama region itself is rich in semiprecious stones and copper ores mined in the pre-Columbian era (Bird 1979; Graffam et al. 1996; Lechtman 2000). Together, the region's strategic location and mineral resources would have been important attractions to Tiwanaku.

Tiwanaku's interaction with San Pedro has attracted interest since the early twentieth century (Latcham 1938; Uhle 1912). Most investigation of San Pedro Tiwanaku has focused on materials recovered from over three thousand burials excavated in forty-seven cemeteries by Father Gustavo LePaige in the 1950s and 1960s and on a smaller number of subsequent tomb excavations by professional archaeologists (Benavente et al. 1986; Berenguer 1978, 1985, 1986; Bittman et al. 1978; LePaige 1964, 1965; Llagostera et al. 1988; Llagostera 1996; Mujica 1985; Orellana 1984, 1985; M. Rivera 1985, 1991; Tarrago 1976, 1977, 1984; Thomas et al. 1985; Torres 1985). The overwhelming majority of these tombs produced entirely local-style grave offerings. Tiwanaku-style artifacts appear in San Pedro as one of several minority styles of exotic offerings. LePaige believed that atypical tomb lots from San Pedro consisted of objects of pure Tiwanaku style (Bittman et al. 1978: 36). Over time this led to an assumption of a Tiwanaku colonial presence in San Pedro as the prelude to imperial conquest (Ponce 1972:78).

Tiwanaku grave offerings found in San Pedro include pottery, tapestry textile tunics and four-pointed hats, carved wooden and gold drinking vessels, and snuff tablets, brushes, and tubes used in the taking of hallucinogenic drugs (fig. 4.3). The few imported Tiwanaku ceramic vessels found in San Pedro all come from similar mortuary contexts. These polychrome keros,

Figure 4.3. Tiwanaku hallucinogenic snuff tablets, San Pedro de Atacama. PSG photo.

Figure 4.4. Tiwanaku *tazón*, San Pedro de Atacama. PSG photo.

tazones, and small pitchers correspond to Tiwanaku IV and V styles in the core region (fig. 4.4). Considering the enormous number of excavated tombs, these vessels are rare, probably accounting for no more than a handful of vessels in the Gustavo LePaige Museum's vast collections. The high incidence of pre-Columbian repairs to cracked Tiwanaku vessels further attests to their rarity and high value there.[6]

Tiwanaku textiles found in San Pedro include polychrome tapestry tunics and *mantas* and warp-striped plainweave wool tunics, mantas, and bags, and four-pointed hats (Conklin 1983; Frame 1990; Oakland 1986). As is the case with pottery, Tiwanaku textiles are actually rare in San Pedro and are always found in association with local grave offerings. Oakland has distinguished two local textile groups in part by their relationship to these Tiwanaku imports. Group A includes garments of San Pedro local styles and seldom co-occurs with Tiwanaku offerings. Group B grave lots are distinguished by pile hats, warp-faced plainweave tunics with embroidered selvages and checkered neck plaques, tie-died tunics with lozenge designs, and hafted stone hammers. This group B assemblage was more often associated with Tiwanaku-style tapestries and snuff trays and a lower incidence of cranial deformation (Llagostera 1996:34). Oakland argues that the group B textiles marked an ethnic enclave of Bolivian Tiwanaku colonists who deliberately maintained a minority identity through dress (Oakland 1992:336; Kolata 1993:277). It must be kept in mind, however, that only six Tiwanaku tapestry tunics were found among the 216 excavated burials in the Coyo Oriental cemetery (Oakland 1992:321). Another plausible reconstruction might consider the group A and B ensembles as the distinctive dress of two local lineages, one of which enjoyed preferred access to Tiwanaku and other trade goods. A temporal sequencing has also been proposed (Llagostera 1996:35).

Elaborate wooden snuff tablets, often with inlays of semiprecious stones or spondylus shell, and other paraphernalia associated with the use of hallucinogens are among the best known Tiwanaku-style artifacts found in San Pedro. Snuff kits are found in approximately 15 percent of San Pedro burials overall (Berenguer and Dauelsberg 1989:155; M. C. Torres 1984, 1985, 1987). Although few wooden snuff tablets are preserved in the highlands, stone snuff tablets and imagery of tablets on stone stelae indicate that the hallucinogen complex also appeared in the Tiwanaku core region at approximately the same time (Berenguer 1985). It is often forgotten, however, that the overwhelming majority of snuff kits in San Pedro are of local style, and only a small proportion of kits from the Coyo Phase bear Tiwanaku iconography (Torres 1987). The snuff complex appears to have concentrated on derivatives of *Anadenanthera colubrina*, a tryptamine alkaloid hallucinogen related to the nightshade. Use of this powerful hallucinogen, known to the Inca as *vilca*, certainly predates Tiwanaku influence in San Pedro and had a wider distribution during the Middle Horizon (Llagostera et al. 1988; Knobloch 2000:397; Torres 2001).

There is general agreement that these trade goods from the Tiwanaku core region found among San Pedro mortuary offerings might be characterized as rare, portable, highly exotic, and sumptuary goods rather than household items (Browman 1980, 1985:64, 1997; Mujica 1985:116; 1996:97; Torres et al. 1984). These were used as status signifiers in mortuary and other ritual contexts. Because a high proportion of the Tiwanaku imports in San Pedro bear iconographic elements of the staff god of Tiwanaku and his entourage, believed to be the deities associated with the Tiwanaku state, it is often assumed that the selective diffusion of these elements expressed Tiwanaku hegemony in the region (Berenguer et al. 1989:159; Torres 1987). Indeed, finds of Tiwanaku gold vessels in the Doncellas River valley of Jujuy and a Tiwanaku stylistic influence on the Isla ceramic tradition could suggest the transfer of highly valued Tiwanaku ideas and trade goods as far as northwest Argentina (Berberian 1977; DeBenedetti 1912; Tarrago 1977:61).

Figure 4.5. San Pedro *negra pulida* bottle. PSG photo.

Figure 4.6. San Pedro *negra pulida keros*. PSG photo.

If this were the case, some evidence of hegemonic control might be found in Tiwanaku's effect on the indigenous traditions of San Pedro. At the time of Tiwanaku contact, San Pedro was populated by agrarian settlements with a well-established ceramic industry. During the San Pedro III or Quitor Phase (A.D. 400–700), the local ceramic style was characterized in mortuary assemblages by *negra pulida* (black polished) serving wares dominated by face neck bottles, cylindrical jars, and incurving bowl forms (fig. 4.5). This black polished ware, which accounts for roughly 82 percent of the total funerary pottery in San Pedro, appears to represent an entirely local technology, and the vessel forms show no relationship to those of altiplano styles (Tarrago 1976:61). Indeed, it has been suggested that exposure to San Pedro *negra pulida* vessels may have inspired Tiwanaku potters to introduce blackware ceramics in the Tiwanaku core region (Browman 1980b:117; Tarrago 1984; Thomas et al. 1985).

In the subsequent Coyo Phase (A.D. 700–1000), potters of the San Pedro tradition emulated Tiwanaku keros and other forms in local red-slipped or black *casi pulida* wares (Berenguer and Dauelsberg 1989:155, 160, fig. 4.6)). The wide acceptance of the kero, a drinking goblet with no precedent in San Pedro, indicates that emulation of Tiwanaku style may have gone beyond material culture per se and implies the adoption of Tiwanaku culinary and drinking practices—notably the popular and ceremonial consumption of maize beer.

Although exotic trade goods and the appearance of keros support culture contact via Tiwanaku and Atacaman travelers, there is no evidence that this Tiwanaku influence significantly changed local settlement patterns or household production. Because no Tiwanaku utilitarian pottery or implements have been found in San Pedro, it seems unlikely that culturally Tiwanaku populations were resident in the region (Mujica 1996:93). Indeed, despite the Tiwanaku textiles found in nearby cemeteries, a settlement survey at the Coyo Aldea has failed to find any Tiwanaku ceramics in domestic midden or habitation scatters (Stovel 1997). Overall, the continuity seen in local ceramic assemblage suggests little change in domestic economy due to Tiwanaku influence.

While it is tempting to posit that enterprising Tiwanaku traders were the agents of these transfers, it is equally likely that San Pedro's own intermediaries controlled the cross-Andean trade. Ideas and grave goods moved freely among diverse cultures in the southern Andes, and it is not necessary to suppose state intervention. It often escapes attention that only some of the imported mortuary offerings in San Pedro's ayllus came from Tiwanaku. Equally exotic trade pieces of the Isla Tricolor, black on red, and other styles of northwest Argentina have been identified in the Quitor 5, Quitor 6, and Tchecar Sur cemeteries (Tarrago 1977:56–62) in numbers that equal or exceed those of Tiwanaku imports. Perhaps more significant, Argentine ceramic styles also appear in surface collections from domestic sectors of Quitor Aldea that produced no Tiwanaku pottery (Stovel 1997). Considering this diversity of trade goods, exotic imports may have been received from a variety of sources without the intervention of any foreign trader-agents, and some of the oldest relationships were probably with regions other than the altiplano. Finds of pre-Tiwanaku San Pedro black polished pottery in northwest Argentina confirm that this interregional elite exchange network predated Tiwanaku, and inter-Andean trade also survived the Tiwanaku collapse (Llagostera 1996:37; Tarrago 1976:62).

Clearly, a better understanding of the sociopolitical organization of indigenous San Pedro society is critical to understanding Tiwanaku's influence there. Without convincing evidence of Tiwanaku ethnic colonization, two possible interpretations of the local political landscape might explain the presence of Tiwanaku artifacts.

First, Orellana (1985:249) suggests that San Pedro in the Tiwanaku era was already in "a situation close to a centralized government, like a great lordship on the threshold of a theocratic state."[7] Orellana infers that particularly wealthy cemeteries such as Quitor suggest local social ranking and a single seat of local power. Because these elite individuals enjoyed better access to Tiwanaku sumptuary goods, Orellana concludes that San Pedro was ruled by chiefs who became closely allied to Tiwanaku (1985:250). If this is the case, the political clientage of a local paramount to Tiwanaku patrons could be a reasonable interpretation (Mujica 1985, 1996; Kolata 1993). This supports a view of a hegemonic Tiwanaku world system that co-opted indigenous elites with gifts of valuable, exotic and iconographically charged items. Under a hegemonic strategy, dealing with one local chief could have been the simplest and lowest-cost solution for safeguarding Tiwanaku trade through the San Pedro region.

A second interpretation, suggested by Thomas and colleagues, considers a more segmentary political organization the more likely scenario in indigenous San Pedro, with "a society whose social organization was strictly tied to the concept of lineage or clan and segmented according to territorial patterns (*ayllus*) with a strong connotation of dual management of territory and perhaps bound to the institution of leadership" (Thomas et al. 1985:268).[8]

The shifting power relations of a collection of rival ayllus, as opposed to a unified San Pedro chiefdom, would suggest very different relationships with Tiwanaku. These relationships could have been largely religious, consisting of contacts between foreign priests and local converts to Tiwanaku religious orders (Benavente et al. 1986:72). Alternately, exotic sumptuary goods may have been more important in the political context of local factional competition. Under this scenario, control over status-affirming preciosities would have been a key competitive strategy for San Pedro lineages. It has been suggested that individuals buried in the ayllus of Larrache, Solcor, and Quitor enjoyed preferential access to Tiwanaku ceramics and gold artifacts (Llagostera 1996:32), while Oakland has noted an elevated incidence of imported Tiwanaku tapestries at Coyo Oriental (1992). However, the continuing presence of Argentine styles and other foreign grave goods at these locations suggests that petty local chiefs vied for *any* exotic trade items, not merely Tiwanaku ones. This indicates that the San Pedro elites who possessed Tiwanaku cultural items were more interested in local politics than in globalist Tiwanaku hegemony.

Direct Complementarity and Colonies

Most arguments for Tiwanaku colonization focus on regions of far greater agricultural potential than San Pedro de Atacama. Access to agricultural zones outside the limits of the altiplano would have permitted Tiwanaku to supplement its highland resources with tropical crops such as coca and fruits, marine resources from the Pacific Coast, and cotton, squash, gourds, legumes, and maize from the temperate irrigable valleys of the Andean slopes. According to the archipelago interpretation, Tiwanaku peripheral settlement would have represented a system that moved commodities, bulk produce, and people considerable distances, permitting the intensive economic exploitation of distant regions.

Most studies of the Lupaqa and other post-Tiwanaku cultures in the region of the Garci Diez *visita* have noted that the area of Tiwanaku expansion coincides with the region for which the archipelago construct was first formulated (Lumbreras 1974a; Murra 1972; Rostworowski 1986; Stanish 1989). It is not surprising, therefore, that several seminal articles on the subject explicitly considered it likely that Tiwanaku colonies were the direct prototypes of the Lupaqa colonies of the western sierra (Browman 1978:332, 1984:125; Mujica et al. 1983; Mujica 1985; Murra 1972). Two key regions where recent research has examined the question of Tiwanaku peripheral settlement are the Cochabamba Valley of eastern Bolivia and the Azapa Valley of Arica, in northern Chile.

Cochabamba Tiwanaku

Evidence of Tiwanaku interaction is found in Cochabamba in the intermontane Mizque, Capinota, Santivañez, Sacaba, Valle Alto, and central Cochabamba valleys of eastern Bolivia, approximately 400 to 600 km southeast of the site of Tiwanaku, at elevations from 1,800 to 2,800 m. Environmentally, these valleys of eastern Bolivia are different from the arid coastal valleys of Peru and Chile. Climate variation within the Cochabamba region is largely altitude-determined, with mean annual temperatures between 6 and 18°C and seasonal precipitation (November–March) ranging from 300 to 1,000 mm. Natural biota include arid xerophytic, humid, and subspinous vegetation (Higueras 1996). Rainfall agriculture of maize, potatoes, legumes, and fruits is possible in most of the mesothermal valley bottoms, while upland slopes are used for pasture. The region overall is considered extremely fertile and was a major area of colonization for agricultural production under Inca control. It is presumed that Tiwanaku-contemporary subsistence in Cochabamba would have relied on both rainfall and irrigated cultivation and the herding of camelids.

A degree of Tiwanaku influence in the eastern Andean lowlands has been known since the early twentieth century (Bennett 1936; Byrne de Caballero 1984; Ponce 1972; Rydén 1957; Wassen 1972). Early on, a local style of Cochabamba Tiwanaku polychrome pottery was identified as "Derived Tiahuanaco." This assemblage includes "Cochabamba-style" restricted base keros and an idiosyncratic selection of design motifs with different hues of polychrome pigments and the use of panels on the upper vessel for painted iconography (fig. 4.7; Bennett 1936:402–403; Browman 1997:231; Byrne de

Caballero 1984:70; Higueras 1996; Ibarra Grasso and Querejazu Lewis 1986; Rydén 1957, 1959). Distance from the core region suggests that most of this pottery was made locally. However, many vessels follow Tiwanaku archetypes closely, and the Tiwanaku-style ceramic collections in Cochabamba are very similar overall to those of the Tiwanaku core region and Moquegua (fig. 4.8; Kolata 1993:270; Janusek 1994:127; Goldstein 1989b: 238). Illataco and Piñami Phase vessels excavated in the central Cochabamba Valley correspond stylistically to Tiwanaku IV and V vessels from the core region (Anderson et al. 1998).

As regional archaeology further defined local traditions, it became evident that Tiwanaku coexisted with and influenced the contemporary regional pottery styles of Omereque (also known as Mizque and Nazcoide), Yampara in the southern valleys, and Mojocoyo in the east (Browman 1997: 231; Ibarra Grasso and Querejazu Lewis 1986). The Omereque style is a polychrome with unusually opaque and colorful pigments and local forms such as tripod vessels (Anderson 1997). Later Omereque pottery displays strong Tiwanaku influence (fig. 4.9; Bennett 1936:387, 403; Byrne de Cabal-

Figure 4.7. Derived Tiwanaku-style *kero*, Cochabamba Museum. PSG photo.

Figure 4.8. Tiwanaku-style *keros*, Cochabamba. PSG photo.

Figure 4.9. Omereque-style vessel showing Tiwanaku influence, Cochabamba. PSG photo.

lero 1984). Trade pottery of Cochabamba's Omereque and Yampara styles also appears in low frequency at the Lukurmata and Tiwanaku sites, where it has been interpreted as a potential marker of ethnic enclaves or privileged exchange partners from Cochabamba (Janusek 1993:16; 1994:127; 1999: 122–123). More recently, with Higueras's systematic survey, it has been discovered that Omereque and Gray Ware local pottery is commonly found in association with Tiwanaku wares in the Capinota and Mizque valleys (Higueras 1996). Household archaeology and further research on the relative frequency of Tiwanaku and local wares in Cochabamba domestic sites can help to explain these associations.

In offerings from the Manzanani, Omereque, and Pérez regions, Tiwanaku-style textile tunics, bags, and bands were found in burial contexts in association with Tiwanaku pottery, wooden spoons, and snuff tablets (Oakland 1986:246). Textile finds also included provincial imitations of Tiwanaku garments using local coloring and materials, while local-style cotton garments continued in use as well. The frequencies and contextual relationship of imports, imitations, and local style finds have not been quantified (Oakland 1986:233, 248). Tiwanaku tapestry textile tunics and bags of highland manufacture have been found in dry cave burial contexts such as Niño Korin (Wassen 1972).

Céspedes reports more than three hundred Tiwanaku-affiliated sites in the region, including a major mortuary center at Piñami in Quillacollo and administrative centers at Jarka Pata in the Pocona Valley and Caraparial in Omereque (Céspedes Paz 1982, 1993:65). From a 10 percent survey sample of the Capinota and Mizque valleys, Higueras estimates aggregate Middle Horizon occupations of 159.9 ± 99.7 hectares for Capinota and 365.9 ± 259 for Mizque. Despite these substantial settlement densities and the adoption of Tiwanaku assemblages at many sites, Higueras detected no change in site location from pre-Tiwanaku settlement patterns, nor did the ostensibly agrarian settlement display any settlement preference for the more fertile Mizque Valley in the Middle Horizon (Higueras 1996).

To date, there is little published excavation-based information on Cochabamba Tiwanaku habitation sites. Bennett found the remains of rectangular domestic structures with stone foundations and stone-lined circular storage pits at the Arani site. Habitation middens at Arani included rocking grindstones, stone-lined cylindrical storage cists, grooved axes or hoes for processing and storing crops, and deer antler and bone projectile points and bola stones that suggest supplementary hunting (Bennett 1936:341, 350). Cochabamba Tiwanaku burials at the Arani site were stone-covered, bark-lined cist tombs, typified by ceramic offerings of exclusively Tiwanaku style (Bennett 1936:353). The cist burials represented a marked departure from local pre-Tiwanaku burials, which were typically in ceramic urns.

Interpretations differ on the intensity of Tiwanaku exploitation and integration of Cochabamba. Without household excavations and full coverage survey, it is unclear whether the socioeconomic relationship of Cochabamba to the Tiwanaku core region was one of direct administration, colonization, hegemony through religious proselytizing, or long-distance trade or an even less obtrusive relationship. The low frequency of sumptuary Tiwanaku goods like tapestry tunics and snuff kits and their association with local contexts suggests to some that those were long-distance trade imports for local elites (Browman 1997:232; Oakland 1986:245). These scholars point to Cochabamba Tiwanaku's "Derived" pottery style, and the prevalence of Tiwanaku materials in mortuary rather than domestic contexts, to support an interpretation of indirect trade, elite clientage, and stylistic emulation of Tiwanaku by the region's preexisting local chiefdom societies (Browman 1997:231; Oakland 1986:246). Noting continuity in local settlement pattern, Higueras favors a status quo model that, like Bermann's "local perspective" on Tiwanaku rule in the altiplano, proposes only minimal Tiwanaku influence on local culture change (Higueras 1996).

Others, however, describe a directed Tiwanaku colonization of Cochabamba that effectively set the pattern for the massive Inca occupation that followed. Bennett noted that the adoption of cist burials suggests major culture change and the adoption of highland mortuary practice. Moreover the burial offerings of ceramic keros and tazones at the Arani site were of exclusively Tiwanaku style, rather than mixed local and Tiwanaku contexts (Bennett 1936:353). The predominance of Tiwanaku-style grave offerings at the Piñami site in Quillacollo also supports direct colonization (Céspedes Paz 1993:65), and at least some of the burial contexts reported by Oakland from Manzanani, Omereque, and Pérez may also have had exclusively Tiwanaku offerings (1986:246). The absence of local offerings in these contexts suggests interments by culturally Tiwanaku people, either colonists or fully acculturated local populations. Because of the overwhelming adoption of Tiwanaku stylistic elements and material culture, Céspedes suggest that direct Tiwanaku expansion began as early as A.D. 300, and was followed by full provincial incorporation after A.D. 750 (Anderson et al. 1998; Céspedes Paz 1993:65). This debate can only be settled with future research that includes full coverage survey and household archaeology at Tiwanaku-contemporary sites in the region.

Tiwanaku in the Pacific Coastal Valleys

There is extensive evidence for Tiwanaku interaction with the Pacific coastal valleys of southern Peru and northern Chile from the Azapa Valley of northern Chile (Berenguer 1978; Berenguer and Dauelsberg 1989; Bird 1943; Dauelsberg 1972a,b; Focacci 1969, 1983; Muñoz 1983a,b), in the neighboring Chaca, Camarones, and Lluta valleys (Santoro 1980), and in the Locumba, Sama, and Caplina valleys of southern Peru (Disselhoff 1968; Flores Espinoza 1969; Ishida 1960; Lynch 1983; Mujica 1985, 1996; Mujica et al. 1983; Trimborn 1973; Uhle 1919; Vela 1992), all approximately 300 km west of the site of Tiwanaku.[9] Climate in these coastal valleys is temperate and hyper-arid, with virtually no precipitation, and the absence of any biota outside the river valleys limits human occupation to the immediate area of the floodplains. Nonetheless, with irrigation from mountain runoff, these Pacific-draining oasis valleys at elevations from 0 to 1,000 m are far more productive agriculturally than the San Pedro region and are a more likely candidate for multiethnic colonization on the model of the vertical archipelago. Indeed, ethnohistoric sources indicate that enclaves of an astonishing diversity of highland groups coexisted in the northern Chilean coastal valleys in the late pre-Hispanic and colonial periods (Hidalgo 1996; Hidalgo and Focacci 1986). It is not surprising that direct Tiwanaku exploitation of these regions for irrigation agriculture has been proposed as a precedent for these patterns.

Since early in the twentieth century, there has been considerable interest in Tiwanaku's influence in the Azapa Valley, near the city of Arica in the first region of Chile (fig. 4.10). Azapa's relative proximity to Tiwanaku and the known presence of imported Tiwanaku pottery suggests a qualitatively more direct or socioeconomic interaction than the indirect trade of magico-religious items described for San Pedro. The Tiwanaku-related period in Azapa, designated the Loreto Viejo phase, was typified by the presence of textiles, fine redware pottery, and other artifacts of Tiwanaku IV and V affiliation in cem-

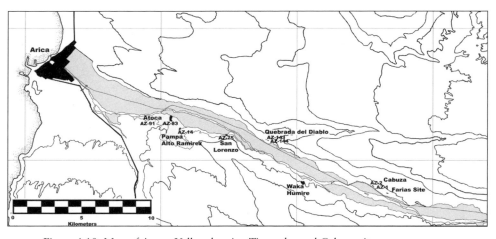

Figure 4.10. Map of Azapa Valley showing Tiwanaku and Cabuza sites.

etery contexts.[10] However, the picture is complicated by Tiwanaku's coexistence in Azapa with peoples using a majority ceramic style known as Cabuza, generally dated from ca. A.D. 500–1000. Cabuza sites, typified by a locally made black on red fine serving pottery that emulated Tiwanaku forms in a noticeably coarser paste than the altiplano Tiwanaku V imports, are considerably more common than site components of altiplano Tiwanaku affiliation.

Azapa Tiwanaku pottery (also known as the Loreto Viejo style) corresponds closely to Tiwanaku IV and V in the core region. Azapa Tiwanaku polychrome keros, tazones, and small pitchers appear at cemeteries and some habitation sites in Azapa (fig. 4.11). Carved wooden vessels, flat-handled decorated spoons (Espouyes 1976), and narrow-stemmed white chert arrow points are also commonly found. Tiwanaku utilitarian *olla* and *tinaja* forms are found at a few habitation sites (fig. 4.12). Azapa Tiwanaku textiles include a limited number of polychrome interlocked tapestry tunics bearing complex iconography of elaborately adorned supernatural figures similar to low-relief carvings at Tiwanaku (Conklin 1983:8–11). These and warp-striped plainweave tunics, mantas, and bags and knotted four-pointed hats were woven of two-ply Z-spun S-plied camelid wool fibers (Frame 1990; Oakland 1986, 1992). While other Tiwanaku-style artifacts abound, few hallucinogenic snuff kits are found in Azapa Tiwanaku (Focacci 1993:81).

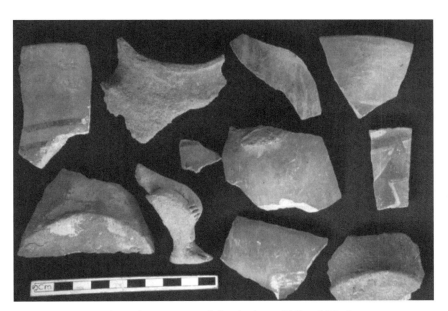

Figure 4.11. Tiwanaku-style serving vessel sherds, Azapa Valley. PSG photo.

Figure 4.12. Tiwanaku-style utilitarian ceramics, Azapa Valley. PSG photo.

Ceramics of the Cabuza style emulated Tiwanaku keros and other forms in local pastes, with decoration in black over a purplish red slip (fig. 4.13). The Cabuza tradition is also characterized by seated flexed cist burials. Cabuza textiles include plainweave and floating-warp decorated tunics, long belts, and four-pointed hats (Ulloa 1982). Part of the subsequent Maytas-Chiribaya polychrome pottery style may also overlap with the Azapa Tiwa-naku (Loreto Viejo) tradition (Focacci 1983, 1993; Mujica 1985, 1996; Muñoz 1983a,b, 1996a,b; Rivera 1991).

Overall, the quantity and contexts of these finds support the presence of an elite Tiwanaku minority in Azapa. Tiwanaku-style crafts do not appear in Azapa in sufficient numbers to confirm local production, and no textile or ceramic workshops have been identified. Pottery of the locally made Cabuza tradition may appear in Azapa as early as A.D. 380, predating the arrival of

Figure 4.13. Cabuza-style ceramics, Azapa Valley. PSG photo.

the Tiwanaku-style ceramics (Berenguer and Dauelsberg 1989:147–148; Dauelsberg 1985), although most absolute dates place Cabuza later (e.g., Focacci 1981; Muñoz 1983b; Schiappacasse et al. 1991:52). Stylistically similar kero-using ceramic styles in southern Peru seldom date before A.D. 900 and are considered products of local craftsmen heavily influenced by Tiwanaku precedents (Bermann et al. 1989; Goldstein 1989a,b; Owen 1994).

While no large Tiwanaku habitation sites, ceremonial structures, or agricultural works have yet been documented, systematic full coverage survey of the middle Azapa Valley by Goldstein (1996) found fifty-four sites with Azapa Tiwanaku or Cabuza sherds. Of these, fifteen produced both styles, twenty-seven produced only Cabuza, and twelve produced only Azapa Tiwanaku fragments. The distribution of the Azapa Tiwanaku occupation closely parallels that of its Cabuza contemporaries, with a marked avoidance of both coastal settlement (Bird 1943) and the incised upper sectors of the valley. Both Azapa Tiwanaku and Cabuza sites were found below km 24 of the Azapa highway, concentrated at locations overlooking open river floodplain, particularly near natural springs at Las Riberas, Alto Ramírez, and Saucache, suggesting a preference for zones optimal for irrigated cultivation. This is markedly different from the coastal focus of the earlier indigenous occupation, representing "the exploitation of microzones such as the mid-valley areas that had previously not been utilized by the local settlers" (Mujica et al. 1983:90).[11] These new microzones are characterized predominantly by their potential for the cultivation of temperate crops, and their settlement implies the presence of maize-producing colonies.

The Tiwanaku and Cabuza economies in Azapa were essentially agricultural, with sites clustering in optimal irrigable zones and little presence on the Pacific littoral. Greater settlement has been associated with "sweet water" (less mineralized) valleys like the lower Azapa Valley of the San Jose River and particularly with locations near natural springs. Cultigens included maize, beans, fruits, and coca, which has been identified in Azapa only after the Tiwanaku arrival. Coca, perhaps of a variety cultivated only in the dry western valleys (Molina et al. 1989:47) could have been a significant economic attraction for the Tiwanaku presence. Other potential trade items for export to the Tiwanaku core region would have included mineral ores and fish and shellfish from the Pacific Coast.

Tiwanaku-contemporary habitation sites consisted of perishable structures, some with stone foundations. Cabuza and Tiwanaku-contemporary dwellings were built of ephemeral materials such as cane, with little surface-visible architecture other than stone terrace facings and platforms (Muñoz 1983a:73–74, 1986:315; Muñoz and Focacci 1985; Piazza 1981). There were only three habitation sites with Tiwanaku household material culture predominant, with an aggregate area of less than 5 hectares. At 3 hectares, site AZ-83 in the Pampa Alto Ramírez was the largest Tiwanaku village. Salvage excavations conducted before the site's bulldozing in 1974 revealed circular and rectangular stone foundations and found Cabuza and Azapa Tiwanaku ceramics and textiles. Radiocarbon dates of 560 ± 110 and 760 ± 70 place the site within the Cabuza/Tiwanaku chronological range (Rivera 1987:12). The site was also centrally located among three Tiwanaku cemeteries (AZ-9, AZ-14 and AZ-19) and nearby geoglyphs and petroglyphs that date to Tiwanaku and later traditions.

Tiwanaku burials in Azapa have received far more attention than settlement sites. It is somewhat surprising to realize that the cemeteries that produce actual altiplano-style Tiwanaku grave lots are few in number and extremely small. Unlike in San Pedro, however, several small cemeteries in Azapa have exclusively Tiwanaku grave goods, while others were typified by tombs with offerings of both Cabuza and Tiwanaku ceramic and textile styles. Azapa Tiwanaku burials were seated flexed individual interments in either pits or stone-lined cist tombs, furnished with ceramic and other offerings and originally marked with wooden poles. Cabuza and later Maytas-

Chiribaya burials adopted these traditions and often added offerings of paws, heads or ears of camelids, entire guinea pigs, coca, textiles, feathers, or wool (Focacci 1993:76). Tiwanaku-style offerings were also placed at locally sacred sites, including pre-Tiwanaku *túmulo* mound burials, Cabuza cemeteries, and rocky hillside promontories (Goldstein 1996; Muñoz 1996b:253). Focacci (1983:112) discovered at least one looted burial with entirely "Classic" Tiwanaku offerings at the AZ-75 cemetery site at San Lorenzo, dated to A.D. 560. Another altiplano cemetery, AZ-143 Quebrada del Diablo, consists of an enclave of fewer than twenty tombs with predominantly Tiwanaku-style offerings adjacent to a far larger cemetery of Cabuza affiliation.

Outstanding even among these cemeteries is Atoca 1, another small cemetery located on a bluff overlooking the western edge of the Pampa Alto Ramírez above the Atoca hacienda (Dauelsberg 1972a; Focacci 1983; Goldstein 1996; Muñoz 1983b 1986:314).[12] The site includes a sector of cist tombs and a separate stone pile of ruined above-ground architecture. In the lower section of the cemetery, Muñoz excavated two decapitated camelid offerings and four cylindrical cist tombs, all badly disturbed by pre-Columbian destruction and colonial corrals (1983b, 1986:311, 320). Cabuza and Tiwanaku sherds and an engraved wooden kero fragment were found in the looted tombs and on the surface nearby.[13] In 1991 I investigated the above-ground stone burial structure. Ceramic fragments on the surface nearby included red-slipped and polished blackware Tiwanaku kero fragments of exceptionally high quality, beads, tapestry textile fragments, and a

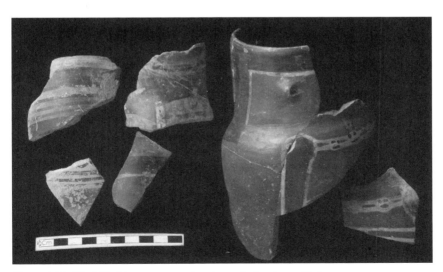

Figure 4.14. Wari Chakipampa ceramics, Atoca 1 site, Azapa Valley.

Figure 4.15. Tiwanaku cemetery at Atoca, Azapa Valley.

Tiwanaku figurine fragment (fig. 4.14). Perhaps the most provocative aspect of the Atoca 1 site was my discovery of fragments of several Wari Chakipampa–style vessels, including a face neck jar (Goldstein 1996; Muñoz 1986:314).

The Atoca sherds are the only Wari-style pottery yet found in Chile and the southernmost known find of Ayacucho-style ceramics. As they were found amidst a majority of Tiwanaku offerings and no Wari sites are known in the Azapa Valley, we must assume that these represent exotic grave goods obtained indirectly via a prestige goods network. Wari pottery is so rare in the Tiwanaku sphere that it must have been a rare curiosity in the Tiwanaku diaspora, supporting an elite status for the occupants of this Azapa Valley Tiwanaku cemetery. With its stone mausoleum structure, precious Tiwanaku offerings, and Wari exotics, the Atoca 1 site supports the picture of a small enclave of particularly high status provincial Tiwanaku elites in Azapa. (Goldstein 1996). Neither large nor more proletarian Tiwanaku cemeteries are found in Azapa, and the small mortuary enclaves sit amidst far larger Cabuza culture cemeteries.

Biological distance analyses of Azapa Valley human populations have been equivocal on the matter of Tiwanaku colonization. Several studies of metric cranial traits have noted similarities between later Azapa Valley populations and those from the Tiwanaku core region (Rothhammer et al. 1986; Rothhammer and Santoro 2001). These studies suggest significant gene flow from the altiplano beginning in the Middle Horizon. However, another examination of skeletal remains from Azapa sites has failed to isolate altiplano individuals from indigenous Azapa Valley residents on biological grounds, suggesting less genetic interaction than is implied by migration models (Sutter 2000). Examining both dental data and nonmetric cranial traits, Sutter concludes that there was genetic continuity throughout the Azapa Valley sequence. This implies that altiplano colonists were not numerous enough to be detected in existing skeletal samples and that they had little genetic effect on local populations. This suggests that Tiwanaku colonists did not significantly intermarry with local populations in Azapa.

The most likely explanation of the Azapa Valley's Tiwanaku occupation is as small enclaves of colonists from the Tiwanaku core region coexisting with a larger local population who emulated the Tiwanaku tradition in the Cabuza style. Many of the Tiwanaku sites in the Azapa Valley are small components of multicomponent cemeteries or habitation sites, suggesting segregated islands in a sea of denser Cabuza settlement. Interpretations of the coexistence of these small Azapa Tiwanaku enclaves with indigenous populations have ranged from a "symbiosis" of ethnic groups (Rivera 1985:17) to a vision of marked social stratification, with the Loreto Viejo ceramic tradition representing a "directive group of the Tiwanaku coastal colony" (Berenguer and Dauelsberg 1989:151).[14] This conception of a Tiwanaku ruling elite was originally based on the quality and quantity of pottery and textiles of elite Tiwanaku style (Berenguer and Dauelsberg 1989:151; Focacci 1981: 70), but it does seem to be supported by systematic settlement data. The minority presence of Tiwanaku peoples in Azapa in coexistence with emulative local groups suggests interaction mechanisms that fall short of direct colonization and that may more closely resemble the enclaves of a trade diaspora. The small, resident, and elite presence of Tiwanaku in Azapa paints a picture of a trade diaspora community whose impressive cultural associations permitted it to attract local clients, inspire emulation, and exert a dominant political influence over its hosts (Curtin 1984:5; Stein 1999b:49).

Summary: In Search of the Tiwanaku Diaspora

Our search for Tiwanaku colonies in a context of early state expansion in the south-central Andes has so far met with only limited success. In distant peripheries like San Pedro de Atacama, any discussion of a "Tiwanaku presence" is really a discussion of the presence of sumptuary artifacts rather than people. Suggestions of Tiwanaku settlers in mortuary contexts simply cannot be convincing without associated bioarchaeological evidence or the identification of ethnic Tiwanaku settlements or enclaves within local settlements. We cannot yet rule out the kind of globalist interpretation of a Tiwanaku world system suggested by the "altiplano model" or other hegemonic interpretations of Tiwanaku sumptuary trade. It is certainly possible that the Tiwanaku core deliberately induced dependent clientage relationships through a conscious program of gift giving and acculturation of elites. Without evidence of a resident trade diaspora or other enclave of Tiwanaku agents, however, there is no proof that this actually occurred, and various alternate explanations are possible. An agency-oriented local perspective could explain the presence of the same exotic goods in a context of factional competition and local elite display.

In contrast, more attractive agricultural regions like the Cochabamba and Azapa valleys, considerably closer than San Pedro to the Tiwanaku core region, would appear better candidates for an archipelago of diasporic colonization. Both regions do provide more substantial evidence of direct cultural contact with Tiwanaku people, including numerous Tiwanaku-style burials with homogeneously Tiwanaku offerings and wide domestic distributions of either Tiwanaku artifact styles or local styles that emulate Tiwanaku at settlement sites. The broad and sudden adoption of Tiwanaku cultural archetypes in these regions is extremely impressive, even if there is no confirmation of major settlement location change. Without further household archaeology at these Tiwanaku-related settlements, there remains considerable uncertainty on the exact nature of Tiwanaku integration or interaction in Cochabamba. For Azapa, we can certainly speak of resident enclaves of altiplano Tiwanaku people, but their small size and elite status resemble a successful trade diaspora more than the productive colonies of a vertical archipelago. Did Tiwanaku really send forth migrant waves to the western valleys? It is with this uncertainty in mind that we turn to another area in our search for a Tiwanaku diaspora—the Moquegua Valley of southern Peru.

5

Agrarian Settlement
in the Middle Moquegua Valley

An excellent dry climate with brilliant sunshine all year, fertile soils, the ideal altitude, and cycles of warmth and cold ideally timed for annual planting are unequaled conditions that give this privileged valley its history and tradition of more than four centuries of viticulture.[1]

Pisco Italia Biondi bottle label, Antonio Biondi and Sons,
Bodega Omo, Moquegua, 1999, author's translation

All is so well provisioned and rich as to appear a paradise.

(Vásquez de Espinosa 1948 [1618], quoted in Kuon Cabello 1981:373, author's translation)

Since Spanish colonial times, the middle Moquegua Valley's agrarian potential has made it an opportune region for settlement by colonists in search of better lands. Of the many irrigable valleys of Peru's desert western sierra, this fertile oasis, defined in colonial land claims as "the valley of Omo and Cupina," is one of the closest to the Tiwanaku homeland; and thus it is an ideal place to study Tiwanaku's influence on peripheral zones. There has been considerable conjecture about the antiquity of altiplano influence in the oasis river valleys of the western slope of the Andes, and Moquegua has long been considered a likely area for Tiwanaku "vertical control" over maize-producing irrigable lands (Mujica et al. 1983; Mujica 1985; Murra 1972). Until recently, this discussion has taken place in the absence of a substantive body of archaeological evidence or a long-term program of problem-specific investigation in the region. This situation has changed dramatically since the late 1980s, when new archaeological studies began to elucidate the history of Tiwanaku influence in Moquegua. Following a review of the natural and agricultural resources of the region known to us since the Spanish colonial period, this chapter introduce this recent research and Moquegua's settlement history.

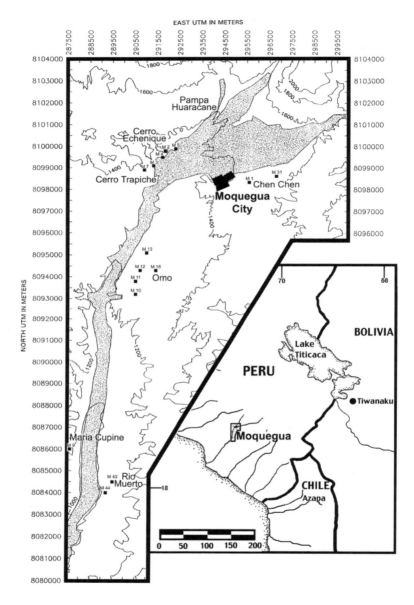

Figure 5.1. Map of Moquegua Archaeological Survey area.

The Middle Moquegua Valley

Like most of the Andean Pacific drainages, the Osmore River is a steep and deeply incised system that carries runoff from the peaks of the Western Cordillera through the arid western slope of the Andes to the Pacific Coast (fig. 5.1). Sectors of the watercourse are also known as Río Moquegua and Río Ilo. I use "Moquegua" to refer to the middle Moquegua Valley region and "Osmore" in reference to the entire drainage. Only the upper 20 percent of the 139 km drainage of the Río Osmore and its tributaries receives regular seasonal rainfall. Annual precipitation in the headwaters above 4,800 m above sea level (masl) approaches 500 mm, principally in the months of December through March (ONERN 1976; Rice et al. 1989:20).

Precipitation decreases drastically at lower altitudes, and the Moquegua and coastal sectors of the Osmore flow through one of the driest deserts in the world. Mean annual precipitation in Moquegua City is even less than the 5.3 mm measured for the nearby coastal port of Ilo. Despite major El Niño flood events that have occurred at irregular intervals, the region was similarly arid throughout its settlement history (Magilligan and Goldstein 2001). The absence of any moisture in the surrounding desert has always limited human occupation to the immediate riverine floodplain. Nonetheless, river-fed canals in the basin of the Río Osmore and its tributaries permit the year-round cultivation of a wide variety of temperate and tropical crops.

Early colonial documents suggest that Moquegua was the seat of an Inca administrative region known as Colesuyu (Rostworowski 1986:127). Since Spanish colonial times, geographic features have been seen to separate the Osmore drainage into an upper valley sector, a middle Moquegua Valley sector, and a coastal Osmore Valley sector. A 1594 petition from Moquegua's *encomenderos* (landholders) used these same features to distinguish their own claim in the fertile "valley of Omo and Cupina" (middle Moquegua Valley) from upper valley lands belonging to the Carumas Aymara and the coastal valley lands then under the jurisdiction of the *corregidor* (governor) of Arica (Pease 1984a:168).[2]

The upper valley zone includes the Huaracane, Torata, and Tumilaca tributary rivers, from their headwaters to their confluence just above the modern city of Moquegua, near 2,000 masl. The steepness and constriction of the upper valley zone has necessitated the construction of extensive terracing since the late pre-Hispanic period (Rice et al. 1989, 1989; Stanish 1985, 1989; Williams 1997, 2002). In contrast, the middle Moquegua Valley is broad and flat, with an irrigable expanse tapering in width from 8 km at the confluence of the tributaries at Moquegua City to 3–4 km in the alluvial plain of the single channel of the Moquegua River. The downstream limit of the

Figure 5.2. View of middle Moquegua Valley, Cerro Echenique site. PSG photo.

middle Moquegua Valley zone is the steep cliffs below Yaral/Los Espejos, the point 45 km from the coast, at an elevation of 900 masl, where the Osmore disappears into a channel deeply incised through rocky canyons. The desolate expanse that separates the middle Moquegua Valley oasis from the Pacific belies any conception of Moquegua as a coastal region. Beyond this barrier the river reemerges from its canyon only 17 km from the Pacific, watering the smaller agricultural oasis of the coastal Osmore Valley before emptying into the Pacific north of the port of Ilo.

Colonial and modern sources agree that the middle Moquegua Valley was and is by far the most productive agriculturally of these regions. Most of Moquegua's 3,200 irrigated hectares in the late twentieth century were located in this zone, at elevations of between 1,000 and 2,000 masl (ONERN 1976; fig. 5.2), where canals permit year-round irrigation agriculture on level ground without artificial terracing. The middle Moquegua Valley was an equally productive agricultural region in the immediate pre-Hispanic period. In the sixteenth century, colonists of the Lupaqa and other altiplano polities cultivated maize, peppers, cotton and other temperate crops (Diez de San Miguel 1964 [1567]; Julien 1985; Murra 1968; Pease 1980, 1984a). When the priest Antonio Vásquez de Espinosa visited the valley in 1618, he was impressed by Moquegua's rich variety of introduced and indigenous crops and by the valley's thriving caravan exchange with the altiplano. He described "very good quinces, peaches, pippins, figs, and other Spanish and local fruits, mills for sugar, and many fields of maize, garbanzo beans, lima beans, and other seeds and much hot pepper that they harvest in this valley, which is very valuable for the export of fruit by llamas to the province of Chucuito and all the high country; they also collect excellent crayfish and all is so well provisioned and rich as to appear a paradise" (Vásquez de Espinosa [1618] 1948, quoted in Kuon Cabello 1981:373, author's translation).[3]

Although native avocados, introduced olives and apricots, and other fruits remained important, much of the middle Moquegua Valley zone was devoted to vineyards throughout the later colonial and republican eras. Wine and distilled *pisco* (grape brandy) shipped by mule trains to the colonial silver mines at Potosí in Bolivia made Moquegua one of Peru's wealthiest provinces (Pease 1984a; P. Rice 1987; P. Rice and Smith 1989). Moquegua's viticulture began to decline with the disruption of Chilean occupation during the War of the Pacific (1879–83), and it virtually disappeared because of *filoxera* blight and a disastrous flirtation with commercial cotton production during the short-term demand of World War I (Kuon Cabello 1981). Today most of the available middle Moquegua Valley land is devoted to the cultivation of alfalfa for dairy cattle. The surviving commercial vineyards today concentrate on the production of pisco.

Mineral deposits, notably of copper, have been economically important in the Moquegua region since the colonial era. Other metals are also present; at the end of the eighteenth century, six silver mines were in operation. Evidence of pre-Hispanic copper mining has been found in northern Chile (Bird 1979; Browman 1984b:125), and similar exploitation cannot be ruled out for Moquegua, although there is as yet no evidence of pre-Hispanic mining or smelting activities.

Colonial sources cite an active trade in coastal resources, such as salt, fish, shellfish, *cochayuyu* (edible algae), and *guano* (seabird droppings), carried by llama caravans to the highlands via the middle Moquegua Valley zone. The best documented of these commodities is guano, a resource of great value to agriculturalists. According to the *visitador* (royal inspector) Garci Diez de San Miguel, who inspected Moquegua in 1567, guano was essential as a fertilizer, particularly for nitrogen-intensive grains such as maize: "The Indians of Moquegua grow a little wheat and maize, although not very much because maize cannot be grown unless bird dung from the coast, that they call *guano*, is put on the fields when the plants are somewhat grown. Without *guano*, the maize does not form kernels. They bring it 20 leagues (100 km) from some islands in the sea" (Diez de San Miguel 1964:245, translation in Julien 1985:185).

While other maritime resources were harvested by ethnically distinct local maritime specialists, guano was so valuable that it was mobilized by the highlanders themselves through a classic vertical archipelago. Colonial documents tell us that enclaves from specific highland ayllus and moieties claimed and exploited particular guano islands off the Moquegua coast (Julien 1985; Rostworowski 1986:131). The dry canyons between the middle Moquegua Valley and coastal Osmore sectors, aptly named Quebrada de los Guaneros, are still occasionally traversed by highlanders' mule trains carrying seabird guano.

Unfortunately, there are no written or epigraphic sources on the Tiwanaku period agrarian exploitation of Moquegua or the region's participation in coastal trade. To reconstruct Tiwanaku settlement history in Moquegua, we must look to the region's rich archaeological record.

Settlement Pattern Research in Moquegua

Analysis of systematic survey data is critical to any discussion of Tiwanaku settlement patterns and the process of Tiwanaku colonization. Ironically, although many of the methods of settlement pattern research were established in the coastal valleys of Peru with Willey's pioneering 1946 survey of the Viru Valley, much of the Andes has only recently seen systematic full coverage reconnaissance (Billman and Feinman 1999).

A Tiwanaku presence in Moquegua has been postulated for some time (Mujica et al. 1983; Murra 1968, 1972), but our knowledge of Tiwanaku settlement patterns in the middle Moquegua Valley has been limited by the sporadic nature of archaeological investigation and publication.[4] Test excavations at the Tiwanaku sites of Tumilaca La Chimba (U4) and Chen Chen (M1) were conducted by members of the University of Tokyo Scientific Mission to the Andes as part of their survey of Peru.[5] The Tokyo Mission described the Tumilaca occupation and associated pottery as Expansive Tiwanaku (V) and postulated that an agricultural colony of that period succeeded an earlier Wari occupation (Fujii 1980; Ishida 1960). Investigations of surface looting and excavations at the cemeteries of Chen Chen and Loreto Viejo by Gary Vescelius and Rogger Ravines in the late 1950s and early 1960s have not been published. The only published account of the Moquegua Tiwanaku excavations of the 1960s is a brief report on investigations at Chen Chen by Disselhoff (1968). Disselhoff excavated several tombs at this huge cemetery. He illustrated a series of decorated keros, flaring-sided bowls now known as tazones, and one-handled pitchers, noting that the majority of Chen Chen artifacts were identical with Bolivian Tiwanaku V materials.[6] Sporadic reconnaissance and excavations conducted by archaeologists from the Universidad Católica de Santa María and Universidad Nacional San Agustín, Arequipa, in the 1970s cataloged some twenty sites in Moquegua of Tiwanaku affiliation (Pari 1987).[7] In 1983, Programa Contisuyu, a binational archaeological research consortium cosponsored by the Museo Peruano de Ciencias de la Salud in Lima and Field Museum of Natural History in Chicago, began a reconnaissance of archaeological resources in the Department of Moquegua. By 1986, Programa Contisuyu's site catalog for the middle Moquegua Valley, based on nonsystematic survey, recorded some forty-four sites, which were numbered M1 through M44. Because this inventory included twenty-six sites of Tiwanaku affiliation and few sites of other periods, it was speculated that the valley was largely unoccupied at the time of the Tiwanaku arrival (Goldstein 1989). The discrepancy between these assumptions and the results of full coverage survey demonstrate the importance of systematic coverage in settlement pattern studies.

Since 1993 the Moquegua Archaeological Survey has systematically surveyed the middle Moquegua Valley between 900 and 2,000 masl (Goldstein 1994, 2000a,b). The middle Moquegua Valley survey area encompasses some 150 km², making it small in comparison to other regional survey areas. This allows me to take a particularly fine-grained full-coverage survey approach. During the survey phase of this project, from 1993 through 1995, a systematic walkover reconnaissance was covered by a team of six archaeologists walking in straight lines at 20 m intervals. Full 100 percent coverage extended from the floodplain to the ridgeline overlooking the valley on either side, a survey area that extended 2 km from the current river course. All settlement site components and related roads, agricultural works, geoglyphs, and cemeteries were recorded on Servicio Aerofotografía Nacional air photos and 1:10,000 Catastro Rural maps. Standardized survey forms and Brunton compass maps were completed and photographs taken of each site component. Selected sites were mapped in greater detail with plane table or EDM theodolite. Data on site size, function, and cultural affiliation from field observations and laboratory analysis have been coded as a database compatible with a Geographic Information System (GIS) for the Moquegua Valley. GIS mapping permits spatial analysis of each of the valley's occupations as well as consideration of different site types, resources, terrain, and environmental variables. In concert with Owen's surveys of the coastal Osmore valley, and of the Torata and Tumilaca valleys (Owen 1993a; Goldstein and Owen 2001; Owen and Goldstein 2001), the Moquegua Archaeological Survey project has now extended 100 percent coverage throughout the main Osmore drainage.[8]

Analysis of the settlement patterns revealed by the systematic survey is revealing a wealth of data on density and organization of human occupation in Moquegua since the late Archaic period. A total of 531 pre-Columbian site components was recorded. Sites of all types and cultural affiliations totaled 280 hectares valley-wide. Components were named according to a site-sector nomenclature—that is, 224 "sites" numbered from M1 through M224, with a capital letter suffix for each component.[9] As each component was spatially distinct, the "site" designation was largely for convenience and the lettered components, known as sectors, are treated independently in all analyses. Sites and components were also named descriptively, using the nearest place name or a geographical feature appearing on existing maps when available. All sites were functionally classified as habitation sites (207 components, covering 220 ha), cemeteries (168 components, covering 47 ha), agricultural fields and canals (20 components), ceremonial structures (11 components) and *apachetas* (small ritual or offering sites, 6 components).[10] For the current discussion of settlement patterns, habitation sites have been considered in terms of area alone, although future analyses may consider architectural and artifact densities to refine population estimates. If we assume a rough equivalence to Wilson's "moderate" density sites of the Santa Valley, an estimate of 100 people per hectare of occupation is not unreasonable (Wilson 1988:79).

The survey coverage of the Osmore has been complemented by a number of problem-oriented excavation projects since the mid-1980s. Extensive work at the largest Tiwanaku site group at Omo permitted the preliminary reconstruction of Tiwanaku influence in the area and interpretations of the colony's sociopolitical and economic structure (Goldstein 1985, 1989a, 1989b, 1990a, 1990b, 1993a, 1993b; Moseley et al. 1991). Knowledge of Tiwanaku sites in the region expanded further with subsequent Instituto Nacional de Cultura rescue excavations of the vast Tiwanaku cemeteries at Chen Chen in 1987 directed by Vargas (Blom 1999; Blom et al. 1998; Vargas 1988, 1994); further salvage excavations of now-destroyed cemeteries, habitation, and industrial areas of the same site in 1995 by Owen, Goldstein, Oquiche, Cardona, and Pari; and test excavations by Goldstein at the newly discovered Río Muerto Tiwanaku complex in 1998. Excavations have also shed light on smaller Tiwanaku settlement components at Los Cerrillos (R. Feldman and L. Watanabe, pers. comm. 1984), La Cantera, and Cancha de Yacango (Goldstein and Owen 2001; Owen and Goldstein 2001); post-Tiwanaku Tumilaca phase components at Tumilaca La Chimba (Bawden 1989, 1993), Loreto Viejo, Algodonal, and Algorrobal (Owen 1993a) and in the Otora Valley (Stanish 1985, 1987, 1992); Chiribaya occupations at La Yaral (García Marquez 1989; Rice et al. 1989, 1993) and Chiribaya (Buikstra 1995; Lozada 1998); Late Intermediate Estuquiña occupations at Estuquiña (Clark 1993; Conrad 1993; S. Williams 1990); and the Inca occupation at Torata (Van Buren 1996).

Some substantial differences between archaeological research in the Tiwanaku core region and in Moquegua may be attributed to differences in site formation processes in the rainy altiplano compared to desert regions. In contrast to the Lake Titicaca basin, the desert environment of the middle Moquegua Valley permits no soil development and produces few water-borne sediments outside the river floodplain. Moquegua's desert conditions and strong southerly winds prevent the accumulation of strata, and except for cultural superposition at a few sites, there are few possibilities for stratigraphic relative dating.[11] As is typical in hyperarid deserts without vegetation to check erosion, cultural deposits from these eroded desert sites tend to be deflated and extremely shallow, consisting of patinated stone and "palimpsests" of debris from many occupations that are difficult to interpret (Schiffer 1987:239). Earlier sites show the most extreme effects, with exposed structures and sherds scoured by wind action and solar radiation. Later sites exhibit less patination and better preservation of organic materials and midden deposits.

A significant source of deposition was the eruption of the volcano Huayna Putina, near Omate at the boundary of the departments of Arequipa and Moquegua, between February 18 and 28, 1600. Contemporary accounts state that six towns in Moquegua and Arequipa were buried and that the region was shrouded in darkness for fifteen days (Cobo 1890:202–213; Kuon Cabello 1981:135). The lasting effect in the middle Moquegua Valley, some 250 km southwest of the volcano, was a covering of fine pale gray ash. Intact ash layers provide a *terminus ante quem* basis for relative dating. In Tiwanaku tombs the volcanic ash lens is typically found near the surface, with a greater accretion of sediments below the ash. While the Huayna Putina ash does not preclude the possibility of early Spanish colonial disturbance, the relative thickness of sediment laminations below the ash layer suggests that tombs were looted well before 1600.

By and large, Moquegua archaeology is archaeology without appreciable stratigraphy. On the other hand, the extensive surface exposure of sites in Moquegua's desert conditions offers an unparalleled opportunity to study regional settlement patterns and map within-site relationships. Many prehistoric sites outside the limits of modern cultivation are fully visible on the surface and in air photos, facilitating their location, mapping, and systematic surface analysis. The extremely arid conditions allow superior preservation of organic materials, permitting the recovery of many types of architectural and subsistence remains and artifact categories that are not preserved in the rainy altiplano Tiwanaku core region. In particular, as has been noted for other hyperarid regions of Tiwanaku influence, preserved costume and artistic media such as textiles, feathers, and wood can provide a more complete perspective on Tiwanaku dress, art, and the expression of identity in crafts (Oakland 1992).

The results of excavation and survey work in Moquegua demonstrate that Tiwanaku followed on the heels of a long period of complex relations between indigenous peoples and foreign influences in the middle Moquegua Valley. A brief discussion of Moquegua's indigenous cultural traditions sets the stage for a more detailed examination of the preexisting social landscape upon which Tiwanaku settlement was imposed.

Tiwanaku's Antecedents in Moquegua

Investigation of the scope and character of indigenous early agrarian societies has been an important goal of the Moquegua Archaeological Survey (MAS) since 1993. The valley's role as a complementary resource zone for highland populations may have originated in the late Archaic with seasonal camps of hunter-gatherers in the upper reaches of the valley. The Moquegua Valley was included in a seasonal round by the time of introduction of llama pastoralism at about 4500 B.P. (Aldenderfer 1993a,b, 1998; Kuznar 1990:65). Early agrarian occupation and the first indigenous ceramic tradition in the Moquegua began in a pre-Tiwanaku ceramic phase first defined at the type site of Pampa Huaracane. The Huaracane ceramic inventory consists largely of neckless or short-necked *ollas* and fine serving bowls (Feldman 1989; Goldstein 1989a, 2000b) (fig. 5.3).

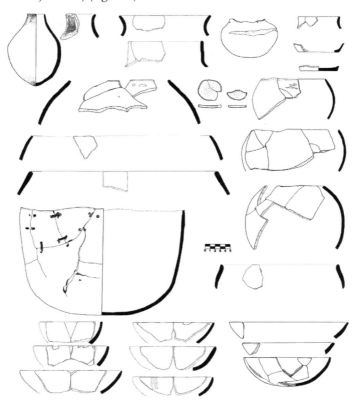

Figure 5.3. Huaracane sand- and fiber-tempered *ollas*, Huaracane fine paste serving bowls, various sites.

Despite early attempts to associate the Huaracane tradition with altiplano colonization (Feldman 1989), the Huaracane pottery has more in common with plainware ceramic styles of the far south coast, such as the Carizal and Pocoma phases; of the Moquegua coast near Ilo (Bolaños 1987; Tello 1987) and the Early Ceramic Phase of the coastal Osmore Valley (Owen 1993a, 1993b); and more distant styles such as Arica's Faldas el Morro tradition (Rivera 1975) and plainware pottery of Ica, Ocucaje, and Callango in the Paracas culture area (DeLeonardis 1997; Massey 1991:333). Huaracane material culture (Cohen et al. 1995; Goldstein 2000b), and dietary analysis (Barrionuevo and Goldstein n.d.; Sandness 1992) indicate a local Moquegua tradition that was closely related to autochthonous indigenous populations throughout the far south coast of Peru.[12]

The distribution of Huaracane Phase habitation sites supports the interpretation of an indigenous agrarian occupation of long standing in the middle Moquegua Valley. Full coverage systematic survey indicates substantial Huaracane population density in Moquegua (fig. 5.4). All the Huaracane sites were located close to the margins of modern agriculture, along the rim of the valley floodplain, at an average distance of only 421 m from the Osmore River and at elevations averaging only 48 m above the riverbed. The close relationship of Huaracane settlement to areas of floodplain cultivation indicates a reliance on simple canal irrigation. This indicates that Huaracane agricultural exploitation seldom extended beyond the natural limits of the valley bottom and did not entail complex land reclamation that required centralized regulation.

The Huaracane villages were small and uniform in size, yet represent a surprisingly dense aggregate population. Represented by 169 habitation site components, the Huaracane occupation totaled 73.5 hectares in residential area (table 5.1). Huaracane habitation sites typically consisted of small semi-

Table 5.1. Moquegua Valley survey results by cultural affiliation

Cultural Affiliation	Number of Habitation Components	Total Habitation Area	Number of Cemetery Components	Total Cemetery Area
Huaracane	169	73.5 hectares	70	20.2 hectares
Wari	3	4.2 hectares?	1	0.1 hectares
Tiwanaku Omo	12	28.7 hectares	3	0.1 hectares
Tiwanaku Chen Chen	31	50.5 hectares	39	10.4 hectares
Tiwanaku Tumilaca	45	42.0 hectares	10	0.8 hectares
Chiribaya	21	11.6 hectares	13	1.2 hectares
Estuquiña	14	9.0 hectares	12	2.6 hectares
Other Late Intermediate	3	1.1 hectares	1	0.1 hectares
Estuquiña-Inka	4	1.7 hectares	3	1.4 hectares

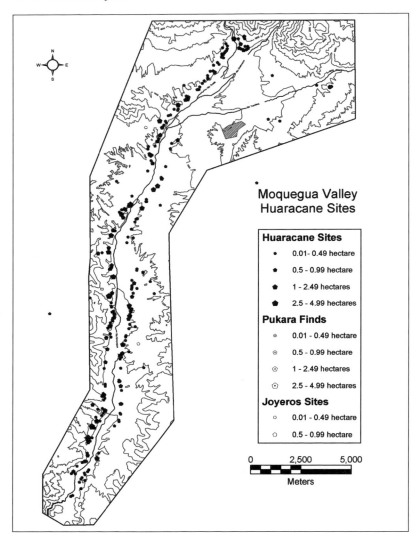

Figure 5.4. Huaracane settlement distribution map.

circular residential terraces without stone facing, with some form of house superstructure built of organic material. On the basis of their small scale and dispersion, Huaracane settlements all fall within the categories of hamlets or small villages (Wilson 1988:79). Generally, settlement areas were small, with a mean area of only 0.44 hectare per domestic component. All but five settlements were less than 2 hectares in area. Huaracane village sites seldom had defensive architecture, and only a few of the larger sites, notably Cerro Trapiche, Yaway, and Montalvo, exhibited modest public architecture or elite

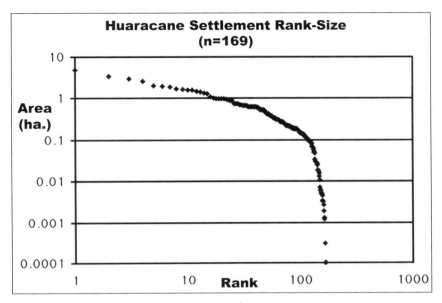

Figure 5.5. Huaracane settlement rank-size graph.

mortuary components. None of these sites resembles a valleywide para-mount, although some of the larger village sites could correspond with local centers of power. A logarithmic graph of Huaracane site size for rank-size analysis shows a notably convex relationship of settlement size to rank (fig. 5.5). This indicates the absence of any single primate center and a low level of political and economic integration.

Systematic survey also recorded an additional seventy Huaracane cemetery sectors, covering 20.2 hectares. Several distinctive Huaracane burial types have been noted. Burials at Pampa Huaracane and Tres Quebradas M73 included both individual and multiple interments of seated, flexed individuals in cylindrical cists or pits, and an extended burial was found at Tres Quebradas M73 (fig. 5.6).[13] No pottery offerings were found in any of these tombs, though a variety of tubular and disc-shaped bone or shell beads did appear. *Túmulo* or mound burials similar to those of the Alto Ramírez tradition of Chile's Azapa Valley (Muñoz 1987) were also found at Tres Quebradas and at forty-four other sites in the middle Moquegua Valley and several sites in the coastal Osmore (Owen 1993b), usually in association with adjacent Huaracane terrace habitation areas. Túmulos are clustered circular or irregular mounds of sand and rock of between 2 and 7 m diameter and up to 3 m in height. Cross sections indicate construction of alternating layers of sterile fill and mats of vegetal material identical to the Alto Ramírez túmulos (fig. 5.7a). Pottery or other offerings are extremely rare in the túmulo cem-

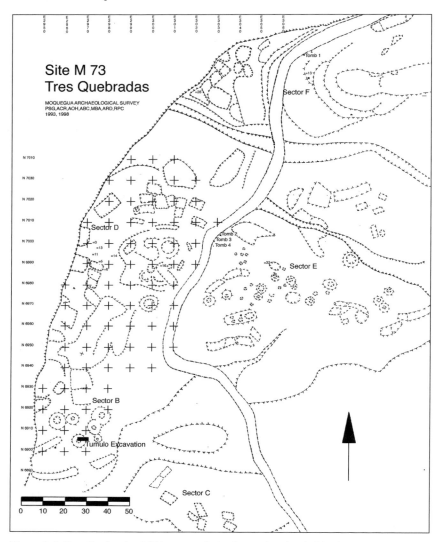

Figure 5.6. Tres Quebradas M73 map and air photo, showing habitation terraces, *túmulos*, and other burials.

eteries, although diagnostic early textiles of vegetable fiber, cotton, and wool, most of nonloomed techniques, are commonly found. It appears that at least some túmulos contained multiple burials, and some burials may have been secondary interments (Goldstein 2000b). This suggests a pattern of reuse over time consonant with extended families or clans, and dated samples from a foundation log and a secondary burial at M73 túmulo 1 support such a long-term usage (fig. 5.8, table 5.2). All told, the 2 sigma calibrated ranges for

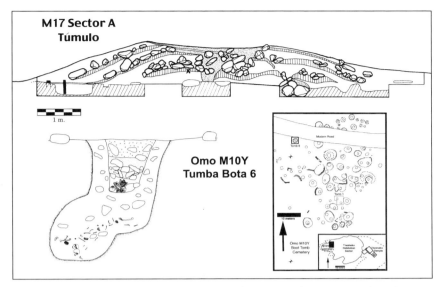

Figure 5.7. (a) *Túmulo* cross section, site M17; (b) Boot Tomb cemetery and tomb 6 cross section, site M10Y.

middle Moquegua Valley túmulos extend from 385 cal B.C. to cal A.D. 2 (Goldstein 2000b). This fits well with dates for the similar túmulos of the Alto Ramírez tradition of Chile's Azapa Valley, which has been dated from ca. 500 B.C. to A.D. 300 (Muñoz 1987:93, 1996:121). Dates between 100 B.C. and A.D. 675 (calibrated) have been reported for components associated with Early Ceramic neckless *ollas* at the Algorrobal and Algodonal sites in the coastal Osmore Valley (Owen 1993b:14, 354, 417).

In contrast to the túmulos, Huaracane "boot tomb" cemeteries were rare and appear to be a burial type reserved for high status individuals. Boot tombs were marked by massive stone surface rings up to 4 m in diameter, with wattle and daub debris that suggests the foundations for organic surface constructions (fig. 5.7b). The tombs inside the stone rings were roofed subsurface shafts up to 3.5 m in depth, with small rounded chambers at the base of the shaft, producing a characteristic boot-shaped profile. The tomb chambers housed family groups of multiple adult and juvenile interments. Fragments of Huaracane pottery were discovered along with beads, decorated baskets, wooden objects, and elaborate textiles (Goldstein 1989a, 2000b). The two available dates suggest that the boot tombs date between cal A.D. 20 and cal A.D. 135. This would suggest that boot tombs appeared late in the Huaracane tradition, either replacing or supplementing túmulo burials.

Several of the looted boot tomb cemeteries produced Pukara zoned incised polychrome sherds in surface collections.[14] Pukara ceramics were found at

Table 5.2 Radiocarbon dates from the middle Moquegua Valley

Sample number	Phase/Style	Context	Material
AA38030;	Huaracane túmulo;	Tres Quebradas M73, túmulo 1	wood
Beta-120262;	Huaracane túmulo;	M17 sector A, M17=1, túmulo post	wood
AA38029;	Huaracane túmulo; túmulo 1	Tres Quebradas M73–1034, branch	wood
Beta-26651;	Huaracane Boot; level 8	Omo M10=2197, Boot Tomb 6, tomb roofing	wood,
Beta-120263;	Huaracane Boot/Trapiche;	Trapiche M7=2, Sector C, looted boot tomb	wood post
AA37978;	Pink Flood Unit;	Rio Muerto, Spring Channel Site, Lower pink flood unit	wood
Beta-124115;	Pink Flood Unit;	Rio Muerto, Spring Channel Site, Lower pink flood unit	wood
Beta-36639;	Omo;	Omo, M12=1617, M12 Structure 2	wood post
Beta-129938;	Omo;	Omo, M16=5500, tomb D-15	wood post
Beta-129939;	Omo;	Rio Muerto, M70=1509, Unit 6	wood post
AA38032;	Omo;	Rio Muerto, M70–1245, Unit 4	wood post
Beta 12721;	Omo;	La Cantera, 283=82–16, pit with blackware ceramics	wood charcoal
Beta-120264;	Omo;	Omo, M12=3016, Structure 7	wood post
Beta-60762:	Omo;	Omo, M12=3388, Structure 7	wood post
Beta-39679;	Chen Chen;	Omo, M10=4014, Lintel of temple	wood
AA38031;	Chen Chen;	Rio Muerto, M43–1067, Unit 1	carbon
Beta-26650;	Chen Chen;	Omo, M10=1758, Structure 13	wood post
AA40628;	Chen Chen;	Omo, M10=1121, Structure 11	wood

Radiocarbon age B.P.	Uncalibrated date	Calibrated intercept date(s)	1 Sigma calibrated result	2 Sigma calibrated result	Source
2220 +/- 42 log	270	354, 291, 256, B.C.	364–207 251, 232, 217, and 213 cal B.C.	385–181 cal B.C.	a cal B.C.
2140 +/- 50 B.C.	190 B.C.	180 cal cal B.C. (340–320)	205–100 cal B.C.	365–45	a
2112 +/-42 B.C.	162 and 121 cal B.C.	163, 129, B.C.	198–54 cal cal B.C.	349–2	a
1990 +/- 70 B.C.	40 20	cal A.C. B.C.– cal A.C. 80	55 cal B.C.– cal A.C. 140	170 cal	a, b
1860 +/- 70	90	cal A.D. 135	cal A.D. 75–240	cal A.D. 5–340	a
1325 +/- 42	625	cal A.D. 679	cal A.D. 660–763	cal A.D. 644–777	c
1290 +/- 50	660	cal A.D. 700	cal A.D. 670–775	cal A.D. 655–870	c
1470 +/- 80	480	cal A.D. 610	cal A.D. 535–655	cal A.D. 420–685	d:31
1290 +/-70	660 700	cal A.D. 665–785	cal A.D. 635–890	cal A.D.	e
1160 +/- 60	790	cal A.D. 885	cal A.D. 785–970	cal A.D. 705–1005	c:433
1132 +/-39	818	cal A.D. 896, 923, and 940	cal A.D. 887–979	cal A.D. 780–997	c
—	870	cal A.D. 981	cal A.D. 892–1020	cal A.D. 779–1152	f
1060 +/- 70	890	cal A.D. 995	cal A.D. 900–1025	cal A.D. 815–1150	e
1040 +/- 70	910	cal A.D. 1005	cal A.D. 965–1030	cal A.D. 875–1160	e
1160 +/- 60	790	cal A.D. 885	cal A.D. 785–970	cal A.D. 705–1005	d:34
1122+/-44	828	cal A.D. 899, 920, 957	cal A.D. 888–982	cal A.D. 780–1017	e
1120 +/- 70	830	cal A.D. 910 (920 and 955)	cal A.D. 870–1000	cal A.D. 765–1025	b:69
1101 +/- 35	849	— 894–987	cal A.D. 886–1017	cal A.D.	e

Sample number	Phase/Style	Context	Material
Hv-1076;	Chen Chen or Tumilaca;	Chen Chen, Tomb?	Cotton
Hv-1077;	Chen Chen or Tumilaca;	Chen Chen, Tomb?	Charcoal
Beta-26649;	Tumilaca;	Omo, M11=1406a, Structure 5	Wood post
Beta 51068;	Tumilaca (Ilo-Tumilaca/Cabuza);	Algodonal, AD 525–15–11/1	Wood post
AA40629;	Tumilaca;	Omo, M11=1406b, Structure 5	wood
Hv-1091;	Tumilaca; (Ilo-Tumilaca/Cabuza);	Loreto Viejo, Tomb?	Cloth (wool)
Beta 51070;	Tumilaca (Ilo-Tumilaca/Cabuza);	Loreto Alto, LA 1518–2–2, Hearth	Wood charcoal
Beta 51072;	Tumilaca (Ilo-Tumilaca/Cabuza);	Loreto Alto, LA 1530–5–4, wall trench	Woody twigs
Beta 51061;	Tumilaca (Ilo-Tumilaca);	Algodonal, AD 363.05, Mummy wrapping	Wool textile
Beta 51065;	Tumilaca (Ilo-Tumilaca);	Algodonal, AD 383-1-1.10, Mummy wrapping	Wool textile
Beta 51060;	Tumilaca (Ilo-Cabuza);	Algodonal, AD 354.06, Mummy wrapping	Wool textile
Beta 51069;	Tumilaca (Ilo-Tumilaca);	Loreto Alto, LA 1506-5-2, Midden	Woody twigs
Beta 51071;	Tumilaca (Ilo-Cabuza);	Loreto Alto, LA 1525-5-1, Floor around hearth	Wood charcoal
Beta 51059;	Tumilaca (Ilo-Cabuza);	Algodonal, AD 339.01, Mummy wrapping	Wool textile
Beta-133794;	Gray Flood Unit, Miraflores Event;	Rio Muerto, flood gravels near M70, channel base	wood
Beta-142835;	Gray Flood Unit, Miraflores Event;	Rio Muerto, Spring Channel Site, upper gray flood unit	wood
Beta-142834;	Gray Flood Unit, Miraflores Event;	Rio Muerto, GeoProfile Site, Upper gray flood unit	wood
Beta-124116;	Gray Flood Unit, Miraflores Event;	Rio Muerto, Spring Channel Site, upper gray flood unit	wood

Note: The sources are as follows:

a. Goldstein 2000b, b. Goldstein 1989a, c. Magilligan and Goldstein 2000, d. Goldstein 1993, e. Golds

Radiocarbon age B.P.	Uncalibrated date	intercept date(s)	calibrated result	calibrated result	Source
1040 +/- 65	910 1000	cal A.D. 903–1027	cal A.D. 887–1158	cal A.D.	g
930 +/- 65	1020 1043, 1091, 1119, 1140, 1155	cal A.D. 1020–1213	cal A.D. 978–1275	cal A.D.	g
1170 +/- 80	780	cal A.D. 880	cal A.D. 770–980	cal A.D. 675–1015	b:77
1100 +/- 80	850				h:407
1061 +/- 37	889	982–1018	cal A.D. 902–1023	cal A.D.	e
1060 +/- 80	890				g
1040 +/- 50	910				h:407
990 +/- 80	960				h:407
980 +/- 60	970				h:408
970 +/- 60	980				h:408
880 +/- 60	1070				h:408
870 +/- 60	1080			h:407	
860 +/- 50	1090				h:407
780 +/- 60	1170	cal A.D. 1165, 1166, 1188	cal A.D. 1043–1241	cal A.D. 1022–1279	h:408
750 +/- 60	1200	cal A.D. 1275 (1365–1380)	cal A.D. 1235–1290	cal A.D. 1185–1310	c
730 +/- 60	1220	cal A.D. 1280	cal A.D. 1255–1295 (1350–1390)	cal A.D. 1205–1315	c
620 +/- 70	1330	cal A.D. 1310 (1360 and 1385)	cal A.D. 1290–1410	cal A.D. 1270–1430	c
620 +/- 40	1330	cal A.D. 1310 (1360 and 1385)	cal A.D. 1300–1400	cal A.D. 1290–1410	c

, f. Owen et al. 2001, g. Geyh 1967, h. Owen 1993

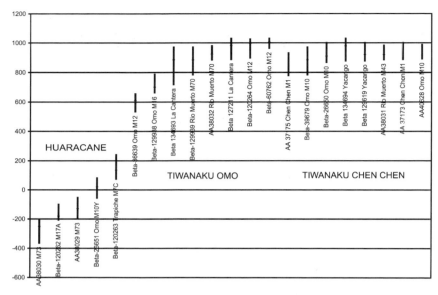

Figure 5.8. Calibrated radiocarbon dates for Huaracane and Tiwanaku occupations in Moquegua.

only seven sites in the middle Moquegua Valley (fig. 5.9), usually in association with Huaracane majority assemblages. These Pukara finds, as well as a small number of early Nasca-style textiles and ceramics (fig. 5.9a), represent a diverse prestige trade phenomenon associated with Huaracane elites, rather than a colonial occupation or dependent clientage (Goldstein 2000b). The elaboration of the boot tombs and their offerings, which include locally made as well as imported sumptuary goods, suggests the interments of elite family groups within Huaracane society. Moquegua's indigenous elites may have played a key role in the cultural interaction of Nasca with Pukara and the Titicaca basin (Mujica 1985), and competition for exotic sumptuary goods from both the south coast and the altiplano may have contributed to the formation of Moquegua's first chiefly power centers.

The reaction of Moquegua's indigenous peoples to the Tiwanaku colonization is not yet understood. No Huaracane site in the middle Moquegua Valley has yet produced dates that overlap with the Tiwanaku occupation, and the issue of late Huaracane contemporaneity with Tiwanaku has not been resolved by settlement pattern or household archaeology. The radically different settlement patterns of the two groups leave no examples of on-site cohabitation, conflict, or reoccupation. Neither is there any evidence of cross-cultural exchange in the form of artifacts traded between sites. This separation could be interpreted as the social segregation consonant with the multiethnic partitioning suggested by Murra as a normative model. The first

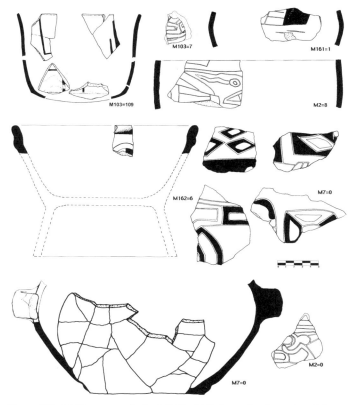

Figure 5.9. (a) Nasca vessel, site M103; (b) Pukara sherds, various Moquegua Valley sites.

Tiwanaku colonists may have been pastoralists who avoided the Huaracane farmsteads of the floodplain, permitting distinct and spatially separated lifestyles. However, the absence of Tiwanaku interaction with native peoples contrasts with Tiwanaku relations in Cochabamba, Azapa, and San Pedro de Atacama, where indigenous cultural traditions emulated aspects of Tiwanaku style or absorbed Tiwanaku trade goods or mortuary offerings within a local cultural context. The separation of the two cultures in the middle Moquegua Valley may be a temporal phenomenon. Perhaps Huaracane peoples were either already gone or were forced to vacate shortly after the moment of Tiwanaku colonization. Because Tiwanaku never established a beachhead in the coastal Osmore, the later dates for Early Ceramic sites there could indicate that Huaracane's coastal compatriots were not displaced when the highlanders arrived and may even have received refugee Huaracane populations. The continuity of coastal Formative traditions into the Middle Horizon suggests that indigenous populations there were unaffected by the Tiwanaku colonization.[15]

The best evidence for any Tiwanaku consciousness of the Huaracane heritage comes from mortuary patterns. All of the Huaracane boot tomb cemeteries were disturbed during later occupations, beginning with Tiwanaku. It is possible that the Tiwanaku were simply looting and curating curiosities from already ancient tombs. However, the reuse of one tomb at the Omo M10Y boot tomb cemetery by the placement of a seated flexed burial suggests that Tiwanaku people may have been responsible not only for the destruction of the boot tombs but also for their reuse and possible veneration. A similar tendency to reuse Alto Ramírez burial grounds has been noted for Tiwanaku settlers in Azapa and could suggest a conscious decision to associate with presanctified local sites. This may not imply contact between Huaracane farmers and Tiwanaku colonists, but it does suggest a Tiwanaku interest in appeasing or appropriating local *huacas* (sacred sites or shrines) that were still understood to be important. Even if the Tiwanaku newcomers could ignore the Huaracane, they apparently could not ignore their ghosts.

Tiwanaku Settlement Patterns

The Tiwanaku occupation of Moquegua is marked by sudden valley-wide changes in settlement, agricultural and cultural patterns. The MAS survey found that Tiwanaku settlement collectively occupied over 141 hectares in the middle Moquegua Valley (figure 5.10), indicating a greater population than that of the Huaracane period. This Tiwanaku occupation was also dispersed and organized in fundamentally different ways than its precursor. I will argue that this occupation represents a colonial diaspora that dominated this fertile valley for half a millennium.

Moquegua's Tiwanaku occupation may be subdivided into three distinct stylistic components. These were named after local type-sites as the Omo, Chen Chen and Tumilaca styles. Site preservation, cross dating with the sequences for altiplano Tiwanaku Core Region, and a small number of absolute dates permitted a preliminary sequencing of the settling of the Moquegua Valley by altiplano Tiwanaku settlers. Additional radiocarbon dates now suggest that the Omo and Chen Chen stylistic units may overlap in time. Nonetheless, occupations of each style are found in marked segregation at distinct, though often adjacent, sites. This indicates simultaneous colonial settlement by different subsets of the Tiwanaku population with distinct ethnic allegiances and different pastoralist and agriculturalist lifeways.

Altiplano Tiwanaku settlement in Moquegua was restricted to densely populated enclaves in locations that were not inhabited previously. Virtually all Omo and Chen Chen style settlement was concentrated at the four large multicomponent Tiwanaku site groups of Omo, Chen Chen/Los Cerrillos, Río Muerto, and Cerro Echenique, with virtually no occupation elsewhere in the valley. This pattern changed with the appearance of more dispersed settle-

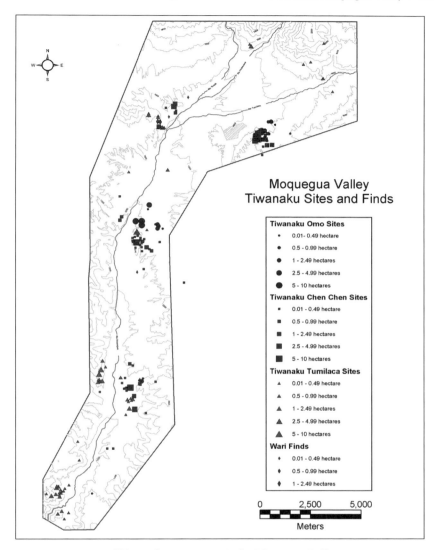

Figure 5.10. Principal Tiwanaku site groups in the Moquegua Valley.

ment of the Tumilaca phase. The following reconstruction considers new data from each of these site groups, as well as a number of smaller Tumilaca phase sites distributed throughout the valley.

The *Omo* site group has seen the most intensive and prolonged study since its discovery in 1983. Omo is a multicomponent settlement group in which three distinct Tiwanaku ceramic styles are represented at five distinct bluff top settlement areas (designated M10, M11, M12, M13 and M16 (fig. 5.11). The largest Tiwanaku site group known outside of the Bolivian altiplano,

Table 5.3 Tiwanaku sites of Moquegua (Omo- and Chen Chen-style occupations only)

Site-Sector	Site Name	Stylistic Affiliation
M1-11	Chen Chen Habitacion Rockpile 11	Chen Chen
M1-12	Chen Chen Habitacion Rockpile 12	Chen Chen
M1-13	Chen Chen Habitacion 13	Chen Chen, Omo?
M1-14	Chen Chen Sector Ceremonial 14	Chen Chen
M1-15	Chen Chen Sector Ceremonial 15	Chen Chen
M1-16	Chen Chen Habitacion Alta 16	Chen Chen
M1-17	Chen Chen Habitacion Alta 17	Chen Chen
M1-18	Chen Chen Habitacion Alta 18	Chen Chen
M1-19	Chen Chen Habitacion Alta 19	Chen Chen
M1A	Chen Chen Cementerio A	Chen Chen
M1B	Chen Chen Cementerio B	Chen Chen
M1C	Chen Chen Cementerio C	Chen Chen
M1Ch	Chen Chen Cementerio Ch	Chen Chen
M1D	Chen Chen Cementerio D	Chen Chen
M1E	Chen Chen Cementerio E	Chen Chen
M1F	Chen Chen Cementerio F	Chen Chen
M1G	Chen Chen Cementerio G	Chen Chen
M1H	Chen Chen Cementerio H	Chen Chen
M1I	Chen Chen Cementerio I	Chen Chen
M1J	Chen Chen Cementerio J	Chen Chen
M1K	Chen Chen Cementerio K	Chen Chen
M1L	Chen Chen Cementerio L	Chen Chen
M1M	Chen Chen Cementerio M	Chen Chen
M1-O	Chen Chen Cemetery O	Chen Chen
M1P	Chen Chen Cemetery P	
M1R	Chen Chen Cemetery R	
M1-21	Chen Chen Cementerio 21	Chen Chen
M1-22	Chen Chen Cementerio 22	Chen Chen
M1-23	Chen Chen Cementerio 23	Chen Chen
M1-24	Chen Chen Cementerio 24 (formerly Ch)	Chen Chen
M1-25	Chen Chen Cementerio 25	Chen Chen
M1-26	Chen Chen Cementerio 26	Chen Chen
M1-27	Chen Chen Ex-Cementerio 27 (formerly Q)	Chen Chen
M1-28	Chen Chen Cementerio 28 (Formerly Z)	Chen Chen
M1-29	Chen Chen Cementerio 29	Chen Chen
M1-30	Chen Chen Cementerio 30	Chen Chen
M1-31	Chen Chen Cementerio 31	Chen Chen
M1-32	Chen Chen Cementerio 32	Chen Chen
M1-33	Chen Chen Cementerio 33	Chen Chen
M1-34	Chen Chen Cementerio 34	Chen Chen
M1-35	Chen Chen Cementerio 35	Chen Chen

East UTM	North UTM	Site area, m²	Site Type
295600	8098300	28,300	Habitation, Rockpile
295600	8098000	86,400	Habitation, Rockpile
295500	8097875	33,000	Habitation
295900	8097950	24,500	Ceremonial sector, Habitation
296025	8097950	14,200	Ceremonial sector, Habitation
296100	8097875	3,500	Habitation
296100	8097650	21,500	Habitation
295900	8097575	800	Habitation
296350	8097675	22,100	Habitation
		7,000	Cemetery, Vargas 1994
		7,000	Cemetery, Vargas 1994
		7,000	Cemetery, Vargas 1994
		3,000	Cemetery, Vargas 1994
		1,000	Cemetery, Vargas 1994
		1,000	Cemetery, Vargas 1994
		500	Cemetery, Vargas 1994
		3,000	Cemetery, Vargas 1994
		3,000	Cemetery, Vargas 1994
		6,000	Cemetery, Vargas 1994
		3,000	Cemetery, Vargas 1994
		4,000	Cemetery, Vargas 1994
		4,000	Cemetery, Vargas 1994
		3,000	Cemetery, Vargas 1994
		4,000	Cemetery, Vargas 1994
		4,000	Cemetery, Vargas 1994
		1,000	Cemetery, Vargas 1994
295975	8098075	3,500	Cemetery, Cists
296025	8098125	300	Cemetery, Cists
296000	8098150	200	Cemetery, Cists
296000	8098175	1,100	Cemetery, Cists
295900	8098250	200	Cemetery, Cists
295850	8098275	200	Cemetery, Cists
295550	8098350	4,400	Habitation, Storage bin cists
295500	8098200	7,600	Cemetery, Cists
295550	8098200	1,300	Cemetery, Cists
295500	8098000	15,200	Cemetery, Cists
295500	8097950	2,400	Cemetery, Cists
295650	8097925	1,100	Cemetery, Cists
295750	8097925	3,300	Cemetery, Cists
295850	8097950	2,300	Cemetery, Cists
295750	8097850	700	Cemetery, Cists

continued

Table 5.3 continued

Site-Sector	Site Name	Stylistic Affiliation
M1-36	Chen Chen Cementerio 36	Chen Chen
M1-37	Chen Chen Cementerio 37	Chen Chen
M1-38	Chen Chen Cementerio 38	Chen Chen
M202A	Estanque, Chen Chen Campos	Chen Chen
Total, Chen Chen Group		
M31	Los Cerrillos	Omo
M206B	Cementerio Altiplanico	Omo
M206C	Cementerio Altiplanico, Los Anillos	Omo?
M208	Los Cerrillos Alto	Omo /Chen Chen
Total, Los Cerrillos Group		
M2A	Cerro Echenique, Cumbre	Chen Chen, Tumilaca
M2B	Cerro Echenique, Terrazas Altas	Chen Chen
M4A	Cerro Echenique, Planicie Baja A	Chen Chen
M4C	Cerro Echenique, Planicie Baja C	Chen Chen?
Total, Echenique Group		
M10A	Omo Sur, Templo	Chen Chen
M10B	Omo Sur, Cementerio B, Plataforma	Chen Chen
M10C	Omo Sur, Area Habitacional	Chen Chen
M10H	Omo Sur, Cementerio H	Chen Chen?
M10I	Omo Sur, Cementerio I	Chen Chen?
M10J	Omo Sur, Cementerio J	Chen Chen?
M10K	Omo Sur, Cementerio K	Chen Chen?
M10L	Omo Sur, Cementerio L	Chen Chen?
M10M	Omo Sur, Cementerio M	Chen Chen
M10P	Omo Sur, Cementerio P	Chen Chen
M10R	Omo Sur, Cementerio R	Chen Chen
M10S	Omo Sur, Cementerio S	Chen Chen
M10T	Omo Sur, Cementerio T	Chen Chen
M10U	Omo Sur, Cementerio U	Chen Chen?
M10V	Omo Sur, Cementerio V	Chen Chen?
M10W	Omo Sur, Cementerio W	Chen Chen?
M10X	Omo Sur, Cementerio X	Chen Chen?
M12	Omo Clasico Habitacional (N,S,W)	Omo
M13	Omo San Antonio Bodega	Omo?
M16A	Omo Alto Habitacional A	Omo
M16B	Omo Alto Habitacional B	Omo
M16C	Omo Alto Habitacional C	Omo
M16D	Omo Alto Cementerio D	Omo

East UTM	North UTM	Site area, m²	Site Type
295675	8097850	4,400	Cemetery, Cists
295550	8098200	5,800	Cemetery, Cists
295550	8098200	5,800	Cemetery, Cists
295851	8097145	308	Reservoir, canal
		368,908 (36.8908 hectares)[a]	
296500	8098700	3,353	Domestic structures, Terraces
296300	8098870	10,500	Scatter, Habitations?
296160	8098850	9,000	Ceremonial Structure
297245	8098258	180	Cemetery or Ceremonial structure
		23,033 (2.3033 hectares)	
291570	8099780	20,525	Habitation or Ceremonial structure
291500	8099640	26,475	Habitation, Terraces
291600	8099420	4,775	Ceremonial structures or Habitations
291580	8099310	7,495	Fields, Canals
		59,270 (5.9270 hectares)	
289960	8092700	6,000	Ceremonial structure
289860	8092750	1,650	Ceremonial structure, Cemetery platform
289650	8092650	79,800	Domestic structures, midden
289460	8092730	450	Cemetery Cistas
289700	8092580	120	Cemetery Cistas
289610	8092370	352	Cemetery Cistas
289570	8092940	300	Cemetery Cistas
289720	8092990	150	Cemetery Cistas
289579	8092570	990	Cemetery Cistas
289860	8092890	1,320	Cemetery Cistas
289910	8092400	300	Cemetery Cistas
289910	8092610	300	Cemetery Cistas
289830	8092510	300	Cemetery Cistas
290040	8092820	400	Cemetery Cistas
289480	8092670	190	Cemetery Cistas
289510	8092740	460	Cemetery Cistas
289460	8092880	110	Cemetery Cistas?
289920	8093550	162,500	Habitation, Plazas
290290	8094590	45,000	Domestic structures, Scatter?
290700	8093380	13,000	Habitation
290750	8093500	10,000	Habitation
290700	8093600	14,500	Habitation
290590	8093600	200	Cemetery, Cists

continued

Table 5.3 continued

Site-Sector	Site Name	Stylistic Affiliation
M16E	Omo Alto Cementerio E	Omo or Chen Chen
M96A	Los Gallineros	Chen Chen
M96B	Los Gallineros	Chen Chen
M96C	Los Gallineros	Chen Chen
M96D	Los Gallineros	Chen Chen
M96E	Los Gallineros	Chen Chen
M158A	Los Adoradores Del Templo	Chen Chen
M158C	Los Adoradores Del Templo Bajo	Chen Chen
Total, Omo Group		
M43A	Rio Muerto	Chen Chen
M43B	Rio Muerto	Chen Chen
M43C	Rio Muerto	Chen Chen?
M43D	Rio Muerto	Chen Chen
M43E	Rio Muerto	Chen Chen?
M43F	Rio Muerto Domestico	Chen Chen
M46A	Grifo Volante Sur, Scatter	Chen Chen
M47A-D	Grifo Volante Alto	Chen Chen
M48A	Rio Muerto, Chamos Alrededores A	Chen Chen
M48B	Rio Muerto, Chamos Alrededores B	Chen Chen?
M48C	Rio Muerto, Chamos Alrededores C	Chen Chen?
M52	Hachas De Cobre	Chen Chen
M54	Chapi Solitario	Chen Chen
M70A	Rio Muerto A, Habitacion Principal	Omo
M70B	Rio Muerto B, Cementerio	Omo
M70C	Rio Muerto C, Habitacion con Wari	Omo, Wari
M70D	Rio Muerto D, Habitacional Oeste	Omo, Chen Chen
M70F	Rio Muerto F, Manantial Alto	Chen Chen
Total, Rio Muerto Group		
M7B	Trapiche, Domestic terraces	Chen Chen
M60	La Bomba	Chen Chen
M61	Sin Nombre	Chen Chen
M65C	Pampa Del Molle	Omo
M72A	El Santuario, Cumbre	Chen Chen
M72B	El Santuario, Base	Chen Chen
M85	Camino Alto al Baul	Chen Chen?
M94	Los Keros	Chen Chen
M129	Sacata Oeste	Chen Chen, Huaracane
M163	Sin Nombre	Chen Chen, Huaracane
M174	Cerro Medio	Chen Chen
M175	Los Vidriados	Tiwanaku
Other Tiwanaku Sites		

a. Total for Chen Chen includes estimates for destroyed cemeteries mapped by Vargas in the 1980s

East UTM	North UTM	Site area, m^2	Site Type
290950	8093370	500	Cemetery, Cists
290160	8092400	13,529	Scatter, Domestic structures
290410	8092210	5,490	Scatter
290300	8092300	3,810	Scatter
289930	8092190	3,030	Scatter, *Apacheta*
290804	8092670	482	*Apacheta*
288840	8093800	9,190	Habitation or *Apacheta*
288920	8093980	8,840	Habitation or *Apacheta*
		383,263 (38.3263 hectares)	
289350	8085200	2,938	Cemetery, Cists
289270	8085200	1,808	Cemetery, Cists
289150	8085200	4,140	Cemetery, Cists
289110	8085170	2,040	Cemetery, Cists
289040	8085150	2,480	Scatter
289350	8085200	53,235	Domestic structures, scatter
288940	8085440	240	Scatter
289090	8085700	40	Trails, ceramic scatter
289540	8084780	24,000	Cemetery, Cists
289160	8085050	3,000	Cemetery, Cists
289470	8084700	900	Cemetery, Cists
289570	8084100	38,000	Scatter, Habitation
290120	8083900	4	*Apacheta*
289920	8085530	22,768	Domestic structures, Scatter
289980	8085670	627	Cemetery, Rockpile
289820	8085600	4,560	Scatter, Domestic structures?
289790	8085570	280	Scatter
290600	8085500	1	Scatter
		161,061 (16.1061 hectares)	
290760	8098600	20,900	Scatter
288500	8082120	2,020	Scatter
288210	8082120	190	Scatter
287450	8079850	15	Scatter, Trail
289320	8086400	8,900	Domestic structures or Ceremonial structure
289470	8086320	42	Scatter
292000	8090600	80	Scatter, Trail
290020	8091280	1,432	*Apacheta*
287845	8084985	1,880	Scatter
288830	8095020	758	Scatter
291100	8099570	100	*Apacheta* or Cemetery
291805	8100330	80	Ceramic workshop?
		36,397 (3.6397 hectares)	

Table 5.4 Tumilaca Phase sites of the middle Moquegua Valley

Site-Sector	Site Name	Stylistic Affiliation
M7E	Trapiche, Cumbre Baja	Tiwanaku Tumilaca, Wari
M7F	Trapiche, Cumbre Antennae	Tiwanaku Tumilaca, Huaracane, Wari
M7H	Trapiche, Cementerio	Tiwanaku Tumilaca?
M7I	Trapiche, Cementerio	Tiwanaku Tumilaca
M7J	Trapiche, Campos De Cultivos?	Tiwanaku Tumilaca?
M7M	Trapiche, Terrazas Habitacionales	Tiwanaku Tumilaca or Chen Chen
M9A	Maria Cupine	Tiwanaku Tumilaca
M9B	Maria Cupine	Tiwanaku Tumilaca
M9C	Maria Cupine	Tiwanaku Tumilaca
M9D	Maria Cupine	Tiwanaku Tumilaca
M9E	Maria Cupine	Tiwanaku Tumilaca
M9F	Maria Cupine	Tiwanaku Tumilaca
M10N	Omo Sur, Cementerio N	Tiwanaku Tumilaca
M10Q	Omo Sur, Cementerio Q	Tiwanaku Tumilaca
M11A	Omo Garibaldi, Sitio Amurallada	Tiwanaku Tumilaca
M11B	Omo Garibaldi, Cementerio	Tiwanaku Tumilaca
M44A	Cerro Chamos, Terrazas Bajas	Tiwanaku Tumilaca
M44B	Cerro Chamos, Cuesta Mediana	Tiwanaku Tumilaca
M44C	Cerro Chamos, Terrazas Altas	Tiwanaku Tumilaca
M44D	Cerro Chamos, Cumbre Alta	Tiwanaku Tumilaca
M44E	Cerro Chamos, Cementerio	Tiwanaku Tumilaca
M50A	Conde Alto	Tiwanaku Tumilaca
M50B	Conde Alto	Tiwanaku Tumilaca
M68A-E	Cerro Terminal	Tiwanaku Tumilaca
M68F	Cerro Terminal	Tiwanaku Tumilaca, Chiribaya
M68H	Cerro Terminal	Tiwanaku Tumilaca
M68I	Cerro Terminal	Tiwanaku Tumilaca, Chiribaya
M69	Grifo Volante Sur	Tiwanaku Tumilaca
M106	Huello Dactil Alta	Tiwanaku Tumilaca
M107A	Rodriguez Piedra Yaral	Tiwanaku Tumilaca
M107B	Rodriguez Piedra Yaral	Tiwanaku Tumilaca
M107C	Rodriguez Piedra Yaral	Tiwanaku Tumilaca, Chiribaya
M107D	Rodriguez Piedra Yaral	Tiwanaku Tumilaca
M107F	Rodriguez Piedra Yaral	Tiwanaku Tumilaca
M107G	Rodriguez Piedra Yaral	Tiwanaku Tumilaca
M108	Cerro Yaral Cumbre	Tiwanaku Tumilaca

East UTM	North UTM	Site area, m²	Site Type
290720	8099100	5190	Ceremonial structure, habitation
290260	8099200	22930	Habitation
290735	8098540	1290	Cemetery
290890	8098580	940	Cemetery
290760	8098600	20900	Fields and canal
291030	8098550	1930	Habitation
287750	8085480	5620	Habitation, terraces
287765	8085600	2480	Habitation, terraces
287965	8085550	14680	Habitation
287820	8085570	46950	Habitation
287810	8085890	35980	Habitation
287900	8086125	35470	Habitation, terraces
289850	8092850	90	Cemetery, cists with rings
289990	8092760	80	Cemetery
289680	8093220	60000	Habitation, low terraces
290180	8093320	1000	Cemetery cists with rings
289206	8084588	5250	Habitation, terraces
289366	8084657	3125	Habitation, terraces
289402	8084553	2000	Habitation, terraces
289483	8084610	5150	Habitation, terraces
289253	8084485	938	Cemetery, cists
289300	8084150	21160	Habitation, scatter
289120	8083840	670	Cemetery
285960	8078955	6600	Habitation, terraces
285760	8078820	5000	Habitation, terraces, cemetery, offerings
286300	8078870	1200	Scatter, terraces, road
286090	8078560	550	Scatter
288870	8085720	6760	Scatter, terraces
285450	8079730	20520	Habitation
285920	8079870	1557	Cemetery
286050	8079980	1670	Habitation
285950	8079970	2500	Habitation
285855	8079690	7200	Habitation
285900	8080040	3080	Habitation
286120	8080110	600	Habitation
285200	8079840	1920	Habitation

continued

Table 5.4 continued

Site-Sector	Site Name	Stylistic Affiliation
M109A	Los Espejos Alto	Tiwanaku Tumilaca
M109B	Los Espejos Alto	Tiwanaku Tumilaca
M109C	Los Espejos Alto	Tiwanaku Tumilaca
M109D	Los Espejos Alto	Tiwanaku Tumilaca
M109F	Los Espejos Alto	Tiwanaku Tumilaca
M109G	Los Espejos Alto	Tiwanaku Tumilaca
M109H	Los Espejos Alto	Tiwanaku Tumilaca
M109I	Los Espejos Alto	Tiwanaku Tumilaca
M111	Rodriguez Piedra Horno	Tiwanaku Tumilaca
M116	Quien Sabe	Tiwanaku Tumilaca?
M122	Chincha Alta, Roca Negra	Tiwanaku Tumilaca?
M132A	Soledad-La Merced	Tiwanaku Tumilaca
M133	Testamento Desperadero	Tiwanaku Tumilaca
M167	La Mesa Cuadrada	Tiwanaku Tumilaca?
M191D	Yaway	Tiwanaku Tumilaca
M192	Yaway	Tiwanaku Tumilaca, Huaracane
M195	Belen	Tiwanaku Tumilaca
M214	Mariposa Baja	Tiwanaku Tumilaca
M216A	Corralon	Tiwanaku Tumilaca? Huaracane
M217A	Cerro Los Angeles	Tiwanaku Tumilaca
M218	Estuquiña Alto	Tiwanaku Tumilaca
Total		

Omo is located approximately ten kilometers south of the modern city of Moquegua, atop bluffs that overlook and control a wide expanse of valley bottom land. Omo is the location of the region's most productive natural springs. It is not surprising that the valley's first Spanish inhabitants named the entire valley after this fertile place (Pease 1984a:168). Omo's five principal settlement areas are situated along a 2.5 km stretch of the eastern margin of the floodplain, above the river-fed irrigation canals that define the limits of both modern and pre-Hispanic cultivation of the valley bottom. Including additional habitation areas discovered to the east and west in 1994, Omo's Omo and Chen Chen style architectural remains and artifact scatter covered over 38 hectares (382,630 m²), with an additional 6 hectares of Tumilaca style occupation. This makes Omo the largest of the Moquegua Tiwanaku site groups (tables 5.3 and 5.4).

East UTM	North UTM	Site area, m²	Site Type
285710	8080200	4000	Habitation
285780	8080210	6530	Habitation
285700	8080140	24340	Habitation
285710	8080235	3500	Habitation
285820	8080185	2026	Habitation, scatter de ceramica
285840	8079890	440	Habitation
285840	8079780	3000	Habitation
285660	8079820	7000	Habitation
286325	8080280	450	Cemetery
286835	8081550	335	Habitation, terraces sin ceramica, litico, etc.
286760	8082480	4	Apacheta/ofrenda o tumba aislada
288135	8086250	2800	Scatter
287980	8086560	8510	Habitation
289270	8096270	16	Ceremonial structure
295230	8102820	2240	Habitation
295305	8102720	14910	Habitation
291200	8096380	5810	Habitation?
298860	8101100	5750	Habitation
298250	8101930	4000	Scatter
297900	8101810	1200	Habitation terraces
298900	8102890	4620	Habitation?
		454461 (45.4461 hectares)	

Unlike the Huaracane settlements, the bluff top Tiwanaku settlement areas at Omo are all located some distance from the valley edge. This location, although removed from the valley bottom itself, lies near natural springs that are the most productive sources of groundwater in the Moquegua. These springs have been a significant supplementary source of irrigation and drinking water since the colonial period. Presumably would have been developed by the Tiwanaku colonists as well. Unfortunately, the digging of horizontal wells, canals and storage tanks since Spanish colonial times has disturbed any evidence of pre-Hispanic irrigation structures that may have been present.

In the desert to the northeast of the Omo sites, several paths converge to follow a direct route to the city of Moquegua and the Tiwanaku sites of Chen Chen and Los Cerrillos. This desert path is likely to have been part of an important Tiwanaku caravan route from the altiplano to the Pacific coast.

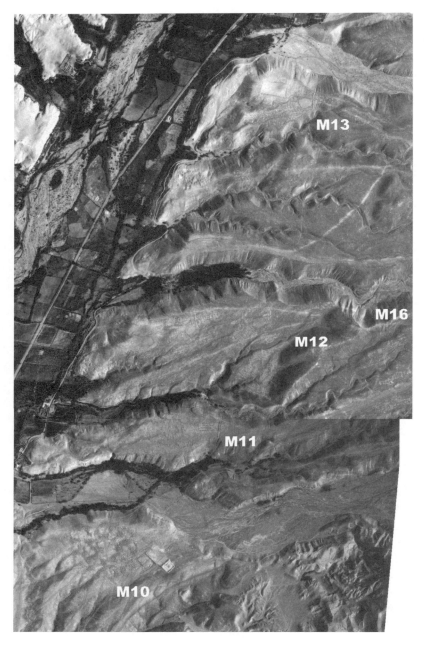

Figure 5.11. Omo site group air photo showing sites M10, M11, M12, M13, and M16.

Figure 5.12. Chen Chen geoglyphs.

The presence of artifacts such as mule shoes and wine and olive jars indicates that these tracks were in use in the Colonial and Republican period as part of a system of wine caravan routes. Tiwanaku "pot-busts" are found as well, and large stones carved with pictographs removed from this area are now displayed at the headquarters of the 3rd Armored Division in Moquegua. These indicate that the trails were in use at the time of occupation of the Omo and Chen Chen site groups. A series of associated geoglyphs are still visible on hillsides along the edge of the agricultural fields at the Chen Chen end of this 10 km route (fig. 5.12). The geoglyphs, most of which represent llamas, appear to have been guideposts along the caravan track that connected the Omo and Chen Chen site groups.

The Chen Chen M1 site group, the type-site for the Chen Chen ceramic style, was located immediately northeast of the modern city of Moquegua. Chen Chen M1 is best known for its mortuary component, which covered well over 10 hectares distributed among 29 independent cemeteries, making it the largest known Tiwanaku necropolis (fig. 5.13, table 5.3). The Chen Chen tombs have been pillaged for years, and numerous Tiwanaku vessels in local private collections almost certainly originated at Chen Chen. A rough estimate of looted tombs visible on the surface and in aerial photographs may have approached 10,000 by the late 1980s. Early mortuary excavations by Disselhoff, Neira, Vescelius and Ravines stylistically placed the site late in the Tiwanaku sequence (Disselhoff 1968; Geyh 1967) Salvage excavations of the northernmost Chen Chen cemeteries A through L by Vargas in 1987 exca-

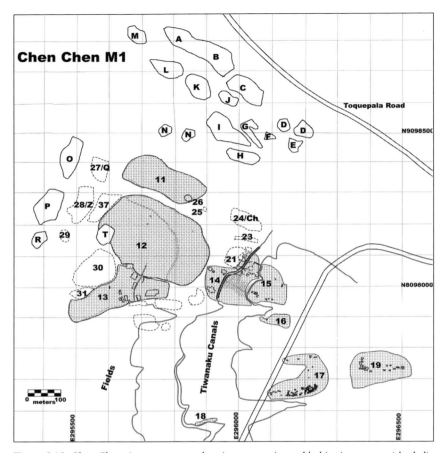

Figure 5.13. Chen Chen site group, map showing cemeteries and habitation sectors (shaded).

vated a total of 334 intact tomb grave lots and numerous disturbed tombs of Tiwanaku affiliation (Blom et al. 1998; Blom 1999; García Marquez 1990; Vargas 1988, 1994). Mortuary rescue excavations directed by Bruce Owen in 1995 extended this sample to represent most of the site's cemetery sectors.[16]

The lesser-known habitation sectors at the Chen Chen site were first mapped during the 1995 season of the Moquegua Archaeological Survey (Goldstein 1995). Chen Chen M1 was also the largest Moquegua Tiwanaku settlement site group of a single cultural affiliation, with some 20 hectares of settlement area distributed among ten distinct sectors. Associated with the site was a succession of canals and a remarkable 90–hectare system of agricultural fields (Williams 1997, 2002). Except for an irrigation tank (M202) and various "pot busts," careful survey by the MAS team found no evidence of habitation within the field systems themselves.

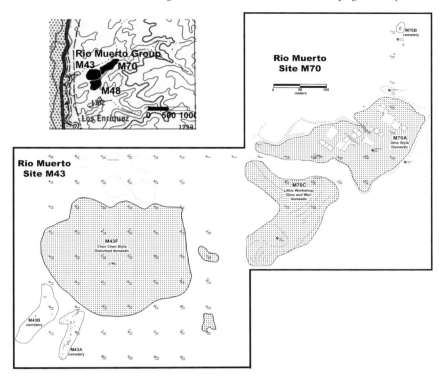

Figure 5.14. Río Muerto site group, map showing sites M43, M48, and M70 habitation sectors.

The Río Muerto complex is Moquegua's third largest Tiwanaku settlement group (fig. 5.14, table 5.3). Río Muerto, which was discovered and mapped by the MAS team in 1993 and 1994, consists of three site areas of Chen Chen style (M43, M48, M52), one of Omo style (M70), and one site of Tumilaca style affiliation (M44). The Río Muerto sites are located in or above a vast dry *quebrada* that lies over a kilometer east of the limits of modern canal irrigation. As at Omo, the Río Muerto sites' proximity to springs may have been a significant factor in Tiwanaku site location. However, geomorphological investigations in 1998 determined that the springs that emerge above the Río Muerto normally would have been inadequate to irrigate the quebrada, except perhaps in years of anomalous floods. Two such floods, dated to A.D. 700 and A.D. 1300, bracket the Tiwanaku occupation at Río Muerto (Magilligan and Goldstein 2001).

The Cerro Echenique site group is the smallest Tiwanaku site group and the only one located on the west side of the Moquegua river (figure 5.15). It consists of hillside residential terraces that completely cover the peak and south face of Cerro Echenique (M2) and a complex of structures on a flat

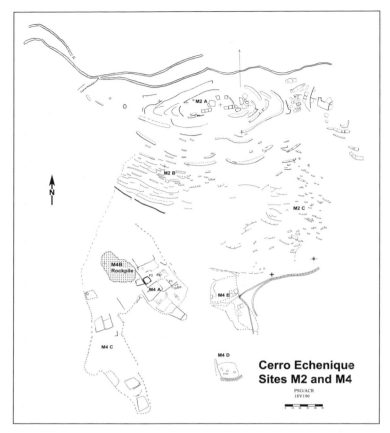

Figure 5.15. Cerro Echenique site group, map showing sites M2 and M4 habitation sectors.

geological terrace at the hill's base (M4). Together, these constitute some 6 hectares of settlement associated with the Chen Chen–style occupation. Echenique is unique among Chen Chen–style settlements in that its hillside terraces are protected by a defensive wall, while structures on the peak could serve as a redoubt in case of attack. This is the only Tiwanaku site built with defenses, a fact almost certainly related to its proximity to a Wari outpost at Cerro Trapiche (discussed later).

The Omo Style Occupation

The earliest dated Tiwanaku occupations in the Moquegua Valley were settlements of Tiwanaku colonists who used pottery of the Omo style. This stylistic complex, first identified at Omo site M12, was originally designated the Omo Phase (Goldstein 1989a,b) because aspects of the Omo ceramic

Figure 5.16. Omo-style redware and blackware serving vessels.

style correspond to attributes ascribed to the middle to later part of Phase IV of the Bolivian Tiwanaku sequence (ca. A.D. 375 to A.D. 725). The Omo style encompasses red-slipped and black polished fine serving wares (fig. 5.16). Both fine wares were used for a suite of liquid serving vessels consisting of keros, jars, and zoomorphic forms that differ stylistically from the Chen Chen style. Omo-style redware and blackware vessels are indistinguishable from altiplano Tiwanaku vessels of the same period and may represent actual imports, or at least pieces made by Tiwanaku-trained potters. Both serving wares are consistently represented in individual household contexts at Omo-style sites, indicating that Tiwanaku ceramic vessels were not reserved for elites or special contexts. This suggests a level of exchange intensity that far surpasses that represented by the minimal number of vessels in San Pedro, the isolated concentrations of Tiwanaku vessels in the Azapa Valley, or the emulation of Tiwanaku style by local traditions in Cochabamba. Moreover, the majority of the Omo-style ceramic inventory consists of exact copies of Tiwanaku utilitarian plainwares (fig. 5.17). This

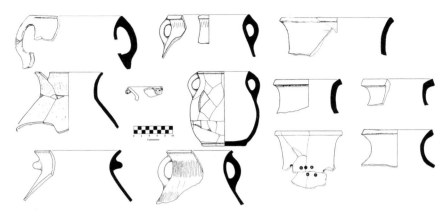

Figure 5.17. Omo-style plain utilitarian vessels.

contrasts with the limited trade in highly valued goods seen elsewhere in the Tiwanaku sphere and instead suggests that the entire ensemble of Tiwanaku material culture was transplanted from the altiplano to warmer climes.

Initially, an "Omo Phase" was dated to a 1 sigma range between cal A.D. 538 and cal A.D. 648 by a single radiocarbon date from Omo M12.[17] A series of additional dates for contexts with Omo-style pottery now suggests a more complex picture, with a 1 sigma range from cal A.D. 538 to cal A.D. 1030 (table 5.2). The preponderance of Omo-style dates follow the major flood event in Moquegua dated to A.D. 700 (Magilligan and Goldstein 2001). There is some contextual evidence that at least one Omo-style site, Los Cerrillos M31, was abandoned early in the Tiwanaku occupation, before its associated canal was recut on a higher level to feed the vast Chen Chen raised fields downstream (R. Feldman, pers. comm., 1985; see also Williams 2002). However, the later dates indicate a long duration for the Omo style, overlapping temporally with the Chen Chen style (Goldstein and Owen 2001).

The major settlements with Omo-style ceramics were located in the middle Moquegua Valley in open areas between 1,000 and 1,400 masl. Fifteen site components covering a total of 28.7 hectares have been associated with this style in the middle Moquegua Valley. Most of the Omo-style settlements were clustered in large residential sectors at Omo, Los Cerrillos, and Río Muerto (fig. 5.18). A rank-size analysis shows no particular hierarchy to the settlement pattern and a surprising absence of small village sites (fig. 5.19). The only smaller Tiwanaku Omo settlements appear to have been located along trade routes or at ritually important spots.

There is evidence for Omo-style occupations on a smaller scale in the higher elevation valleys of Torata and Tumilaca.[18] These valleys are among the few areas of flat agricultural land in the upper valley zone and also lie on the direct route from Moquegua to the altiplano. Owen reports a small Omo-

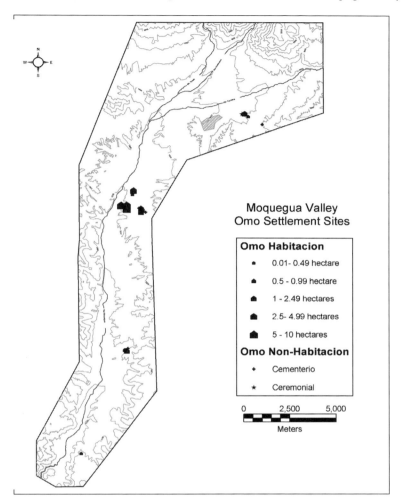

Figure 5.18. Omo-style settlement map.

style Tiwanaku site at La Cantera at the foot of Cerro Baúl that included domestic middens composed of Omo-style blackware. La Cantera is located on the slopes of Cerro Baúl, a peak that had a substantial Wari occupation, yet a collection of over 7,500 sherds from surface collections and test pits included only four Wari sherds.[19] The site's small Tiwanaku ceremonial structure may indicate the veneration of the Cerro Baúl massif by Tiwanaku people (Goldstein and Owen 2002; Owen 1997). The lack of defensive works at La Cantera, as at all of the Omo-style sites, belies any major hostilities among the Huaracane, Chen Chen, or Wari peoples.

It is probable that the first pioneer Omo-style Tiwanaku colonists were pastoralists, following on a long tradition of transhumance by highland

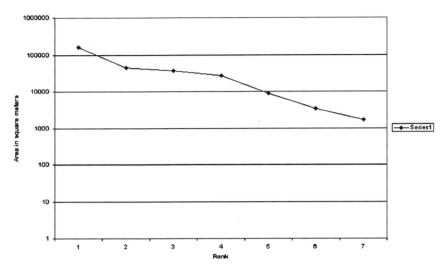

Figure 5.19. Omo-style settlement rank-size graph.

camelid herders. The settlers of the Omo style settled in exactly the kind of places that pioneer llama pastoralists might choose. It is probably no coincidence that the villages of the Omo style are consistently the most distant from the Moquegua River floodplain of all pre-Columbian settlements. Present-day highland herders passing through Moquegua stay close to desert caravan routes that avoid the farms and the farmers of the valley floodplain. Herding camps are typically located near groundwater springs several kilometers from the valley itself, where livestock could be watered without angering local agriculturalists. The Omo-style Tiwanaku towns at Omo, Los Cerrillos, and Río Muerto are all located near these same caravan routes, as much as 2 km east of the floodplain. Omo-style settlements also had few cemeteries, arguably because they were short-term settlements and had no dead to bury. It is possible that the Omo-style colonists had alternate mortuary treatments for herders who died while in Moquegua, again setting them apart from their Chen Chen–style neighbors. As is the case with many present-day pastoralists worldwide, these may have included trailside burial or death rituals of exposure or cremation.

Pastoralist origins are also indicated by the tentlike houses of Omo style settlements, designed with skeletal pole frames to accommodate hanging panels. The Omo house design could be set and struck as the herdsmen's camp moved. The construction did not require finding scarce timbers for roof support and probably incorporated animal skins or woven cloth panels for walls, both pastoralist products. Even after the Omo-style settlements became more permanent towns, the design was retained, perhaps as a marker of the settlers' ethnic and occupational identities. Omo-style houses also lacked many permanent features or furniture that would signify major construction investment, and even portable facilities like grinding stones are smaller and less frequent than in other Tiwanaku occupations. The absence of formal storage features is notable in comparison with the stone-lined storage cists of the Chen Chen–style households, again suggesting a traditionally less settled lifestyle.

The type sites for the Omo style are Omo sites M12, M13, and M16 (figs. 5.20, 5.21). Omo-style residential remains at Omo consist of hundreds of freestanding, multiroom structures arrayed in community sectors centered on distinct public plazas. Topographical features or empty spaces separated each site's residential sectors, delineating socially independent spaces (Goldstein 1993a). Site M13 covered about 4.5 hectares on the northernmost of the Omo bluffs. When discovered in 1983, M13 manifested extreme effects of wind deflation and had already been disturbed by a modern cemetery, a soccer field, and an access road. Aerial photographs taken in 1946 indicate house platforms and two plazas as light areas that had been cleared of the naturally patinated stones of the desert surface. The soccer field was on the site of a rectangular plaza measuring approximately 60 × 100 m. A second plaza of an irregular shape 45 m in diameter was located 55 m southeast of the rectangular plaza. This smaller plaza contained a perfectly circular ring 25 m in diameter, visible in 1986 as a shallow depression one meter in width. Radiating westward from the second plaza, approximately fifty rectangular house platforms can be seen in the aerial photograph as small lighter colored rectangles. Toward the southeast these rooms were larger and well-defined, while those near the rectangular plaza were less distinct. To the east of this second plaza group, a deep trench defined the eastern limit of the M13 site. The M13 site was bulldozed at some time between 1987 and 1993 before it could be surface mapped or collected.

The M12/M16 bluff is located 1.5 km to the south of M13 and is separated from it by a deep gorge and two steep razor-backed ridges. M12 is situated atop one of several open, flat bluffs that rise above the eastern margin of the irrigated valley, adjacent to Moquegua's most productive natural springs. Two paths cross the site from east to west, connecting with the desert path to Moquegua City and the Chen Chen site.

Omo M12 is 16.25 hectares in area, making it the largest single settlement in Moquegua. Housing at the M12 village was concentrated in three distinct communities, which together comprised some 133 buildings divided into 369 rooms. These three clusters have been designated as the west, north, and south communities (M12W, N, and S). The west community consisted of 148 rooms arrayed in 56 structures, the north community of 114 rooms in 40

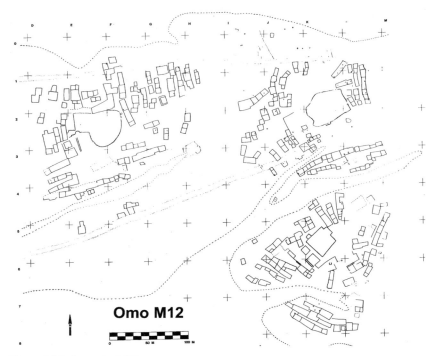

Figure 5.20. Omo site M12 map.

structures, and the south community of 107 rooms in 37 structures. Each community was segregated from its neighbors either by a natural feature like the quebrada that cuts off the south community or by a deliberately unoccupied "no-man's-land" like the one that separated the north and west communities. Each community group was also oriented around a cleared central plaza area. The plazas themselves were virtually free of artifacts and, except for two benchlike features in the south plaza, had no internal constructions. Their extremely low sherd densities suggest that these plazas were kept clean as areas for public assembly. Considering their clear boundaries and separate public spaces, M12's plaza-centered community divisions appear to define social or ethnic groups within the town plan.

The smaller Omo M16 site is located on a dissected plateau to the east of M12, separated from the M12 bluff by a steep 30 m hill. M16 consists of three elongated residence groups that are separated from one another by quebradas. The northernmost of these three communities has a small (25 m wide) plaza and approximately seventy rectangular rooms. The central and southern groups each comprised some forty rooms, and at least the southern group included another plaza. Together, M16's three building groups cover some 3.75 hectares. Surface investigations and household archaeology con-

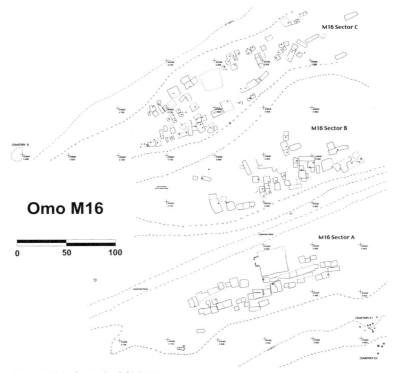

Figure 5.21. Omo site M16 map.

ducted at M12 in 1986 and 1987 and at M16 in 1999 are discussed at length in the following chapter.

Los Cerrillos, a second cluster of Omo-style sites, was found northeast of Moquegua City and the Chen Chen site. Separated from Chen Chen site by a deep canyon, this Omo-style settlement group included sites M31, M206, and M208. These settlement and ceremonial components were already disturbed when first encountered by the author in 1984 and are today almost totally effaced. Earlier aerial photographs suggest that they comprised an extensive complex of settlement and ceremonial space.[20] At Los Cerrillos M31, houses were arrayed individually on shallow terraces on slightly sloping ground. As at Omo M12 and M16, the Los Cerrillos M31 settlement sectors appear to align with cleared plaza areas and ring-shaped depressions visible at site M206. The Los Cerrillos group was also associated with fields and a sequence of preserved irrigation canals. Because this settlement and field system lies upriver from the Chen Chen site, it is possible to trace its occupation sequence through the succession of canal abandonment. It appears that much of the site was abandoned when the principal canal was relocated to service the Chen Chen fields.

The Río Muerto site group included a smaller Omo-style component in its site M70. The Omo-style occupation at Río Muerto consisted of habitation site M70A and a small cemetery, M70B. The M70A habitation component was centered on two small rectangular plazas, surrounded by rectangular house foundations. As the following chapter details, excavations at Omo M12 and M16, Los Cerrillos M31, and Río Muerto M70 have confirmed that the rectangular clearings correspond to wooden post foundations, sub-surface features, and in situ artifacts and organic materials.

The Chen Chen–Style Occupation

The Chen Chen style is the most widespread Tiwanaku ceramic style in the Osmore drainage and coincides with the most substantial provincial occupa-tion by Tiwanaku colonists anywhere in the Andes. The style is named for the heavily looted cemeteries at Chen Chen, the first published site of Tiwanaku affiliation in Moquegua (Disselhoff 1968; Ishida 1960). Chen Chen–style ceramics, like those of the Omo style, are visually indistinguishable from altiplano Tiwanaku prototypes (figs. 5.22, 5.23). Although vessels of the serving and utilitarian assemblages of both styles are functionally similar, there are noticeable variations in ceramic technology, form, and decoration. Most dramatic is the absence of polished blackware serving vessels from Chen Chen–style assemblages. Chen Chen–style redware serving vessels tend to exhibit lower firing, a slightly greater median vessel thickness, less careful surface burnishing, and a lighter range of red surface slip colors. Serving ceramics are also more standardized in form and painted decoration, and some of the Omo style's more elaborate modeled variants are not repre-sented. Chen Chen–style keros tend to be taller, wider-mouthed, and more flared than those of the Omo style. The most striking formal distinction is the widespread appearance in the Chen Chen redware assemblages of the tazón, a flaring-sided bowl shaped like a half kero, and the less common *fuente*, a thick serving platter. Overall, the Omo- and Chen Chen–style assemblages represent two distinct subsets of the larger Tiwanaku IV–Tiwanaku V stylis-tic continuum of the core region. Because these two styles are not found separately in the Tiwanaku core region, it is not entirely clear whether the stylistic distinction is temporal, regional, ethnic, or status-related. The Mo-quegua Valley is unique in the Tiwanaku sphere for the spatial segregation of two Tiwanaku styles at adjacent sites. Calibrated dates for the Chen Chen style in the middle Moquegua Valley cover a 1 sigma range from cal A.D. 785 to cal A.D. 1000 (table 5.2).[21]

Chen Chen–style settlements in the middle Moquegua Valley covered 54.6 hectares of domestic area, with an additional 10.4 hectares of cemeteries (table 5.3, figs. 5.24, 5.25). Chen Chen settlement is found primarily in sec-tors of the four large towns of Chen Chen, Omo (M10), Río Muerto (M43,

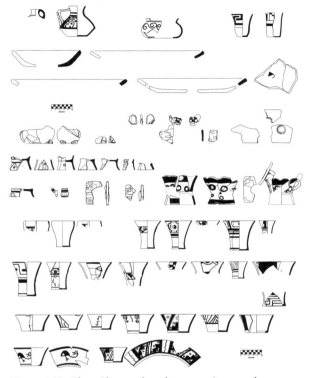

Figure 5.22. Chen Chen–style redware serving vessels.

M48, and M52), and Cerro Echenique (M2 and M4). These principal towns were located near large artificially irrigated pampas (Williams 1997:90) or productive natural springs suitable for agricultural intensification (Goldstein 1989a). The typical village plan included one or more habitation areas with cemeteries located around the site's periphery.

The majority of the Chen Chen–style domestic settlement area was characterized by a surface phenomenon described as "rockpiling." All the Omo M10 habitation area (sector M10C, fig. 5.26) and the largest habitation areas of Chen Chen (sectors M1–11 and 12, 11.5 hectares) were covered by irregular stone mounds and excavated pits dating to before the A.D. 1600 ashfall. The habitation sector of Río Muerto M43 displays similar disturbance in a sandier substrate, while the architecture at Cerro Echenique (M4A) was also destroyed. These rockpile areas coincide with the sites' densest midden deposits and the areas of most intensive occupation. As a result, it is difficult to define the housing plan of the central settlements from surface indications. Excavation indicates that Chen Chen houses consisted of autonomous patio groups with functionally specific activity areas, contiguous roofed rooms, open patios, and storage units (mud-plastered stone cists or

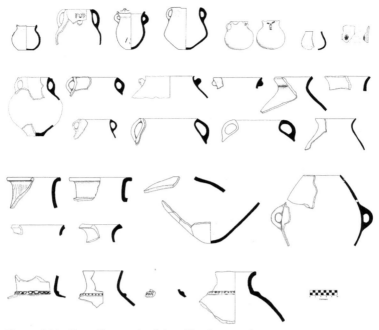

Figure 5.23. Chen Chen–style plain utilitarian vessels.

rectangular cribs). This domestic compound, which appears only in Chen Chen sites, may indicate significant differences from the Omo-style occupation in household organization, size, and productive activities.

The main Chen Chen–style settlements were often accompanied by outer rings of "suburban" habitation. At Chen Chen, sectors 16, 17, 18, and 19 were located to the east of the main body of the site, in the direction of the caravan route and geoglyphs. These suburban sectors covered 4.4 hectares with light artifact scatter and cleared rectangular house platforms. A similar spillover settlement area occupied a low-lying area to the east of Omo M10 (M96). These areas were impermanent settlements, compared to the principal town sectors, and their locations near caravan routes suggest that they may represent temporary housing for transient populations of laborers or traders.

Some site locations in the Chen Chen settlement patterns appear to have been determined by spatial perceptions of alignments of shrines with one another and across sacred landscapes. The Omo M10 site is unique in that it has a large temple that may have served as a ritual and administrative center for the Moquegua settlement (chapter 8, and see Goldstein 1993b). The site of the temple is one of the few locations in the middle Moquegua Valley from which Cerro Baúl can be viewed. The significance of the M10 temple's northwest-facing orientation is yet unknown; however, the structure does appear

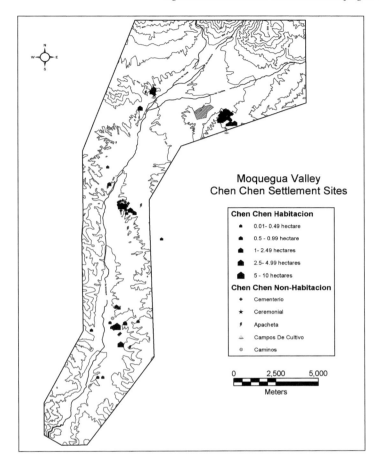

Figure 5.24. Chen Chen–style settlement map.

to have dictated the location of subsidiary ritual sites. The M158 site, one of the only Chen Chen–style sites found on the west side of the valley, is located on an inaccessible peak that aligns with the central axis of the M10 temple, visible at a distance of 3 km. The site is characterized by high surface frequencies of keros and serving wares, evidence of campfires, and an absence of domestic architecture or remains. Ritually significant alignments that could correspond with pilgrimage paths have also been identified within Tiwanaku towns among shrine structures in the Chen Chen and Río Muerto site groups (chapter 8). Finally, several smaller mountaintop sites with surface evidence of feasting or ritual offering behavior were categorized as *apachetas*. Apachetas are among the few Chen Chen–style sites encountered outside the four Tiwanaku towns. Their locations suggest shrines along ritual paths and sightlines and a concern with celebrating the features of the valley landscape.

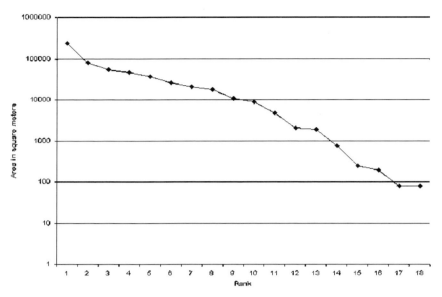

Figure 5.25. Chen Chen–style settlement rank-size graph.

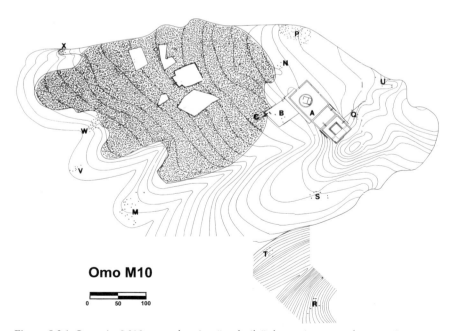

Omo M10

Figure 5.26. Omo site M10, map showing "rockpile" domestic area and cemeteries.

Site locations may also have been influenced by cultural norms that represented ethnic identity in directional spatial organization. At all three Moquegua Tiwanaku site groups where sectors of both the Omo and Chen Chen stylistic groups were represented, settlements of each of the two diaspora communities were arranged in a northeast-southwest opposition. The Omo-style settlement sectors were consistently situated to the northeast while the Chen Chen phase sites were located to the southwest. It has already been noted that this locational consistency placed the Omo-style settlements farther from the valley floodplain, as might be expected for pastoralist communities. However, this pattern persisted over time even after Omo settlements were permanent and presumably agricultural. As noted in chapter 8, ceremonial structures and shrines appear to align along the same axis. This suggests that identification with one of the two great diasporas of Tiwanaku settlement may have been encoded in their settlement locations relative to one another—literally a definition through opposition. This kind of association of social segments with cardinal directions may have been an antecedent of Aymara concepts of *tinku* or joining of complementary opposites and of the Inca *ceque* system, which functioned as both a cosmological and a social map of the ayllus of Cusco.

Other aspects of Chen Chen–style settlement patterns responded more to material considerations than to cosmological or social ones. Site location and preserved irrigation works suggest that the Chen Chen settlements adapted to changes in the organization of agricultural production associated with extensive land reclamation. Extensive canal systems like the one above the Chen Chen site irrigated outlying desert pampas as well as the valley bottom lands. This preference for open lands and the general avoidance of agricultural terracing throughout the Tiwanaku occupation of Moquegua is not surprising, considering the raised fields that characterize Tiwanaku agriculture in the altiplano. Intensified agricultural production is further attested to by the introduction of chipped stone hoes and large rocker *batanes* or grinding stones at Chen Chen–style sites (see following chapter). The heightened labor demands of bringing new lands into production, maintaining canals, and cultivating multiple annual crops may have placed considerable labor demands on the Chen Chen colony and could explain the population growth at the principal towns and their spillover suburbs.

The intensive Tiwanaku occupation of the Moquegua Valley contrasts with the absence of colonial settlement in the coastal Osmore. Owen's systematic survey and excavations at Loreto Viejo and other coastal Osmore sites failed to find any evidence of Tiwanaku state occupation. Even at the height of the Omo and Chen Chen settlement of the middle Moquegua Valley, the coastal Osmore valley was occupied by non-Tiwanaku maritime and agricultural peoples of the local Early Ceramic tradition, dated to cal A.D.

675–950. Indigenous agricultural and maritime traditions in the coastal valley appear to have continued with little change, perhaps only incidentally affected by Tiwanaku state settlement 45 km upvalley. Despite interpretations of direct Tiwanaku control of maritime resources (e.g., Mujica 1985; Ponce 1972) and the unfortunate misuse of the Loreto Viejo site as a type site for Chilean Tiwanaku, it is clear that Tiwanaku colonists never enjoyed a presence on the coast comparable to their direct agricultural occupation of the middle Moquegua Valley.[22] If Tiwanaku colonists of the middle Moquegua Valley enjoyed access to maritime products, these appear to have been obtained indirectly.

Using early Spanish documents, Rostworowski has identified a distinct ethnic group of fisherfolk called Camanchacas, who lived along the coast of Arequipa and Moquegua in the colonial period. Rostworowski suggests that the Camanchacas, like other coastal specialists, were ethnically distinct from valley agriculturalists and spoke a distinct language shared along the length of the littoral (1986:128). Although the ayllus of valley and highland agriculturalists may have exploited the guano islands, all other coastal activities were left in the hands of these indigenous maritime specialists. Tiwanaku access to fish, shellfish, and sea mammals was likely through contact with the ancestors of these fishers and collectors who maintained their own traditions and economies.

An even more surprising aspect of Chen Chen Tiwanaku's provincial system is the absence of militarism or defensive posture. There are no site walls or defensive works in most of the Tiwanaku sites of Moquegua, nor indeed is there evidence of organized conflict in any other region of Tiwanaku V colonization. If Tiwanaku expanded through military conquest, we might expect to see the effects of violence along Tiwanaku's frontiers with other peoples. The rarity of site fortifications, garrisons, barracks, or stores of weapons in Tiwanaku Moquegua point to the migration of peoples of the Tiwanaku core region rather than conquest and exploitation of indigenous peoples. The nondefensive posture of the Tiwanaku settlements, their site size hierarchy, intensified household involvement in state production, the large permanently resident populations evident in cemeteries, and the corporate building of a temple all suggest that no external threat was felt and that between-site competition was minimal under a "Pax Tiwanaku." The absence of overt coercion as agricultural systems grew and production was intensified also suggests that the Tiwanaku colonists themselves consented to these developments. The absence of conflict in the Tiwanaku colony is even more remarkable considering that these settlements faced outposts of Tiwanaku's contemporary, the Wari state, across a poorly understood frontier.

Wari Settlement Patterns

Few phenomena are as puzzling as the interaction of the Wari and Tiwanaku of the Middle Horizon. While both cultures share certain elements of iconography, they were utterly unlike in domestic organization, ideas of urbanism, monumental architecture, mortuary and offering traditions, and ceramic, lithic, and textile technology. Wari and Tiwanaku also display radically different attitudes toward territorial expansion. Wari is seen as a conquest empire assembled through militaristic means (e.g., Schreiber 1992). In contrast, Tiwanaku expansion proceeded through the colonial occupation of new regions. Moquegua represents the Wari-Tiwanaku frontier, and the Osmore drainage is the only valley system that has distinct settlement patterns of both cultures. An examination of these patterns in middle Moquegua can illuminate the interplay of conquest, colonization, and coexistence between the two polities (Moseley et al. 1991).

If the Osmore drainage and the middle Moquegua Valley sector in particular represent an imperial frontier, it was a frontier like few others. Despite the vast no-man's-land areas offered by the empty deserts between Peru's oasis valleys, the two polities occupied different parts of the same drainage in the Osmore. The Wari occupation is best known for the mountaintop city of Cerro Baúl, located at 2,800 masl, in the upper reaches of the Osmore drainage between the Torata and Tumilaca tributaries. The site's characteristic Wari stone architecture and MH 1A, 1B, and 2A ceramics place it squarely in the expansive Ayacucho Wari tradition (Lumbreras et al. 1982; Feldman 1988; Moseley et al. 1991; Watanabe 1990). Like Cerro Baúl, most Middle Horizon domestic sites of the upper Osmore are also characterized by Ocros and Chakipampa B styles, dating them to Middle Horizon Epoch 1B. Excavations by Feldman (1988) and Williams, Nash, and Isla (Williams et al. 2001) are elucidating both the culture history and site functions of Cerro Baúl's Wari occupation. At present, radiocarbon dates place the Cerro Baúl Wari occupation between the sixth and ninth centuries A.D.. This makes the Wari site roughly contemporary with the Moquegua Tiwanaku settlements that lie only 20 km to the southwest.

Cerro Baúl's impressive defensible location and its proximity to Tiwanaku territory suggested early on that it was an intrusive fortified settlement. At the same time, traditions of offerings and veneration of the Cerro Baúl massif that continue to the present day support a conception of the mountain as a spiritually charged ritual center. From the colonial period into the twenty-first century, the site has been a pilgrimage destination for supplicants from as far as Puno and Cusco who make offerings and build family shrines on the summit. Even the ever-practical Inca appear to have constructed a small *ushnu* ritual platform on the summit. Especially as the dimensions of nearby

Tiwanaku settlement became more apparent, Cerro Baúl has traditionally been seen as a settlement anomaly, an isolated Wari military and religious sanctuary within territory populated by Tiwanaku (Lumbreras et al. 1982; Feldman 1988; Moseley et al. 1991; Watanabe 1990).

However, the Wari settlement in the upper Osmore drainage may be explicable by more mundane strategies of resource exploitation and political expansion. The Wari occupation of the upper Osmore represents the first economically viable exploitation of a previously unoccupied agronomic niche. The Wari made this possible by introducing a new agricultural technology that they had perfected in their Ayacucho homeland: agricultural terracing (Schreiber 1992:131). In contrast to the simple floodplain canal agriculture practiced by Huaracane and the flat- land intensification strategies of Tiwanaku, agriculture in the upper reaches of the southern Andean river valleys is constrained by steep slopes. Slope would have represented a formidable new challenge to Tiwanaku agriculturalists, whose altiplano raised fields did not prepare them for farming precipitous hillsides. Indeed, Bruce Owen's survey of Cerro Baúl's immediate hinterland in the upland Torata and Tumilaca valleys found neither a significant Huaracane occupation nor large Tiwanaku sites. In contrast to the model of an invasive Wari intrusion, Owen concludes that Wari moved into an "empty or underpopulated region adjacent to Tiwanaku territory" (Owen 1994). This steep dry region must have seemed inhospitable to Tiwanaku caravans or farmers passing through on their way to lower, warmer climes.

Wari colonists, on the other hand, would have brought a cultural template for creating flat planting surfaces by constructing irrigated benched terraces. The earliest irrigated bench terraces appeared in the southern Andes in the sixth century A.D. (Denevan 2001:198). In the Colca Valley, although simpler unirrigated terracing technologies predate them at higher elevations above 3,790 masl, irrigated bench terraces represent an agricultural shift to drier and warmer downslope areas (Denevan 2001:199). Probably not coincidentally, the advent of irrigated bench terracing correlated with both a period of drought and the general expansion of the Wari culture. Terracing brought the Wari multiple benefits of retarding erosion, facilitating both irrigation and dry farming through better water control, and minimizing the effect of killer frosts by banking solar energy in the stone terrace walls (Schreiber 1992: 131). It also opened previously unattractive regions like the Colca and the upper Osmore to expansive agricultural settlement. The attraction to Wari agriculturalists of new middle elevation regions like the upper Osmore was thus based on both strangeness and familiarity. While Cerro Baúl's exotic form and dramatic setting may have inspired pilgrims, priests, and warriors, Wari farmers would have found themselves on familiar ground building new fields in the surrounding hillsides.

At lower elevations in the middle Moquegua heart of the Tiwanaku colonization, Wari settlement was far more limited (see fig. 5.10). Wari sites cover less than 6 hectares of domestic occupation in the entire MAS survey, all on the steep slopes of Cerro Trapiche (sites M3, M5, and M7). This intrusive Wari occupation consisted of terraced habitation components on the high peaks and ridges of the 1,500 m Cerro Trapiche (M7D, E, and F). These residential components overlook a substantial stone structure built on the site of a Huaracane boot tomb cemetery component (M7C, fig. 5.27). Among the ceramics associated with this structure were Wari-style utilitarian vessels and Ocros and Chakipampa decorated pottery that included face neck vessels and straight-sided bowls (fig. 5.28). A second Wari structure of similar construction but larger in plan was located on a lower ridgetop to the northeast (M3).

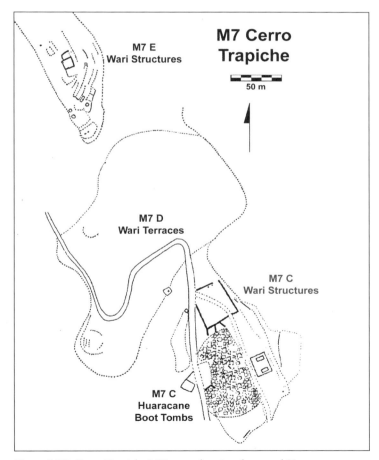

Figure 5.27. Cerro Trapiche M7, map showing destroyed Huaracane cemetery and Wari structures.

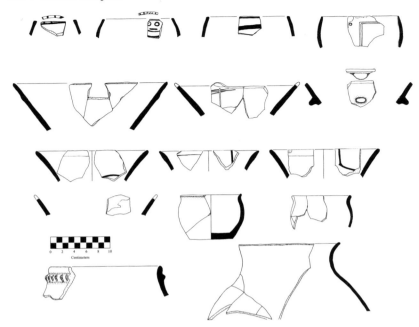

Figure 5.28. Wari ceramics, Cerro Trapiche M7 surface collections.

It is notable that all of these components were located on the higher peaks of imposing hills, at elevations between 100 and 225 m above the elevation of the river. These would appear to be highly defensible outposts that were limited to the northern corner of Tiwanaku's agricultural territory. The Cerro Trapiche outposts afford an excellent view of the middle Moquegua Valley, and the peak occupation can look down on the Tiwanaku settlements at Echenique. Although Trapiche and Echenique are only 2 km apart, the terrain effectively isolates the two site groups, and the Cerro Echenique sites were defended by walls and steep slopes. The Wari sites may have connected to the Cerro Baúl site by an escape route of paths from Trapiche up the Torata river.

The paucity of trade between the two settlement systems also suggests an uneasy truce, if not outright hostilities between the outliers of the Wari and Tiwanaku cultures of the Osmore drainage. Wari sites like Cerro Baúl and Cerro Trapiche have no evidence of a Tiwanaku domestic presence, while Tiwanaku village sites like Omo, Río Muerto, and Chen Chen betray no Wari influence on architecture or domestic life. Nonetheless, as discussed in chapter 4, there is some evidence for trade between Wari and Tiwanaku in the form of minuscule numbers of Wari artifacts found in elite Tiwanaku mortuary contexts in Chile's Azapa Valley.

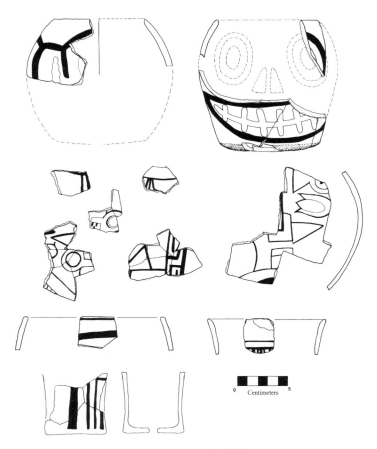

Figure 5.29. Wari ceramics, Río Muerto site M70.

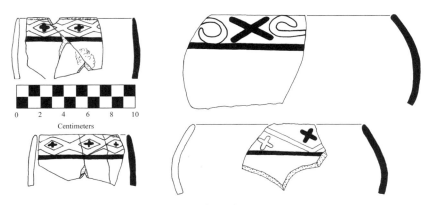

Figure 5.30. Wari Qosqopa ceramics, various sites.

Figure 5.31. Obsidian lithics, Omo site M16. PSG photo.

In Moquegua's Tiwanaku towns, a minimal exchange with Wari sources is supported by the appearance of occasional decorated serving ceramics and obsidian artifacts and lithic raw materials sourced to the Peruvian Andes. Wari Chakipampa and Ocros ceramics similar to those found in Cerros Baúl and Trapiche occur at the Río Muerto M70 site in sector C, a lithic production and domestic area (fig. 5.29). Only slightly more common in Tiwanaku sites are ceramics of the Qosqopa (Coscopa) style, a later Wari variant best known from the Department of Arequipa (fig. 5.30; Lumbreras 1974b:157, 174). Chakipampa and Ocros sherds have been found at Omo-style Tiwanaku sites, and small numbers of Qosqopa pottery items are associated with sites of both Omo and Chen Chen style. A few Qosqopa-style vessels appear as isolated offerings in Tiwanaku tombs of the Chen Chen cemetery. A critical review reveals that this amounts to a total of about a dozen vessels out of a sample from twelve hundred tombs (Vargas 1988, 1994; García Marquez 1990). Qosqopa-style ceramics also appear occasionally in Tiwanaku household contexts at Omo. At the Omo M16 site, Qosqopa vessels were found in habitation areas along with obsidian artifacts and debitage that has been sourced to areas of Peru that were likely under Wari control (fig. 5.31). The significance of obsidian exchange and the occurrence of Wari artifacts within colonial Tiwanaku lithic workshops and domestic contexts are discussed in the following chapter.

The Tumilaca Phase

The collapse of the Tiwanaku polity led to the reemergence of regional political units and leadership. The salient feature of the geopolitical landscape at this time was the disintegration of Tiwanaku's political and economic preeminence, accompanied by the disruption of the existing settlement system and a more gradual waning of Tiwanaku's cultural influence (Bermann et al. 1989; Stanish 1992:86).

I have adopted the term "Tumilaca style" to describe the diversified ceramic traditions that reflect the ongoing imitation of Tiwanaku themes by local potters in Moquegua (Goldstein 1989a). The Tumilaca phase derives its name from Programa Contisuyu site U4 at Tumilaca, which had been investigated by the University of Tokyo Andes Expedition (Ishida 1960; Fujii 1980), Romulo Pari of Arequipa (Pari 1987), and in 1983 by members of Programa Contisuyu (Bawden 1989, 1993). Future refinements in dating will permit correlating the disparate post-expansive Tiwanaku-derived traditions of the south-central Andes under a common rubric. The Tumilaca style in the middle Moquegua Valley overlaps somewhat with both the previous Chen Chen Tiwanaku style and the subsequent Chiribaya tradition (table 5.1). However, Tumilaca-style occupations persist well after the Tiwanaku collapse, permitting us to use the term "Tumilaca Phase" to refer to these post-expansive settlements. In the coastal Osmore Valley, Owen reports nine calibrated dates, suggesting a range from cal A.D. 950 to 1050 for his Ilo-Tumilaca ceramic style and a related Ilo-Cabuza style lasting from cal A.D. 1000 to 1250 (Owen 1993b:415, 418).

One prominent feature of the Tumilaca settlement pattern is the first appearance of Tiwanaku-derived ceramic traditions in previously uncolonized upper valleys and coastal valleys of the Osmore drainage. The migration of Tumilaca-style settlement beyond the optimal middle Moquegua Valley lands into more marginal zones has been described as one result of the balkanization of the Moquegua Tiwanaku colony (Bermann et al. 1989). The Tumilaca type site, U4, located at 2,000 masl near where the Tumilaca River first emerges from its highland canyon, was part of the upper valley focus of this secondary colonization (Bawden 1989:289). Another group of Tiwanaku-derived sites (T8, T9) is located on the flanks of Cerro Baúl, facing the fertile Torata Valley, while Stanish reports a late Tiwanaku occupation in the Porobaya Valley (Stanish 1992:114).

Most Tiwanaku-related settlement in the coastal Osmore may also be ascribed to the appearance of refugees from the Tiwanaku state collapse in the middle Moquegua (Owen 1993a,b). These settlers appear to have maintained social distance from local populations and did not engage in marine pursuits, continuing to rely instead on irrigation agriculture (Sandness 1992:

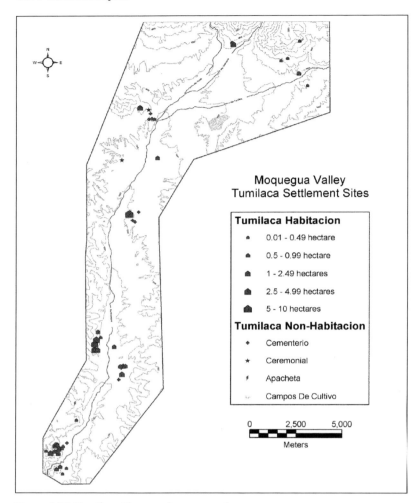

Figure 5.32. Tumilaca Phase settlement map.

29). A similar tendency has been noted for the post-Tiwanaku "Regional Development" sites of the Azapa Valley, with higher, strategically placed villages and new settlements in the *cabeceras del valle*, or headwater areas (Muñoz 1983). This refugee migration to the coastal and upper tributary valleys from the wreckage of Tiwanaku's Moquegua Valley province signals substantial settlement realignment in Moquegua following the Tiwanaku state collapse.

In the middle Moquegua Valley itself, Tumilaca settlement was both reduced in total population and transformed in pattern. The Tumilaca occupation is characterized by the disappearance of monumental architecture and the replacement of the concentrated settlement pattern of the Omo- and Chen

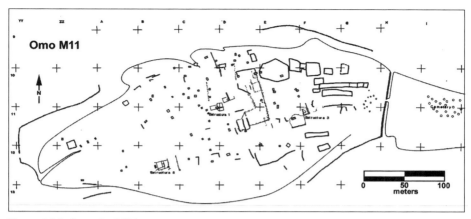

Figure 5.33. Omo site M11 map.

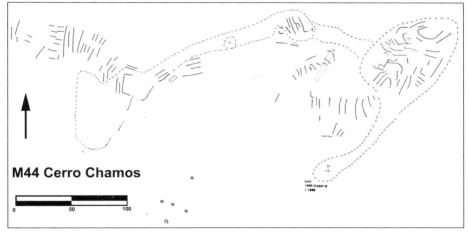

Figure 5.34. Cerro Chamos site M44 map.

Chen–style Tiwanaku colonies with a pattern of smaller, dispersed, and defensible sites. Aggregate habitation site area is reduced to 42 hectares, considerably less than that of the state-contemporary colonies of the Omo and Chen Chen styles (table 5.1, 5.4; fig. 5.32). Tumilaca occupation continues at the great Tiwanaku colonial centers, but they are reduced to shadows of their former selves. At Omo, sites M10 and M12 are largely abandoned, and settlement is removed to site M11, a site completely surrounded by a defensive wall. At Chen Chen, the minority presence of Tumilaca-style pottery suggests that there was continued occupation at the site following the state collapse. This is likely to coincide with the final stages of the progressive abandonment of canal systems and retraction of agricultural field system (Williams 2002). At Río Muerto, settlement shifted from low-lying sectors to the defensible

Cerro Chamos (M44) site, where residential terraces were perched on the high slopes of a steep hill.

Except for these terminal occupations at the Omo, Chen Chen, and Río Muerto sites, most Tumilaca populations who continued to live in the middle Moquegua Valley retreated to fortified or strategically located settlements. The forty-five Tumilaca-style settlement sites were more widely distributed and far smaller, with a mean habitation area of under one hectare. Characterizing the period are defensive site walls as at Omo M11 (fig. 5.33) or steep, inaccessible site locations as at La Yaral (M8), Maria Cupine (M9), and Cerro Chamos (M44; fig. 5.34); or both, as in the walled steep hillside sectors of Echenique M4 and hilltop fort at Tumilaca (U4). This supports a scenario of increasing competitive tensions within the Moquegua Valley following the collapse of Tiwanaku state control. With the withdrawal to more defensible site locations, steep residential terracing replaces the bluff top residential sectors of the Omo and Chen Chen occupations throughout the middle Moquegua Valley. Tumilaca-style residential terraces at Río Muerto/ Chamos M44, Yaral M9, and Los Espejos M106 are distinguishable from later Chiribaya terraces by their narrower width, use of smaller facing stones, and more eroded and patinated condition. As demonstrated by excavations at Omo site M11 and Maria Cupine (M9), where the residential architecture is extraordinarily well preserved by deep windblown sand, Tumilaca houses used the same *quincha* cane construction that typified the Chen Chen occupation (chapter 6).

The diversification of Tumilaca Phase ceramic styles suggests the development of at least three distinct geographic foci of ceramic production during this period (figs. 5.35, 5.36). An upper valley focus encompasses assemblages from several defensible sites in the Tumilaca and Torata valleys that share a similar ceramic style. In the middle Moquegua Valley, the pottery of Tiwanaku-descendant populations display a transformation from Tiwanaku precedents to locally produced derivations. Tumilaca Phase serving pottery from middle Moquegua Valley sites includes oversized keros, with considerable variability in base slips ranging from purple reds to mustard yellow. The Maria Cupine focus of the Tumilaca style is represented in the lower half of the middle Moquegua Valley at the Maria Cupine (M9), La Yaral (M8), and Cerro Chamos (M44) sites. This ceramic substyle is most closely related to contemporary developments in the coastal Osmore Valley. Serving ware includes nubbed-rim keros in an assortment of variant shapes.

Despite this divergence of local ceramic styles, enough details are shared among Tumilaca Phase pottery to indicate a common cultural heritage and perhaps some continued contact with the altiplano. The main vessel forms—keros, tazones (flaring-sided bowls), and one-handle pitchers—are present in

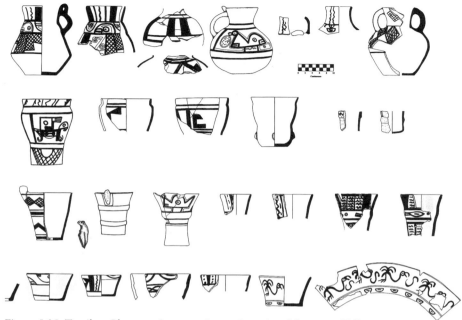

Figure 5.35. Tumilaca Phase serving ceramics, various sites, Moquegua Valley.

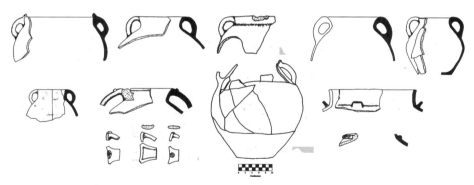

Figure 5.36. Tumilaca Phase plain utilitarian ceramics, various sites.

approximately the same proportions as in the Chen Chen style. This indicates a general continuity in quotidian cultural practice and domestic functions and categories between the two ceramic styles. Continuity is also evidenced by other aspects of Tumilaca Phase material culture. Tumilaca Phase peoples continued the Moquegua Tiwanaku mortuary pattern, domestic architecture continued to use the same wall trench and quincha techniques seen in the

Chen Chen style, and fundamental household patterns remained largely constant. For example, Stanish reports that housing at the Porobaya Valley site of P5 continued in a "normative pattern" of abutting rectangular rooms on terraces, with no tombs in habitations (Bawden 1989:289; Stanish 1992: 114). Throughout the Tumilaca Phase, domestic architecture, burial practices, and cranial deformation seem to indicate the maintenance of ethnic, religious, and symbolic identity with the Tiwanaku tradition even after the disintegration of the Tiwanaku provincial administration.

The Late Intermediate and Inca Periods

Occupation of the middle Moquegua Valley continued to decline following the Tumilaca Phase. The entire Late Intermediate and Inca Period occupation of the MAS survey area never exceeded 28.5 hectares. This represents a significant decline from the scale of occupation during the Tiwanaku era, and even pales in comparison to the Formative occupation of the Huaracane tradition. In part, this retraction may arise from the political realignment of the valley from a series of mutually competitive small villages sharing a common Tiwanaku-derived culture into two distinct and separate settlement groups. The clustering of the settlements of each group at the lower and upper ends of the middle Moquegua Valley correspond to two different cultural affiliations, known as Chiribaya and Estuquiña (fig. 5.37).

Chiribaya was the dominant culture of the coastal Osmore Valley in the Late Intermediate, and the Chiribaya cultural complex extended to the southern valleys of Locumba, Sama, Caplina, and Azapa, where it is also known as the Maytas culture. The early dates for Chiribaya are in dispute, and it is possible that the culture's origins may be contemporary with the Tumilaca Phase or even Tiwanaku V occupations of the middle valley (Rivera Díaz 1991; Lozada and Buikstra 2002). Chiribaya became a major chiefdom in the coastal Osmore Valley, with a dense agricultural population and a large center at the Chiribaya site (Buikstra 1995; Lozada 1998; Owen 1993a,b; Rice 1993). In the middle Moquegua Valley, however, Chiribaya appears to have arrived late and never became a dominant occupation. Chiribaya settlement was limited to twenty-one habitation components and thirteen cemeteries, totaling only 12.9 hectares valleywide. Moreover, almost all of this settlement was confined to the lower end of the middle valley, primarily in the two sites of La Yaral M8 (6.7 hectares) and Ramadón M59 (2.6 hectares).

At approximately the same time, Estuquiña became the dominant culture of the Tumilaca and Torata valleys of the upper Osmore drainage. Estuquiña terraced agricultural systems succeeded and expanded upon the Wari's pioneering use of terraced agriculture in the upper valley (Williams 1997). Exca-

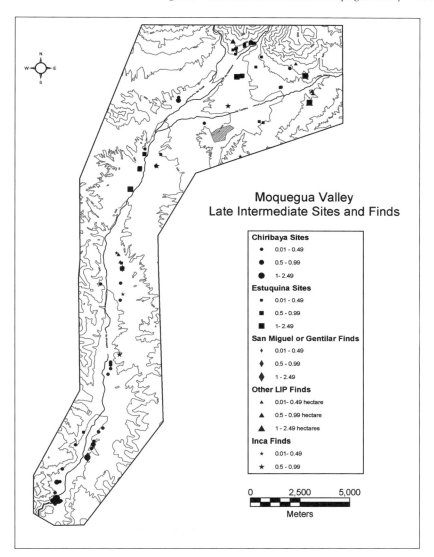

Figure 5.37. Late Intermediate Period settlement map.

vations at several Estuquiña sites indicate a cultural complex of walled sites with agglutinated compounds of stone and quincha architecture and largely undecorated ceramic and textile assemblages that are markedly different in form and function from the Tiwanaku-derived assemblages of Tumilaca Phase sites (Bawden 1993; Conrad 1993; Rice 1993). Systematic survey suggests a settlement system of unprecedented density in the steep valleys at between 2,000 and 3,000 masl (Owen 1994). Stanish (1992) has suggested that these high elevation descendant settlements became the nuclei of new smaller-scale vertical exchange networks. In the middle Moquegua Valley, Estuquiña settlement was considerably more limited, comprising only fourteen habitation sites and twelve cemeteries covering 11.6 hectares in total. These Estuquiña settlements were concentrated in the upper reaches of the middle Moquegua Valley, and many of the larger sites were located on defensible hilltops and surrounded by walls and trenches. Two of the Estuquiña habitation sites included some Inca sherds, suggesting their continuous occupation into the Late Horizon.

The cultural contrast between the Chiribaya and Estuquiña settlements offers one explanation for the overall depopulation of the middle Moquegua Valley following the Tiwanaku collapse. Estuquiña sites in the middle Moquegua were located on inaccessible bluffs and hilltops and heavily defended with walls. Also apparent with the results of the MAS full coverage survey is an unoccupied buffer zone or no-man's-land in the middle stretch of the valley, between most of the Chiribaya and Estuquiña sites.

The vast agricultural terracing projects that supported the upper valley Estuquiña settlements provide a second explanation for the decline of the middle Moquegua. Calculations of the total hydraulic output of the Osmore drainage indicate a limited water budget. It is suggested that high altitude runoff sources are insufficient to water agricultural lands simultaneously in highland terraces, the middle valley floodplain, and the coastal valley (Williams 2002). The enormous water demands of the Estuquiña and Estuquiña-Inca terrace systems upvalley would have strangled the middle Moquegua Valley and severely challenged the water resources of the coastal Osmore as well.

This situation did not change with the advent of Inca control, as the Inca seem to have shown little interest in this highly depopulated zone. There is only a token presence of Inca pottery in most of the middle valley, either as minority presence in Estuquiña sites or at small sites that could be road system *tambos* or messenger stations. Pottery finds by local informants suggest that there may be additional Inca remains beneath modern Moquegua City and the town of Samegua. However, no Inca architecture or Inca cemeteries have yet been located, and the principal focus of Inca efforts appears to have been at the centers like Camata and Torata Alta (T5). Terraced agricultural systems and pasture lands in the Torata and Tumilaca valleys between 2,000 and 3,000 masl remained the primary productive infrastructure for wealth and tribute. The watering of the upper valley terraces turned the once-crucial middle Moquegua Valley into both an agricultural backwater and a political buffer zone between highland and coastal cultures until the Spanish colonial period.

Summary

Settlement pattern studies demonstrate the unique nature of Tiwanaku colonial settlement when compared to other pre-Columbian utilization of the Moquegua Valley. Before Tiwanaku, Huaracane agrarian settlements had developed in place over centuries, creating a continuous landscape of small settlements. Their location indicates that these settlements were organically integrated with small-scale floodplain agriculture. Archaeological evidence shows a nascent social hierarchy, represented by elite access to exotic imports from the Pukara and the Nasca regions and a new minority mortuary tradition of boot-shaped tombs. Although some of these boot tomb cemeteries may have been associated with emerging elite power centers, the absence of one significantly larger primate or ceremonial center suggests that Formative sociopolitical development probably never enfolded the entire valley under a single chiefdom.

In contrast, the settlement pattern of the Tiwanaku colonies indicates that people of exogenous origin came to dominate the valley by occupying a different ecological and social niche. First, the Tiwanaku settlements were all located at previously unoccupied sites without any cultural continuity from the Huaracane tradition. This settlement shift echoes the pattern introduced with Tiwanaku incorporation of the Titicaca basin, where Late Formative sites were often abandoned as more populous political centers were established (Bauer and Stanish 2001:149; Stanish 1999; Stanish et al. 1996). Second, settlements tended to be located at a considerable distance from the floodplain, adjacent to intensive agricultural systems that exploited subterranean springs, extended canals laterally, and brought new fields to desert *pampas*. Third, the Tiwanaku colonies offered no evidence of militarism or defensive works, nor indeed is there evidence of organized conflict. Fourth, virtually all Tiwanaku settlement was physically enclaved at four major midvalley settlement groups at Chen Chen, Omo, Río Muerto, and Echenique. If one of the advantages of full coverage systematic survey is its ability to provide negative evidence, the results of the MAS project confirm a surprising absence of small Tiwanaku villages or hamlets.

Fifth, the settlement patterns of the Tiwanaku colonies were profoundly segmented socially, with residential and cemetery enclaves separated spatially at a variety of levels of scale. This suggests that colonies representing distinct maximal ayllus, moieties, or other segmentary groups operated autonomously within the greater Tiwanaku colony. The coexistence of the Omo and Chen Chen ceramic styles may mark two such overlapping but separate ethnic or cultural spheres. This supports both Murra's archipelago conception of multiethnicity under highland control and interpretations of the Tiwanaku state as a confederation rather than a centralized system. The completely open and undefended nature of all these settlements suggests a powerful consensus of coexistence among these confederated ayllus. It may be significant that the Omo-style occupations were all located to the northeast of adjacent Chen Chen–style settlement clusters. The two groups may even have had structurally complementary roles similar to the binary opposition often noted among indigenous highland societies (e.g., Platt 1986).

This program of tolerance may even have extended to the culturally foreign enclaves of Wari settlers established upvalley of the Tiwanaku colonies in the upper Osmore. However, only one Wari settlement group actually penetrated Tiwanaku's middle valley territory, and that was at a high and defensible location. Even if we accept the contemporaneity of Wari and Tiwanaku settlements in different parts of the same drainage, we may see the limits of multiethnicity in the minimal overlap between the distinct Wari and Tiwanaku settlement patterns.

The end of the Pax Tiwanaku splintered the middle Moquegua Valley towns into smaller mutually hostile settlements. Tumilaca Phase villages were invariably built in defensible locations, sometimes distant from the valley bottom and often with defensive works. Ironically, settlement patterns after the Tiwanaku collapse have more in common with pre-Tiwanaku settlement of the Huaracane than with that of the Tiwanaku state colonies, as settlement dispersed to defensible locations. The process of local chiefly development that had been interrupted for four hundred years began anew from the wreckage of the Tiwanaku system, ultimately producing a realignment of power into two or more dominant señoríos based in the upper valleys of Torata and Tumilaca and the coastal Osmore Valley. Even the advent of Inca control did not restore the middle valley's economic importance, as the Inca limited their administrative presence to the existing coastal and sierra seats of power and economic productivity (Covey 2001; Van Buren 1996).

Although settlement pattern studies can be highly instructive, they provide an incomplete picture of the processes of state integration and the character of colonial populations. Only the analysis of specific archaeological contexts can demonstrate how Moquegua's Tiwanaku settlements worked as communities. Did provincial settlers maintain direct cultural, political, and economic ties to the homeland on the level of the individual household? In mortuary traditions? In public ceremony? And how did these relationships change over time? In the chapters that follow, I demonstrate that Moquegua was populated by people maintaining a direct and enduring identity to altiplano Tiwanaku—people who lived in Tiwanaku houses, worked with Tiwanaku tools, played with Tiwanaku gaming pieces, cooked and carried their water in Tiwanaku pots, worshiped in Tiwanaku temples, and chose to be buried in Tiwanaku clothing when they died.

6

Homes Away from the Homeland

Communities and Households of the Tiwanaku Diaspora

"Estos vecinos son malos, muy malos" (Those neighbors are bad, very bad).

Cecilia Mamani, squatter from Muylaque describing squatters
from Cuchumbaya; Moquegua, 1999

Doña Cecilia's complaint about the neighbors typifies the complexity of establishing a new household in a diasporic setting. Her own experience as a highland colonist in the Moquegua Valley began in a tiny *chosa*, the reed shack she built to claim an unused sliver of desert hillside. Gradually, she brought her younger brothers and their families to Moquegua from their highland village of Muylaque to dig an irrigation canal and cultivate their marginal plots. After fifteen years of struggle, the slopes of Trapiche were green and Doña Cecilia and the Mamanis had turned her pioneering land claim into a going concern.

Suddenly in 1998, however, new *chositas* appeared even higher on the dry hillslopes of Cerro Trapiche. The new colony was from a town near Cuchumbaya, another Aymara-speaking community in the Moquegua highlands. The new squatters hoped to build an ambitious canal to reclaim even more marginal land above the Mamanis. The newcomers' chositas perched directly above the Mamanis' homes, yet the two enclaves kept their distance and inhabitants had little to do with one another. Although they literally spoke the same language and their aspirations and histories were remarkably similar, Doña Cecilia made it clear that the Cuchumbaya colony was an alien and unwelcome presence in the eyes of the Muylaque enclave. While the households of each group maintained strong ties to their own homeland and kin, each group also took pains to segregate itself from its neighbor on the slopes of Trapiche. In diaspora, the Muylaqueños not only maintained their differences from the new colonists but celebrated and accentuated them with harsh glances, closed doors, and separation by an uneasy no-man's-land. The present-day Aymara colonization of Moquegua is no melting pot.

In this chapter, I consider the results of household archaeology in order to evaluate the economic and social organization of Tiwanaku diasporic colonization. The fundamental faith of household archaeology is that the patterns of residence, affiliation, and productive activities in the domestic setting are reliable indicators of a society's mode of economic production and its ethnic and cultural affiliations. Most household archaeology in the Andes has concentrated on the former, focusing on the variable economic integration of nuclear family households into state-level political systems (D'Altroy 1992; D'Altroy and Earle 1985; Stanish 1989). While this perspective has greatly expanded our understanding of Andean states, it is only part of the story that household archaeology has to tell. I argue that in addition, household archaeology can illuminate shared social and political identities that mediated between the household and state. But can household patterns also help to identify the role of cultural identity in shaping diasporas? Or, to put it another way, can the archaeological study of households and communities illuminate the kind of cultural identity through opposition that Doña Cecilia found so compelling?

Households and Archaeology in the South-Central Andes

Following Bourdieu's definition of *habitus* (Bourdieu 1977, 1990), many archaeologists accept that cultural identity and the definition of social relationships are enacted and negotiated through the structured dispositions of material conditions and the repetitive actions of daily practice. Much of daily practice is directly reflected in conscious and unconscious choices made about domestic activities that are in turn reflected in the contexts and assemblages of the archaeological record. Writing of the persistence of Zapotec cultural features in the Tlailotlacan enclave in Teotihuacán, for example, Spence suggests that the use of familiar homeland pottery in the domestic context was a major factor in the maintenance of a beleaguered ethnic identity in a Zapotec barrio. Pottery items "had become instruments of enculturation and visible expressions of conformity, so change in them would have been perceived as a rejection of the community's values and ways" (Spence 1992:74).

In reaction to static structuralist models, however, Bourdieu's theory of practice suggests that actors also actively participate in, reproduce, and transform the culture around them. Household traditions, rules, and conventions are not simply conservative constraints on human agency or some kind of essentialist peasant conservatism. Household practices, like other cultural traditions, can be "enabling" in that they are both the medium and the outcome of the practices they recursively organize (Giddens 1984). This kind of interplay of structure and agency, described by Giddens as "structuration," posits that societal rules can be manipulated as human agents put their structured knowledge into practice. Putting the two concepts together, we see that habitus is socially generative because conscious or unintended acts of production and consumption can either reproduce or transform social structure (Dietler and Herbich 1998:247). Household practices and traditions thus do more than simply reflect cultural affiliations. The household is the only arena in which cultural and social roles are negotiated on a daily basis. It is the fertile soil in which cultural identities take root and from which social change springs.

Simply by their pedestrian nature, then, architecture and archaeological remains found in household contexts have a democratic advantage over remains found in other contexts. Although they tend to be aesthetically unimpressive, household assemblages are numerous and therefore quantifiable. Most important, because domestic contexts represent the casually deposited detritus of daily life, they are far less likely to be biased by exhibitionist intent than are other kinds of contexts. While mortuary offerings and ritual caches produce more impressive artifacts than the lowly household midden, these have the disadvantage of having been deliberately chosen for public or sacred display. Consequently, the contrast between the mundane households and special contexts can highlight differences between an archaeological population's everyday identity, grounded in habitus, and those identities they consciously chose to display. Household archaeology is a window on who ancient people were, instead of who they imagined themselves to be.

Because the household is the fundamental unit of social reproduction, as well as economic production, the physical remains of household residences, or household units, can provide the most reliable archaeological signals of group identity. To demonstrate a diasporic colonization, peripheral habitation sites must first and foremost reflect the immigration of peoples of ethnic identities that are distinct from local populations. The ongoing ethnic relationship of the diasporic household to its homeland counterpart should be recognizable by comparing the domestic assemblages of colony and homeland. The functional and stylistic aspects of artifacts and their domestic context are good indicators of ethnicity because they reflect the minutiae of daily life. Sites with exchange relationships that are ethnically distinct are unlikely to exhibit similarities in domestic architecture and material culture beyond certain classes of exotic artifacts. Sites that are ethnically identical should show similarities in domestic architecture and activity patterning and in both domestic and nondomestic assemblages of material culture (Stanish 1989). To take this further, beyond similarities between individual artifacts, ethnically related colonial and homeland populations should have similar domestic assemblages or functional arrays of domestic material culture. For example, ceramic collections from homeland and diasporic domestic sites should have not only similar ceramic types but also similar ratios of serving to cooking and storage wares, distributions of functional types in different household contexts, and consumption and discard patterns.

The Household and the State

Household archaeology also provides a powerful tool with which to study the integration of communities in larger political economies. Because the household is the fundamental unit of economic production, domestic assemblages indicate the economic and political relations of ancient peoples. The effects of state intervention on the household economic enterprise may be considered in light of how people produce and consume food and make crafts and other material products in their everyday lives. In terms of production, the household is the smallest locus where skills and physical energy are pooled and allocated for agriculture, herding, crafts, and other productive activities. In the pre-Columbian Andes, the household was the social nexus through which reciprocal labor services, gifts, and ceremonial exchanges were coordinated. The nature, intensity, and directness of the integration of a household's material production should thus vary in direct relation to the settlement's incorporation into a state political economy (Bermann 1997:95; Costin 1991). In cases where peripheral peoples were integrated through direct state incorporation or hegemonic indirect control, households should reflect suprahousehold tribute or asymmetrical exchange. Any state bent on overarching control of tribute as suggested by imperial or world systems models would be obliged to articulate the household economy into its own larger political economy. The household's participation as a productive unit in state political economies is variable. According to Chayanov's rule, households will not produce surplus unless coerced by external forces. Evidence of increases in household agricultural and craft production beyond the needs of the household can therefore be interpreted as a marker of increased demands on the household by state or community. The intensified production of craft items or agricultural surplus may be manifest in equipment, tools for bulk processing, expanded storage facilities, production debitage, or botanical remains of larger-scale productive activities in or around the household unit.

Another phenomenon associated with the incorporation of peripheral households into state political economies is the specialization of productive units (regions, sites, neighborhoods, or households) in particular industries. For example, agricultural production might concentrate on a single staple crop of peculiar importance to the state and on the relocation of settlements to new productive zones more suitable for particular cultigens. Settlement pattern shifts suggest that this was a typical concomitant of the incorporation of valleys under Inca land tenure and tribute systems (Bauer 1992:104; D'Altroy 1992:213; Hastorf 1990). Such specialized agricultural production could also be reflected within the household by changes in both processing activities and the local diet. Specialization in household craft production should be evident in changes in the features of tools and changes in production debris related to particular tool assemblages (Costin and Earle 1989; D'Altroy 1992:12; Johnson and Earle 1987). In the case of Inca control of the Mantaro Valley, frequencies of stone hoes, spindle whorls, ceramic wasters, and stone blade production debitage have been used as indices for markers of specialization of agriculture, textile, ceramic, or lithic production (D'Altroy 1992:66, 161).

Household participation in state political economies also often leads to new relations of domestic production. The extraction of tribute from households is not a simple tithing and is often only part of larger patterns of accentuated household inequality under state political economies. Interhousehold status inequalities between elites and commoners may be evident in distinctions between their household structures and contents. Under the Inca, for example, households were the organizing units for reciprocal labor obligations (*mita*) owed to the state (Stanish 1992:26–28, 37). At the same time, changes in domestic production may foster intrahousehold inequalities due to changing gender roles and family structure and even unequal access to food (e.g., Brumfiel 1992; Hastorf 1991:150). For the Sausa society of the Mantaro Valley, a region that had no strong central governance before the Inca conquest, Hastorf notes that previously gender-balanced diet took on gendered patterns under Inca control. Dietary analysis of pre-Inca skeletons showed no gender differences in carbon and nitrogen isotope ratios, suggesting that both sexes participated equally in maize-concentrated feasting, and thus in ritual, community, and political events (Hastorf 1991:150). In contrast, analysis of Inca-contemporary individuals found a marked difference in delta C and delta N values between the sexes, indicating a male diet enriched in maize and meat. Thus, even though *chicha* and other maize foods were probably produced by females, as is ethnographically common in the Andes, Inca-contemporary provincial males enjoyed a significantly enriched access to both products. This suggests that males in provincial households under Inca state control disproportionately enjoyed both ritualized feasting and the political power that implies, even as they disproportionately shouldered the labor tax burden of state tribute (Hastorf 1991: 152; Murra 1982:256).

On the other side of the equation, households more closely associated with state political economies would be greater consumers of manufactured items affiliated with the state core. In pre-industrial political economies, states often distributed finished goods in compensation for household labor or tribute. As households were drawn into state political economies, we would expect increased penetration of imported goods to the level of the household.

The household consumption of Inca-style pottery in Wanka III sites of the Mantaro Valley, for example, has been cited as an index of Inca political and economic control (D'Altroy 1992:213; Earle et al. 1987). Fine Inca-style pottery in the Inca provinces is easily distinguished from local wares and would have been a self-evidently labor-intensive good associated with state power. Access to Inca state pottery varied among provinces and among villages in the same province, with the strongest representation in large settlements with elite residential architecture. Within provincial centers like Hatunmarca, Inca pottery was associated with community sectors containing high status residences (D'Altroy 1992:181, 196–207). The local distribution of Inca state wares thus paralleled the lines of political relationships, reflecting both status and the degree of local integration into the imperial administration.

A second effect of state intervention on household consumption could be increased homogeneity among imports. Specialized production and exchange in state systems could limit the variability of products available in the peripheries. The standardization of imported artifacts produced for peripheral consumption might be accentuated by the limitations of bulk distribution over distance, eliminating heavy, awkward, or delicate items. Even where state-style goods were made locally, the state might mandate the standardization of finished products to distinguish them from local goods (Earle et al. 1987). In either case, increased demand may lead to a streamlining of production processes, eliminating some of the more elaborate artifact variants (Costin 1991; Sinopoli 1991). Thus some of the more idiosyncratic artifact types of the homeland assemblage might not appear in provincial settlements.

The effects of state integration on household consumption may also be evident in dietary change. Despite the gendered inequality already described, the overall population of the Mantaro Valley underwent significant dietary change under Inca state control with a shift to maize cuisine over the tuber crops of their pre-Inca ancestors. At the same time, local access to diverse subsistence commodities may correlate with the efficacy of state integration. During periods of greater regional integration, some household consumers may enjoy access to a greater range of imported foods that assume particular importance as delicacies or as complementary resources. In the Estuquiña-Inca Period in the Otora Valley, for example, abundant marine fishbone found in highland households suggests an improvement of subsistence exchange under Inca indirect control. Noting the complexities of preparing and transporting fish, Stanish (1992:147) correlates this new dietary presence of marine fish with interregional exchange spurred by the advent of social differentiation.

Household Archaeology in the Tiwanaku Core Region

Archaeologists have only recently begun to show interest in the nature of Tiwanaku households and communities in the altiplano homeland. Only at two sites in the core region, Tiwanaku and Lukurmata, have excavations exposed entire household building plans. This small sample is due in part to the depth of the Titicaca basin sites and in part to the priorities placed in the past on monumental exposure or chronological testing. Although the excavated household sample is still limited, the record now shows considerable diversity in architecture and activities in urban sites of the Tiwanaku core region (Bermann 1994, 1997; Janusek 1994, 1999, 2003). Domestic structures normally consisted of adobe walls over stone foundations with floors of packed earth or prepared clay. Informal hearths appear in most habitation rooms. House plans varied, but dispersed unattached single-room household units were typical of earlier occupations. Although circular structures are reported in later levels at Lukurmata, rectangular structures predominated.

Household organization in the Tiwanaku core region appears to have been transformed profoundly as Tiwanaku and Lukurmata grew into urban centers. Distinct community and family groups appear to be represented by the advent of walled domestic compounds in Tiwanaku's Akapana East residential center after A.D. 600 (Janusek 1999). Similar compact patio groups, typically consisting of two domestic structures, a storage building, and subfloor burials, appear at Lukurmata between A.D. 700 and 850. In both cases, it is believed that the reorganization from a minimal household plan into larger compounds corresponds to a modification to family structure that maximized household production under Tiwanaku's "vertical integration" of the region's political economy (Bermann 1994, 1997). It is not inconceivable that Bermann's conception of an increasingly formal template for Tiwanaku patio groups was a distant ancestor of the *kancha*—the building block compound of imperial Inca towns (Hyslop 1990). Both household architectural compound forms may have developed as a backdrop to vertically integrated state tribute.

It is possible to define the highest status residences at Tiwanaku by their elaborate stone architecture. The Tiwanaku palace precincts of Putuni and Kalasasaya were surrounded by a moat to separate them from the rest of the city (Kolata 1993:90). Elite residential complexes have also been identified on the summit of the massive Akapana pyramid (Manzanilla 1992a,b) and possibly in the Akapana East residential district (Janusek 1999). These high status residential precincts support an interpretation of a hierarchical social class structure at Tiwanaku. It is likely that the monumental center of the site was reserved for royal or high status residence, much as was the case with the core of the city of Cusco under the Inca Empire.

There is abundant evidence, however, that status was not the only determinant of residential location in Tiwanaku. In non-elite residential sectors at Tiwanaku, it appears that perimeter walls separated socially and functionally differentiated neighborhoods. This pattern suggests a segmentary social substructure, perhaps with ethnic barrios like those described for Classic Teotihuacán in Mexico. At Tiwanaku, barrios were further subdivided into patio groups. The subdivision of these community sectors suggests that urban Tiwanaku was composed of ayllu-like corporate segments (Albarracin-Jordan 1996a,b; Janusek 1999). Recent excavations at Tiwanaku and Lukurmata also suggest that some of these walled *barrios* corresponded to co-residential craft specialists, foreign ethnic groups, lineages, or ayllus (Janusek 1999, 2003).

Accepting the cosmopolitan nature of the Tiwanaku capital, one question is whether similar community segmentation characterizes settlements in the Tiwanaku periphery. The Moquegua Tiwanaku sites are uniquely suited to address this question because of their extensive surface exposure of architectural remains and artifacts. In what follows, I review the household archaeology at Omo, Chen Chen, and Río Muerto that helps us illuminate community and household patterns of settlement and economy in peripheral Tiwanaku.

Household Archaeology in Moquegua Tiwanaku

Our strategy of domestic archaeology at the Omo, Chen Chen, and Río Muerto site groups was to analyze settlement patterns on the nested levels of town site, community, and household. As discussed in the previous chapter, the Omo-style sites in particular offered a unique opportunity to examine settlement through mapping and surface collections as well as excavation. The sites' brief occupations, surface visibility, and abandonment with only minimal reoccupation and postdepositional disturbance allow us an unusual glimpse into the workings of Tiwanaku towns.

Town and Community Plan

The Moquegua Tiwanaku sites were particularly suited to town and community level analysis because desert conditions have preserved entire town site plans and associated artifact distributions on the surface. The most successful architectural mapping efforts have been at sites where wind erosion has left exposed house platform outlines, providing an unparalleled opportunity to map an entire Tiwanaku town plan. At these sites, notably Omo M11, M12,

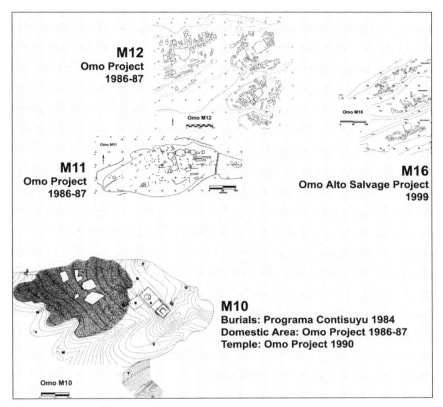

Figure 6.1. Map of Omo site group.

M13 and M16, Chen Chen M1 sectors 14 through 19, and Río Muerto M70, house platforms are partially visible in aerial photographs as lighter-colored rectangles. Field mapping provided ground truth and additional details on structural divisions and hearths within structures.[1] As mapping progressed, certain diagnostic artifacts including projectile points, beads, metal objects, modeled vessel fragments, sherds with incised decorations, and reconstructible vessels were collected as "spot finds."

Because of the surface exposure of artifacts and architecture at the Moquegua Tiwanaku sites, systematic surface collections provide an ideal method for comparing distributions of artifact assemblages within and between sites. Between 1986 and 1998, my Omo and MAS projects surface-collected the Omo, Chen Chen, and Río Muerto site groups in 10 m × 10 m square units located on systematic grids at 50 m intervals. Total surface pickup collections of 432 such units were made, and approximately 127,000 surface sherds were tallied in the field by the MAS team (table 6.1).[2]

Table 6.1 Surface collections at Moquegua Tiwanaku site groups

	Units	Unit size	Areal coverage	Total sherds collected	Average sherd density
Omo M10, M11, M12, M16	204	100 m2	4%	54,149	2.65 / m2
Chen Chen M1	89	50 m2	2%	17,847	5.03 / m2
Rio Muerto M43, M48, M52, M70	139	100 m2	4%	55,429	3.99 / m2
Total	432			127,425	3.89 / m2

My analysis of the systematic surface collections from all three Moquegua Tiwanaku site groups indicates that living space was separated on two levels: into distinct towns and communities. First, a general pattern of segmentation may be discerned between town sites. The maximal level of distinction was between sites of Omo-style and Chen Chen-style affiliation. At the Omo site group, hills and deep canyons divide the town sites of M10 and M11 from the Omo-style sites of M12, M13, and M16 (fig. 5.16). Artifacts at these adjacent sites are stylistically distinct; that is, the Chen Chen ceramic style of M10 is distinguishable from the Omo style of M12, M13, and M16. The coexistence of towns with each of the two styles of Tiwanaku material culture suggests that neighboring towns were populated by distinct ethnic groups within Tiwanaku. As discussed in chapter 5, town sites of each ethnicity within each of the Tiwanaku site groups consistently group on opposite sides of a northwest-southeast axis.

The second level of community segregation is evident within many of these town site components. Typically, artifact density mapping and surface indications show community habitation areas separated by no-man's-land areas—devoid of material culture—even when no topographical boundaries were present. Many Tiwanaku town sites also include multiple spatially distinct cemetery sectors. This segregation appears to be the pattern for habitation sites as well. Within both M12 and M16, the two Omo sites with the best-preserved town plans, housing is clustered in distinct community sectors arrayed around common plazas (fig. 5.16). Unlike the broad stylistic distinctions noted between Omo- and Chen Chen–style town sites, these community and cemetery sectors share common artifact styles. More subtle variations in the artifact assemblages point to distinctions in function and status among community groups within each town. Ravines separate many of these neighborhoods, but it is notable that the north and west communities of M12 are

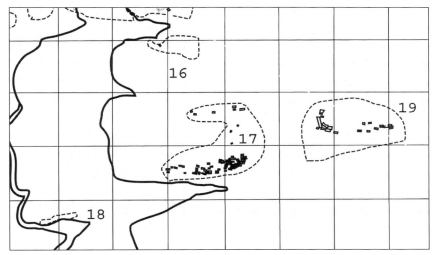

Figure 6.2. Map of Chen Chen M1, suburban sectors 16–19, showing domestic structure platforms.

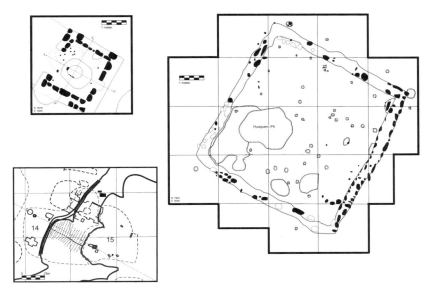

Figure 6.3. Map of Chen Chen M1, ceremonial sectors 14 and 15, showing ceremonial structures 14-1 and 15-1.

located on a perfectly flat bluff top, yet separated by a wide area with no architecture or artifact scatter. This confirms that the separation of community groups within Tiwanaku towns was by social intent rather than topographical accident.

Similar levels of town and community segregation are evident at the Chen Chen M1 site among the three most intensively occupied habitation areas (Sectors 11, 12, and 13) and between these and a series of low-density habitation sectors far to the east of the site (Sectors 16 through 19; figs. 5.17, 6.2). Extensive intervening areas devoid of cultural material indicate that these sectors were socially segregated from the main settlement. It is possible that these lightly occupied "suburban" areas were for seasonal visitors, individuals of different ethnicities, or transients associated with the adjacent caravan route to Omo to the south and the altiplano to the north (Bandy et al. 1996). However, unlike Omo, the Chen Chen site group does not demonstrate a gross stylistic distinction between town sites, as all habitation areas share Chen Chen–style pottery. Instead, ceramic distributions suggest spatial distinctions that are functional and status-related. For example, lower densities of utilitarian and serving ceramics combined with a high incidence of *incensarios* (incense burners) characterizes Sectors 14 and 15, indicating specialized ritual activities within these areas.

Figure 6.4. Río Muerto M70 sector A, unit 6 before excavation. PSG photo.

At the Río Muerto site group, social divisions are also evident in the site layout and the surface distribution of ceramics and other artifacts. Ceramic density coincided with the field survey's site divisions of sites M43, M48, M52, and M70, suggesting distinct and segregated town sites (figs. 5.18, 6.4). Site M70 has an Omo-style ceramic assemblage, while M43, M48, and M52 have Chen Chen–style assemblages. Extensive areas void of architecture or artifacts separate these habitation areas. Assuming the four sites are contemporary, this suggests an intentional spatial division among social or ethnic groups within the Tiwanaku colony at the Río Muerto group as well. At least two distinct Tiwanaku communities may be discerned within the M70 site. One of these, M70C, a small area to the south of the M70A residential sector, was characterized by a minority of Wari Chakipampa–style ceramic fragments and dense lithic production material. As is discussed later in this chapter, this suggests a situation similar to the socially distinct foreign-connected communities of crafts workers noted by Janusek at Tiwanaku.

Household Units in the Tiwanaku Colonies

On the face of it, there seems to be little resemblance between domestic structures of the Tiwanaku core region and the houses of the Moquegua colonies. Lowland Tiwanaku settlers used cane wattle-and-daub walls and timber post construction rather than adobe in most houses. The climate difference between the cold rainy altiplano and the desert Moquegua Valley may explain the differences in building materials and features. More important to the study at hand is what Tiwanaku domestic architecture can tell us about the cultural affiliation of its builders and occupants and what the evolution of the Tiwanaku household reveals about Tiwanaku social, political, and economic systems.

To compare structure, form, and content among household units at the Moquegua Tiwanaku sites, we selected representative domestic structures at Omo, Chen Chen, and Río Muerto for excavation.[3] Excavation strategy targeted better-preserved structures in the hope of obtaining a representative sample of architectural plans and subsurface. At Omo M11, M12, and M16, and at Río Muerto M70, house clearings mapped in surface survey helped guide the selection of structures for excavation. Elsewhere, the ephemeral nature of Moquegua Tiwanaku houses left few surface landmarks for architecture before excavation. At Omo M10, Chen Chen M1, and Río Muerto M43, site disturbance made definition of house plan impossible prior to excavation, and selection of test locations was arbitrary. At all sites, structure excavations advanced in a cardinal grid of 2 m × 2 m squares, which included exterior as well as interior space, and all excavated fill was screened through a quarter-inch-mesh screen.[4]

The ephemeral nature of the Omo architecture necessitated excavation in an arbitrary grid, a policy that had two indirect benefits. First, grid excavation forced a wider scope of excavation than the house buildings themselves, lessening the risk of missing ephemeral outbuildings, middens, and other features of the "household cluster." Second, at least in the case of M11 and M12, the absence of standing stone walls may have minimized secondary deposition of postoccupational trash. Indeed, abandoned stone or adobe buildings serve for a long time as convenient trash containers, and few archaeological household contexts accurately reflect true "primary deposits" (Schiffer 1987:58, 74). In the archaeology of stone and adobe household structures, the upper fill of a locus seldom has a direct relationship with the original function of the locus. In contrast, *quincha* (cane-walled) and other ephemeral domestic buildings do not remain standing long after abandonment, and thus their fill may more accurately reflect actual room activities.

Deposits were shallow, and most domestic structures at the Omo-style sites were covered by deposits less than 15 cm in depth. Often, much of the soil matrix had blown away, leaving a palimpsest of sherds and lithic material on the surface and preserved subsurface pit features. Only at Omo M10, Chen Chen M1 sectors 11 and 12, and Río Muerto M43 was there sufficient midden depth and stratigraphy to indicate superposition of floors or features. Excavated levels followed such cultural layers whenever possible. As soon as walls or other within-structure spatial divisions became apparent, "rooms" were numbered sequentially and analyzed independently within each structure. Features included pits, postholes, hearths, in-situ vessels, special offering contexts, and storage bins; these were likewise numbered sequentially and treated as separate cultural contexts. Human burials were also considered as features; however, no human burial was ever found in domestic area excavations at Omo, Chen Chen, or Río Muerto.

Moquegua Tiwanaku houses often featured unlined subfloor pits. These were usually intrusions into the light-brown or orange sterile subsoil, filled with organic silty fill. Following the distinction between "trash pits" and "trash-filled pits" (Schiffer 1987), it is unclear whether any of these pits contained fill related to their original use. Subfloor pit features were artifact traps for residual primary refuse and "loss refuse"—household debris, artifacts that escape from sweeping, and lost items. For this reason, pit feature fill was considered to correlate with floor fill in determining room function and activities. All feature fill was fine screened and soil samples were collected.

The most important element of household archaeology is the careful contextual study of house and room contents in tandem with architecture and features. Artifacts were analyzed in order to characterize houses, rooms, and activity areas through comparison of their collected lots. After artifacts were cleaned, cataloged, and curated, they were drawn and photographed for qualitative comparative analysis. Ceramic, faunal, lithic, botanic, or-

Table 6.2 Excavated sherd frequencies by ware at Moquegua Tiwanaku sites

	Tiwanaku Plainware		Tiwanaku Redware		Tiwanaku Blackware		Wari		Total
Omo M12	17,590	91.66%	867	4.52%	734	3.82%	0	0.00%	19,191
Rio Muerto M70[a]	5,168	98.01%	72	1.37%	10	0.19%	23	0.44%	5,273
Omo M10	21,749	89.48%	2,492	10.25%	66	0.27%	2	0.01%	24,307
Chen Chen M1	15,418	88.21%	1,997	11.43%	63	0.36%	1	0.01%	17,478
Rio Muerto M43	5,058	98.50%	76	1.48%	1	0.02%	0	0.00%	5,135
Omo M11	3,960	81.20%	917	18.80%	0	0.00%	0	0.00%	4,877

a. Wari ceramics are from M70 sector C excavations.

ganic, and textile collections were assigned binomial specimen numbers and coded to facilitate concatenation and sorting.[5] All ceramics were sorted into utilitarian plainware (storage and cooking vessel sherds) and redware and blackware serving categories (table 6.2). The relative frequency of these ware categories proved useful in defining room functions and activity areas, and utilitarian and serving ware frequencies were comparable with those in published reports from the Titicaca basin (Alconini 1995; Bennett 1934, 1936; Rydén 1957). To refine this basic tally, we have begun a sherd-by-sherd diagnostic coding system on a sample of diagnostic sherds to permit statistical analysis of functional type distributions, vessel size, and stylistic frequencies. We also separated a small sample of sherds for thin section petrography to compare them to Bolivian and other Tiwanaku pottery (Barnett 1991).

House and Community in the Omo-Style Sites

Settlements characterized by ceramics of the Omo style mark the onset of Tiwanaku's long dominion in Moquegua. The Omo style saw the earliest introduction to Moquegua of Tiwanaku architecture, town plans, and material culture that indicate direct residence by colonists affiliated with the altiplano civilization. Domestic activities introduced to Omo by these settlers directly reflected the political and social order of Tiwanaku's earliest productive colonies in the western sierra.

Among the Omo M12 and M16 and Río Muerto M70 sites, Omo-style houses shared a consistent range of floor plans and construction techniques. Although there is no standing architecture, each of these sites is distinguished by surface scatters of ceramics and wind-deflated plazas and house platforms distinguishable in air photos as rectangular lighter-colored areas. On surface examination, these are silty areas that were cleared of the patinated small stones of the natural desert pavement. These darker stones were removed from the house sites and plazas and mounded in low piles along their borders. In the structures excavated at Omo M12 in 1986 and 1987 by the Omo project, and at Río Muerto M43 in 1998, surviving lines of wooden post foundations paralleled the inner boundaries of these cleared house platforms, permitting us to generalize about house construction and layout. Subsequent excavations of Omo-style houses at Omo Alto M16 in 1999 and at Río Muerto M70 have confirmed these generalizations on plan and construction details.

Omo-style houses were built with frameworks of closely spaced thin posts.[6] These posts averaged only 3 to 5 cm in diameter and were spaced at intervals of between 60 and 70 cm. The walls must have been suspended from this skeletal framework, which also supported the roof. Wall panels may have consisted of woven vegetable-fiber mats, textiles, or skins. Without substantial wall trenches, foundations, or roof posts, dwellings of the Omo style might be considered more like tents than houses. This contrasts sharply with the more permanent quincha (cane wattle and mud daub) houses of the other Tiwanaku settlement sectors at Omo, which had nonload-bearing cane walls with independent roof structures supported by heavy posts. Floors were generally compacted earth, although evidence from Omo M12 and Río Muerto M70 suggests that some Omo-style rooms may have had prepared clay floors. Their tentlike construction suggests temporary residence by people who regarded themselves as having primary homes as elsewhere. Although it appears that Omo-style houses were designed to house families for short periods of time, the extraordinary ceramic density at some Omo-style sites suggests intensive long-term use. This situation could correspond either to frequent periodic returns or to a single long-term occupation of a village site by a group with a pastoralist architectural tradition.

Houses at the M12 site consisted of from two to eight contiguous rectangular rooms, usually arranged linearly. Structures at M16 and M70 tended to be similar, though often consisting of fewer rooms. Unfortunately, although room divisions were readily apparent, it was seldom possible to determine access patterns. Mounds of removed stones completely separated some rooms, suggesting that there may have been narrow spaces between walls rather than shared party walls. Household facilities and artifacts indicate that all structures were primarily domestic units for cooking, eating, and sleeping and household productive activities. Most rooms had one or two hearths. These were simple shallow fire pits on the ground, contained with two or three large stones visible on the surface. A similar range of activities was represented in most rooms, and no obvious facilities identified any single-activity spaces. However, higher frequencies of plainware ceramic storage and cooking vessels and organic and faunal remains in some rooms suggest that food preparation may have been concentrated in one room in each structure (Goldstein 1989a:131). This may imply a more extended family group, rather than small autonomous nuclear families.

Household Consumption and Tiwanaku Cultural Identity

Tiwanaku's earliest peripheral colonial villages were first and foremost agricultural settlements, but the available evidence suggests a less specialized subsistence strategy than that of the Chen Chen style. Botanical and faunal remains in each of the Omo-style communities indicate a diet based on maize, beans, pumpkins, and squashes, with limited evidence of *quinoa*, tubers, and hot peppers. In contrast to Chen Chen–style sites, Omo-style maize cobs were smaller and appear in only 28 percent of macrobotanical samples. The Omo-style sites produced *manos* and *metates* only of a flat "push-pull" variety associated with general domestic use. The absence of storage or processing infrastructure for needs beyond those of the household suggest primarily domestic production and at most a limited surplus production of cultigens for export to the altiplano. As compared with Huaracane settlements, Omo-style sites may have emphasized camelid herding, but the faunal density appears to be lower than that of the Chen Chen–style sites. This could represent the incidental slaughter of caravan llamas rather than intensive herding, or it might imply that animals, like their Omo-style pastors, may have been seasonally transhumant. The small number of Omo-style burials makes it impossible to assess Omo diet directly from isotopic dietary analysis of human skeletons at this date. Archaeobotanical and faunal remains suggest a household economy dependent on maize in combination with a mixed group of cultigens, a moderate amount of camelid and other meat, and no significant access to coastal resources.

The Omo evidence suggests that maritime access was not the major factor in Tiwanaku expansion. The Middle Moquegua Valley's location, 90 km from the littoral, places it beyond the range of direct maritime exploitation, and investigations on the coast indicate that this economic niche was already occupied by peoples of a specialized coastal tradition. The absence of Tiwanaku state settlements on the littoral suggests that Tiwanaku access to coastal resources must have been through trade with these indigenous specialists or intermediaries. The tenuous nature of coastal contacts for Omo-style Tiwanaku colonists is demonstrated by the absence of marine mollusks from the M12, M16, and M70 settlements. Virtually all of the marine shell found at these sites was olive shell (*Oliva peruvianus*), a species used for adornment rather than subsistence. This contrasts the Tiwanaku settlers with indigenous Huaracane Phase agriculturalists, whose diet included a significant maritime component (Sandness 1992). The contrast indicates that the Omo-style Tiwanaku colonists had no reliable access to coastal subsistence resources.

Artifact assemblages from the Omo-style household contexts indicate that an effective system of exchange between the Moquegua midvalley and altiplano Tiwanaku was in place by late Tiwanaku IV. An impressive quantity of Tiwanaku fine serving pottery was found in domestic contexts at Omo-style sites, constituting 10 percent of the excavated household sherd count. The Omo-style ceramic assemblage tends to emphasize the smaller and less elaborate vessel forms of the Tiwanaku core region. Petrographic analysis supports the attribution of the mineralogy and technology of the Omo redwares to the Titicaca basin (Barnett 1991). This suggests a limited assemblage of vessels selected for export to colonial consumers by altiplano ceramic workshops, or at least the local preparation of clays and vessels by Tiwanaku-trained potters.

The high proportion of blackware, which comprised nearly half of the fine serving ware inventory at Omo M12, also differs markedly from Tiwanaku, where redware predominates and blackware is rare. Blackware may be a regional as well as a temporal marker for Tiwanaku ceramic trade. Mineralogical examination of Omo-style blackware showed it to differ in composition from the redware, suggesting separate sources of manufacture (Barnett 1991). Adolph Bandelier's excavated collections from Ciriapata and other Tiwanaku cemeteries on the Island of the Sun include numerous blackware vessels, and blackware is common in Tiwanaku collections from the Copacabana area. The blackware phenomenon appears to represent a limited stylistic subgroup within Tiwanaku ceramics, with a distribution that included the southwestern Titicaca basin and the Moquegua Valley. This appears to be a key marker separating the Omo-style from the Chen Chen–style assemblages and could represent distinct trade networks and stylistic preferences consonant with distinct ethnicities within the larger Tiwanaku polity.

Standard household furnishings at the Omo-style settlements included ceramic vessels often thought of as ceremonial in nature, such as kero drinking goblets for maize beer, and a smaller number of zoomorphic incensarios, vessels believed to have been used for burning offerings. Other ritual paraphernalia, such as pigments used for face painting, altiplano flamingo feathers, and metal objects of adornment and jewelry, were also represented in many houses (fig. 6.5). Some of the most valuable imported Tiwanaku-style objects were found cached in contexts of household dedicatory rituals. One silver *tupu* (brooch pin) found in M12 Structure 7, had been intentionally "killed" and torn into three separate pieces, each of which was carefully rolled up and buried beneath the entryway of the house.[7] Such extravagant destruction of imported wealth suggests that households participated fully in Tiwanaku's exchange system and ceremonial practices. Imported material

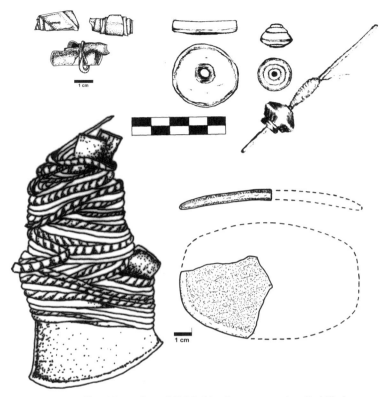

Figure 6.5. Small artifacts, Omo M12 habitation sectors: ritually killed *tupu*, camelid mandible tool, ceramic sherd polisher, spindle whorls, reconstruction drawing.

symbols used in dedicatory rituals were important to the maintenance of a Tiwanaku cultural identity in the Moquegua colonies.

One everyday example of the identity-affirming nature of household practices in structuring habitus is a peculiarly Tiwanaku hafted bone tool fashioned of a camelid mandible (fig. 6.5). The working edges of these mandible tools were the polished surfaces of dense bone left by snapping the toothed section off from the mandible ramus. Although the function of these idiosyncratic Tiwanaku household tools is unknown, the identity of the Moquegua mandible tools to altiplano ones from Tiwanaku and Lukurmata is manifest (Bermann 1994:188–189; Janusek 1993:15, 1999; Webster 1989). Assuming that these items had a specific function, this indicates a commonality in technology and ordinary domestic activities. However, especially because camelid mandible tools have never been reported outside Tiwanaku cultural contexts, it also means rather more. It has been noted that the intensely tactile and personal connection of tools to their users creates a world of meaning and a powerful link to ancestors, community, and society (e.g., Dietler and

Herbich 1998; Spector 1996). The acts of making these tools, learning to use them, using them, and even just having them around the house from child-hood, amidst a myriad of small signs, sights, and smells of everyday actions could be among the most powerful reminders and signposts of Tiwanaku identity.

The reproduction of identity through quotidian material culture is most striking in the everyday cooking and storage plainware vessels that account for over 90 percent of excavated sherds in Omo-style domestic contexts. Apparent differences in paste and temper suggest that these vessels, unlike the decorated redware and polished blackware serving vessels, were probably not direct imports from altiplano Tiwanaku. Nonetheless, the Omo-style plainwares display a formal, technical, and functional identity with altipl-ano Tiwanaku prototypes such as those collected by Bennett and Rydén at the type site, indicating their manufacture by Tiwanaku-trained ceramicists for the needs of Tiwanaku consumers. The absence of Huaracane Phase sherds or of any non-Tiwanaku plainware forms at the Omo-style sites pre-cludes the integration of any local groups and strengthens the image of daily culinary practices and customs derived from Tiwanaku.

In sum, there is no indication of within-site cultural or ethnic diversity that would suggest a contemporary non-Tiwanaku population component at the Omo-style sites. Instead, a consistency in house form and structure and in both the sumptuary and mundane aspects of the domestic material inventory imply shared concepts of household organization and, presumably, common ethnicity with altiplano Tiwanaku. As we shall see, the Omo-style sites may represent colonies of one of several ethnicities or maximal ayllus coexisting within the greater Tiwanaku polity, each distinguished by distinctive ceramic styles. Even within sites that shared the Omo style, household level evidence from systematic surface collections and excavation supports the physical segmentation of these sites and suggests several important social differences among their component communities.

Crafts and Trade in Moquegua Tiwanaku Households

Beyond family subsistence and household ritual activities, there is evidence of household craft production throughout the Omo-style settlements. Textile preservation was poor, but unspun camelid wool, spun threads, and tools such as cactus spine needles and ceramic spindle whorls were found in most rooms of all structures. This suggests that spinning and other textile work were universal activities in all parts of the community. This universality of household wool textile production activities reinforces the prominent role of pastoralism in the Omo-style Tiwanaku colonies. At the same time, there is no evidence of cotton textile production in the Omo-style sites. This contrasts with the processing of both wool and cotton textiles in the Chen

Chen–style settlements, supporting some economic distinction between the two groups.

Most lithic production at the Moquegua Tiwanaku sites took place in the household. This is in keeping with the household production of basalt hoes and chipped-stone tools at the Tiwanaku type site (Giesso 2000, 2003). However, certain households or neighborhoods appear to have specialized in more skilled lithic production like the production of arrow points and lapidary work. Specialized craft workshop activities are evident from surface collections and excavations at the Omo-style sites. At Omo M12's west community, 1986 investigations of the Omo project discovered fish vertebrae, shark teeth, and worked marine shell, primarily drilled and sawn fragments of *Oliva peruvianus*, and a number of reworked ceramic sherds that had been ground into rectangular and oval-shaped tools (fig. 6.5). These appear to indicate that one community group specialized in lapidary production.

Obsidian, Lithic Crafts, and the Wari–Tiwanaku Interface

A small household obsidian workshop at Omo M16 may shed some light on a link between community craft specialization and the exchange of exotic materials with non-Tiwanaku partners. Concentrations of obsidian flakes in M16 Structure 4 suggest that obsidian reduction took place in one household in habitation sector C. Analysis of the obsidian debitage indicates mostly fine pressure retouch or bifacial thinning and the production of stemmed micropoints. These obsidian micropoints, found in small numbers throughout the Tiwanaku sites, were fashioned from flakes measuring well under 2 cm in length and appear to be a variation on the longer white chert stemmed points that dominate the Tiwanaku assemblage. Their rarity and small size attest to the rarity of obsidian generally in Tiwanaku contexts. In the M16 Structure 4 workshop, the absence of raw material with cortex and a number of broken biface fragments further suggest the possibility that larger obsidian tools rather than raw nodules were being reworked to produce these micropoints. One large laurel-shaped point found in sector B to the south is of a Wari type. This indicates the reduction of obsidian preforms or even finished Wari bifaces by specialized households in the Tiwanaku colonies. It is possible that this material was obtained through indirect trade, pillage, or curation of small quantities of raw material or finished pieces from Cerro Baúl. However, the M16 habitation area also produced several bowls of the Qosqopa style, a Wari style from Arequipa. This suggests that the Tiwanaku colonists obtained obsidian and ceramics together through interaction with Wari traders.

A larger Tiwanaku lithic workshop associated with Wari Chakipampa and Ocros-style ceramics was discovered adjacent to the main domestic sector of the Río Muerto M70 site in 1998. Sector C is a workshop area of intensive lithic production of Moquegua Tiwanaku-style arrow points from chert preforms. Here we found dense concentrations of white chert flakes, point preforms, broken points, hammerstones, and a deer antler chipping tool (fig. 6.6). Low numbers of finished points compared to the high quantity of lithic debitage indicate that this was a workshop producing finished projectile points for distribution in the Tiwanaku colony. The high proportion of fine retouch flakes to cortex flakes and cores suggests that raw material was quarried and reduced elsewhere in the valley and brought to this workshop for final finishing by specialists.[8] We also found fragments of several imported vessels of Wari Chakipampa style in the M70C workshop. These are some of the few Chakipampa imports yet found at any of the Tiwanaku sites, and their association with lithic manufacture is striking considering the parallel evidence from Omo M16.

These rare points of contact between Wari and Tiwanaku may be explicable in the context of a special trade network for the strategic material obsidian. While both Wari and Tiwanaku used obsidian, the Wari industry is much more impressive in the quantity, size, elaboration, and source diversity of obsidian artifacts. Locally, at Cerro Baúl, the excavators have found over 150 large and small points, knives, "micropoints," and large quantities of debitage. Moreover, Wari obsidian lithic production at Cerro Baúl seems to have been an almost ubiquitous household activity, occurring in residential, administrative, and ceremonial areas (Williams et al. 2001).

Although obsidian was prized as a raw material in the Tiwanaku lithic tradition, there were no sources of the volcanic glass closer than 200 km from the type site. As a result, imported obsidian was a rare and exotic material in the core region, accounting for less than 1 percent of lithic debris and artifacts recovered in systematic surface collections at Tiwanaku (Giesso 2003:365). Obsidian imported from the Cotallalli source, near Chivay in the Colca Valley in Arequipa, dominated the Tiwanaku site's obsidian assemblage. Cotallalli-Chivay obsidian, which tends to be transparent, accounted for 90 percent of the obsidian found at Tiwanaku and in the core region (Brooks and Giesso 1997; Burger 2000; Giesso 2003:368). From the dominance of this single source in the core region, Giesso concludes that the Tiwanaku state held a monopoly on obsidian procurement (2003:382). It is notable that this source is located in an area likely to have been under Wari control (Jennings and Yepez 2001; Malpass 2001).

Obsidian finds at Moquegua Tiwanaku sites are similarly rare and normally limited to extremely small points and utilized flakes. Surprisingly, however, obsidian from the Cotallalli source near Chivay was not the dominant type in a neutron activation analysis of eight obsidian flakes from the Omo sites. The Omo obsidian represents four distinct sources, a remarkable diversity, considering the small numbers and colonial nature of this settlement.

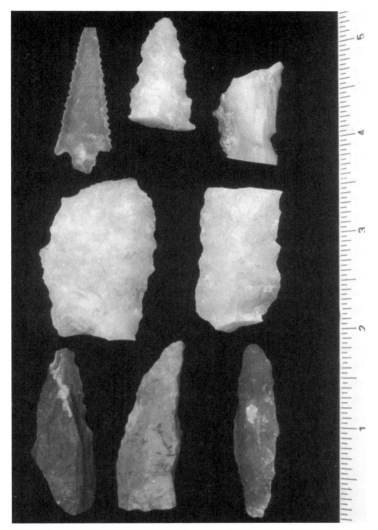

Figure 6.6. Lithic raw materials, preforms, and points, Río Muerto M70 sector C.

The Cotallalli-Chivay source was represented by only two samples from a household context at Omo-style site M12.[9] The remaining six fragments were sourced to the Alca (two), Andahuaylas A (three), and Quispisisa (one) sources.[10] All of these sources are located considerably farther within Wari territory and are seldom represented in obsidian from the Tiwanaku core region (Burger et al. 2000:338; Giesso 2003:369). This nexus suggests that the Tiwanaku colonies, unlike the core region, may have enjoyed a direct and independent interface with diverse obsidian sources deep within Wari territory.

What could account for this connection? It is possible that Wari entrepreneurs set up workshops in the Tiwanaku colonies. Foreign-affiliated enclaves of craft specialists have been suggested for Lukurmata and at the Tiwanaku site (Janusek 1999) and similar patterns are possible in colonial Tiwanaku towns like Omo M16 and Río Muerto M70C. However, there is no evidence beyond a small number of decorated Wari vessels and obsidian to indicate that households of an ethnically foreign group lived within the Tiwanaku colonies. In the absence of a full domestic assemblage, it is difficult to argue for even a small presence of Wari migrants. Alternatively, Moquegua Tiwanaku knappers may have obtained the material either through trade or marriage alliances with Wari counterparts. An ayllu of Tiwanaku knappers could have cultivated trade partners deep within the Wari sphere. Or perhaps Tiwanaku knappers simply curated raw material or finished pieces from abandoned Wari sites in Moquegua. In either case, Wari pottery does not seem to have been a status signifier within the Moquegua Tiwanaku domestic context. Instead Wari imports in Tiwanaku households had a specific association with lithic craftspeople. Their demand for obsidian may have constituted one of Wari and Tiwanaku's few interfaces across a tense cultural boundary.

Elites and Tavern Keepers—Elite Households in the Omo Sites?

If the various plaza-centered communities of the Omo-style sites reflect social divisions in the Tiwanaku town plan, evidence suggests a status of paramount, or at least *primus inter pares*, for the Omo M12 south community. Circumscribed by topographic features, the south community appears noticeably more congested than the other communities, and the corners of some of the structures appear to overlap, suggesting crowding and the reuse of buildings. The public architectural features of the south community's plaza and its associated infrastructure also suggest more care and elaboration than the irregular circular open spaces of the other community plazas. The south plaza itself is considerably smaller than those of the other communities, and more care is evident in its rectilinear layout. The plaza is also flanked by three smaller subsidiary courtyards bounded by low stone bench structures.

The higher frequency of the most elaborate ceramic vessels is the strongest indication that residents of the south community enjoyed privileged status. In the north and west communities, fine Tiwanaku IV decorated redware and polished blackware ceramic vessels were limited to a few vessels per household and seldom included the most elaborate types. The most elaborate vessel found was a wooden kero buried in Structure 7 (fig. 6.7). In contrast, the south community enjoyed greater frequencies of fine serving wares and nearly exclusive access to several of the most elaborate Tiwanaku artifacts, such as modeled zoomorphic figures and portrait head ceramic vessels (figs. 6.8, 6.9).[11]

This disproportionate distribution of the most elite ceramic categories

Figure 6.7. Wooden *kero*, M12 Structure 7, M12=3152.

Figure 6.8. Zoomorphic blackware vessels, Omo M12 south community surface (top) and Titin Uayani, Island of the Sun, Bandelier Collection, AMNH. PSG photos.

Figure 6.9. Ceramic *kero*, M12 site, south community sector.

was further emphasized by at least six specific drinking vessel types uniquely found at specific locations in the south community.[12] The excavation of M12 Structure 2, a small two-room building, exemplifies these and demonstrates the uniqueness of these specific ceramic types to certain elite residences (fig. 6.10). The remarkable nature of the artifacts and features in Structure 2 qualitatively distinguishes this otherwise undistinguished house from other purely domestic buildings at the site. Some twelve polished blackware portrait vessels point to this small structure's special significance as the location of ritual beverage consumption (fig. 6.11). These remarkably naturalistic vessels seem to represent actual personages and appear to be the work of a single artisan or shop.[13] The spatial distribution of these portrait vessels suggests that they were part of a "use assemblage" associated with functions exclusive to M12 Structure 2, and not an offering cache.

Many of the portrait head vessel fragments were associated with three very large plainware vessels that had been cemented in place in Structure 2 (fig. 6.12). These vessels had at their bases deposits of dark organic sediment that appeared to be the dregs from *chicha*, or maize beer. Ceramic reconstruc-

Figure 6.10. Omo M12 Structure 2 excavation. PSG photo.

Figure 6.11. Polished blackware portrait head vessels, M12 Structure 2 excavation. PSG photo.

tion indicates that the vessels each held up to 90 liters, a capacity far beyond any imaginable demand of a two-room household. Thus, certain houses of M12's south community were well equipped for ceremony with large vessels for brewing and storing quantities of maize beer and elaborate sets of

Figure 6.12. Plainware *chomba* filled with feasting debris, M12 Structure 2 excavation. PSG photo.

matched drinking vessels. Additional finds in Structure 2 included a puma-headed incensario, an unusual quantity of red ochre pigment, and M12's only preserved examples of coca leaves. Collectively, this household assemblage suggests a ceremonial *chichería* or household tavern for the brewing and ritual serving of maize beer.

Analogy with historic and contemporary Aymara communities suggests that the hosting of *ch'alla* (libation) rituals can be critical to economic, social, and political relations. Such ritual hospitality seldom entails permanent formal officeholding and can be fluid over time (Abercrombie 1986; Buechler and Buechler 1971; Platt 1980). Thus the household-based rituals of the Omo style may have been sponsored or presided over by elite yet informally selected male community leaders. These commensal rites solidified Omo-style ayllus' articulation with their lineage or moiety ties in altiplano Tiwanaku without the intervention of a permanent priestly or administrative class. Nonetheless, the patrons of ritual events in the Andes, through their mastery of esoteric knowledge and managerial experience, tend to assume powerful political roles. In his explication of K'ulta Aymara ch'alla rituals, Abercrombie has described how a ritual's sponsor "takes the place of the gods in provisioning bounty," giving specific form to the relations of social production (Abercrombie 1986:164).

Must a centralized state play a major role in the sponsorship of these feasts of bounty? To help us imagine how the tavern houses of the south community were used, we can consider chicherías in other Andean contexts. Moore (1989) discusses in detail what he learned about chicha production at the Chimu site of Manchan. The Chimu were a state-level society and Moore expected evidence for sequestered specialist producers, perhaps like the Inca *mamakuna* or the male *chicheros* reported for the central coast. Instead, chicha production at Manchan took place in nonspecialized social contexts, similar to the household production in ayllu communities described in ethno-historic accounts (Moore 1989:691). The intensity of household chicha production varied considerably from house to house at Manchan. One household, for example, had a production capacity of 513 liters, a supply Moore estimates sufficient for 171 people; more than enough to meet household needs (Moore 1989:688). However, equipment was widely distributed throughout Manchan's residential barrios, and there was no evidence of specialized institutional settings for chicha production.

At Omo M12, the context of similar facilities and objects suggests that some elite houses doubled as chicherías for their community. While domestic functions are evident in their otherwise undistinguished houses, these Tiwanaku households hosted events of ritualized hospitality. Indeed, the naturalistic portrait vessels found in M12 Structure 2 suggest that aspects of the Tiwanaku ideology reified power relationships at the community level. Each of the M12 portrait head drinking vessels depicts a turbaned figure with the characteristic *piqchu* or bulging cheek of a coca quid—most likely an allusion to both the individual's rank and access to the precious leaf. Moquegua's Tiwanaku citizens were invited to drink, literally as well as figuratively, the maize beer flowing from the head of a coca-chewing authority. This is in keeping with the "feasts and drinking bouts" that several scholars have suggested accompanied the redistribution of goods as essential mechanisms of state provincial administration in other Andean states (e.g., Isbell 1987; Isbell and Cook 2002; Morris 1986).

The fact that Omo M12's chicherías were also homes, given the absence of any public buildings of entirely "governmental" nature, suggests that administrative mechanisms above the level of informal community leadership were absent from the Moquegua Tiwanaku colonies of the Omo style. The colonial representatives of such authority may have arisen from the ranks of the colonists themselves. Modern Aymara leaders achieve a metaphoric "elder brother" status through the competitive sponsorship of ritual activity and the organization of successful llama caravan expeditions (Abercrombie 1986:156). In a context where both the bounty of ritual and the bounty of everyday life were linked to a patron's close ties to the Tiwanaku state, the traditional role of leader/sponsor might be transformed into a more permanent administrative position for particularly successful hosts and provisioners. If this is correct, the ceremonial concerns of the proprietors of the

Omo chicherías may have coincided ever more closely with those of a maturing colonial administration and an ideology that was increasingly state-centered.

In summary, investigations at the Omo-style domestic sites show the presence of households with a material culture and domestic activities identical with those of altiplano Tiwanaku. These colonists' lifestyle and settlement patterns suggest that they may have originated in an ethnic group with a tradition of nomadic camelid pastoralism. The Omo-style diaspora is characterized by towns that were spatially divided into distinct ayllu-like community divisions at several nested levels of scale. The role of a centralized state seems to be minimal in this migration, and the households of the Omo-style settlements were primarily integrated with their homeland counterparts at the level of ayllu and community. This is consistent with the conception of a socially diverse archipelago of Tiwanaku colonies. However, as the settlements grew and became more permanent, maize cultivation and the chicha cult became more important. Provincial elites emerged as ayllu leaders who hosted public ceremonies and enjoyed better access to wealth objects supplied by powerful homeland exchange partners. These developments indicate a tension in Tiwanaku's periphery between the traditional heterarchy of a folk diaspora and the emergence of hierarchy as the colony grew. The expression of hierarchy and centralized Tiwanaku control in the Moquegua periphery was far more pronounced in the agricultural settlements of the Chen Chen style.

House, Community, and State in the Chen Chen–Style Sites

The incorporation of households in peripheral regions into an imperial political economy should have profound repercussions in the domestic economy. The standard interpretation of the Tiwanaku state would suggest that Tiwanaku elites systematically extracted agricultural surplus from Moquegua and distributed Tiwanaku manufactured goods in the Moquegua province. As we have seen, productive activities beyond the level of the household in the Omo-style settlements were organized at the level of the ayllu or community group. Generally, the level of intensity of production was moderate. In contrast, intensified and reorganized household production in support of a state superstructure is detectable in the Chen Chen–style sites of Chen Chen M1, Omo M10, and Río Muerto M43.

In the Tiwanaku core region, the state literally changed the orientation of domestic life, effectively redesigning it from the ground up. Little is known about Tiwanaku urban domestic life in the core region before Tiwanaku V, yet research on monumental and domestic sectors of the type site suggests that a consistent cardinal orientation was imposed under a planned urban renewal program between A.D. 780 and 900 (Kolata 1993:153). The Tiwanaku V rebuilding at the Tiwanaku site may have taken its cue from the orientation of the formal palaces in the site's elite sector and may have coincided with the rebuilding of the Putuni and Multicolored Rooms palaces in finely dressed stone circa A.D. 800 (Kolata 1993:166).

Chen Chen–Style Town Plan and the "Rockpile" Sites

The Chen Chen–style settlements of Moquegua were large bustling towns of rectangular cane-walled houses. Site M10 at Omo, covering some 7.75 hectares of the southernmost bluff of the Omo site group, is typical in its deep midden deposits and extraordinarily high density of ceramic sherds, organic matter, textiles, and other cultural materials.[14] Eighteen distinct cemeteries ring the domestic site. Omo M10 is unique among peripheral Tiwanaku settlements for the presence of a Tiwanaku temple structure. At M10, as well as at Chen Chen M1 and Río Muerto M43, the density and greater depth of cultural deposits and the multiple floor levels encountered in excavations all suggest a denser and more permanent occupation than that of the Omo-style sites. In chapters 7 and 8, I argue that the corporate architecture and large cemetery population associated with the Chen Chen–style sites also attest to a social and economic reorganization of Tiwanaku's corporate subunits under increasingly hierarchical territorial control. In the present chapter, I examine how these sites indicate an intensification of agricultural production and Tiwanaku economic control of the provincial town and household.

All three Chen Chen–style villages were heavily disturbed at the time of abandonment, and it is difficult to read much order into these sites' town plans from the surface. At Omo M10, irregular open areas with leveled surfaces and minimal surface scatter suggest plazas that anchored community sectors, much as they did at Omo-style Omo M12. One such plaza, a 35×50 m keyhole-shaped area, was defined by a substantial stone wall. These community plazas at M10 indicate the continuity of an independent community focus and, by implication, a continued importance to autonomous ayllu groups.

Nonetheless, it appears that sitewide town planning was imposed at the Chen Chen–style sites to a degree that did not occur in the Omo-style occupation. Excavations in Omo M10's domestic structures found the later structures to share an orientation of 30 degrees off the cardinal axes, suggesting a grid plan aligned with the axes of the M10 temple. A similar alignment was also noted at the Chen Chen between two structures of ritual function.[15] Provincial households thus followed patterns set by ruling elites. Houses of the periphery, like those of the Tiwanaku metropolis, were realigned to parallel structures symbolic of state centricity. We can therefore consider the later Chen Chen occupation as a planned settlement not only on the local level but according to more generalized canons of Tiwanaku urban alignment.

Life History of a Household Unit: A Chen Chen–Style example from Omo M10

Our understanding of the habitus of Tiwanaku colonial life may be informed by household archaeology at three sites of Chen Chen–style affiliation: Omo M10, Chen Chen M1, and Río Muerto M43. The domestic architecture and assemblages of these sites indicate villages of solely Tiwanaku affiliation that used pottery of the Chen Chen style.[16] While referring to features common to all three site groups, what follows is focused particularly on the results of household unit excavations in the M10 domestic area by the Omo Archaeological Project in 1986 and 1987 and on work in habitation sectors of Chen Chen M1 by the Chen Chen Salvage Project in 1995. The M10 excavations found superimposed episodes of occupation and a considerable depth of midden. In three of the four excavated structures at Omo M10, distinct phases of construction and occupation were discerned on the basis of architectural and depositional sequences and not indicated by gross changes in pottery, which is predominantly of Chen Chen style.

Surviving fragments of cane walls, wooden posts, wall trenches, and post molds indicate that Chen Chen–style homes were rectangular, multiroom structures with walls built of mud-daubed river cane set into wall trenches. Chen Chen–style homebuilders included both cane and intermittent thin wooden posts in their walls. Structurally, this technique represents an intermediate form between the skeletal thin-post frames of the Omo-style houses and the true quincha structures of the Tumilaca Phase, which had freestanding cane curtain walls and a separate system of stout wooden pillars for roof support. More substantial roof-support posts are also found in some Chen Chen–style houses, particularly in the later phases of construction. These substantial wooden posts, typically greater than 10 cm in diameter, had not been used in Omo-style architecture and seem to increase in frequency and size over time. This could indicate the fruition of a local forestry program under Chen Chen Tiwanaku control or improved access to lumber brought from forested areas.

One particularly well preserved household structure excavated at M10 in 1987, Structure 13, allows us to consider the configuration of a Chen Chen–style household unit over time and to speculate on one household's productive, consumptive, and even spiritual life history. Structure 13 underwent at least two major rebuilding episodes, designated phase A and phase B (fig. 6.13). The phase A floor was a packed-earth living surface with deposits of bone and other midden fill. Four 10 cm diameter posts located in the middle of the floor area served as central roof pillars. Traces of parallel walls and

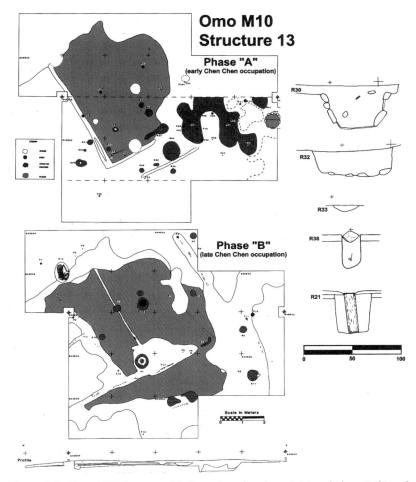

Figure 6.13. Omo M10 Structure 13, floor plans for phase A (a) and phase B (b) and storage cist and posthole profiles.

wall trenches suggest numerous small rebuilding events within this early period, although subsequent construction obscured much of their configuration. Throughout the major construction phase, a small hearth (R40) located near the east edge of the phase A floor served the structure. Guinea pig guano, found throughout the house in both burnt and unburnt condition, had been used as fuel.

Throughout Structure 13's history, the eastern exterior of the house was used for storage, some domestic activities, and trash disposal. This "backyard" area included several pit features and storage cists that were carefully lined with cobblestones sealed with mud plaster. The backyard served as the household's general disposal area, and the pits, cists, and the entire east exterior area were incrementally filled with trash, which was leveled and packed down by traffic into a stratified midden. Artifacts of Chen Chen style typified this midden, although a small amount of Omo-style pottery appeared in the earliest midden levels, presumably contemporary with construction phase A.[17]

The phase B reconstruction of Structure 13 began with the disassembly of the roof supports and the sealing of the earlier occupation floor below a layer of fine clean gravel and a prepared floor surface of poured and packed red clay (known locally as *moro moro*). An area of yellow clay floor to the east was carefully separated from the red clay floor area by a narrow border or thin wall trench. Walls and posts from the phase A occupation were either removed or cut off below this new surface. Fragments of new cane walls built after the pouring of the floor indicate that Structure 13 was enlarged by relocating the south wall and adding new rooms to the west. Overall, this suggests the expansion and subdivision of the household group to accommodate family expansion across a second generation.

Other features of Structure 13's rebuilding indicate distinct room-specific activities and new divisions of labor within the family that accompanied the household expansion. The most unusual reconstruction feature of the phase B occupation was the replacement of the structure's four central pillars with a single large wooden post. This massive central pillar suggests that the rebuilt structure had a high pyramidal, hipped, or pointed roof. The addition of the carefully prepared floor and the absence of floor fill deposits suggest that the phase B occupants valued this roofed space highly and took pains to keep the area clean. Notably, the interior hearth that had been present in phase A was floored over and not replaced, and it appears that cooking activities were removed to a small hearth in the backyard area at this time. It is not insignificant that the only domestic feature evident in this newly roofed area was a large storage vessel base set into the red clay floor in the southern interior.

The importance of the reconstruction of Omo M10 Structure 13 is further supported by two animal offerings that coincide with the dedication of the new structure. These animals were particularly well preserved and offer some insight on household dedicatory ritual. A juvenile camelid was interred on its side beneath the structure's probable entrance in the northwest corner of the construction (fig. 6.14).[18] A mummified guinea pig also found in association with the floor of Structure 13 was buried with coca leaves and colored yarn in its mouth (Dittmar 2000).[19] Similar offerings of young camelids and dogs were found buried beneath floors and entryways in household excavations at Chen Chen M1 and Río Muerto M43. A number of llama sacrifices were found in excavations in the Omo M10 temple (chapter 8).

Because of their wide distribution in domestic contexts, it is unlikely that animal dedicatory sacrifices necessarily marked sacred spaces to the Tiwa-

Figure 6.14. Camelid dedicatory offering, Omo M10 Structure 13.

naku. Instead, they seem to have been integral to the ritual life of ordinary households. Animal sacrifice in household dedicatory rituals has been widely reported ethnographically in the south-central Andes, specifically among the Aymara (Abercrombie 1986; Palacios Ríos 1982; Miller 1977; Platt 1986). To this day, llama fetuses for dedicatory rituals may still be purchased from "witch's markets" throughout the south-central Andes.[20] In the post-Tiwanaku period, camelids were buried as house dedicatory offerings in the corners of *every* house at the San Lorenzo site in the Azapa Valley, and guinea pigs and dogs were found in identical corner dedicatory contexts (Muñoz 1983:11, 1983b:66; Muñoz and Focacci 1985:24). Entire camelids have also been encountered beneath house floors at the Chiribaya site of Yaral in the Moquegua Valley (D. Rice 1993) as well as in Chiribaya cemetery contexts.

Overall, Structure 13's dedicatory offering, its fancy new floor and roof, and the removal of ordinary domestic functions from the space suggest that the remodeling entailed a functional reapportionment of household space as well as an expansion. The general-purpose interior space appears to have been converted to a political or ritual meeting area, and ordinary domestic functions were banished to the outdoors. One potential clue to the nature of this change was a fragment of *copal*, a resinous tree sap that is still highly valued by Quechua and Aymara speakers for medicinal and offering purposes (Abercrombie 1986:306). According to the sixteenth-century chronicler Martín de Murúa, copal was used in *mesas* or ritual offering packages and as incense for offerings to ancestors and earth spirits like *pachamama* (Girault 1987:243–244). Given the removal of ordinary domestic functions and the addition of a *chomba* or beer storage vessel to this fancy room, the room may also represent a "gendered" household space, reserved for adult male social, political, and ritual activities. We may speculate that the later Chen Chen–style colony saw new categories of household space that paralleled new divisions of labor and privilege within the household, much like those earlier described for the Inca period.

Domestic Subsistence and Household Food Production

Household food production and consumption in the Chen Chen–style towns indicate a shift to intensified subsistence, storage, and exchange patterns. Throughout the occupation, the dominant macrobotanical finds in virtually all contexts were maize cobs, kernels, and husks. Maize was present in over 45 percent of excavated contexts at M10, close to double its incidence in Omo-style M12. Maize cobs from the M10 household clusters also appear to be considerably larger than those excavated at M12; improved varieties may have allowed for further intensification of production. Beans, gourds, *pacae* pods, *lucuma*, peanuts, quinoa, potato, *oca* and *chuño* (freeze-dried tubers), and cottonseed were also represented, as well as a surprising number of nonedible plants that may have been used medicinally or for animal fodder.

All Chen Chen–style households enjoyed access to meat, as shown by dense concentrations of camelid bone in household middens at Omo M10, Chen Chen M1, Cerro Echenique M2/M4, and Río Muerto M43. Chen Chen–style camelid remains cover a wide range of ages, including yearling animals left as household dedicatory offerings and fetal or neonate animals in temple offering contexts. The presence of a wide age range suggests that herds exploited at the Chen Chen–style sites were breeding populations available year-round rather than through occasional or seasonal slaughter of caravan animals.

The frequency of shells of edible marine mollusks and crustacea indicates that the Chen Chen–style colony enjoyed better access to marine resources than the settlers of the Omo style, who apparently used shellfish only for ornaments. Marine mollusks of seven edible species comprised a small but significant proportion of the excavated faunal remains at Chen Chen–style sites.[21] Shell represented 3.14 percent of the total weight of faunal remains at M10, a settlement of highland people, 95 km from the ocean. Isotopic analysis of human skeletal samples from M10 indicates that marine resources contributed less than 13 percent to the lifelong diet of Chen Chen–style Tiwanaku individuals (Sandness 1992:51), and it is possible that it was consumed as a delicacy for ceremonial purposes. Shellfish may have been brought to Omo by the same people who delivered the seabird guano fertilizer that was critical to the Chen Chen–style colony's intensive maize agriculture (chapter 3).

As was noted in the previous chapter, Chen Chen–style maize agriculture is associated with extensive irrigation canal systems, notably those at the site of Chen Chen. The Chen Chen–style sites were further distinguished by the proliferation of stone-lined storage cists. Storage cists are distinguishable from tombs by their generally larger diameter, smaller stones, and complete

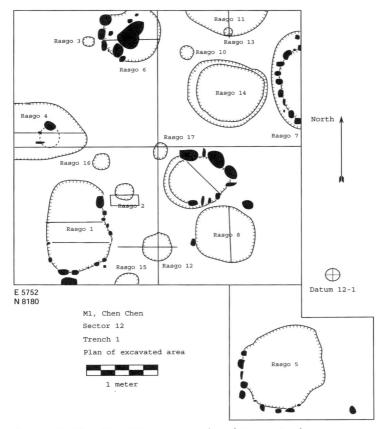

Figure 6.15. Chen Chen M1 excavation plan of storage cist cluster.

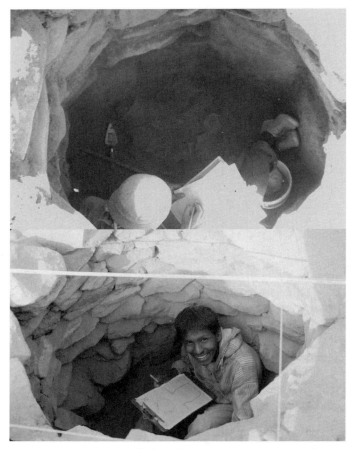

Figure 6.16. Omo M10 and Chen Chen M1 storage cists. PSG photos.

internal plastering. This Chen Chen–style innovation appeared in the back-yard activity areas of individual household clusters and grouped in special-ized warehouse locations. Tiwanaku storage cists were identified at Omo M10 in 1987 and during the 1995 Chen Chen Salvage Project. Excavation of one concentration of twelve storage cists at Chen Chen suggests that much of the site may have been devoted to these roofed clusters of storage units (figs. 6.15, 6.16). Extrapolating the observed density of one cist per 4 m² across 6.1 hectares of similar "low rockpile" topography, we estimate 7,500 storage cists and a sitewide storage capacity of 5,140 m³ (Bandy et al. 1996). This suggests a level of storage well beyond the needs of the site's inhabitants.

Intensified food production at the Chen Chen–style sites is also attested to by the proliferation of stone agricultural implements and tools dedicated to maize processing in these sites. Systematic surface collections in domestic

Figure 6.17. Ground stone manos, hammerstones, and hoe fragments, surface collection unit, Chen Chen site.

sectors of all three Tiwanaku centers found a high density of *manos*, *metates*, and stone hoes in the Chen Chen–style sites. Enormous *batanes*, or rocker metates, were noted throughout the domestic areas at Chen Chen M1, Omo M10, and Río Muerto M43. Unlike the small, flat push-pull metates of the Omo style, the Chen Chen–style batanes are massive boulders as large as a meter in diameter, with deep concavities for grinding with a rocking motion. In contrast to the general household tasks associated with push-pull metates, the proliferation of rocker metates suggests maize grinding in industrial quantities well beyond household needs. The Chen Chen–style batanes show heavy wear: many had been turned and worked from the opposite side when their concavities became too deep, and a few were worn through entirely. At Chen Chen, particularly high densities of manos and metates were noted in the vicinity of the storage unit clusters, suggesting maize processing in specialized mill and warehouse districts.

The high frequency of chipped-stone hoe or *taclla* (foot plow) blades was also notable in the Chen Chen–style domestic areas (fig. 6.17). These crudely chipped bifaces, ranging from oval to axe-shaped in form, are similar to the basalt hoes reported by Giesso at Tiwanaku (2003). At Omo M10 and Chen Chen, they were found by the hundreds and often showed sheen and wear from intensive use. The surface density of hoes at Omo M10 (.01016/m^2) and at Río Muerto M43 (.0078/m^2) indicate the widespread adoption of this tool type in the Chen Chen–style sites, while it was totally absent at the Omo-style sites. The highest frequency of hoes was at Chen Chen M1, where the systematic surface collection found a density of .0694 hoes/m^2. The proliferation of these hoes throughout Chen Chen–style domestic areas indicates that household agricultural production was intensified in part through a widespread agricultural technology that permitted greater plowing efficiency. The highest domestic concentration of hoes also appears to coincide with the Chen Chen site's specialized storage areas. Considering the vast adjacent field systems, this suggests that the farmers of Chen Chen cultivated, received, and processed maize far in excess of their population's needs.

The florescence of maize-processing tools and infrastructure suggests that Chen Chen–style agriculture was both more specialized and more intensive than that of sites of the Omo style. A heightened emphasis on maize may also be indicated by the increased prevalence of keros in the Chen Chen–style ceramic inventory. The ubiquity of the kero in all domestic contexts at Omo M10, Chen Chen M1, and Río Muerto M43 reminds us that significant quantities of maize were consumed via chicha drinking in the household setting. It also appears that the cult of chicha became more prevalent over time. In the Omo M10 Structure 13 excavation, the frequency of redware keros, serving bowls, and jars increased from under 9 percent in phase A to 13.8 percent of the ceramic count in the upper levels. Maize may also have been consumed in other ways. Only in the Chen Chen style does a smaller category of two-handled ollas become commonplace. These vessels are usually found in burnt condition, and it may be significant that they were the only plainware type used as burial offerings. The small ollas appear in the tombs of females and juveniles, while keros were reserved for males (chapter 7).

The strongest support for the intensification of maize agriculture comes from dietary analysis via carbon and nitrogen isotope studies of human bone chemistry for pre-Tiwanaku and Tiwanaku populations. A dietary simulation using a linear mixing model suggests that before the Tiwanaku colonization, both Huaracane and Early Ceramic coastal Osmore diet relied on C3 plant foods, such as legumes, and animals grazing on C3 vegetation for approximately 50 percent of their diet, with a heavy dependence on marine resources, such as fish, shellfish, and algae, comprising 23 to 50 percent of the diet. Maize made only a minimal contribution (3 to 18 percent) to the Huaracane diet (Sandness 1992:49). In contrast, analysis of a sample of ten adult individuals from Chen Chen–style burials at M10 indicated positive ^{13}C values and low ^{15}N values, consistent with a diet emphasizing C4 plant consumption (Sandness 1992:51). The estimated dietary proportion of maize, ranging from 46 to 76 percent, suggests an enormous dependence on a single crop. Significant dietary changes might be expected with the economic specialization, large-scale demographic movements, and changes in cultural practice associated with Tiwanaku expansion. The implication is that with new Tiwanaku settlement came a monoculture emphasizing maize to the exclusion of other cultigens.

Craft Production, Exchange, and the Chen Chen–Style Household

Colonial Tiwanaku produced a variety of craft items on a household basis. Some products were universally produced in all households, while others were produced by specialists in a limited number of household or extra-household settings. The production of various types of stone tools offers some examples. The presence of hoe flakes and preforms indicates in situ production of hoes in most households, and we might assume that ground stone tools were also produced locally in most communities, if not by every household. However, few cores or flakes of the fine white quartzite used for making arrow points were found in most household contexts. This suggests that fine lithic production was the province of specialists.

In 1994, the MAS project discovered a well-preserved lithic and lapidary workshop in a sector of the M52 site at the extreme south of the Río Muerto group (fig. 6.18). Raw materials, artifacts, and debitage of exotic materials including worked and unworked *Oliva peruvianis, turitela,* and *Choromytilus* shells, green stone, lapis lazuli, and sharks' teeth indicate bead working and jewelry work in exotic imported materials at this location (fig. 6.19). The lapidary sector at M52 was located adjacent to but slightly south of the main domestic sector, in an area separated by a slight gulley. As there was little surface indication of full-time residence at the immediate location of the lapidary shop, it would appear that craftspeople resided in the adja-

Figure 6.18. Río Muerto site M52, showing location of lapidary workshop. PSG photo.

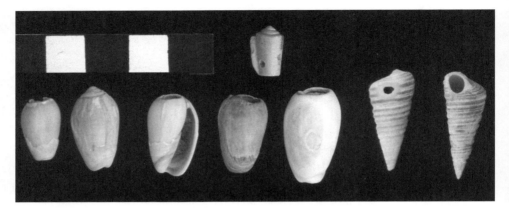

Figure 6.19. Turquoise bead in the shape of a shell, *Oliva* and *turitela* shells, M52 lapidary workshop.

cent domestic area and commuted to work. Shops like this one may have processed raw materials from colonized regions both for local consumption and to supply a growing demand in the altiplano for craft items of exotic raw materials.

It has long been taken for granted that Tiwanaku's textile industry made only fabrics of camelid wool fibers. Because llamas and alpacas are native to the Tiwanaku core region, the Moquegua colonies seemed an unlikely textile crafts center for Tiwanaku. An unexpected discovery from M10 household excavations was that cotton fabrics were not only worn by Chen Chen–style Tiwanaku colonists but produced by most households. Finds of cottonseeds, unspun cotton, spun cotton yarn, and finished cotton fabrics were common in Chen Chen–style domestic contexts. Cotton textiles do not appear in any Tiwanaku burials and had escaped notice in most studies of Tiwanaku textiles.[22] Tiwanaku people wore wool tunics, hats, and other attire when buried (chapter 7) and presumably for other formal occasions as well. However, cotton fabrics were evidently the everyday clothing of choice for the Chen Chen–style Tiwanaku colonists and may have been an important export to altiplano Tiwanaku. The discoveries of cotton raw materials, along with wool, cactus spine needles, ceramic and wooden spindles, and weaving tools in all Chen Chen–style Tiwanaku households suggests an active domestic production of textiles of both materials. For the Chen Chen–style agricultural colonists, cotton textiles could have been one of the Moquegua province's most important exports. This contrasts with the exclusively wool fabrics produced by households of the Omo-style settlements, which may have had a more pastoralist economy.

Another aspect of Tiwanaku colonial economy was the diaspora's consumption of goods from highland Tiwanaku. Caravans carrying maize, guano, shellfish, or cotton fabrics from the midvalley to the altiplano returned with manufactured goods that would have reinforced the identity, loyalty, and dependency of the Moquegua agriculturalists. Tiwanaku V was indeed an "Expansive" period, not only in geographical extent but also in terms of the expansion of trade. Long-distance exchange of prestige craft objects may have supported Tiwanaku elite ideology and encouraged compliance with tribute demands. However, unlike the luxurious diplomatic gifts given to faraway chiefs of San Pedro, Tiwanaku's Moquegua caravan goods satisfied the demands of its own working people, who wanted to dress, eat, and drink like their ayllu back home. Most important, the imported craft items helped to form and maintain the common identity of colonists and homeland.

The artifact assemblages of the Chen Chen–style sites indicate an enormous consumer demand among the new colonial diaspora for pottery that was functionally and stylistically identical to the serving, ritual, and cooking wares of the altiplano. Plainware ollas, *tinajas* and storage vessel fragments comprised roughly 90 percent of the sherds in all Chen Chen–style domestic contexts. Redware keros, bowls, and jars recovered in M10 excavations comprised 10.25 percent of the sherd count, exceeding the combined frequencies of the two fine serving ceramic categories at M12 (4.5 percent redware, 3.8 percent blackware). The Tiwanaku redware sherds found in domestic excavations include fragments of keros, tazones, everted bowls, small pitchers, and occasional fragments of portrait head vessels and modeled zoomorphic incensarios.

This demand for home-style vessels and tools for the more populous Chen Chen colonies appears to have coincided with changes in ceramic production and distribution. Ceramic standardization, a function of stronger state control over production and exchange, is evident in the Chen Chen–style decorated wares. The great similarity of Moquegua's Chen Chen–style artifacts to those of contemporary Tiwanaku occupations from as far away as Cochabamba (Byrne 1984; Céspedes 1993; Oakland 1986) indicates exchange of detailed standardized information among artisans, if not actual coordination of workshop production and centralized distribution. Moquegua Tiwanaku serving vessels of the Chen Chen style are indistinguishable from pottery from Tiwanaku itself, and many were probably imported from the altiplano.

From a production standpoint, it is important to see this standardization of pottery as a streamlining of manufacturing processes rather than a decay of artistic integrity. The key element of this streamlining was the elimination of some of the more idiosyncratic vessel types that required complex individual processing. As ceramic output increased, Tiwanaku ceramic shops must have been divided into separate forming, painting, and firing operations. The more complex modeled vessels that characterized the Omo style, particularly those in polished blackware, could only be created by skilled sculptors who tracked their work through laborious postfiring engraving and special firing and finishing. This level of individual attention was abandoned by the Chen Chen–style workshops, which produced batches of identically formed vessels for assembly line painting and firing. Painters churned out red-slipped vessels decorated with simplified versions of iconographic themes painted in blocky panels, instead of the Omo style's fine line drawings.

From a distribution standpoint, standardization is also evident in the emphasis in the Tiwanaku provinces on smaller mass-produced and more portable vessel forms. The epitome of this trend in the Chen Chen style is the widespread dominance of the flaring-sided bowl, or tazón in Tiwanaku redware. These bowls are easy to nest for transport, suggesting that the ceramic industry responded to the needs of stacked storage and export through caravan exchange. The flaring-sided bowls, like other Tiwanaku V fineware vessel categories, also cluster within particular ranges of size and volume, suggesting standard units of measure. In Mesopotamia, a similarly stackable, standard-sized vessel known as the bevel rim bowl is considered a marker for the state expansion associated with the city of Uruk in the Protoliterate period. It has been suggested that bevel rim bowls are associated with daily laborers' rations, perhaps in a temple context (Adams 1974:459; Wright and Johnson 1975:282). Such vessels would appear to represent participation in a centrist economic system with some redistributive entity beyond the simple reciprocity of the ayllu.

No craft item is more identity-affirming than clothing, and Tiwanaku colonists placed high value on Tiwanaku-style woolen garments. Unlike the cotton fabrics of everyday use, some woolen clothing types were extremely limited in distribution and may be considered prestige exchange goods that were emblematic of high status. The most labor-intensive textiles were fine knotted polychrome hats and interlocked tapestry tunics with figures depicting mythical themes. These are rare and usually associated with elite mortuary contexts. Only one fragmentary example each of a polychrome hat and a tapestry tunic were found in the domestic excavations at Chen Chen–style sites. These conspicuously elite artifacts were not typical of Tiwanaku peoples at large and appear to be markers of leadership and prestige.

In contrast, woolen warp-faced plainweave fabrics, ranging from coarse blankets to finely woven tunics in dyed or natural yarns, were ubiquitous in Chen Chen–style burials and were found in fragmentary form in many domestic contexts. Warp stripes in natural whites and browns or dyed reds, greens, blues, and yellows were the predominant decorative element in these plainweaves. Most decorated textiles were of camelid wool or occasionally cotton-wool composites. Characteristic loop stitch embroidery of geometric or figural motifs was used to finish selvages and edges with geometric designs (Oakland 1986, 1992). These techniques typify Tiwanaku textile production elsewhere in the south-central Andes (Oakland 1992). Particular stripe designs on wool plainweave tunics may have represented specific ayllu, moiety, or sodality identity or even been uniforms for soldiers or civil servants.

The redistribution of textile and pottery artifacts may be one part of more pervasive patterns of habitus that supported a common identity among Tiwanaku colonists. The allegiance of the Tiwanaku diaspora to ayllu, state, and culture was maintained through these patterns of shared identity. With time, the production and exchange networks that made this possible may have been dominated increasingly by the extraction of agricultural and crafts tribute from the colonies to support the growing state. At first, there is no evidence that the colonists were coerced to contribute to the state political economy—no military garrisons or administrative mechanisms of tax collecting, for example. However, the Chen Chen–style sites offer evidence of violent upheaval that led to the collapse of that provincial system and the end of the Tiwanaku colony.

Chen Chen Site Destruction and Abandonment

The intentional destruction of all of the Chen Chen–style domestic sites is one of the most enigmatic phenomena in the Tiwanaku expansive period. The domestic areas were deliberately pitted, mounding stones and cultural fill in irregular piles. The effects of subsequent deflation of their surfaces by wind left the sites looking like fields of silty pits and patinated rockpiles. Deliberate and systematic site razing has been hypothesized by some investigators (Moseley et al. 1991). Considering this to be behaviorally unlikely, I expected to find that these irregular rockpile formations reflected some unusual form of perishable architecture that had undergone melting, collapse, and weathering. Instead, I found the configuration of rockpiles had no correspondence to surviving traces of rectangular cane buildings, nor are the small stones of the rockpiles suitable for any kind of construction. Both at Omo M10 and at Chen Chen, my 1987 and 1995 excavations found most of the original ground surface honeycombed with irregular pits filled with a jumble of loosely packed soil, organic debris, artifacts, ash pockets, and air spaces. The presence of adobe fragments and grasses from thatched roofing implies that the destruction of the site occurred while the structures were still standing. This kind of intentional disturbance cratered all the Chen Chen–style settlements at Omo M10, Chen Chen M1, Echenique M2/M4, and Río

Muerto M43, churning and piling midden and building materials in a seemingly haphazard manner.

A study of site formation processes through artifact analysis provides independent support for the seemingly implausible scenario of intentional site destruction. Excavated sherds at rockpile habitation sites like Omo M10 and Chen Chen were noticeably smaller and more battered than those of M12. Moreover, while reconstructible groups of sherds, sometimes of entire vessels, were extremely common at M12, few such clusters were discerned in rockpile excavations. This observation was tested quantitatively by a study of mean sherd weight (i.e., the ratio of total sherd weight to total sherd count). The average weight per sherd in the M10 surface collection (25.01 grams for plainware diagnostics) was less than half that of surface sherds at M12. This markedly lower average sherd weight was confirmed for M10 excavation contexts in contrast to the more intact houses of Omo M12. Pottery from Chen Chen–style houses and domestic middens probably had been broken up during the intensive site disturbance that created the rockpiles.

The intentional disturbance of Chen Chen–style midden and domestic contexts is difficult to explain. Though this sort of activity has been reported for cemetery contexts in Chile (Focacci 1983; Muñoz 1983b; and see chapter 7), the Chen Chen–style sites are the first known cases of the deliberate destruction of Tiwanaku residences. The scale of the site destruction suggests ferocity and thoroughness that far surpass anything expected from simple looting. However, there is no evidence of intruders who did not share the material culture of the Tiwanaku colonists; thus the sites were probably not destroyed by any party from outside the Tiwanaku cultural sphere.

Indeed, excavations indicate that the final Chen Chen–style occupation at Omo M10 may have been coeval with the pitting phenomenon. The absence of pitting in Structure 13 suggests that the red clay floor of the later occupation may coincide with or at least survived the site destruction. In M10 Structure 12, a rectangular above-ground storage bin, similar to the type used at Omo site M11 in the subsequent Tumilaca Phase, was superimposed over earlier below-ground storage cists (fig. 6.20). As is detailed in what follows, stones from the destruction of the Omo temple were reutilized in Chen Chen–style Tiwanaku tombs. All artifacts from these contexts are well within Chen Chen–style Tiwanaku norms, and there is no evidence that any of these terminal occupations involved any non-Tiwanaku agents.

However, the continued occupation of the M10 site after its destruction as a state center was short-lived. Eventually, the M10 village, like its temple—a symbol of a state that no longer existed—was abandoned, and the former citizens of Tiwanaku's provinces turned to new patterns of integration that were local rather than global in character.

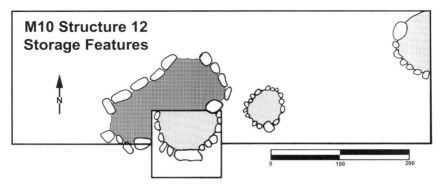

Figure 6.20. Omo M10 Structure 12, showing superposition of rectangular storage bin above cylindrical cist.

State Collapse and Household Continuity in the Tumilaca Phase

If the hand of the Tiwanaku state may be discerned in the orientation and activities of the Chen Chen–style provincial household, the decline of the Tiwanaku system and the resurgence of locally based political systems is epitomized by the subsequent Tumilaca Phase. I have suggested that the Tumilaca style parallels the emergence of local production and distribution spheres in the Moquegua Valley as Tiwanaku's economic and political control waned. Tumilaca settlement sites were characterized by the absence of monumental architecture and a settlement pattern of dispersed and defensible sites. Following the destruction of the Chen Chen–style sites, valleywide habitation site area in the Tumilaca Phase was reduced to 42 hectares, less than half the Chen Chen occupation area, as many descendants of the Tiwanaku colonies left the valley.

The Omo M11 village site typifies this period of fading Tiwanaku peripheral influence in the middle Moquegua Valley. M11 was a village 6 hectares in area, located on the central bluff of the three at Omo (fig. 6.21). The site is distinguished by a stone perimeter wall that surrounded the domestic area and separated it from an associated cemetery to the east. This double-course stone construction surrounds the M11 bluff on its north and south cliffs. To the east and west of the village, the wall crosses the bluff top, with a deep trench on its exterior. The eastern wall and moat were traversed by a gateway 3 m in width and an earthen bridge leading to the cemetery.

M11's enclosure wall and moat constituted the most obvious representation of the site's autonomy. The Tumilaca Phase inhabitants of Omo M11 did not enjoy the security that had typified the Tiwanaku colonies for centuries. But what of village life within that enclosure wall? Did the Tumilaca house-

Figure 6.21. Omo M11 Structure 5, compound plan.

holds similarly close themselves off from the outside in the face of Tiwanaku collapse?

The Tumilaca Phase Village of Omo M11

Within its defensive walls, the M11 village was an unremarkable community of separated residential compounds. Domestic structures on the M11 bluff top were grouped on leveled house platforms, typically terraced with low retaining walls of a single course of stones. The house platforms step downward with the bluff's topography, sharing an alignment several degrees south of west. Leveling of residential compounds involved removal of surface stone and occasionally the building up of low areas with midden fill. Most of the house compounds were bordered by rectangular stone storage bins. Surface architecture gives no indication of any special-purpose buildings or elite sectors of town.

Tumilaca Phase houses were of true freestanding quincha curtain wall construction, with substantial wooden posts to support an independent roof structure. Except for stone storage bins and retaining walls, house superstructures were built entirely of closely spaced river canes ranging from 1 to 3 cm in diameter set vertically into excavated wall trenches that extended to a depth of up to 30 cm below the floor level. In contrast to *quincha* houses of the Inca and Late Intermediate periods from Arica and Tacna (Piazza 1981), Tumilaca Phase wall canes were individually implanted in handful-sized bunches and not prefabricated as mats. Horizontal cords of twisted vegetable fiber secured the walls (see Piazza 1981: figs. 8, 9, 10), and cane-impressed clay indicates the use of mud daub on the walls and roofs, particu-larly those of the storage bins.

Unlike the small posts of Omo and Chen Chen–style houses, Tumilaca Phase structures of M11 used substantial timbers between 10 and 22 cm in diameter as roof pillars. These pillars were set in postholes outside the wall trench lines, producing a freestanding roof support independent of the walls. The roof posts were not precisely aligned with the cane walls, suggesting that walls were added after the roof was already built. Roofed space was spanned in at least two ways. In Structure 1, excavations found three particularly large postholes aligned from east to west across the center of the structure's largest room. This suggests a peaked roof supported by a central beam. In contrast, the builders of Structures 3 and 5 avoided interior pillars, relying instead on smaller posts placed around the perimeter. This suggests a flat roof structure.

The Tumilaca Phase Household Unit

Structure 5 was the best-preserved structure excavated at M11 and serves as a prototype for household clusters of the Tumilaca Phase. With an excavated area of 215 m², this cluster was the largest single block excavation of the Omo project. Structure 5 was characterized by an unusually clear building plan and a full complement of features and materials. This has permitted an understanding of the use of domestic space in a way not possible in other excavated houses. Structure 5's wall, post, and wall pattern divide household space into three categories: the central roofed core, unroofed contiguous space, and exterior space.

Structure 5's central roofed core was an 8.5×7 m cane-walled area divided into three rooms (designated 4, 5, and 7), and surrounded by substantial wooden roof pillars. Smaller wooden posts between 2 and 4 cm in diameter delineated entryways between rooms, suggesting that hinged doorways pro-vided access to the central roofed rooms. The roofed core was the primary locus of the household's daily domestic and industrial activity. Subsurface features and artifacts found in rooms 5 and 7 include the structure's primary hearth, a very large pit filled with ash and burnt bone and surrounded by hard-packed reddened soil. A separate lenticular pit contained a wide variety of botanical remains, suggesting household storage of immediate food re-quirements. Three medium-sized plainware olla vessels were cemented into the floor (fig. 6.22). These two-handled vessels were considerably smaller than the huge vessels found in the Omo- and Chen Chen–style structures. The

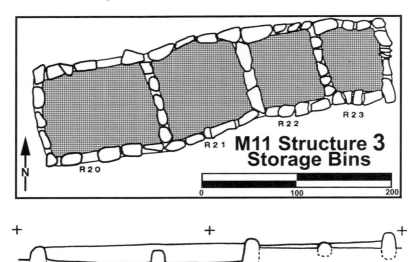

Figure 6.22. Omo M11 domestic storage bin.

kitchen storage pits and cemented-in vessels indicate that at least some house-hold foodstuffs were stored within the roofed living area. × near here}

Artifacts and food remains in the central roofed core also point to food preparation and consumption, particularly in room 7. Some 43.7 percent of Structure 5's faunal remains were found in Room 7, where bone density was more than double the density structure-wide (Goldstein 1989a). This bone was burnt and highly fragmented, suggesting that animals were cooked and consumed in this part of the house. Macrobotanical remains were plentiful in this room, which also contained the structure's only stone mano and a hammerstone. The larger central roofed rooms also display a disproportion-ately high incidence of redware serving vessels, suggesting daily serving ac-tivities and ritual drinking within the household. The lower representation of redware compared to faunal remains and utilitarian plainware in room 5 could indicate that this small room was an area for food preparation rather than consumption. It may have been a space of predominantly female use, while males may have participated in chicha drinking rituals in room 7.

The overwhelming majority of dedicatory offerings, luxury items, and items of personal adornment were also found in the central roofed core. One item, a small five-color striped *inkuña* or carrying cloth appears to have been intentionally placed with a stone hoe as a dedicatory offering in a small pit below the floor. Other items, including a bronze pendant (fig. 6.23), worked olive shell, turquoise and mica beads, and flamingo feathers appear to have been lost in their loci of use. Ceramic disks described as "game counters"

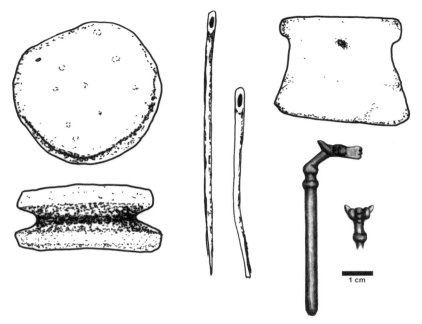

Figure 6.23. Tumilaca Phase small artifacts: quartz disk, cactus spine needles, bronze pendant, and *tupu* in form of llama, M11 Structure 5.

(Rydén 1947) and a small ceramic whistle were also found adjacent to the hearth. The presence of a dedicatory offering and lost objects of adornment, gaming pieces, and musical instruments in the household suggests that Tiwanaku household ritual continued with little change into the Tumilaca Phase. Indeed, the ceremonies that had always occurred in the central rooms of ordinary households may have taken on greater importance with the destruction and abandonment of the Omo temple at this time (chapter 8).

Surrounding the roofed core of Structure 5 was a group of cane-walled rooms that showed no evidence of roof supports. These unroofed contiguous spaces held lower densities of ceramic sherds, artifacts, and debris than the roofed core (table 6.5).[23] The less fragmented state of the faunal debris suggests that these rooms saw less traffic than the roofed rooms, where only small residual debris was found.[24] Guinea pig and camelid droppings indicate that these areas doubled as household corrals.

The unroofed contiguous rooms also were the location of bulk storage features in each of the M11 household units. In most structures, these were sets of two or three contiguous rectangular bins with substantial stone foundations and mud-plastered walls and floors. Mud plaster fragments with cane impressions show that considerable care was taken in sealing the stone foundations, cane superstructure, and roof.[25] The carefully plastered floors and the presence of camelid paws, *poroto* and *pallar* beans, gourds, maize, and *lucuma* indicate that these bins were used for the long-term bulk storage of produce for the individual household unit. This contrasts with the clusters of below-ground cists of Chen Chen–style sites, which indicate storage that was controlled by the state or its component ayllus. All indications are that the households of the Tumilaca Phase lived in a more autonomous fashion than their Chen Chen and Omo predecessors.

Household Economy in Tiwanaku's Decline: The New Self-Sufficiency

Did Tiwanaku's imperial collapse result in a shift from a single-crop export economy to a more diversified self-sufficient economy? Household evidence indicates that Tumilaca Phase farmers grew the same crops as those of the Chen Chen–style sites and seem to have continued most of the same agricultural practices. As in the Chen Chen–style sites, chipped stone *taclla* or hoe blades were found throughout M11 surface collections, albeit in lower density. The M11 village consumed maize and a variety of beans, squash, gourds, and fruits and the presence of potato and *chuño* in M11 household structures suggests ongoing subsistence exchange with the highlands.

Nonetheless, it appears that maize declined in importance to the Tumilaca agricultural economy, and diverse crops were managed and stored by each household instead of at the community level. This return to household self-sufficiency would appear to coincide with the ultimate contraction of the irrigation maize agricultural systems of the Chen Chen site and a return to smaller community and household forms of agricultural organization. Although human remains from Tumilaca Phase cemeteries have not yet been subjected to carbon and nitrogen isotope dietary analysis, this hypothesis is supported by other data. Maize cobs and kernels were less prevalent in M11 than in household contexts of the Chen Chen style. There is a conspicuous scarcity of metates at M11, and the huge rocker batanes of the Chen Chen–style sites are nowhere to be seen. This suggests the abandonment of industrial-scale maize grinding, as agricultural production reverted to providing for a single family group rather than producing a specialized surplus for a distant elite.[26] Equally significant is the appearance of the rectangular stone- or cane-walled bins that accompany each household unit. While villagers of the Chen Chen–style Tiwanaku colony may have participated in communitywide systems for storing, staging, and redistributing agricultural surplus, each Tumilaca Phase household was responsible for gathering and storing its own. This shift to house-by-house storage suggests a fundamental breakdown of the state system of surplus management and exchange.

The effects of increased isolation from exchange networks are also apparent in complementary aspects of household subsistence production. An over-all decline in the presence of camelid bone at Omo M11 suggests that access to camelid herds was limited during the Tumilaca Phase. There was also a marked increase in the ratio of rodent bones to those of large mammals, and guinea pig guano was also particularly plentiful. This indicates increasing reliance on guinea pigs to compensate for the loss of domesticated camelids as interregional transhumance and caravan trade with the highlands de-clined. Guinea pigs may even have supplanted camelids in the ritual sphere. No camelid offerings were discovered in the M11 habitation excavations, while at least one guinea pig mummy was found.

The weakness of interregional exchange ties is also apparent in the disap-pearance of shellfish remains from Tumilaca Phase domestic contexts. While Chen Chen–style colonists enjoyed marine mollusks and shellfish, these items virtually vanished from midvalley households in the Tumilaca Phase. Shell-fish remains comprised only 0.92 percent of the total faunal remains by weight at M11. This near-disappearance of marine resources from the do-mestic economy is also reported for contemporary sites such as P5 in the Otora Valley (Stanish 1992:115). It represents a dramatic interruption of the Chen Chen–style sites' exchange of guano and shellfish with coastal special-ists. Remembering the age-old relationship among coastal collecting of sea-bird guano fertilizer, llama caravan transport, and intensive maize agriculture in the midvalley, it comes as no surprise that maize production declined at the same time as did access to camelids and shellfish.

The profound changes in household economic patterns that accompanied the collapse of Tiwanaku's provincial administration in the Tumilaca Phase went beyond a reversion to agricultural self-sufficiency. Most aspects of Omo M11 point to a scenario of independence from the Tiwanaku state. M11's defensive wall and moat suggest increased levels of internecine hostilities commensurate with the loss of Tiwanaku's regulatory role in local conflict resolution. The Tumilaca Phase sites have no monumental architecture or public plazas. Moreover, state iconography such as the front-faced god icon disappears from Tumilaca Phase portable art. This suggests that the descen-dants of the Tiwanaku diaspora no longer needed to call on the Tiwanaku gods to intercede with the cosmos at large. In the next chapter, I discuss how the appearance of new mortuary markers suggests the emergence of local elites in the absence of altiplano ritual suzerainty.

Trade independence from the altiplano is also reflected in the marked decrease in highland-style ceramic vessels and other artifacts and their re-placement with local manufactures. Actual ceramic imports seem to disap-pear almost entirely, and all Tumilaca Phase redware appears to be locally made by a developing local ceramic industry.[27] The decline of caravan trade in manufactured commodities and coastal resources may have fostered increasing regional self-sufficiency and the development of household craft industries in the Tumilaca Phase. Tools for spinning, sewing, and weaving and remains of unspun wool and cotton, threads, and yarn as well as finished textiles in excavated households indicate that textiles continued to be made in midvalley homes. It is unclear whether the two metal artifacts found in Omo M11 Structure 5 represent contemporary local products, imports, or curated "heirlooms" from the heyday of Tiwanaku metalwork. However, beads, olive shell, obsidian, mica, and Andean flamingo feathers suggest that some personal ornamental crafts continued at the household level. Textiles and other ornamental objects continued to be emblems of labor investment, wealth, and status, but they no longer carried any iconographic association with a Tiwanaku state or state religion. Where imported Tiwanaku craft items once reified membership and place in a hegemonic system, the focus of craft production in Tumilaca Phase Moquegua hints that crafts production shifted its role to validating status under a distinctly local rather than a regional system.

Cultural Continuity after State Collapse

Despite the breakdown of Tiwanaku's provincial administration and economy, a remarkable degree of cultural continuity in the former Tiwanaku political sphere is evident at the household level. The midvalley province was not conquered or repopulated by foreigners but was the home to inheritors of a Tiwanaku cultural tradition who had opted out of their political affiliation. Evidence of a "post-expansive" Tiwanaku legacy may be seen in specific items such as the punctate shoulder band plainware pitcher, which is found at Omo M11 as well as at late Tiwanaku sites in the altiplano (Bermann et al. 1989; Goldstein 1985, 1989; Rydén 1947: figs. 6A, 41 I, J and H, 66H). In Tumilaca Phase redware, the characteristic formal categories of serving ware —keros, tazones, and one-handled pitchers—continue to be represented in roughly the same proportions as in earlier phases (fig. 6.24). Despite stylistic changes in vessel form, such as the introduction of the "Coca-Cola glass"–shaped kero, there was an overall continuity in household ceramic formal categories. Local adaptations of Tiwanaku V painted motifs, such as the omnipresent step-stair geometric motif, continue to dominate.

Although imported ceramics, and notably ceramic vessels bearing icons of state control, drop out of the picture, some imported Tiwanaku artifacts do seem to be highly valued. Particularly telling is the curation in an apparent offering context in Structure 5 of a portrait vessel (fig. 6.24).[28] Stylistically, from the modeling of the eyes and other facial features, this appears to be an "heirloom" piece of the Omo style. Significantly, the vessel's rim had been broken off and the vessel had been reworked by polishing along the break. As

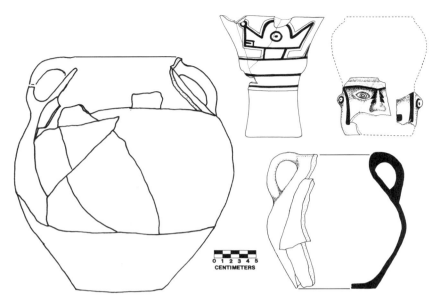

Figure 6.24. Tumilaca domestic ceramic assemblage, including repaired Omo-style portrait vessel, Omo site M11, Structure 5.

with the few heavily repaired Tiwanaku ceramics of San Pedro de Atacama, this is a strong indication of the value placed on what had become a rare and coveted symbol of cultural affiliation. The vessel appears to have been deposited as part of a dedicatory sacrifice buried at the southeast corner of Structure 5 and also including a guinea pig mummy, two stone hoes, a stone ball, and a bronze *tupu* pin in the form of a llama (fig. 6.33).[29]

Continuity in Tiwanaku traditions is also indicated by textile techniques, such as some of the diagnostic Tiwanaku colors used in wool fabrics and the use of undyed cotton plainweaves. Warp-faced woolen plainweaves with vertical stripes and embroidered selvages were still the norm for tunics, blankets, and bags. A knotted hat fragment found in Structure 3 appears to be stylistically transitional between Tiwanaku polychrome four-pointed hats and later monochrome Chiribaya-style hats (e.g., Eisleb and Strelow 1980:fig. 344). The same cultural continuity is also evident in everyday implements such as cactus spine needles in which the eye end was beveled before the drilling of the eye itself, a technique peculiar to Tiwanaku needles. Continuity in domestic architecture, household activities, and material culture can be traced from the Tumilaca Phase into subsequent regional traditions. These include the black-on-red ceramic traditions of Chiribaya, Maytas, San Miguel-Gentilar, Churajón, and Chuquibamba that are generically referred to as the "Tricolor del Sur" tradition (Lumbreras 1974b).

Summary: Keeping House in the Tiwanaku Diaspora

In this chapter, we have seen how household archaeology can trace the historical transition of Tiwanaku's peripheral towns from a segmentary collection of folk colonies through a province laboring under economic hegemony to a postcollapse situation of no external control. Throughout, Tiwanaku settlers were united by an enduring cultural identity that was enacted on a daily basis through the rhythms of household practice. Tiwanaku colonists brought their own uniquely Tiwanaku habitus in ways of cultivation, cuisine, couture, craft, and cult. The practice of being Tiwanaku was enacted not only on feast days and in conscious ritual practice but every day, in the myriad mundane motions of daily existence.

Household patterns also linked colonists to more specific subtraditions represented by distinct technological and material styles. Most notable was the distinction in many aspects of household construction, layout, activities, and material culture between sites associated with the Omo and Chen Chen ceramic styles. The segregation between these two styles is so pronounced that it was formerly considered to be a chronological distinction. Although some Omo-style contexts do precede the Chen Chen occupation, the two occupations now appear to overlap temporally. If this is the case, the presence of two contemporary, yet highly segregated, highland Tiwanaku styles represents precisely the kind of "multiethnicity" predicted by John Murra and described in chapter 2. What is most intriguing is the possibility that there were in fact two Tiwanaku diasporas coexisting in the lowlands, each representing one of two distinct maximal ayllus within the Tiwanaku cultural sphere.

Colonists of these two Tiwanaku diasporas further marked their positions in communities, clans, and families by a complex and segmented residential pattern. The colonists settled in loosely organized yet assiduously separated enclaves, each with its own plazas for collective ritual and favored locations for commensal feasting. Each individual enclave was integrated through regular patterns of ceremony that also served to reinforce social solidarity with distant compatriots. It would thus appear that the finer spatial divisions of these colonial communities followed the nested finer-scale social divisions of the homeland, perhaps at the level of minimal ayllus.

Did this heterarchical system change with external demands placed on household and community by agricultural intensification for export? With the vast land reclamation projects undertaken by colonists of the Chen Chen occupation, aspects of the Moquegua Tiwanaku domestic economy did become more like extractive tributary systems over time. The proliferation of highly specialized agricultural tools and facilities indicates an intensification of domestic production, just as their association with larger clusters of storage banks indicates new modes of surplus accumulation. There is good evidence that this activity was dedicated to the cultivation, processing, and export of maize and cotton and a probability that peppers, coca, and other cultigens were exported as well. By the end of the Chen Chen occupation, a significant part of household production appears to have been dedicated to some sort of state finance.

In at least one site, the reorganization of household production was paralleled by a physical realignment of the settlement to follow the cardinal orientation of the Omo M10 temple, a clear symbol of Tiwanaku hegemony (Goldstein 1993b and chapter 8). A reapportionment of household space between construction phases suggests that the division of household labor also changed, as some productive activities associated with females were moved to exterior spaces and finely appointed interior spaces were created for male ritual activities and feasting. It is possible that tensions inherent in increasing household inequality, along with communitywide resistance to Tiwanaku's extractive political economy, had a great deal to do with the collapse of the colonial system and the emergence of the Tumilaca Phase autonomous village communities from the Tiwanaku colonial populations.

In the end, household archaeology of the Tiwanaku colonies illuminates two contradictory aspects of highland Tiwanaku colonization. First, the ample household evidence for shared and nested Tiwanaku cultural identities confirms many of the predictions of a vertical archipelago model of ayllu-organized diasporic colonization. On the other hand, economic data from the Chen Chen–style households suggest some aspects of an extractive political economy that we can associate with globalist models of political control. Can we presume that a Tiwanaku polity at its height dispensed with segmentary forms of integration in favor of a centralized administration headed by a state hierarchy? Unfortunately, the poor preservation and visibility of town plans in the Chen Chen–style sites do not permit us to answer this question through residential patterns alone. Fortunately, the Tiwanaku colonists buried their dead in spatially distinct cemeteries, each with a rich record of distinctive mortuary practices. In the next chapter, I explore this tension between ayllu heterarchy and state hierarchy by examining the mortuary practices of the Tiwanaku colonies.

7

Death in a Faraway Land

The most extraordinary thing to be seen here in the Collao is, in my opinion,
the graves of the dead. When I went through, I stopped to set down what seemed
to me the most noteworthy things about the Indians. And it truly amazes me to think
how little store the living set by having large, fine houses, and the care with which
they adorned the graves where they were to be buried, as if this constituted their
entire happiness.

Cieza de León (1959 [1553]:274)

Ancient Andean peoples furnished their loved ones' tombs with great care
and took pains to make their deceased ancestors comfortable, as Cieza de
León noted. The extraordinary veneration of the dead in the south-central
Andes suggests that funerary practices played an important part in the affirmation of beliefs, identity, and status among the living. For this reason, the
study of burial practice can shed light on the processes of migration and state
expansion in the Andes. In this chapter I examine how mortuary archaeology
in the Tiwanaku peripheries can elucidate burial practices that reflect the
cultural affiliation of resident populations, their beliefs about an afterlife,
and aspects of the political and social structure of the Tiwanaku civilization.

Mortuary archaeology is a distinctive method of social analysis that can
go beyond characterizing the normative death rituals of a culture to illuminate many aspects of its political and social organization. Burial and funerary
treatment can represent the life identities of a deceased individual or may
have more to do with the needs of the living survivors (Brown 1995:393). The
nature and meaning of mortuary treatment is variable across cultures, but
ethnographic analogy and cross-cultural studies suggest that there is a correlation between complex societies and more "representationalist" mortuary
treatments. Complex societies have more complex stories to tell about their
dead, and they tend to develop complex funerary practices that can represent
more information about the dead person's identity. More often than not,
variations among forms of burial relate to the status and affiliations of the
deceased and reflect the social position and roles held by an individual in life
(Tainter 1975; Ucko 1969:270). Binford described the complete package of
an individual's roles and status as a *social persona*, "the composite of the

social identities maintained in life and recognized as appropriate for consideration at death" (Binford 1971). These include age, sex, and a wide range of social positions and affiliations. Accepting the generalization that "who you are affects how you get buried," the challenge of mortuary archaeology is to distinguish how these separate aspects of social identity were represented in burial practice (Pearson 1999:29).

The Mortuary Record

In assessing mortuary variability, it is useful to consider the mortuary expressions of the social persona to vary in "vertical" and "horizontal" dimensions (Tainter 1977:331). Vertical, or hierarchical, mortuary variability is that part of differentiation in mortuary contexts that reflects social inequality in society, or social rank for the individual. Vertical mortuary variability can be read as an expression of the decedent's membership in one of several ranked segments of society. Mortuary archaeology provides particularly well honed theoretical tools for examining the marking of social rank, social differences, and political claims to control over resources within a population (Brown 1995: 392). Most methodologies stipulate that the rank of an individual in a society will be expressed by the degree of community investment and involvement in his or her funerary rituals. It is assumed that the greater the energy expended on funerary constructions, furniture, and ritual, the higher the status of the individual (Binford 1971:21; Pearson 1999:31; Tainter 1975:2). This straightforward logic lends an elegant theoretical simplicity to mainstream mortuary archaeology and provides a data set that is amenable to quantification and sampling. Perhaps because of this inherent accessibility of mortuary distinctions in rank and wealth to scientific analysis, arguably more attention has been paid to social rank than to any other subject in mortuary studies (Brown 1985, 1995; Shennan 1989; Tainter 1975, 1978, 1980). On the other hand, it may be no coincidence that the emphasis in mortuary archaeology on rank, status, and class distinctions corresponds with their predominant role in neoevolutionary theory on social complexity.

Studies of vertical mortuary variability have been particularly successful in illustrating social hierarchy in early Andean state societies. Andean mortuary traditions display considerable variability in the quality of tomb construction and the number and nature of offerings. In the Moche culture area, the most successful region for this type of study, hypotheses on social hierarchy have been tested through the excavation of significant numbers of tombs. Although Moche burial practices were closely adhered to for all members of society, the expression of these practices can be ranked on a continuum from the simple to the elaborate on the basis of variation in how the body was encased, the nature of the burial chamber, the quantity and quality of grave goods, and the grave's location relative to major monuments. These variations support a close correlation of mortuary treatment to social roles and positions of the deceased (e.g., DeMarrais et al. 1996; Donnan 1995:154; Rowe 1995).

Mortuary archaeology has been less successful in analyzing "horizontal" dimensions of variability among and within ancient cemeteries. Horizontal variability describes categories of distinctions among mortuary populations that are exclusive of status differentiation. Tainter describes this horizontal dimension as mortuary variability among "structural components that are equivalent on identical hierarchical levels and between which there are no major institutionalized differences in rank" (Tainter 1977:331). Horizontal variability may include gender roles and the operation of crosscutting social segments such as "sodalities, individual descent groups of segmentary descent systems, task groups, territorial bands and the like" (Tainter 1977: 331). Given that mainstream neoevolutionary theory considers inequality to be a hallmark of social complexity, it is understandable that archaeologists have not chosen to emphasize aspects of ancient treatment of the dead that manifest these kinds of nonranked social affiliations. Even in the Andes, despite the availability of well-preserved cemeteries that show horizontal variability in burial contexts, mortuary archaeologists have been relatively reluctant to examine issues of corporate group membership, descent orientation, moiety affiliation, and society membership (Dillehay 1995:11). Recent years have begun to see this change, largely because of new bioarchaeological methods that can provide exciting new perspectives on genetic and social relationships in ancient societies (Blom et al. 1998; Buikstra 1995; Hoshower et al. 1995). The promise of these methods and the rich social diversity that they reveal within complex societies should remind mortuary archaeology to give greater consideration to dimensions of social complexity outside the straightforward variables of status, prestige, and wealth. In the following discussion of what mortuary practices can tell us about Tiwanaku society, I aim to keep both the vertical and horizontal dimensions in mind.

Provincial Tiwanaku Social Structure and Burial Practice

With Tiwanaku, for perhaps the first time in any Andean state society, settlement and household archaeology suggest that whole communities of immigrants had come to live permanently, to have children, and eventually to die in new lands far away from their kin and their cultural roots. We may expect the mortuary record to reflect not only the cultural practices and beliefs of these people but something of the social organization and internal variability of provincial Tiwanaku society as well.

A first task in analyzing provincial Tiwanaku mortuary contexts is to define the cultural affiliation of cemetery populations. As we have seen in chapter 4, provincial Tiwanaku cemetery populations can represent (a) acculturated local populations, (b) interspersed separate populations of local peoples and Tiwanaku elites, traders, or their local clients, or (c) the kind of diasporic popular migration of a highland population suggested by the archipelago model. The first possibility is that the provincial Tiwanaku cemeteries simply represent acculturated local populations. If this were the case, we might expect to see gradual and selective modification of local traditions of tomb construction, mortuary treatment, and interment and the introduction of a proportion of Tiwanaku-style, prestige-enhancing grave goods or their imitations. Such innovations could associate with tombs of higher status individuals, while the majority of burials might not vary from preexisting local traditions, as appears to be the case in the Chilean oasis of San Pedro de Atacama. Both cultural and biological markers should support the majority populations being of indigenous descent and not composed of migrants from Tiwanaku or their descendents.

A second scenario of separate contemporary populations might be inferred if one segment of the burial population displayed strong ties with Tiwanaku while others displayed indigenous cultural or ethnic affiliations. Multiethnicity should be represented in distinctive burial practices and offering assemblages and through skeletal evidence of biological distance and culturally manipulated factors such as diet and cranial deformation. An important consideration would be whether enclaves of Tiwanaku colonists could be distinguished from local populations in particular cemeteries, as appears to be the case in the Azapa Valley. Most Azapa Tiwanaku burials are found either in isolated small cemeteries or in small sectors within larger cemeteries of local affiliation (Goldstein 1996). This situation might typify a trade diaspora or other minority settlement operating within the context of a local majority population. If such a community were too small to be self-reproducing, one might expect a gender imbalance among the culturally Tiwanaku burials or a scarcity of child burials.

A third situation in which the entire burial population of a peripheral site displays exclusively Tiwanaku burial practices would suggest the presence of a self-sustaining population culturally identified with the homeland. Here we would expect to see men, women, and children of all ages represented in Tiwanaku-style cemeteries, accompanied by exclusively Tiwanaku grave goods and clothing. Settlement and household data discussed earlier appear to support this diasporic migration scenario. If this is indeed the case, we would be interested in the internal composition of cemeteries and their implications for understanding patterns of social hierarchy and heterarchy within the Tiwanaku culture. Is there evidence for a range of mortuary practices for different individuals or groups? If so, do these differences indicate distinct status classes within a state hierarchy? Do burials of some high status individuals, perhaps Tiwanaku governors or nobles, imply a framework of imposed social stratification, as might be expected in globalist imperial models? Or does the burial population represent a more egalitarian immigrant population, without evidence of a ruling elite? If so, can horizontal distinctions be discerned among members of distinct ethnic identities, kin groups, or other nonhierarchical corporate groups? Could mortuary patterns reflect the nested array of coexisting ayllus and ethnicities suggested by the vertical archipelago model?

Moquegua's large and well-preserved Tiwanaku cemeteries present a unique opportunity to explore the meaning of mortuary variability in Tiwanaku society. Considered in the light of the settlement and household patterns already discussed, mortuary archaeology can indicate the degree of segmentation among distinct social subunits within Tiwanaku society and can provide a powerful test of a diasporic model of early state colonization.

The Moquegua Tiwanaku Cemeteries

The majority of Tiwanaku burials in Moquegua are associated with sites of the Chen Chen style. Chen Chen–style habitation sites all included numerous cemeteries of clearly Tiwanaku affiliation, and thirty-nine Chen Chen–style cemeteries are known, covering well over 10 hectares valleywide (table 5.1). Considering the number and size of its habitation sites, the Omo-style settlement pattern is notable for its scarcity of cemeteries. By comparison to the Chen Chen–style pattern we would predict a number of cemeteries roughly equal to the number of settlement sectors valleywide and a ratio of about 1 hectare of cemetery for every 5 hectares of settlement area. Only three cemeteries have been discovered in association with Omo-style residential sites, however, and these cover only a minuscule area.

The absence of large Omo-style cemetery populations is perplexing. One possible explanation may be that the large Omo-style residential sites of Omo, Río Muerto, and Los Cerrillos represent shorter occupations than those of the Chen Chen style or seasonal occupations by pastoralist communities who regularly returned to the highlands. If this is the case, it is possible that relatively few people died during their short stays at these sites. Alternatively, Omo-style settlements may have had distinctive mortuary practices that reflected their cultural and social difference from the Chen Chen–style sites. As is often the case in pastoral societies, Omo-style mortuary practices may have included exposure, cremation, or other treatments that left no remains. It is also possible that burials at locations more distant from the community are yet to be discovered. As is detailed in what follows, tomb construction and grave goods suggest that two of the three known Omo-style cemeteries represent a high status segment of the population. Lower status Omo-style burials may have received distinctive treatment outside these cemeteries and may be missing from the archaeological record.

There is also a possibility that this imbalance is due to Tiwanaku funerals that involved long-distance transportation of the deceased. Could the Tiwanaku diaspora have shipped some of their dead by caravan to the Tiwanaku core region for burial? Especially if the Omo-style sites represent settlers of a more prestigious affiliation, one of the rights and privileges of their enclave could have been return for burial in the altiplano. This intriguing possibility is impossible to test with the existing evidence, but it would give a different meaning to the "expectation of return" criterion in Clifford's definition of diaspora! Alternately, it is possible that the Chen Chen–style mortuary population was skewed upward by postmortem migration. The Chen Chen site's cemeteries alone contained over thirteen thousand burials (Goldstein and Owen 2001). This may represent a population far greater than is suggested by the occupation's habitation area. Desert areas like Moquegua could have been preferred burial sites because of their superior preservation in comparison with the rainy altiplano. If natural mummification were important to the Tiwanaku, deceased individuals could have been shipped from the Tiwanaku core region for burial in the necropoli of Moquegua.

One of the most important aspects of the Moquegua Tiwanaku mortuary tradition is that burials were distributed among spatially distinct cemeteries surrounding each settlement site. Chen Chen–style Tiwanaku burials at Omo, Chen Chen, and Río Muerto were always located in discrete cemeteries situated around the fringes of the domestic settlements. Typical locations were on hillsides, ridges or fingers of land, or in *quebradas* contiguous to the town sites. No human burials have been found under household structures or elsewhere within the habitation sectors of Moquegua Tiwanaku settlements.

At Omo, fifteen of the nineteen spatially distinct cemeteries at the Omo M10 habitation site and temple could be associated with the Chen Chen–style occupation (table 5.3, fig. 5.26).[1] Nine cemeteries were located within 100 m of the limits of the M10 town site. The remaining cemeteries were either in quebradas at the base of the M10 bluff or on more distant ridges or slopes up to 250 m south of the domestic areas. A similar pattern held at Chen Chen M1, where twenty-eight Chen Chen–style cemeteries clustered around the main settlement sectors. The Chen Chen cemeteries covered over 9 hectares in total, distributed among ridges, quebradas, and slopes around the edges of the town site (fig. 5.13). The Chen Chen–style sectors of Río Muerto M43 and M48 were associated with seven cemeteries covering almost 4 hectares on the slopes of a steep hill overlooking the habitation sector.

What do these discrete cemeteries represent? Cemeteries could be specific to a particular sex or age group, social class, corporate kin or ethnic group, or chronological unit. The association of spatially distinct cemeteries with particular residential wards is another reasonable hypothesis. Without far more extensive residential excavations, direct linkages between domestic groups and cemeteries are not yet possible. A preliminary study of cranial deformation styles by Hoshower et al. (1995) suggests that the Omo cemeteries represent different corporate groups, perhaps similar to ayllus. I return to these questions of gender, age, class, kin, and ethnic representation after a general review of Moquegua Tiwanaku burial practice.

Moquegua Tiwanaku Burial Practice

Tiwanaku colonists introduced a distinctive mortuary tradition to the Moquegua Valley. Unlike the region's indigenous burials, virtually all Tiwanaku burials in Moquegua were individual primary interments. These contrast markedly with the collective *túmulo* and boot tomb interments of Moquegua's indigenous Huaracane Phase described in chapter 4.[2] Unlike the majority of Huaracane burials, which were either primary or secondary interments in earth-filled túmulos, Tiwanaku tombs were sealed chambers with visible capstones that permitted future access to the deceased.[3] Tiwanaku's different social response to death was reflected in a mortuary liturgy and burial structures and practices that facilitated the periodic reopening of tombs for ceremonies or new offerings. This underscores a distinct notion of an individual rather than collective spiritual destiny and a distinct conception of the afterlife. Conceptions of ancestor worship that were prevalent in highland south-central Andean ayllu societies like Tiwanaku required "open sepulchers" (Isbell 1997), tombs that were both visible and visitable. Unlike túmulos, Tiwanaku tombs allowed remains to be taken in and out and permitted postmortem rituals and offerings not possible with other types of burial. The sealed chambers of Tiwanaku tombs suggest a Tiwanaku tradition of an active afterlife, like those that fascinated Spanish chroniclers who had contact with the Inca (Cobo 1984 [1653]:111). It is probable that Tiwanaku dead were visited, regaled with gifts, and removed from their tombs for consultation or festivities on special occasions.

The basic tenets of the Tiwanaku burial tradition were consistent from the Omo- and Chen Chen–style occupations into later Tumilaca times. Despite the political changes that resulted from the collapse of the Tiwanaku polity and the realignment of altiplano-descended settlement in Moquegua, Tumilaca Phase burial practice continued to follow time-honored Tiwanaku traditions, with only minor innovations. Canons of interment, including furnishings, offerings, and positioning of the body suggest a strong continuity in beliefs about the afterlife. Interments were arranged in a seated position, tightly flexed with the arms placed within the fold of the body, hands on the chest, and elbows in the lap. The compact burial bundle was trussed with braided vegetable fiber ropes, producing the characteristic tight flexing of the knees and hips.[4] Where body orientation could be determined, the bodies at Omo were buried facing east in all but one burial, and Vargas reports east-facing orientation for most burials at Chen Chen (Vargas 1994).

East-facing orientation is common to interments throughout the Tiwanaku sphere, and it outlasted the Tiwanaku state in subsequent south-central Andean traditions. Bermann (1994) reports an east-facing orientation for most Tiwanaku burials at Lukurmata, 10 km northeast of Tiwanaku, while Kolata reports the same for Tiwanaku's monumental precinct (Kolata 1993: 156). In the Tiwanaku peripheries, LePaige (1977) reports that a majority of burials at the Coyo Oriental and Quitor cemeteries of San Pedro were east-facing (though it is not clear whether this applies specifically to Tiwanaku-influenced tombs). Both the Akapana and Pumapunku, Tiwanaku's two principal temple platforms, were accessible only by stairways along an east-west axis (Kolata 1993:97–98). Long after the Tiwanaku collapse, Cieza de León observed that the *chulpa* burial towers of Inca-era Aymara rulers were oriented with their doorways toward the rising sun (Cieza 1959 [1553]:284).[5] East-facing, seated interment in individual cist burials constitutes a dominant south-central Andean burial tradition that spread with Tiwanaku diaspora but persisted long after the collapse of the Tiwanaku state. We may surmise that all Tiwanaku peoples shared a complex vision of the afterlife that endured well after the demise of the Tiwanaku state ideology.

Tomb Construction

Tiwanaku individuals were buried in a seated, flexed position in roughly cylindrical graves that seldom exceeded 120 cm in depth. Excavations indicate four formal types of tombs and several variations on surface structures.[6] The simplest tomb type is the *fosa* or unlined pit, an unadorned cylindrical hole excavated in sterile soil. Fosas represent 28.5 percent of a sample of 4,291 tombs in the nine cemeteries examined by Vargas at Chen Chen (1994; see also Blom 1999:81). Fosas have no surface indications and may be discerned on the surface only as depressions of looser fill. Consequently, they are probably underrepresented in the present sample for Omo M10, which includes only six such tombs.

The majority of Moquegua Tiwanaku tombs were *cistas*, roughly cylindrical tombs with some kind of stone lining (fig. 7.1). At Chen Chen, Vargas reports that 70.6 percent of her total sample were cistas, though the frequency of cista tombs varied considerably from cemetery to cemetery.[7] Cistas

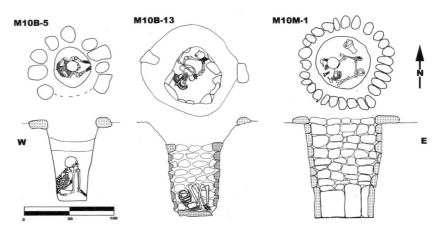

7.1. Moquegua Tiwanaku tomb types: *fosa* with surface ring only, stone-lined *cista*, and slab-lined *cista* with collar.

also varied in the care and complexity of their construction. Many tombs at Omo were marked only by single rings of cobbles or stones that outlined their mouths.[8] These surface ring tombs may be less common at Chen Chen. More elaborate cistas were partially or fully lined with stones. Some twenty-five examined tombs at Omo M10 (41 percent) were completely lined with boulders measuring between 15 × 30 and 30 × 40 cm. Stone was occasionally used for tomb floors, but more often the pavement consisted of sterile soil or packed mud. In several cases, adobe bricks similar to those of the M10 temple complex were used for tomb linings, perhaps indicating the borrowing of materials from the temple after its abandonment. The most elaborate variant of the cista was the slab cist, found at Chen Chen and in seven tombs in the Omo M10 sample (12 percent). In these tombs, large flat-sided stone slabs were carefully fitted to line the base of the tomb, with rows of smaller cobbles sometimes used for upper layers. Fragments of cut-stone blocks removed from the Omo M10 temple were used in a few tombs in the Omo M10B and M10S cemeteries, and the use of stone taken from temples has also been reported for Tiwanaku tombs at the site of Lukurmata (Bermann 1994:331).

Markers that made them visible on the surface distinguished all Tiwanaku burials. Fragments of wooden posts found in many Omo and Chen Chen tombs indicate that poles marked most tombs.[9] Similar wooden poles or canes were used as markers for contemporary tombs in the Azapa Valley (Focacci 1983:106: Muñoz 1983b:93) and in the Solcor 3 and Coyo Oriental cemeteries of San Pedro de Atacama (LePaige 1977:114–124; Llagostera 1996; Llagostera et al. 1988; Oakland 1986:84). None of the Omo tombs was found with its marker pole in its original position.

An alternative surface marker prevalent in some cemeteries was a stone collar wider than the tomb diameter. This surface feature originated in tombs of the Chen Chen style, where it was a minority variant among cista tombs. Considering the substantial surface structures that distinguished Tiwanaku elite tombs (see later discussion), the energy invested in these collar markers could indicate higher status burials. On the other hand, the prevalence of surface collars in the tombs of the Omo M10S cemetery, where distinctive styles of textile tunics and cranial deformation styles have also been noted (discussed later), suggests that some intercemetery variation in tomb styles may correlate with horizontal distinctions of social identities. However, the most significant factor in the distribution of aboveground stone collar tombs seems to be chronological.

Even though Post-Tiwanaku burials indicate continuity in mortuary practice, a trend toward increasingly elaborate tomb markers parallels the reemergence of locally defined elites following the Tiwanaku collapse. Collar tombs increase in frequency in Moquegua's Tumilaca Phase, and they are relatively common at the Tumilaca type site (Bawden 1993). In the cemetery of Tumilaca Phase site Omo M11, twenty-seven of seventy-two tombs were marked by stone collars on the surface. Arguably, a continuum can be traced from these increasingly elaborate collared tombs to the aboveground tombs and chulpa burial towers of the Late Intermediate Period (Stanish 1985:144, 1992:136, 150, 155; Bermann et al. 1989). The spread of post-Tiwanaku collared tombs represents the appearance of new status markers of a locally constituted elite in the face of state collapse.

Prehistoric Cemetery Disturbance

Almost all of the Tiwanaku tombs excavated in Moquegua show signs of prehistoric disturbance. An important distinction might be made between tombs subjected to modern looting and this prehistoric disturbance. Prehistorically looted tombs had their capstones removed and appear today as shallow, silt-filled circular depressions in the desert surface. Thick lenses of volcanic ash demonstrate that these tombs have remained undisturbed since sometime before the eruption of the volcano Huayna Putina in February 1600. Usually, these volcanic ash lenses are found near the surface. Numerous water laminations in the fill below the ash layer and the minimal accretion above the ash indicate that the tombs were opened well before A.D. 1600.

Taphonomy supports this relative dating of prehistoric tomb looting. The removal of the tomb capstones and subsequent silting in of tombs caused considerable deterioration of cadaver soft tissue and associated textiles. Despite this accelerated decay, no intentional disturbance of the interred individuals was indicated. Indeed, the majority remained in their original seated, flexed positions, except for predictable slumping due to gravity. Once tomb capstones were removed, the decay processes in Moquegua Tiwanaku tombs were a race between the disintegration of the remains and their encasement and immobilization in silt. Most interments were found almost fully articulated; however, loose and unstable bones from the upper part of a seated cadaver (crania, mandibles, patellae, and occasionally cervical vertebrae, scapulae, clavicles, and sternae) were often found out of position in the tomb fill. This indicates that the individuals' soft tissue and textile and fiber rope wrapping were left intact in a semi-mummified state when the tombs were opened and only began to disintegrate over the course of the filling in of the tomb.

Decorated ceramic and wooden artifacts are often found intact in these tombs, indicating that the looters were not interested in these materials. In contrast, virtually no metal or jewelry objects were found in any prehistorically disturbed Tiwanaku tomb. The only metal object recovered was a single silver earspool from tomb M-7, found hidden in the folds of a blanket (see later discussion). As earspools might be expected in pairs, it is extremely likely that this artifact was simply left behind by the pre-1600 looter who removed its companion.[10]

In summary most of the Moquegua Tiwanaku tombs were ransacked at some time before A.D. 1600. Because of the extensive deposition below the Huayna Putina ash fall in tombs, most of this valleywide disturbance of Tiwanaku burials must have taken place earlier than the Spanish colonial era. Similar prehistoric looting of Tiwanaku tombs has been reported at the AZ 75 cemetery near San Lorenzo in Chile's Azapa Valley (Focacci 1983; Muñoz 1983a), and it would appear to have been a widespread phenomenon. Caution must be observed in discussing Moquegua Tiwanaku tomb offerings, as the lack of certain grave goods may indicate their prehistoric removal by looters. Usually, Moquegua's prehistoric looters, guided by the Tiwanaku tombs' clear wooden markers and capstones, removed metal and jewelry objects but left ceramics, textiles, and mummies undisturbed. The few known elite tombs may have been singled out for particularly violent and thorough desecration. The Tiwanaku collapse was a time of iconoclasm—as seen in the rejection of state motifs in the arts and in the destruction of the Omo temple and settlements. It would appear that the rejection of the Tiwanaku political collectivity was accompanied by a particularly violent uprooting of the mummies of dead leaders, either at the hands of the colonists' own descendants or by later Late Intermediate or Inca-contemporary looters.

The Dress Code of Tiwanaku Burial

Regarding cultural practice, ethnic orientation, and social affiliations, few aspects of material culture carry as much significance as clothing. Textiles may be the most important material signifier of rank, status, and cultural identity in Andean societies (Murra 1962). Indeed, the Quechua term for "foreigner," *q'ara*, also means naked, uncultured, or uncivilized (Meisch 1997:7). Considering the interweaving of Andean textile production and social identity, the examination of mortuary textile style can support the kind of horizontal social segmentation suggested by the domestic patterns. Andean textile technologies and style have been seen to define corporate segments such as distinct ethnic groups localized in distinct cemetery groups.

In the altiplano Tiwanaku core region, wet conditions inhibit the preservation of clothing. In contrast, the arid sites of the western Tiwanaku periphery offer a rich source of information on Tiwanaku textile art and technology and present us with a category of artifacts that may be highly diagnostic for social affiliation and identity. For San Pedro de Atacama, Oakland argues that a distinctive group of textiles associated with the Coyo Oriental cemetery marked an ethnic enclave of Bolivian Tiwanaku colonists who explicitly maintained a minority identity through dress (Oakland 1992:336; Kolata 1993:277; Llagostera 1996:35). Because it can be compared with the textile inventory of household contexts, the range of burial dress in the Moquegua Tiwanaku cemeteries also offers a unique opportunity to compare the clothing of the dead and living for insight into funerary preparation among Tiwanaku colonists.

In Moquegua, Tiwanaku men, women, and children were buried wearing woolen tunics, blankets, and shawls. Tunics were worn as in life or placed over the folded arms and knees of the flexed bundle and sewn shut. Some individuals wore two or more tunics or an additional shawl or carrying cloth. There is no evidence that Tiwanaku people wore undergarments, in contrast to the Late Intermediate Estuquiña culture where males wore *taparobas* or loincloths beneath their tunics (Clark 1993). Finally, most Tiwanaku interments were wrapped in thick camelid wool blankets of a coarse plainweave type. These blankets were decorated with wide warp stripes in undyed yarn colors of brown and tan. Cactus spine sewing needles or unelaborated spines (*Browningia candelabris*) were often used to affix the blankets, which in some cases were loosely stitched to the tunics with a heavy natural yarn. Bronze *tupu* brooches were occasionally found in the Chen Chen cemeteries (Vargas 1994), but metal artifacts of all types were rare and may have been removed by early looters.

Andean garments in general are distinguished by the fine weaving of fabric panels that were assembled intact and seldom tailored, cut, or pleated. Tiwanaku tunics, which were the only fitted garment, were sleeveless, untailored rectangular shirts made from four intact panels sewn together at the selvages with slits left open for the neck and arms. Because most individuals wore formally identical tunics of warp-faced plainweave construction, most of the variability in dress was in the fineness of the weave and the colors and technical elaboration of warp stripes and added embroidery. Although some of these elements, like decorative embroidered selvages, do reflect added energy input and skill, most of the textile assemblage from the Omo M10 tombs suggests variation within a range that would be available to the general Tiwanaku population.

Textile offerings that suggest significant vertical status distinctions are rare in Moquegua Tiwanaku. The key indicator here is the absence of tunics made in the tapestry technique in most of the Chen Chen or Omo tombs. Tapestry is a labor-intensive technique in which a design is woven directly into the fabric as numerous separate sections of differently colored wefts. Tiwanaku tapestries were particularly fine, often with very high weft thread counts, and usually distinguished by a complex "interlocked" technique of joining color sections (Conklin 1983; Oakland 1992). We know from the Inca period that tapestry would have been instantly recognizable as a prestige fabric in a society that valued weaving and that it may well have been limited to certain classes by sumptuary laws (Murra 1962). Tapestry was also the only Tiwanaku textile medium capable of incorporating design elements into the weave itself. Despite the attention paid to small numbers of Tiwanaku tapestry tunics found in San Pedro and elsewhere for their iconographic content (chapter 4), it is notable that tapestry is almost absent in the vast majority of Tiwanaku tombs in Chen Chen and Omo M10.

Totally absent from Moquegua Tiwanaku burials are garments of cotton, which appear to occupy the lowest end of the prestige scale. The discovery of cotton fabrics in Tiwanaku domestic contexts presents a fascinating new perspective on the contrast of dress for the living and the dead in the Tiwanaku diaspora. Cotton, a lowland product, was a common provincial garment material but it was clearly considered inappropriate for the afterlife. One cannot help but wonder why the dress code for the Tiwanaku dead excluded cotton, a lowland, warm-weather fiber, in favor of tunics and heavy blankets of wool. Such stubborn adherence to woolen burial wear may have been a symbolic link to highland Tiwanaku, with its frosty climate and wool-producing camelid herds. The colonists of Tiwanaku physically remained in the *yungas* lowlands for eternity, yet they may have thought of the afterlife as a place akin to their ancestral homeland, a high frigid land to the east. In death, the Tiwanaku diaspora dressed as if they were going home.

Grave Offerings

Moquegua Tiwanaku tombs were typically furnished with a variety of grave goods to accompany the interment. Excavations at Chen Chen found that tombs varied from no offerings to a maximum of nine, with a mean of 1.5 offerings per tomb (Blom 1999:82). Only a limited range of artifact types were placed in Tiwanaku tombs, suggesting that there were conservative conventions about suitable grave furnishings in the altiplano Tiwanaku tradition. Many categories of artifacts and materials that were ubiquitous in Tiwanaku domestic contexts, such as cotton textiles, utilitarian pottery, agricultural implements, and food items, were clearly considered profane and inappropriate as offerings. Conversely, some offering categories that were ritually appropriate for temple or household dedicatory offerings were also excluded from burials. Foremost among these are offerings of sacrificial camelids or guinea pigs, for which there is ample evidence in domestic and temple contexts at Omo and Chen Chen and in ceremonial contexts at the Tiwanaku site (Manzanilla and Woodard 1990; Manzanilla 1992a,b). Animals or animal parts were not included as offerings in any human interments in Moquegua Tiwanaku. This apparent taboo conflicts with Late Intermediate Period cultures, in which burials included hoofs, heads, and on occasion entire llamas.[11]

Ceramic vessels are the best-preserved component of the Moquegua Tiwanaku grave offerings. Intact ceramic vessels were usually found above or at the same level as the body, suggesting that they had rested on the mummy bundle itself. Vegetal or faunal food offerings were seldom found in ceramic or basketry vessels, suggesting that it was the vessels themselves, rather than their contents, that were the significant offerings. Vessels often show signs of use and none appears to have been manufactured specifically for burial, suggesting that the vessels represent the deceased individuals' personal implements. As with clothing, the ceramic offerings represent a conscious selection from the vessel types used in everyday contexts. In order of frequency, the primary Chen Chen–style mortuary ceramic offerings were Tiwanaku red-slipped keros (flaring drinking goblets), tazones (flaring-sided bowls), and one-handled pitchers (fig. 7.2). In addition, small plainware ollas (two-handled cooking pots, always soot-covered) were found in the tombs of females and children. Of 37 identified vessels from the M10 tombs, 14 (37.8%) were keros, 11 (29.7%) tazones, three (8.1%) pitchers, and three (8.1%) plainware ollas. A 1984 examination of Tiwanaku redware vessels in private collections (Goldstein 1985) and finds from Vargas's Chen Chen excavations confirm a similar order of distribution for these four principal types.[12] Other decorated types, like round-based open bowls, straight-sided cups, hollow-base libation bowls and incensarios, and portrait or zoomorphic vessels account for only a small proportion of mortuary offerings, while some serving types such as *fuentes* and most utilitarian plainware vessels are absent altogether.

Wooden and basketry implements and containers were also common inclusions in Moquegua Tiwanaku burials. Again, these represent a subset of

7.2. Ceramic grave offerings, Omo M10M cemetery, tomb 1.

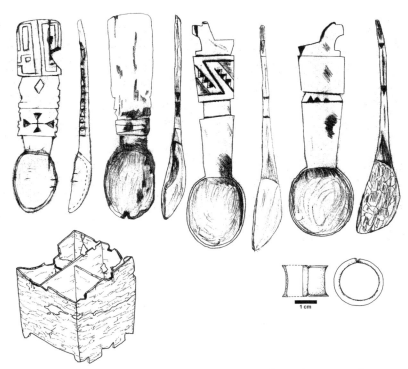

7.3. Omo M10 grave offerings: wooden spoons, pigment box, silver earspool.

artifact types also found in everyday domestic contexts. Carved wooden spoons were the most frequent offerings, often found placed inside ceramic tazones. Most spoons were of the flat-handled variety typical for the Chen Chen style, usually decorated with notched or scalloped edges, incised cross-hatched designs, and llama-shaped silhouettes on the tip of the handle (fig.

7.3).[13] Carved wooden keros and pitchers and small, finely woven poly-chrome baskets were found less frequently in tombs than were their ceramic counterparts. Also found in small numbers were distinctive two- or four-compartment wooden pigment boxes of a style also known from Tiwanaku contexts in Arica and San Pedro, spindle whorls, combs, and gourd vessels (Blom 1999:80). Snuff or *rape* tablets or other components of hallucinogenic drug kits were not found in Chen Chen or Omo's Tiwanaku tombs, nor do they appear in local collections. This suggests that the vast majority of Tiwa-naku colonists did not participate in the magico-religious rites and elite rela-tionships that were represented by finds of drug kits in the rare Tiwanaku-associated tombs of San Pedro de Atacama.

Age and Sex Distinctions in Moquegua Tiwanaku Burials

Excavation at Omo and Chen Chen has shown that each cemetery includes burials of individuals of all ages and both sexes. There is no evidence for age- or sex-specific burial grounds, nor have we located any nonstandard burial treatment for children in Moquegua Tiwanaku. Generally, age profiles ap-proximate a 50 percent representation of nonadults, as might be expected in preindustrial societies. Among twenty-six sex-identified individuals in the Omo M10 cemetery sample, sixteen were male and ten female. This gender imbalance in the small sample from Omo initially suggested predominantly male trade diaspora, military or diplomatic mission, or a vanguard migrant community (Anthony 1990:905). However, Blom's larger sample of 334 adult individuals from the Chen Chen cemeteries found only 37 percent of the sex-identified adults to be male. Blom posits that the prevalence of female adults could result from a high mortality rate for male children, an emigra-tion of males, or polygynous marital patterns at Chen Chen (Blom 1999: 178). The contradiction between the Omo and Chen Chen populations could reflect some gendered functional distinction between the two sites or may simply be an artifact of small sample size. In any event, the age and sex distributions for both cemetery populations are within the range of a resident reproducing population of complete families (Blom 1999:160). In Moque-gua, as throughout the Tiwanaku world, the incidence of cranial modifica-tion was identical among males and females, indicating that infants of both sexes received similar treatment. The practice of cranial modification, while practiced in infancy, signaled the individual's ethnic origins throughout life. Gender parity in this practice points to a social system that emphasized social distinction to the extent that neither men nor women could ever be fully assimilated by families of another ethnicity. This argues strongly for bilocal residence patterns and a high degree of endogamy.

Male, female, and juvenile interments shared a similar range of tomb types and offerings. At Omo M10, thirty-two adults and twenty-eight juveniles were represented in the sample, a ratio consistent with other pre-Columbian sites in the region. There is no indication of any spatial segregation within cemeteries according to age of the deceased. Generally speaking, juveniles and adults had the same kinds of grave goods, but adults had more goods. Of seven standard tombs that produced two or more vessels, six were of adults, mostly of advanced age. As three females and one male were identified in these "richest" tombs, it seems that gender had no absolute association with the quantity of offerings, although the tombs with the most numerous offerings were burials of adult males.

Some gendered distinctions in the nature of offerings are apparent. Two offering types—plainware two-handled cooking ollas and wooden spindles—were associated with adult female and juvenile burials. The female association of the cooking ollas might suggest that adult women cooked, while spindles suggest that women did the spinning for textile production, as is common today in the south-central Andes. In contrast, ceramic keros, the Tiwanaku goblets associated with the ritual consumption of maize beer, were associated only with males and undetermined-sex juveniles at Omo and never with female burials. At Chen Chen *zamponas* (pan pipes) were only found with male burials (Blom 1999:82). The association of keros and zamponas with male burials supports male participation in ritualized maize beer drinking. A gender-based distinction in diet is also supported by carbon and nitrogen isotope evidence from the Omo burials. A significantly lower C13 value in female skeletons suggests that men consumed more maize products while women in the sample ate more C3 leguminous plants. Males' higher N15 values also suggest greater meat consumption (Sandness 1992:54). Did Tiwanaku males control the production of Moquegua's politically vital maize crop and caravan herds? More likely the dietary distinction results from different patterns of consumption. Considering the political and ceremonial importance placed on ritual drinking in Andean state societies, the association of keros and zamponas with males suggests that chicha drinking, and all the sociopolitical power it implies, was a male activity.

Ayllu and Ethnicity: The Horizontal Dimension

The segregation of segments of the Moquegua Tiwanaku population into distinct cemetery groups and the diversity of Tiwanaku burial offerings suggests that there was significant mortuary variability in the horizontal dimension. At Omo M10, for example, identically patterned blue and red striped tunics were found only in tombs from the M10S cemetery (S-4 and S-5). Assuming a household production of textiles in which stylistic elaboration and weaving techniques were passed down from weaver to weaver, this could be explained by cemetery-specific burials of a distinctive kin group, ayllu, or other horizontal subset of the population. Because virtually no non-Tiwanaku materials were found in any of the Moquegua tombs, it is difficult to isolate these between-cemetery distinctions as "multiethnicity" through gross stylistic differences in tomb offerings. Despite this homogeneity at the level of widely shared cultural norms, future consideration of more subtle stylistic and technical variation among artifacts from different cemetery groups has the potential to isolate some of these distinct segments of the colonial Tiwanaku population (e.g., Oakland 1992). This will be an important avenue of future research.

One approach to identifying horizontal dimensions of mortuary variability is through indications of genetic relationship or biological distance. Some of the most eloquent testimony to the origins of the Tiwanaku colonists of the eighth through tenth centuries comes to us in their own physical remains. Sophisticated new techniques of biological archaeology and physical anthropology offer an entirely independent avenue to discussions of group affiliation in prehistory. A comprehensive study of nonmetric traits by Blom and colleagues (1998) found no significant biological distance among skeletal populations of Tiwanaku, Lukurmata, and rural sites of the Tiwanaku Valley and the Katari basin. This indicates relatively open migration and mating among Tiwanaku populations. The Tiwanaku population of the Chen Chen site of the Moquegua Valley was far closer genetically to that of the Tiwanaku core region than to non-Tiwanaku peoples of Moquegua, confirming that colonists and their descendants peopled peripheral settlements.

One of the most effective methods to approach horizontal segmentation in Tiwanaku society is the study of cranial deformation. Intentional shaping of the skull by deforming it during infancy was a common practice in the pre-Columbian Andes. Cranial deformation marked the individual throughout life according to culture-specific canons of beauty and group inclusion. Sources from the Spanish colonial period indicate that Andean cranial modification styles, along with specific hairstyles, hats, and headdresses, correlated with regional, ethnic, or clan affiliations rather than status or gender (Blom 1999:102). In one case recorded in the sixteenth century, the Collaguas of Arequipa's Colca Valley even used cranial deformation to mark their children's ayllu membership in explicit relation to their ethnic group's mythic origin place. The Collaguas "molded the heads of their newborns to lengthen and narrow them as high and as elongated as they could, so that in remembrance the head would have the form of the volcano from which they came" (Ulloa Mogollón et al. 1965 [1557–86]:327). The chroniclers go on to note that the neighboring Cavanaconde "have very different heads from the Collaguas, because they wrap them tightly and make them squat and wide," and that each group found the other's head shape to be ugly (Ulloa Mogollón et al. 1965 [1557–86]:327). This aesthetic opposition may have reinforced group endogamy and suggests that cranial deformation was used to make an explicit statement of ayllu group identity in a multiethnic or socially segmented environment.

Most Tiwanaku populations practiced cranial deformation by using a variety of implements to modify the developing crania of infants. Deformation techniques may be divided into two general categories: annular or circumferential deformation by binding the head with ropes or turbans to achieve an elongated head shape, or fronto-occipital or tabular deformation produced by flattening the forehead and base of the skull using cradleboards or other devices (fig. 7.4). Stylistic variation at this macro level has been noted between regions and may well reflect ethnic distinctions at the level of maximal ayllus. Among culturally Tiwanaku populations, annular types of deformation predominated in the Katari basin region of the altiplano, while fronto-occipital types dominated in the Moquegua Valley. As might be expected for a cosmopolitan city, the Tiwanaku site itself displays the greatest heterogeneity of styles, with 60 percent of crania showing fronto-occipital and 40 percent showing annular deformation. Moreover, examples of each type were differently represented in sectors of the site that may correspond to distinct ethnic populations (Blom et al. 1998:250; Blom 1999:159).

Cranial modification was extremely widespread in the Moquegua Tiwanaku colonies. Deformation was displayed by all but one of the thirty-five adult crania recovered from Omo M10 and by 82 percent of the 420 Chen

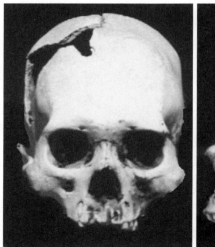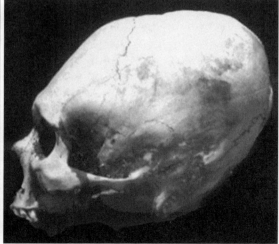

7.4. Moquegua Tiwanaku cranium showing fronto-occipital deformation. PSG photo.

Chen adult crania (Blom 1999:152). All deformation at Omo and Chen Chen was fronto-occipital, involving some kind of cradleboard or other deforming device that produced varying degrees of occipital and frontal flattening and some widening of the parietals. However, a wide assortment of deforming techniques was apparently used, producing considerable variation in cranial shapes. An examination of deformation patterns left in crania by the configuration of pads, straps, boards, and bindings suggests as many as four distinctive deformation styles. Although there is intracemetery variation, the distribution of styles tended to be homogeneous within cemeteries and heterogeneous between cemeteries (Hoshower et al. 1995).[14] For example, the three deformed crania recovered from the M10S cemetery, noted earlier for the similarity of style of some of its textile tunics, all displayed a marked circular "bunning" of the occiput that is most likely due to a doughnut-shaped device placed on the back of the skull in childhood. In contrast, all four crania from the M10R cemetery display triangular deformation, occipital flattening, and circumferential banding. These cemetery-specific types suggest a correlation between cemeteries and deformation practices that can only be tested with a considerably larger sample. Nonetheless, the discovery of both interregional and intrasite segregation of artifact substyles, biological markers, and cranial deformation styles makes a convincing case for strong horizontal divisions of ethnic and ayllu identities that persist in the Tiwanaku homeland and colonies.

Status and Wealth: The Vertical Dimension

Earlier it was noted that the prevalent use of mortuary data is in analyzing differences in the vertical dimension of social status distinctions in ancient societies. "Commoner" burials are expected to show little investment in tomb construction and relatively modest grave offerings, as befits individuals of relatively simple social personae. "Elite" burials are expected to display greater labor investment, more numerous imported or sumptuary offerings, or better nutrition and health than the population at large. Of course, it is possible that some of these variables may reflect horizontal dimensions of the social persona as well. For example, some families' mortuary ritual traditions may simply be less ostentatious than others. However, it is reasonable to conclude that the consistent correlation of spatially or biologically distinct groups with different levels of energy expenditure in death ritual implies some degree of vertical differentiation in society.

If the quantity of offerings is an index of respect for a social persona, we may recognize those adults or children who were buried with no offerings whatsoever as the Tiwanaku colonies' least advantaged individuals. At Chen Chen, only 63 percent of unlined fosa tombs had offerings, while 88 percent of cista tombs had offerings (Blom 1999:82). Considered in terms of energy investment, this suggests that fosas could correlate to an underprivileged segment of Tiwanaku society. Examples of this at Omo may be found in M16E and M10Q cemeteries, which showed a high incidence of the unlined fosa tomb type and had virtually no grave offerings. The Tiwanaku colonies' most marginalized individuals may be represented by a very small number of burials where the bodies were interred in aberrant positions. The only exceptions to the seated flexed burial pattern at Omo were three individuals buried in the M10Q cemetery in a facedown position. One of these was a pregnant female with a well-developed fetus, presumably a death in childbirth. It is conceivable that these negative burial treatments may have been reserved for outcast or taboo individuals. Only further research can determine whether the distribution of burials without offerings reflects a lower class in provincial Tiwanaku or simply idiosyncratic cases of low status achieved in life through impoverishment, widowhood, alienation from kin groups, social transgression, insanity, or disease.

Elite Tiwanaku Burials: The First *Chulpas*

Tiwanaku is not known for elaborate pyramids, mausolea, or other tombs of kings and high status individuals. In the Tiwanaku core region, despite the presence in museum collections of thousands of precious objects that were presumably looted from elite tombs, no intact royal tombs have ever been studied by scientific excavators. The great pyramids and platforms of the Tiwanaku core region appear to have been primarily temple structures, and archaeologists are unaware of any substantial mortuary monuments. Because high status groups apparently resided near monumental structures of the Tiwanaku site (Janusek 2002:43), it is reasonable to assume that their burials might be associated with elite residential compounds. Available evidence suggests that some high status interments were in stone-lined chambers attached to palaces. A series of cut-stone chamber tombs can still be seen in a platform in the Putuni compound at Tiwanaku surrounding what is known as the Palace of the Multicolored Rooms (fig. 7.5 Posnansky 1957). Although these tombs had been looted at the turn of the twentieth century, reexcavation found enough material to indicate that this burial ground was once a "sumptuous, and evidently, coveted final resting place" (Kolata 1993:163).

In the Tiwanaku cemeteries of Moquegua we do see some vertical dimensions in mortuary variability in the form of differential inclusion of prestige goods and labor investment in burials in spatially separated cemeteries. However, most tombs from Omo and Chen Chen show only a limited range in the energy invested in construction or the number or quality of offerings. Fur-

Figure 7.5. Elite tomb at Tiwanaku site. PSG photo.

thermore, there is no direct association of better appointed tombs with high status residences or temples. At Omo M10, contrary to initial expectations, the interments of the M10B cemetery, located in an artificial platform that directly abuts the M10 temple, were not better constructed than tombs in other locations, nor were there distinctive grave goods. Indeed, the random and rather careless placement of the tombs in the southeastern half of the platform and the use in one tomb of cut stones that may have been removed from the temple suggest that this cemetery postdates active temple use. The quality and quantity of tomb offerings were consistent with other Chen Chen–style interments.

One endorsement for the idea of vertical mortuary variability comes from finds of elite regalia that can be identified in the iconography of Tiwanaku. Portrait head ceramic vessels portray males wearing four-pointed hats or turbans, metal earspools, and face paint or facial paint or tattoos of stylized tears or arrows (Eisleb and Strelow 1980: figs. 248, 250, 260; Frame 1990; Ponce 1947:209, 1948: plate 2, 1972: plate 5; Posnansky 1957:114, plate 66). Muñoz (1983a:55) argues that Tiwanaku-contemporary mummies with distended earlobes for earspools, certain types of facial deformation, and a lower frequency of pathologies were associated with more elaborate offerings and represent a chiefly social stratum in the Azapa Valley of Chile. Tiwanaku portrait vessels often depict these individuals with mustaches and coca quid bulges in their cheeks (fig. 7.6). Tapestry tunics complete the ensemble,

Figure 7.6. Portrait *kero* depicting elite male, Chen Chen site M1. PSG photo.

based on their depiction on Wari face-neck portrait vessels that similarly portray high status males with earspools, face paint, and four-pointed hats. Tapestry tunics also adorn the bodies of the great stone stelae of Tiwanaku in low-relief carving, and they were perhaps the most important marker of Tiwanaku-influenced elite burials in San Pedro de Atacama.

Offerings of some of these emblematic high status artifacts were associated with the Omo M10M cemetery, located to the south of the domestic settlement. In terms of tomb construction and offering quantities, this cemetery is noteworthy but not exceptional, as all burials fall within the range of zero to nine offerings per tomb reported for Chen Chen. The fifteen excavated tombs of the M10M cemetery produced a total of fifteen ceramic vessels, six wooden spoons, and a number of other offerings. This is an above-average number of offerings when compared to the Chen Chen sample and to the other fifty-six tombs of Omo M10, which produced only seventeen vessels and nine spoons combined. Tomb M10M-1 is a relatively elaborate slab cista construction that contained a male of over fifty years of age; it was furnished with four unusually elegant ceramic vessels (fig. 7.2), a fine six-color striped *inkuña*, or carrying cloth with embroidered edges, a spoon, and a decorated basket. The only silver object yet found at M10 was the large earspool from tomb M10M-7, the burial of an adult male between thirty-five and forty (fig. 7.3). The surviving earspool and associated fragments of a six-color striped plainweave tunic suggest that this individual may have been of moderately high status. A polychrome Tiwanaku knotted four-pointed hat was found in another tomb in the M10M cemetery (tomb 17). Other M10M tombs had few or no grave goods, and even the richest tombs were within the range described for Chen Chen, so the M10M cemetery's apparent concentration of richer tombs may be the result of a small sample. Moreover, none of the individuals was buried in tapestry tunics, arguably the most significant emblem of all. Nonetheless, the concentration of grave wealth here and particularly of rank insignia like earspools and four-pointed hats indicates moderate vertical distinction of status from Omo M10s other cemetery groups.

Two cemeteries recently discovered in association with Omo-style components at Omo and Río Muerto are unique in Moquegua Tiwanaku as examples of a distinct elite burial type. The Omo M16D cemetery, located on an isolated hillside between the elite south community of Omo M12 and the M16 village, was discovered at the Omo Alto M16 site in 1998 and completely excavated during salvage work in 1999. Eighteen of the nineteen excavated tombs in this small cemetery were cistas of fully stone-lined construction, and no simpler ring tombs or fosas were found. Although M16D, like most Tiwanaku cemeteries, had been looted in antiquity, it was also notable for the surviving grave offerings found. These included Tiwanaku serving ceramics of particularly high quality and an unusual quantity and variety of metal objects, jewelry, and beads. Greenstone beads were found in five tombs, including three tombs of infants or young adults. An adolescent burial, tomb 14, included four silver rings and greenstone beads. One infant burial, tomb 9, was remarkable for the presence of anklets of *Spondylus* shell and greenstone beads and a metal spoon. Both metal and greenstone were quite rare in Moquegua Tiwanaku tombs, and this would appear to be the only occurrence of spondylus beads in a mortuary context. Spondylus, a pink thorny oyster that was highly prized in the ancient Andes, is found only off the coast of Ecuador and represents a valued long-distance import.

The M16D cemetery also included one remarkable Tiwanaku burial structure that is unique in Moquegua in construction and contents. Tomb 15 was detected on the surface as a ring of large stones. The ring was approximately 7 m in diameter, dominating the southern half of this hillside cemetery (figs.

Figure 7.7. Omo M16 cemetery D, view north. PSG photo.

Figure 7.8. Omo M16 tomb D-15 plan.

7.7, 7.8). Excavation showed this to be the circular foundation of a stone or composite enclosure wall that may have been as high as two meters. The interior of the circle was a leveled platform with a packed earth floor. At the center was a single, oval cist approximately 3 × 2 m in width and 2 m in depth. This central chamber was completely lined with rounded cobbles, with flat stone slabs in the floor, all plastered with mud. The tomb had originally been roofed with mud-covered straw and branches supported by a central wooden post or posts. On the southeast side of the tomb, a 60 cm cutout in the rim and impressions of stone slabs in mud mortar indicate a stepped entryway to the inner tomb chamber. This east-facing entryway is consistent with both Tiwanaku tomb orientation and the east-facing doorways of post-Tiwanaku chulpas of the altiplano. A wooden post recovered from the floor of tomb 15 was radiocarbon dated to cal A.D. 635–890 (table 5.14).[15]

Although tomb 15 was thoroughly looted and its contents had been destroyed, even the disturbed offerings recovered in 1999 exceeded the richest tombs of Omo and Chen Chen and indicate a very special burial indeed. The looters were apparently not interested in collecting ceramic vessels, textiles, or beads, yet they took great pains to tear the interred individual and his grave offerings into small fragments. Skeletal material recovered includes an adult male and partial remains of a two- to four-year-old and a younger child (Blom, pers. comm., 2002). Unfortunately, these three individuals were completely disarticulated and scattered, so we can only surmise that the adult male was the principal interment, and the children were either subsidiary burials or intrusions from neighboring looted burials. Fragments of at least seven ceramic vessels were found within the tomb D-15 chamber or in the structure above. These include a portrait head vessel, fragments of a large llama-shaped blackware *sahumario* (censer), cups, keros, tazones, and everted bowls (fig. 7.9). Also present were a decorated wooden spoon and three polychrome baskets in poor states of preservation.

Beyond the quantity of offerings, the M16D interment was set apart from all others in Moquegua by the opulence of jewelry and personal dress that accompanied the interments. Over eight hundred turquoise, onyx, and malachite greenstone beads were recovered, the remnants of numerous necklaces, bracelets, and anklets. Some of these beads were less than 1 mm in diameter, indicating a phenomenal level of craftsmanship. Most important, fragments of three distinct tapestry shirts were found as a mass sandwiched together. This confirms that the adult male mummy had been clothed in three tapestry tunics, layered one atop the other (fig. 7.10). It is worth recalling that tapestry tunics were not found in *any* other Moquegua Tiwanaku burials. Considering the sumptuary laws concerning tapestry tunics in the Inca empire, and their rarity and elite contextual associations elsewhere in the Tiwanaku world, the occurrence of three such tunics in association with a single indi-

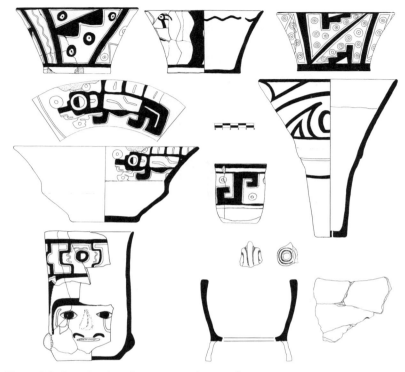

Figure 7.9. Omo M16 tomb D-15 ceramic grave lot.

vidual represents a unique, spectacular, and ostentatious concentration of textile wealth and symbolic capital.

The Omo M16D cemetery probably was not the only elite tomb group in Moquegua. The M70B cemetery, discovered in 1993 adjacent to the Omo-style habitation area at Río Muerto M70, also appeared on the surface as an irregular concentration of piled stone. The quantity of stone and patterning of the 34 × 22 m stone pile indicates a massive aboveground mausoleum structure. While this cemetery has not been excavated, fragmentary keros and polished blackware pottery of Moquegua Tiwanaku's Omo style are visible on the surface.

These cemeteries' aboveground stone construction resembles only one other known cemetery in the Tiwanaku periphery: the Atoca 1 site of Chile's Azapa Valley (Focacci 1983; Goldstein 1996; Muñoz 1983b). The Atoca 1 cemetery is located on a bluff overlooking the western edge of the Pampa Alto Ramírez above the Atoca hacienda (Dauelsberg 1961:283).[16] The site includes a sector of cist tombs and a separate "accumulation of rocks" (Muñoz 1986:314). In the lower section of the cemetery, Muñoz excavated two de-

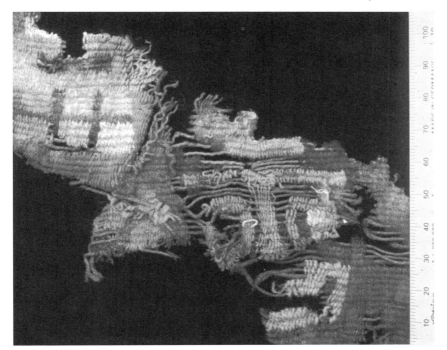

Figure 7.10. M16 tomb D-15 tapestry tunic fragment. PSG photo.

capitated camelid offerings and four cylindrical cist tombs, all badly disturbed by pre-Columbian destruction and/or construction of colonial corrals (1983b, 1986:311, 320). Muñoz reports finding Cabuza and Tiwanaku sherds and an engraved wooden kero fragment in the tombs and on the surface nearby.[17] In 1991 I noted that the stone structures reported by Muñoz were an aboveground stone burial structure. Ceramic fragments on the surface near this disturbed stone structure included red-slipped and polished blackware kero fragments of exceptionally high quality, beads, tapestry textile fragments, and a figurine fragment. Perhaps the most provocative aspect of the Atoca 1 collections was my discovery that a small number of ceramic fragments are of a Wari Chakipampa–style face-neck jar and other vessels, making them the only Wari-style pottery found in Chile (figure 4.14; Goldstein 1995; Muñoz 1986:314). As the decorated Wari pottery appears as a minuscule portion of burial offerings in a site that is evidently of Tiwanaku affiliation, these southernmost of Wari pots must have been status markers that appeared as rare and precious trade goods in the Tiwanaku peripheries. With its surface mausoleum and precious offerings, the Atoca 1 site is a good candidate for particularly high status provincial Tiwanaku burials (Goldstein

1996). Berenguer suggests that Tiwanaku enclaves in Azapa ruled over a
large indigenous population as an elite minority and suggests that this higher
status would be reflected in the Azapa Tiwanaku cemeteries (Berenguer and
Dauelsberg 1989). It is true that Tiwanaku cemeteries in Azapa are smaller
and far rarer than those of Moquegua; indeed Atoca 1 is one of only three or
four Tiwanaku cemeteries that produce altiplano-style offerings. If this were
the case, the elite Azapa Tiwanaku colonies may have been fundamentally
unlike the enormous proletarian occupations of Moquegua, where only a
tiny minority received this kind of mortuary treatment.

Summary: Death and Social Persona in Provincial Tiwanaku

At the beginning of this chapter I proposed that mortuary data could provide
some insights into the social organization of the Tiwanaku state. I suggested
that large cemetery populations with unquestionable material and structural
similarities to homeland burials would be a marker for large-scale permanent
Tiwanaku settlement. Mortuary archaeology in the Moquegua Tiwanaku
cemeteries indeed supports the idea of an ethnically Tiwanaku diaspora that
remained closely connected to the death rituals of its altiplano homeland.
Moquegua Tiwanaku burials had nothing in common with the communal
burial mounds of the Huaracane tradition, and they differ little from those of
the Tiwanaku core region in tomb construction, preparation and positioning
of the deceased, or offerings. All offerings in the Moquegua Tiwanaku cemeteries were of altiplano Tiwanaku types; and there is no evidence of any
legacy from indigenous mortuary traditions. With all interments facing east,
Moquegua Tiwanaku tombs display a further orientation to Tiwanaku tradition. Tiwanaku colonists went to their reward wearing traditional highland
woolen garments according to a strictly formal dress code banning the casual
cotton clothing that was everyday wear in Moquegua. Not only are local
style elements not found, but the Moquegua Tiwanaku mortuary assemblage
seldom includes the magico- religious elements that seem to have been the
vital commodities for the co-option of elite clients in San Pedro de Atacama,
such as elaborate drug paraphernalia. The Omo grave goods overwhelmingly suggest a community of altiplano origins rather than a local population dominated by Tiwanaku overlords. This sets Moquegua apart from
Tiwanaku mortuary influences in Azapa Valley, where graves of Tiwanaku
colonists were a distinct minority, or at San Pedro, where only a small cadre
of local lords adopted Tiwanaku grave goods.

This archaeological interpretation of wholesale colonial immigration has
been supported by biological distance studies that found the Moquegua
Tiwanaku population to be far closer genetically to that of the Tiwanaku core

region than to the pre-Tiwanaku peoples of Moquegua (Blom et al. 1998). Similarly, skeletal carbon and nitrogen isotope ratios indicate that Moquegua Tiwanaku individuals consumed high levels of C4 plants such as maize, contrasting with the more diverse C3 plant diet indicated for pre-Tiwanaku individuals of the Huaracane Phase, suggesting radical differences in diet between the two cultures (Sandness 1991). This substantiates the hypothesis that Moquegua Tiwanaku was a colony settled by altiplano immigrants and their descendants and not by a few foreigners ruling over acculturated local populations.

Furthermore, the size and number of the Omo, Chen Chen, and Río Muerto cemeteries suggest a colonial phenomenon of enormous scale. Full coverage survey of the middle Moquegua Valley has mapped a total of forty-two Omo- and Chen Chen–style Tiwanaku cemeteries, which collectively cover a total of 10.5 hectares. Assuming a cemetery density of only one tomb per 4 m^2, the total burial population could have exceeded twenty-six thousand souls. Even when conservatively averaged over the approximately four-hundred-year duration of the Tiwanaku occupation in Moquegua, this still would come to more than sixty-five Tiwanaku deaths per year, a figure that does not account for individuals buried outside these community cemeteries. Given the potentially "transnational" nature of the Tiwanaku diaspora, the colonial population may even have been higher if some colonists returned home to die or be buried. The sheer size and number of these cemeteries tells us that Tiwanaku's colonies in Moquegua were the endpoint of a migratory settlement phenomenon unprecedented in the south-central Andes. Because their scale surpasses anything implied in Murra's colonial archipelago formulation, I would propose that they represent the maturation of an expansive state's province out of a diasporic migration.

Generally, the horizontal dimensions of social differentiation in mortuary contexts overshadow vertical differentiation in the Tiwanaku provinces. Overall, the strongest patterns in burial treatment, biological distance, and cranial deformation styles suggest subtle differences in social identity among cemetery populations rather than a formalized class system. Perhaps the Tiwanaku polity as a whole was less class-oriented and more horizontally integrated than other states. Such a heterarchical sociopolitical organization could have been dominated by descent groups or ayllus instead of the complex hierarchy of social classes and bureaucracies we associate with states. This heterarchical explanation would emphasize the association of the few known "elite" burials in the Tiwanaku periphery with ayllu leaders rather than with state governors. To arrive at more convincing interpretations of ethnicity and social segmentation within Tiwanaku, far larger samples and more detailed studies of demographics, biological distance, pathology, nutrition, and cranial deformation, along with comparative studies at other sites, are required.

Does the mortuary record point to increasing state control over this densely settled provincial region and the institution of a vertical social hierarchy as the initial colonies grew into a populous province? There is evidence for emergent social stratification within Moquegua Tiwanaku on two levels. First, one group of particularly well appointed cista tombs was associated with offerings that had specific significance as emblems of authority. Artifacts such as earspools and four-pointed hats were restricted in distribution to the graves of a small number of senior adult males who were buried at several cemeteries in Omo and Chen Chen. The distribution of these finds in ordinary "satellite" cemeteries suggests that they were not markers of class membership or elite wealth but representations of community authority vested in ayllu leaders.

Second, the discovery of truly elite tombs at the M16D and M70B cemeteries indicates a more pronounced vertical differentiation in some provincial Tiwanaku burial treatments. These chambered necropoli with aboveground monuments mimicked the chambered construction and lavish offerings of the most elite tombs of the Tiwanaku site. The men buried there were uniquely privileged to wear elaborate jewelry and tapestry tunics bearing images of the most powerful gods of the Tiwanaku culture. However, even the richest of these provincial elite tombs, like the palace tombs of Tiwanaku themselves, pale in comparison with elite burials in other societies of comparable complexity and scale, like the Moche. Furthermore, there is no apparent relationship between these most opulent tombs and state-related monumental architecture in the Moquegua province. Their locations near domestic sites and far from the temple suggest that these elite cemeteries can also be seen as fancier versions of community burial grounds. This implies that even the highest elites of the Tiwanaku colony may have been of leaders of corporate segments of the community rather than governors imposed as representatives of a central government. Or more likely, successful leaders in Moquegua Tiwanaku managed to wear both hats. Even in provincial Tiwanaku at its height, the social persona was the result of a complex negotiation between identities born in segmentary corporate groups like the ayllu and identities that flowed downward from the new institutions of the centralized state. Foremost among these was the Tiwanaku temple.

8

Provincial Tiwanaku Temples and Sacred Landscapes
Touchstones to Power

Pachacutic saw the magnificent buildings of Tiaguanaco and the stonework of these structures amazed him because he had never seen that type of building before; and he commanded that his men should carefully observe and take note of that building method, because he wanted the construction projects in Cuzco to be of that same type of workmanship. Having enlarged his empire with so many and such vast provinces, during the remainder of his life this king devoted himself to improving the provinces by building in the major towns of each one magnificent temples and palaces and some strong castles, all according to the model of the buildings that he had seen at Tiaguanaco.

Cobo (1984 [1653]:141)

Thanks to chroniclers like Bernabé Cobo, we know that even in ruins, Tiwanaku's abandoned monuments so impressed the Inca emperor that he tried to emulate their style and recapture their grandeur in designing his own capital. To this day, Tiwanaku's monuments impress with their sheer scale, with the geometrical perfection of their stone construction techniques, and with the striking sculptures that populated the type site's ceremonial precincts. Tiwanaku may have been not only a direct prototype for the Inca monumental architecture of Cusco but a model for Inca state ideology as well (Cieza de León 1959 [1553]:284). Cobo's comment further suggests that the Tiwanaku civilization was Pachacuti's inspiration for replicating the monuments of his own capital in the Inca provinces. Yet until recently, it was not known whether the Tiwanaku civilization built ceremonial architecture when it spread to regions outside of Tiwanaku's core region.

In this chapter, I examine the Tiwanaku state's growth in the light of its traditions of temple architecture and religious practice. I focus on how temple structures reflect Tiwanaku religious practice and its relationship to social and political systems. None of Tiwanaku's great buildings survived intact and none has decipherable texts describing its history or purpose. As a result, the functions and meanings of the monuments of the Tiwanaku capital and its hinterland are not readily apparent. After reviewing the architectural and archaeological evidence to propose a general model for the form and functions of Tiwanaku temples of the altiplano homeland, I examine the importance of their replication in a distant province by the Tiwanaku diaspora.

Provincial Public Architecture

Leaders build public monuments to turn the idea of the state into physical reality. Because public monuments represent both civil and religious authority, they are among the more tangible residues of ancient ideologies. Temples, palaces, courts, and tombs can inspire awe and associate secular rulers with supernatural power. The capacity of public monuments to impress and to endure helps leaders institutionalize asymmetrical power relations by "materializing" ideologies (DeMarrais et al. 1996:16; Earle 1997:151). Monuments transform cultural ideas into enduring objects that can be experienced by large numbers of people. By building the idea of power into the public arena, leaders can establish an ongoing apparatus for the transmission and negotiation of meaning.

Public architecture becomes a social fact in two ways. First, large numbers of people must be brought together to construct monuments. From the perspective of architectural energetics, the labor input directly reflects the complexity of organizational behaviors and the degree to which leaders can harness surplus energy (Abrams 1994). Second, the purposes of public architecture are encoded in their functional and symbolic design and through the accrued memory of their use. Monumental architecture has an enormous potential as a communicative medium through the "legibility" of its design—its ability to be seen and experienced by informed audiences (Moore 1996:120). Ideologies can be made and reinforced on a regular basis by the public's structured participation in public spectacle or by the public's exclusion from other activities behind the temple door. As experienced by a populace that was aware of the amassed labor they represented and able to read their visual symbols, public monuments advertised the state's ability to exert authority (Paynter 1989:384).

When state societies expand into new territories, public ceremonial architecture often follows. Provincial monuments serve not only as local foci of power but as touchstones to the vitality of the capital. In provincial centers, public structures may be built in the image of major homeland monuments, often as miniaturized representations of the capital. As a form of administrative and political technology, public facilities can "reflect by their size, form and functional context the importance and variety of the decision-making activities with which they are associated" (Spencer 1990:15). Civic ceremonial sites can thus chart the intensity of political activity at nodes in a hierarchical administrative regime (DeMontmillon 1989:154). Provincial ceremonial centers also serve a symbolic role as physical reminders of the "centripetality" of their capital cities (Wheatley and See 1978) and reflect the province's place in the state system. This process of microcosmic representation turns provincial centers into replicas of the state capital, itself often designed to reproduce a celestial reality that lies outside the direct experience of mortals. By incorporating recognizable visual references, ceremonial centers could be "a universally recognized metaphor," symbolic of propositions universally sacred to the state (Townsend 1982:61).

Andean states materialized and transmitted their ideologies in the construction of their capitals and their provincial centers. For the pre-Inca Chimu state of Peru's north coast, the canons of public architecture in capital and provinces were shaped by an ideology of social control. Provincial ceremonial structures were created in the image of the *ciudadelas* (ceremonial precincts) of the capital city of Chan Chan. Many archaeologists have interpreted the ciudadelas as administrative centers that regulated the flow of energy, matter, and information by controlling passage to elite offices known as *audiencias* and to storerooms (Klymshyn 1987; Mackey 1987). Under this bureaucratic scenario the smaller provincial Chimu public structures were miniature ciudadelas of mainly administrative function: "As one descends the administrative hierarchy, centers should become smaller, more simplified, more schematic 'miniatures' of Chan Chan" (Keatinge and Conrad 1983: 258). A less administrative interpretation is indicated by Moore's analysis of "route maps" of room access in the ciudadelas of Chan Chan, Manchan, and Farfan. Moore found little connection between audiencias and storeroom access, suggesting that the ciudadelas' purpose was more symbolic than economic, designed to mark the separate status of elites (Moore 1996:219). Whether Chimu monumental architecture was primarily designed for economic control or to shape ideology through the encounters between rulers and subjects, both schools of thought agree that the Chimu provincial centers replicated the architectural canons of the capital.

Inca provincial centers often featured specialized ceremonial architecture, and many have been seen as symbolic reproductions of ceremonial features of Cusco (D'Altroy 1981, 1992; Dillehay 1977; Morris 1982; Morris and Thompson 1985). Inca ceremonial space is often conceptualized as *ceques*, ceremonial paths that radiate from a sacred center (Bauer 1998; Zuidema 1964). Inca public architecture similarly emphasized gateways, boundaries, and the ceremonial passage through indoor and outdoor sacred space. Provincial Inca ceremonial centers often duplicated this pattern, and some centers like Tomebamba reproduced not only the temple buildings of Cusco but the ceque lines and sacred landscapes of the capital in sufficient detail to serve as second capitals (Idrovo 1986; Uhle 1919). As in Cusco, public ceremonial activities in the Inca provincial centers were often centered on *usnu*, platforms usually located at the centers of public plazas (D'Altroy 1981; Dillehay 1977; Gasparini and Margolies 1977; Hyslop 1990:70; Morris 1982; Morris and Thompson 1985). Processions punctuated by gateways, shrines, and other stopping points were critical to both Inca religious ceremony and Inca political legitimization (Von Hagen and Morris 1993:103). Could the Incas' phenomenal success at materializing an imperial ideology derive from precedents learned at Tiwanaku?

Public Architecture and the Tiwanaku State

In the Tiwanaku heartland, administrative and ceremonial responsibilities were focused through specialized public architecture in the capital city and its lakeside satellite centers. From the outset, we must admit that we know little of how Tiwanaku's monuments worked as religious or political buildings There are no eyewitness reports of rites and ceremonies in the Tiwanaku temples, no inscriptions with the names of their deities, and no genealogies of the priests and rulers associated with Tiwanaku's palaces. Centuries of looting, stone robbing, indifferent excavation, and reconstruction for tourism have irreparably transformed Tiwanaku's monuments, and little of their original floor plans or access patterns survives. Nonetheless, a great deal can be determined from the ruined monuments of Tiwanaku and its hinterland. Tiwanaku architects developed a distinctive and instantly recognizable style that made their monuments not only functional for liturgical and political ends but readable as materialized ideology. The distinctive design canons of this Tiwanaku monumental style might be considered in two parts: as a set of characteristic construction techniques, and as a series of normative conventions on building form and plan.

Construction and Tectonics

Tiwanaku's monuments are justly famous for the superb quality of their stone masonry. Tiwanaku construction techniques illustrate a distinctive Tiwanaku "tectonic" or programmatic intention as to how constructions are to be perceived and read (Protzen and Nair 2000:360, 370). For the capital's finest buildings, Tiwanaku masons cut granite and sandstone into perfect prismatic blocks with sharp right-angle corners. The legends of Emperor Pachacuti's importing of Tiwanaku stonemasons to rebuild Cusco could reflect the Inca's realization of the symbolic value of stone architecture for its permanence and its encoded messages about labor and craft. However, if the Inca were inspired by the idea of Tiwanaku's cut-stone monuments, they adopted few of its specific details. The two architectural traditions differed in their masonry style and in their methods of cutting, fitting, and handling stone (Protzen and Nair 1997:148). Inca monuments often incorporated the living rock of outcrops and caves, and the finest Inca stonemasonry imitated nature by using a variety of polygonal bond types, "pillowing" or outlining each stone with beveled recessed edges. Even in Inca walls that appear to consist of coursed blocks, the courses are not truly planar, and each stone is individually fitted to slight concavities in its neighbors. Inca walls were battered, or inward-sloping by 3 to 5 degrees, Inca doors and niches were trapezoidal, and Inca masonry was seldom ornamented (Gasparini and Margolies 1977; Hyslop 1990). The Incas' unique building aesthetic emphasized the individuality of each stone, perhaps as a reminder of the interplay of human labor and technology and the sacred natural stone of the Cusco landscape.

In contrast, the goal of Tiwanaku's stone carving was to join true ashlars, or prismatic blocks, to produce plumb and continuous wall surfaces of meticulous rectilinear perfection. A variety of masonry substyles may be distinguished among the Tiwanaku monuments, but all of them employed prismatic blocks with precise 90-degree angles to construct walls, doorways, and ornamental details. Some masonry, like the retaining walls of the Akapana and Pumapunku, was built with planar individual courses of consistent height. Although a few of the Pumapunku walls were near isodomic, (i.e., built of ashlars identical in all three dimensions to produce symmetrical bonds), Tiwanaku did not employ a standardized kit of building blocks or bond intervals, and blocks of irregular widths and depths were employed in most walls (Manzanilla 1992a; Protzen and Nair 1997:152; 2000). To join some of the largest building stones, bronze cramps were cast in situ into T-shaped sockets to prevent slipping. Another uniquely Tiwanaku solution to the lack of a standard interlocking bond was masonry of the Kalasasaya style, described as random-range work between orthostats (Protzen and Nair 1997:148). This technique consisted of erecting a series of large vertical slabs at regular intervals and filling the spaces between them with an interlocking puzzle of small blocks of different heights and widths (fig. 8.1). Kalasasaya-style masonry of massive scale surrounded its namesake, a large walled platform at the Tiwanaku site, and smaller walls of random-range masonry, with or without orthostats, may be seen in the neighboring Templete Semisubterráneo and in most of the sunken court temples of the core region.

Tiwanaku's most important buildings, like the temples atop the Akapana and Pumapunku, included massive and intricately carved blocks that were ornamented with precisely carved niches, inset crosses, concentric circles, step moldings, and meander friezes. These complex geometric designs were

Figure 8.1. Kalasasaya-style random-range masonry and false tenon heads at Templete
Semisubterráneo, Tiwanaku. PSG photo.

carved directly into wall-sized blocks of different shapes and sizes to produce
a continuous pattern without regard to the joints and bonds of individual
stones. The most elaborate ornamentation in Tiwanaku's monumental buildings was focused on their doorways, encouraging modern readers of Tiwanaku architecture to emphasize a "doorway cult" as the key to Tiwanaku
temple tectonics and liturgical patterns (Conklin 1991; Protzen and Nair
2000). Whether carved from enormous monolithic blocks or as trilithons,
Tiwanaku's monumental doorways were carefully designed as *chambranle* or
recessed frames with beveled or stepping jambs (Protzen and Nair 2000:361).
Despite the elaboration and enormous size of their component stones, the
doorways themselves were small, none exceeding a meter in width. The great
care taken in carving these full-sized doors was also echoed in perfect half-
scale miniature in diminutive blind doorways or niches in the Pumapunku. A
small number of doorways, including the famed Gateway of the Sun, were
adorned with precious metal inlay and reliefs of human and supernatural
figures on their lintels. These deities seldom appear on other architectural
elements at Tiwanaku, and their presence on Tiwanaku doorways associates
Tiwanaku's most important gods with passage through temple portals.

Ironically, many Tiwanaku builders hid their most masterful and labor-intensive masonry beneath gaudy applications of plaster and paint. Contrary to our austere image of ancient capitals, most of the cut-stone architecture of Tiwanaku's religious centers and elite residences were painted in vivid colors (Conklin 1991:285; Mohr Chavez 1988:18). The intense hues of the Puma-punku temple, for example, included red floors and red, blue-green, and white walls (Escalante 1994:219). Stucco painted in "malachite green, cobalt blue, and electric cinnabar red-orange" was applied to elite buildings like the Putuni and the Palace of Multicolored Rooms at Tiwanaku, and in smaller structures elsewhere in the altiplano like the PK-5 temple in Pampa Koani (Kolata 1993:153, 221).

What was the intended meaning behind the construction style of the Tiwanaku monuments? Tiwanaku's propensity to hide the most exquisite details of its monumental architecture could not be explained by anyone but a Tiwanaku builder. We may surmise that this was a technological style in which the finest work could be hidden, yet remembered and appreciated by those who understood the Tiwanaku tectonic. Smoothing over the bonds of Tiwanaku's magnificent masonry accentuated the unity, mass, and angularity of the overall construction, at the expense of the individuality of each stone. If we take the liberty of considering this style of building metaphorically, does the bringing together of disparate parts to create a smooth and seamless whole capture the tension between pluralism and unity in Tiwanaku? Can we view this as a materialized ideology that was "monolithic" in all senses of the word?

Temple Plans and Processional Paths

Tiwanaku public buildings also shared planning principles that materialized state ideology through ceremonial practice. Formally, the representation of Tiwanaku power crystallized in a characteristic ceremonial architecture, the archetypes of which are found at the Tiwanaku type site and its altiplano satellites. Most of the monuments of the Tiwanaku site's ceremonial core shared a cardinal orientation, suggesting an interest in sunrise and sunset (Kolata 1993:90).[1] The forms of Tiwanaku monumental architecture have been characterized as either *pirámides*, pyramids with elevated religious structures that were related to exclusive ceremony, or *recintos*, open precincts that served as congregation points for the public (Manzanilla 1992a: 21; Manzanilla and Woodard 1990:134). In fact, a more complex tension between public spectacle and private ceremony was a principal theme of Tiwanaku public architecture, and it is seldom possible to separate these two ideal types in architectural reality. Indeed, it is by skillfully articulating pyramids and courts that Tiwanaku architects shaped ceremonial experiences accentuating the drama of passage from the realm of ordinary experience to the exceptional. The key architectural elements of this complex are

(a) stepped platform mounds, (b) rectangular enclosures, including walled precincts and sunken courts, and (c) complexes of staircases and doorways that channeled and controlled access to a ceremonial core.

Stepped Platforms Mounds

The largest structure ever built by Tiwanaku and the model for all of its stepped pyramids is the Akapana, the "man-made hill built on stone foundations" first described to Europeans by Cieza de León (1959 [1553]:283). Carlos Ponce Sanginés has noted that the sheer mass of the structure's terraces dominated the entire site and structured its directional axes (Ponce 1972:81). Although extensive looting, stone robbing, and erosion since the Spanish conquest have destroyed most of the Akapana's summit and façade, excavations confirm that the structure was composed of earthen fill retained by massive terrace walls of carefully fitted masonry.[2] Even disregarding the labor invested in carving the blocks of its stone façade, the structure's 16 m height and its volume of 53,546 m^3 would have been a conspicuous reminder of Tiwanaku's ability to assemble large pools of labor (Manzanilla 1992a: 22). The structure's layout and its tectonic and iconographic presentation would also present a legible message to informed visitors. From the west, the pilgrim, supplicant, or tourist would have ascended a grand staircase lined with sculptures of anthropomorphic feline creatures called *chachapumas* holding human heads. On the summit, the visitor would encounter elaborate gateways and an elite residential complex that faced an enormous cruciform sunken court, now all largely destroyed by Spanish looting. To complete the experience, the visitor would probably contribute to the numerous offerings of precious objects, smashed ceramic vessels, animals, and possibly human sacrifices that covered the Akapana's terraces and buildings of the summit (Alconini 1993; Kolata 1993; Manzanilla 1992; Manzanilla and Woodard 1990:138).

What ideology was materialized by this building and its veneration? One school holds that the Akapana was a deliberate representation of sacred mountain peaks of the Eastern Cordillera (Kolata 1991, 1996; Reinhard 1985, 1990). Kolata conjectures that Tiwanaku was built as a public symbolic text and that its monuments reified Tiwanaku's social order by representing an idealized cosmography. In this view, the Akapana and its smaller replicas at other core region sites were the centerpieces of carefully designed "islands enceinte" separated from vernacular architecture by artificial canals and moats. By building terraced pyramids with elaborate drainage systems that represented life-giving mountain water sources, Tiwanaku elites could connect the power and legitimacy of the natural world to their own vision of a hierarchical social order (Kolata 1993:106; 1996:233).

The symbolic centrality of the Akapana for Tiwanaku is reinforced by its recurrent appearance as a motif in Tiwanaku art and architecture. Posnansky pointed out that the "reentrant and salient angles" of Akapana's "stepped and superimposed terraces" represent an essential leitmotif of Tiwanaku civilization (Posnansky 1957:69–72). Posnansky offered several possible interpretations of this motif's meaning, including a stylized representation of Andean topography, agricultural terracing, lightning, and even the Milky Way. Although stepped motifs appear in earlier altiplano art and architecture, the stair-step design became the single most frequent motif used on Tiwanaku decorated pottery and in other media (Bennett 1934; Goldstein 1985, 1989a, 1989b; Oakland 1986: fig. 17; Rydén 1947; Wallace 1957). The step motif often appears in conjunction with circles, crosses, and other figures that could represent cosmological elements. Perhaps most significant, the front-faced deity, the signature icon of Tiwanaku religion, is often depicted standing on a stepped pedestal that is arguably a direct representation of the Akapana itself (Cook 1983, 1985; Demarest 1981; Kolata 1983:255; Reinhard 1985, 1990:169). The consistent depiction of a stepped pyramid in a motif that literally "supports" the state divinity lends credence to its use as a symbol of state power and legitimacy in architecture and other media.

Sunken Courts and Enclosures

Another diagnostic form of Tiwanaku public architecture is the sunken court temple, for which the archetype is often considered to be Tiwanaku's Templete Semisubterráneo (Bennett 1934; Ponce 1969). While sunken courts have a long tradition as components of earlier highland ceremonial complexes at Chavín, Qaluyu, and Pukara, this feature achieved its highest level of standardization and widest distribution in the south-central Andes during the Tiwanaku period. Tiwanaku's Templete is a rectangular sunken court measuring approximately 28 m by 26 m with walls faced with finely cut stone blocks and a clay floor. The only entry was a single staircase of superimposed stone slabs (Ponce 1969:55). The massive Bennett Monolith and other stelae that once stood at the Templete's center and the collection of sculptured stone heads set into the sunken court's walls represent the greatest concentration of Tiwanaku sculpture found at any site. The sculptures of the Templete Semisubterráneo were such powerful icons that they were evidently still being worshiped at the time of Cieza de León's 1547 visit: "A great stone idol, which they probably worshiped, stands a short distance away in a small recess. It is even said that beside this idol, a quantity of gold was found and around this shrine there were a number of other stones, large and small, dressed and carved like those already mentioned" (Cieza de Leon 1959 [1553]:283).

The rich variety of sculpture in the Templete Semisubterráneo suggests that it may have been a collection point for sculptural *huacas*, or sacred objects (Burger 1992:180; Moore 1996:92), of chronologically or regionally distinct styles (Chavez 1976:12). This may have anticipated the Inca practice of capture, curation, and display of the huacas of subject peoples (Rowe 1946, 1982). Twentieth-century excavators of the Templete noted the stylistic and temporal eclecticism of the stelae at its center and the diverse tenon heads that lined its walls. These diverse sculpted human heads appear to represent a variety of facial features and headdresses and are executed in several distinct styles (Bennett 1934:474; Ponce 1969 figures 20–24, 1972). The installation sequence of these monuments has yet to be resolved. Some, like the Yaya Mama–style "bearded" stela 15, may predate the others by many centuries. Regardless of their antiquity, all were in use simultaneously at the time of abandonment, a remarkable example of the long-term curation of sacred objects. The submissive positioning of these stylistically diverse pieces around the central Bennett stela may have sanctified Tiwanaku's Templete as a model for state control, or even as a microcosmic representation of ethnic components spread throughout the four geographical quarters of the Tiwanaku state (Kolata 1993:142). Whether or not the Templete Semisubterráneo served as a cosmological map of empire, it was surely an important symbolic focus of secular and spiritual power.

There is also archaeological evidence for the physical transport to Tiwanaku of non-Tiwanaku sculpture and not merely sculptural styles. In one celebrated case, the "Thunderbolt" stela, a basal fragment excavated at the Putuni palace of Tiwanaku, was found to refit the upper fragments of a Pukara-style stela from Arapa, in Puno, 255 km away on the Peruvian side of Lake Titicaca (Chavez 1976, 1981; Isbell 1991:304; Posnansky 1945). While the circumstances of the Arapa Thunderbolt stela's "capture" are uncertain, the curation of abducted stone sculpture of a rival polity expressed both a veneration of the past and the subjugation of foreign lands.

Tiwanaku's *Altiplano* Temples: The Courtyard in the Pyramid

The design of most Tiwanaku temples placed concealed sunken courts atop terraced platform mound structures, where they were accessible only by a graduated upward journey from public assembly areas. At Tiwanaku, this pattern held for the Akapana and for the Pumapunku ceremonial precincts. Computer-assisted mapping of the Pumapunku's excavated architectural features and the adjacent local topography now indicates that the temple was entered from an enormous adobe-walled courtyard on the mound's western base, by way of a single grand staircase through a series of doorways (Vranich 1997, 2000, 2001). This new interpretation supports a structuring of Tiwa-

Omo M10 Temple

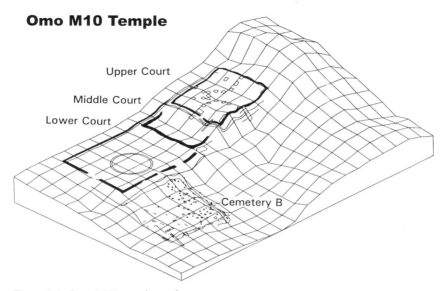

Figure 8.2. Omo M10 temple, surface map.

naku ceremonial space that emphasized a gradual passage from secular public space to increasingly sacred inner precincts.

Mounds with sunken courts are the key architectural elements of many of the "secondary temple centers" of Tiwanaku's core region in the Bolivian Lake Titicaca basin (Browman 1978a:343; Kolata 1986). A map of Tiwanaku sites in Bolivia and Peru shows the distribution of satellite temple mounds believed to have sunken courts (fig. 8:2, table 8:1). Additional mound complexes without cut stone blocks on the surface may have escaped notice in the altiplano, where wet climate favors the preservation of stone over adobe. Surface features suggest other Tiwanaku temple centers at Pajchiri (Bennett 1936), Ojje-puco (Ponce and Mogrovejo 1970:264–265), LLojepaya and Santiago de Machaca (Browman 1978a:328), and Pokotia (Lumbreras 1974:63); at the PK-5, PK-6, and PK-7 mound complex (Kolata 1986: 755–758; 1993:221), Pukuro-uyu (Browman 1978a:328), and Turini, Sikuy Kollu, and Miraflores (Ponce 1972); and at TMV-561 or Wila Pukara at Tiwanaku (Albarracin and Mathews 1990:114; Ponce 1972:81). Potential temple sites on the Peruvian side of Lake Titicaca include Cota, Incatunahuiri, Tuma Tumani, Qenuani, Yanapata, Kajje, and Imicate (Hyslop 1976: 85–87) and Tumuku or "Tucumu" (Rowe and Donahue 1975; Stanish 1991), and Chucaripupata and Wakuyu on the Island of the Sun in Lake Titicaca (Bandelier 1910:225–226; Bauer and Stanish 2001:136; Seddon 1998:465). It has even been suggested that a Tiwanaku-style semisubterranean temple was built in the Moraduchayuq zone of the Wari site in Ayacucho as early as A.D. 580 ± 60, perhaps using imported Tiwanaku technology or labor (Isbell 1991; Isbell et al. 1991:30, 50).

The altiplano satellite centers display strong consistency in layout and construction details. Sunken court temples on Lukurmata's Willakollu hill (Bennett 1936; Ponce 1989; Rivera Sundt 1989) and at Chiripa (Bennett 1936; Browman 1978b), Khonkho Wankani (Portugal 1941; Rydén 1947), Mocachi (Casanova 1937, 1942), and Simillake (Posnansky 1934:295–296; Rydén 1947:153; Hyslop 1976:85) were all set in the summit of a hill or artificial mound that was terraced and faced with stone blocks. Access to the summits and their sunken courts was controlled by staircases constructed of overlapping stone slabs flanked by cut-stone gateways (Bennett 1936:483–485; Ponce 1989). Tiwanaku-style stone sculpture has also been found at many of these sites.

When the Tiwanaku-style sunken court temples were built is something of a mystery. Sunken temples are notoriously difficult to date because of the rarity of datable construction fill or floor deposits and their tendency to fill with unrelated sediment after abandonment (Girault 1990:261). The chronological span of sculptural styles present in the Templete Semisubterráneo range from the early "bearded" stela 15 to the Classic Bennett Monolith (stela 10). This variety of sculptural styles does little to resolve the mystery.

Many Tiwanaku scholars advocate an early date for the sunken courts. Some of the sunken court temple centers might have been constructed as early as Bennett's Qeya or Early Tiwanaku Phase, now known as Tiwanaku Phase III (Browman 1978b:810; 1980:111; Kolata 1993; Ponce 1969:98). Nonetheless, there is little solid evidence in the form of Tiwanaku III sherds or carbon dates for such early construction. The overwhelming proportions of Tiwanaku IV and V pottery in offerings and throughout temple excavations at Lukurmata and Chiripa (Bennett 1936:504; Browman 1978b:810), Khonko Wankani (Rydén 1947:154), Mocachi (Casanova 1942:363) and the Templete Semisubterráneo itself (Girault 1990; Ponce 1969:56) instead suggest that the sunken court phenomenon reached its height during Tiwanaku Phases IV and V. This would make the apogee of the sunken court temple complex contemporary with Tiwanaku's maximal territorial expansion.

Artifacts from the excavated sunken court temples also shed light on the special activities that took place within the temple complexes. Fragments of the otherwise rare elaborate zoomorphic and pedestal-based vessels known as *incensarios*, *sahumarios*, or hollow-base libation bowls comprised 87 percent of the sherds recovered from the Lukurmata temple (Bennett 1936: 493).[3] Present-day Aymara ritual practice employs similar incensarios to burn animal fats in offering contexts (Abercrombie 1986; Buechler and Buechler 1971). Complete or reconstructible incensarios were found behind walls and in the surrounding terraces of the Lukurmata temple complex (Bennett 1936:484; Ponce 1989:283; Rivera Sundt 1989:69). These appear to have been specifically left as offerings. Similarly high concentrations of incensario sherds have been noted in the sunken court temples at Mocachi and Khonko Wankani (Casanova 1942:363; Rydén 1947:154), at the platform mound of Pajchiri (Bennett 1936:464), and at the Chiripa sunken court, where Browman (1978b:810) has noted that they "reaffirm the use of the temple as an important religious sanctuary." Incensarios were also found alongside gold pendants and vessels in Tiwanaku offerings recovered from Lake Titicaca off the Island of the Sun (Reinhard 1992).

The sunken court temples of the Tiwanaku core region also are associated with what might be considered a separate category of "elite" artifacts. The structure at Lukurmata yielded a number of gold, silver, copper, and lapis lazuli beads (Bennett 1936:493). Jewelry fragments of metal and semiprecious stones have been reported in elite architecture on the Akapana summit (Manzanilla 1992; Manzanilla and Woodard 1990:138) and other platform mound centers (e.g., Bandelier 1910:225–226; Kolata 1986:757, 1993:222). Where there is no indication that these status goods were intentionally left as offering caches, they probably represent items lost in everyday elite usage, perhaps by resident temple personnel.

To summarize, existing surface surveys and excavations in the Tiwanaku core region permit us several generalizations about Tiwanaku's temple building program. The height of this architectural and ceremonial tradition coincides with the apogee of Tiwanaku political growth. Evidence from the Lake Titicaca region suggests that two essential formal elements—sunken courts and platform mounds—were most often combined in temple structures. While sunken courts have often been seen as miniaturized reproductions of the *Templete Semisubterráneo*, most are located atop raised platforms that replicate Tiwanaku's man-made mountain, the Akapana pyramid. The summit of the Akapana itself was the site of perhaps the greatest of all sunken courts. In the satellite temples for which plans are available, elaborate staircases and doorways channeled and progressively restricted access to the temple platforms. At their summits we find the sunken courts, inner sancta that housed the state's sacred icons and witnessed a tradition of ritual offering and elaborate ceremony.

All of the previously cited Tiwanaku public structures are located in the Lake Titicaca basin at elevations well above 3,500 m. Considering the importance of provincial ceremonial centers to the Inca and Chimu, the rarity of any of the Tiwanaku monumental architectural forms outside of the altiplano challenges the very conception of Tiwanaku as a true expansive state society.

As we have seen, the initial Omo-style Tiwanaku occupation of the Moquegua Valley, as represented by the M12 settlement, was a system of insular community groups who may have relied largely on llama pastoralism and built neighborhoods clustered around open plazas. These plazas must have been the locations for open public assembly of the entire community or its component moiety or ethnic groups. More private ceremonies confirming leadership and intrasocietal bonding took place in a few elite households. Sponsorship of ritualized hospitality may have conferred prestige on the households serving as conduits between the colonial community and their ayllu. However, these community roles of *primer inter pares* were informal, depending on ritualized face-to-face interactions rather than an imposed ideology of state control. It is not surprising that exclusively public architecture played little or no role.

A very different pattern prevails at site M10, occupied by Chen Chen–style colonists who may have been more specialized in maize agriculture for export to the altiplano. For these intensive agriculturalists, the M10 town plan and household and mortuary excavations indicate a more densely occupied, permanent settlement. Perhaps the most remarkable aspect of the Chen Chen–style occupation of Omo is the construction of the first altiplano temple in this new land.

Omo's Tiwanaku Temple

At first glance, the dry dusty appearance of the Omo M10 temple seems to have little in common with the rain-washed temple mounds of the altiplano. However, this is due more to the differential preservation afforded by the two areas' contrasting environments than to architectural style. Observation of the rapid postabandonment decay of modern Aymara adobe houses in the altiplano suggests that some of the Tiwanaku core region's mound complexes may have melted away long ago in that region's relentless rains. In contrast, desert conditions at Omo have preserved a wealth of detail on architectural form and adobe construction techniques.

Excavations in the Omo Temple

The core of the Omo temple is a set of three adobe-walled courts built on platforms that step up a small hill to the east of the Omo M10 habitation site. The temple's three precincts, designated as the Lower, Middle, and Upper Courts, are aligned facing downhill to the northwest on a bearing of 316 degrees magnetic. An additional platform, known as Platform B, abuts the Lower Court to the southwest. During the 1990 season of the Omo Archaeological Project, a program of topographic survey and test excavations was initiated to verify and date the complex's cultural affiliation and to test for diagnostic Tiwanaku architectural features, particularly a sunken court in the Upper Court. A series of 2 × 2 m test units was located to transect the Upper

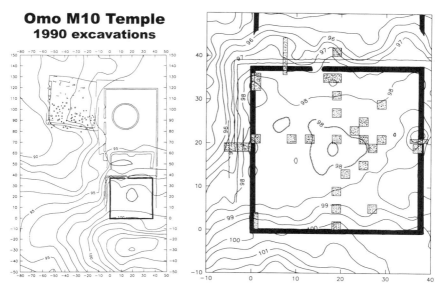

Figure 8.3. Plan of Omo M10 temple 1990 excavations.

Court platform to determine its cultural stratigraphy, construction sequence, and final architectural form (fig. 8.3).

The sterile fill used to build up the three core platforms makes it difficult to date the initiation of construction of the terreplane itself. However, all sherds found on floor surfaces of the Upper Court superstructure are of the Chen Chen style, and there is no evidence that any part of the mound construction was earlier. Superposition indicates that Platform B was added at a later date. A radiocarbon date from the temple's wooden lintel in the Upper Court correlates with dates from M10 domestic area excavations and brackets the final construction and use of the temple superstructure at the apogee of Tiwanaku expansion (Beta-39679, table 5.2).

Stratigraphy indicated two distinct episodes of site destruction—one pre-Columbian and one in the Spanish colonial period. A homogenous mixture of broken adobe fragments and shattered ashlars suggests that the structure's walls were pushed over and systematically smashed during or shortly after its abandonment. This intensive and intentional first episode of demolition could represent the same pre-Columbian site destruction that accounts for the opening of numerous tombs in the M10 cemeteries and the extensive pitting of the M10 habitation site. The pre-Columbian site destruction is unrelated to the Spanish colonial looting that produced the Upper Court's large central crater and corresponding spoils. The two events were separated in time by the intervening lens of volcanic ash from the eruption of Huayna Putina on February 19, 1600. The presence of sherds of Spanish colonial *botijas,* or wine jars, above the volcanic ash layer may be compatible with a directed destruction of the Omo temple and removal of its idols by Spanish colonial authorities during their campaign to extirpate idolatry.

Construction and Tectonics

Excavations found the Upper Court to reflect an unusual concern for detail in its construction and maintenance. The platform constituting the base of the Upper Court terreplane was constructed of walled terraces and cribbing compartments built of mud-mortared adobes set over foundation courses of cobbles. Superimposed terrace faces and fill zones exposed on the southwest exterior of the Upper Court indicate episodes of expansive reconstruction or the buttressing of retaining wall sections that were collapsed by earthquakes or natural slump. Fill alternated between dry gravel and sand from nearby borrow pits and wet-laminated red clay similar to the flooring in the Middle and Upper courts, which was brought from a more distant source. The contrast of the clean fill used in all these reconstruction episodes of the Upper Court platform with the midden fill used in the Cemetery B platform is noteworthy and could suggest a high degree of sanctity for the Upper Court.

The Omo ashlars were all prismatic in shape, although their sizes varied considerably. Unlike the granites and sandstones of Tiwanaku, Omo's masonry was of a soft volcanic tuff that is found in pyroclastic erratics throughout the region. Perhaps because Moquegua had no real quarry of suitable stone and most blocks were reduced from isolated "bombs," the ashlars seldom exceeded 40 cm in length, and no pillars or spanning elements have yet been found. In the tradition of Tiwanaku masons' remarkable control over right angles, each ashlar was dressed to shape and smoothed by abrasion. As at Tiwanaku, some stones were finished on only three faces, while nonvisible sides were left unpolished. Other stones were perfectly squared and smoothed on all six faces (fig. 8.4).

Great care is also evident in the fitting of the basal masonry of the Upper Court superstructure. In the excavated elevations, a single course of finely polished ashlars was used as the foundation for interior walls (fig. 8.5). Because of the intentional destruction of walls, the foundations of the Upper Court superstructure were found intact only in areas buried under particularly deep layers of adobe wall fall. Elsewhere, the outlines and construction of walls could be construed from ashlar fragments and stone-shaped impressions and remnants of mud mortar left in the red clay floors (fig. 8.6). Interior walls, as indicated by impressions in the clay floors, were built atop uniform-width ashlars that spanned the entire thickness of the wall. It is unknown whether these interior walls had more than one course of stone blocks. The vertical edges of each stone were closely fitted to its neighbors without any mortar or space between blocks. In excavated elevations of the perimeter

Figure 8.4. Ashlar from Omo M10 temple, Upper Court façade. PSG photo.

Figure 8.5. Fitted ashlars, M10 temple Upper Court interior foundation (left) and Puma-punku temple, Tiwanaku (right). PSG photo.

Figure 8.6. Ashlar impressions in red clay floor, Omo M10 temple. PSG photo.

Figure 8.7. Random-range masonry, M10 temple Upper Court perimeter wall interior.

walls, ashlars of varying height and thickness clad both faces of the wall base, with adobes above (fig. 8.7). The random-range pattern of the ashlars in the basal course of the Omo temple produces the same puzzlelike effect as the distinctive masonry of the Templete Semisubterráneo (Ponce 1969:63) and Akapana summit structures (Manzanilla 1992a:57) at Tiwanaku, and at the Willakollu temple of Lukurmata (Bennett 1936:471–481).

The adobes of the Omo temple were rectangular and flat, typically measuring $50 \times 40 \times 8$ cm. The adobe matrix included reeds, textile scraps, fibers, fragments of Tiwanaku ceramics, and highly eroded sherds of Huaracane neckless ollas (Feldman 1989; Goldstein 1989a). As no Huaracane sherds were found on occupation floors, their presence in bricks is attributed to the borrowing of adobe mud from old cultural midden deposits. Kolata has reported a similar presence of Chiripa formative sherds above Tiwanaku IV floors at sites in the Pampa Koani (1986:753). All walls, including the stone foundation courses, were finished with covering layers of mud plaster and painted with a well-burnished dark red pigment, with details in green and yellow.

Riverine reeds and fist-sized bundles of cut *ichu* grass 30 cm in length were found directly atop the temple floor (fig. 8.8). These were the remains of roofing and a protective ichu thatching of the wall tops. Use of this technique

Figure 8.8. *Ichu* grass roofing material, M10 temple. PSG photo.

Figure 8.9. Stone carved to resemble thatched roof, Pumapunku temple, Tiwanaku. PSG photo.

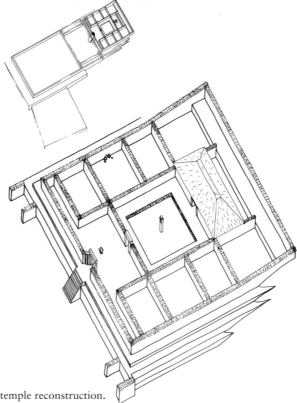

Figure 8.10. Omo temple reconstruction.

to protect adobe walls from rain is diagnostic for altiplano architecture. Since the Moquegua area is a hyperarid zone, this might be a vestigial continuation of altiplano tradition and a marker for the cultural orientation of the builders. The cultural significance of thatched roofs to the Tiwanaku tectonic ideal is supported by a series of carved stones found in the vicinity of the great western stairway of the Pumapunku at Tiwanaku that were carved to replicate cane or grass roofing (fig. 8.9).

The Temple Plan and Ritual Procession

While environmental and preservation differences make it difficult to compare the Omo temple's construction technique and materials directly with those of the altiplano temples, it is possible to trace parallels in architectural design. A preliminary reconstruction of the complex as it stood during its final occupation gives us some idea of how the temple was utilized by Tiwanaku provincial worshipers and how it functioned to materialize Tiwanaku ideology (fig. 8.10).

Just as in the Tiwanaku temples of the core region, the Omo temple was transected by a single line of access through doors aligned on its central axis. Visitors traveled from lower, profane, and more public space to higher, sacred, and very private precincts. As in the Pumapunku, a visit to the Omo temple began in the Lower Court, a large and unadorned public plaza at the structure's base. The Lower Court was the largest of the three courts along the principal axis of the complex. This 42 × 57 m courtyard was built on an artificially leveled rectangular platform that separated the Omo temple from the M10 town site. Like the large adobe-walled courtyard recently discovered by topographic mapping west of the Pumapunku temple at Tiwanaku (Vranich 2000), the Omo Lower Court had no internal divisions or prepared floors and was surrounded by a low wall. The only visible feature within Omo's lower court is a shallow trench or depression that forms a ring-shaped circular feature 23 m in diameter. Similar ring-shaped depressions appear in the open plazas of Omo sites M12 and M13 and in ceremonial sectors at the Chen Chen site. The function of these ring-shaped circular features is not known, but they may have been used for community dances or processions. As did the Pumapunku's recently discovered western plaza, Omo's Lower Court probably served as an area of unrestricted public assembly and celebration. It was also the first stage for those seeking access to the temple's inner precincts.

Off the main temple axis, a rhomboidal platform, known as Platform B, abuts the Lower Court on its southwest side. Platform B was superimposed on the Lower Court mound as the latest temple construction phase, after which seventy Tiwanaku tombs were located in the southeastern half of the platform. No cut stone was used to construct Platform B, and its construction

290 / Andean Diaspora

fill, unlike the clean fill of the Upper Court, contained organic midden deposits, pottery, and other artifacts of the Chen Chen style. As discussed in the previous chapter, the Platform B cemetery comprised standard Chen Chen–style Tiwanaku interments with typical offerings of this style. Because both the platform and the burials in it postdate the construction of the main temple, it is possible that the temple had already been abandoned when this cemetery was in use.

Passing from the Lower Court through a central doorway in the southeast wall, temple traffic funneled into the smaller Middle Court, a 20 × 37 m precinct that was surrounded on three sides by substantial adobe walls. The Middle Court's construction was more elaborate than that of the Lower Court, with a floor of smoothed red clay locally called *moro moro* and walled galleries on either side of the central atrium. On its uphill (southeast) side, the Middle Court was dominated by the 3 m high terraced face of the Upper Court. Fragments visible on the surface and intact blocks found in excavation indicate that this interface with the temple's highest level once boasted a striking facade of perfectly dressed ashlar blocks.

Architecturally, the Upper Court was the most imposing and complex part of the temple structure and the most isolated from public view. The only access to the Upper Court complex was from the Middle Court via a central staircase constructed of overlapping stone slabs.[4] A splendid façade of cut-stone blocks once faced the Middle Court on either side of the staircase. Shattered stone block fragments indicate that the interior superstructure of the Upper Court had been faced with the same carefully dressed ashlars.

At the top of the stairs, entrance to the Upper Court complex was controlled by a single doorway less than 1 m in width. The door's sill, indicated by three in situ stone blocks, was marked by a deep circular pivot hole and semicircular grooves that suggest a swinging door.[5] Adjacent to the door sill, the impressions of blocks set in the clay floor indicate the location of door jambs that stepped inward in the classic *chambranle* or recessed frames that typify the stone portals of the Pumapunku (Protzen and Nair 2000). Plaster fragments reveal that the surfaces of the Omo door jambs were painted in vivid red, cream, yellow, and green pigments. The green pigment resembles a rare fugitive green pigment that is found only on zoomorphic incensario vessels and may have been a color reserved for religious purposes.

In trying to recapitulate the grand entryways of the altiplano tradition, Omo's architects were faced with a lack of raw material in lengths sufficient to span doorways. The tuff that was used for the temple's ashlar blocks is a volcanic erratic that appears commonly on the surface in the middle Moquegua Valley but usually in the form of pyroclastic bombs less than 1 m in diameter. To solve this problem, the Upper Court's colorful doorway was capped by an unusual architectural element that might be described as an imitation stone lintel. The lintel was constructed of three heavy wooden logs bound together with braided vegetable fiber, with interlaced tufts of ichu grass used to anchor a covering of mud plaster (fig. 8.11). The mud plaster surfaces were carefully smoothed and painted with gray-white and yellow pigments, apparently to resemble the smooth stone of the altiplano gateways. Some plaster fragments found near the doorway included modeled square depressions, perhaps in imitation of carved stone decoration in the Pumapunku at Tiwanaku. Omo's combination of real ashlar blocks and faux stone represents a unique solution to the problem of re-creating an authentic Tiwanaku structure from local materials.

The Omo temple's doorway, like its altiplano archetypes, must have conveyed tectonic messages that were readable by the Tiwanaku colonists. Physically, the doorway's small size and its location atop a flight of stairs indicate the same kind of "funneling" of traffic to the inner sanctum of the temple that is suggested by the monumental gateways and tiny doorways of Tiwanaku's Kalasasaya, Akapana, and Pumapunku. Stylistically, with its faux stone lintel the Omo gateway was intended to mimic the famed stone entryways of the Tiwanaku site. It is plausible that the Tiwanaku tradition of chambranle recessed doorway, echoed in simpler materials at Omo, was a symbolic statement of this restricted access.

Those visitors who passed through the Upper Court's gateway would have arrived in an antechamber flanked on either side by galleries of small rooms with well-plastered floors and lightweight, post-supported roofs. Finds of

Figure 8.11. Omo temple entryway showing sill and fallen lintel. PSG photo.

minuscule jewelry fragments and the absence of standard domestic debris suggest that these rooms served for storage of sumptuary goods, as administrative or priestly offices, or perhaps as a vestry or robing rooms.

Through another axial gateway, the visitor would have entered the 16 × 15 m walled inner sanctum of the temple complex. The mud-plastered walls of this inner sanctum were painted a bright red, with decoration in green. In the center of the inner sanctum was a sunken court 10.5 m square and 50 cm deep. Although the center of the court was damaged by both the original site destruction and the colonial looting, impressions left in the surviving parts of the red clay floor indicate that it was once lined with an inner façade of finely cut ashlar blocks.

The center of attention in the sunken court, and indeed, the focus of the entire temple complex, was a massive idol that was once located in the court's center. A test excavation in the center of the sunken court found the outlines of a deep pit that extended 2.7 m into sterile soil beneath the court's clay surface. This is considerably deeper than the deepest penetration of either looting episode, indicating that some large object, presumably an idol of unknown material, had originally been set in the center of the sunken court and later removed. The otherwise clean clay fill of this builder's trench contained isolated human bones, suggesting the possibility of dedicatory ritual associated with this idol.

What did this focal idol of the Omo province look like? Fragments of stone sculpture found elsewhere at the M10 site represent local derivations of the Classic Tiwanaku stone carving style. The broken-off head of one stone stela, crudely carved of a local volcanic tuff, was found in the M10 domestic area.[6] Though the piece is badly weathered and exfoliated, it depicts a human figure carved in the rectangularized Classic Tiwanaku style. A smaller stone sculpture of the same volcanic tuff material, attributed to the Omo site and now at the Catholic University of Santa Maria (UCSM) museum in Arequipa, represents an oval human face with a protruding nose, round eyes, and a large grin. These faces correspond with two of the many distinct styles depicted on the carved false tenon heads of Tiwanaku's Templete Semisubterráneo (fig. 8.1). While the diverse origins of the Templete Semisubterráneo tenon heads are unknown, the two Omo heads, carved from the same local volcanic tuff, were both made in Moquegua as part of a single sculptural ensemble. If so, they could represent a conscious attempt to imitate the diversity of the Templete Semisubterráneo group. The architects and sculptors of the Tiwanaku diaspora sought to evoke not only the tectonic forms of their homeland temples but the eclectic nature of their icons. If Tiwanaku temples were centers where pluralistic ayllu-based ethnic and social groups came together, the reproduction of diverse icons at Omo could indicate that this symbolic pluralism was replicated in diaspora temples as well.

Behind the sunken court, test excavations found the clay floor and cut-stone foundations of a substantial temple building. Without excavation, it is impossible to confirm the structure's form, but the stonework of the foundation is of exquisite quality and could indicate an impressive façade, long destroyed. The depth of wall fall indicates a structure with massive adobe upper walls and a thatched roof that may have been of two stories and was certainly tall enough to enjoy a commanding panorama, not only of the sunken court chamber and galleries but of the entire ceremonial complex, the village site of M10, and the world beyond.

Temple Models

The architectural plan of Omo's Upper Court takes on greater significance in view of a small carved stone model or *maqueta* found near a looted tomb at Omo in the 1970s (fig. 8.12). This 15 × 13 cm fragment was carved from the same lightweight porous volcanic tuff material used for other stone sculpture found at Omo. Now in the UCSM collection in Arequipa, the *maqueta* exhibits a number of strong similarities in proportion and details to the Omo ceremonial structure. Depicted is an approximately square structure, consisting of a central walled and sunken court surrounded on three sides by ten

Figure 8.12. Stone *maqueta* (architectural model) of temple, Omo site M10. PSG photo.

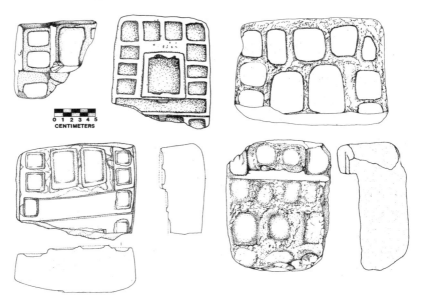

Figure 8.13. *Maquetas* from Moquegua Valley sites. Top: Echenique M2B, Omo M10, Huaracane M22B. Bottom: Conde Alto M50A, Calaluna M104A Calaluna.

smaller rooms separated from one another by lower walls. On the fourth side, a single walled room runs the entire width of the square structure. The maqueta fragment indicates adjacent to this long room a miniature central staircase that descends to the central room of three on a lower level. Although the maqueta is broken at the base of the staircase on this lower level, its resemblance to the Upper and Middle courts of the Omo temple is striking. With the "real life" confirmation of the gallery rooms of the Middle and Upper courts, the central sunken court of the Upper Court, the transverse antechamber, and the central staircase, there is little doubt that the Omo maqueta is a model of the actual M10 structure.

Four additional stone maquetas were discovered by the MAS team at other sites in the middle Moquegua Valley (fig. 8.13). Of the five Moquegua maquetas, the Omo M10 example is the only one that corresponds to a specific known structure. All were similarly carved from the local volcanic tuff and appear to represent stepped platforms with multiple compartments. The creation of carved architectural miniatures was an established Tiwanaku practice. The best known is a massive stone block depicting a sunken court with miniature staircases, visible today in the Kantatayita section of the Tiwanaku site (fig. 8.14). Posnansky (1945:109, 111, 123) made the case that the Kantatayita stone, a 4 × 4 m single slab, was an accurate model of the Putuni, a semisubterranean court that faced the western terrace of Kalasasaya. Unfortunately, Courty's 1903 excavations and subsequent looting have

Figure 8.14. Kantatayita stone temple *maqueta*, Tiwanaku.

Figure 8.15. Stone *maqueta*, Copacabana regional museum.

left this "sanctissimum" on the east side of the "Palace of the Sarcophagi" too disturbed for more exact comparison. More recently, Protzen has identified a series of diminutive doorways among the cut stone of the Pumapunku as examples of half-scale miniatures of the principal doorways of the structure (Protzen and Nair 2000). Smaller portable models of domestic and ceremonial architecture have also been reported at the site (Ponce 1972:73) and on the Copacabana peninsula (fig. 8.15).

What was the function of these Tiwanaku maquetas? Miniature replicas of sacred places were more than just ancient equivalents of an Eiffel Tower souvenir. In the Andes, sacred propositions were celebrated through mimesis, and even the great architectural monuments of Tiwanaku themselves may have been sacred precisely because they were seen as miniatures of cosmogonic reality (Kolata 1996). Portable miniatures permitted worshipers to carry the idea of the temple with them and would have been an important component of pilgrimage experiences. Carved stone miniatures of houses and farms are commonly used today to invoke prosperity in Aymara festival contexts. Typically, they are included with coca leaves, llama fat, and alcoholic libations in offering packages or as amulets for prosperity (Girault 1987:564). The ritual building of model houses and farmsteads has been reported in twentieth-century Aymara offering ceremonies on the Akapana itself (Reinhard 1990:161). In the Bolivian altiplano, Aymara families still celebrate the January festival of Alacitas by creating models of their lands, roads, and homes and decorating them with an astonishing variety of miniature animals, cars, appliances, consumer products, and even tiny deeds, college degrees, passports, and currency. Similar practices continue to this day in Moquegua atop Cerro Baúl, the massive natural outcrop still considered sacred by local residents. From the colonial period into the twenty-first century, the site has been a major pilgrimage destination, and visitors build elaborate stone models of ideal homes and make offerings to propitiate earth and mountain spirits.

Ritual Activities and the Tiwanaku Offering Assemblage

Careful analysis of excavated contexts in the Omo temple offers insight on the ritual activities and practices of Tiwanaku provinces and a glimpse of elite life in the Tiwanaku colonies. The temple excavations found few of the features and artifacts associated with domestic life, and the scarcity of cultural material on the Upper Court's prepared floor surfaces indicates fastidious cleaning during the temple occupation. Where present, primarily in the peripheral rooms adjacent to the sunken court area, floor deposits were limited to thin layers of compacted organic soil. Among the few artifacts present in floor deposits, it is possible to discern a distinct assemblage that is associated with sacred spaces in Tiwanaku. Plainware vessels and even fine serving vessels such as keros were rare. This indicates that drinking and feasting, like domestic activities, did not take place in the temple. Instead, ritual-related objects that were rare in domestic contexts comprised a disproportionate part of the temple assemblage.

The first element of this ritual offering assemblage consists of vessels designed for the burning of offerings. Fragments of Tiwanaku zoomorphic incensario vessels were represented throughout the temple excavations, just as they were in the Lukurmata and Chiripa sunken courts and in Akapana (Manzanilla 1992:70). At Omo, these include two size categories of the pedestal-based vessels that Bennett (1934) called hollow-base libation bowls and a category of smaller incensario vessels with flat oval bases shaped like a shoe. Analogy with present-day Aymara practices suggests that incensarios were probably used as censers for the burning of llama fat during rituals. The Tiwanaku vessels were adorned with heads and tails of either pumas or raptorial birds, often ingeniously designed with baffles and perforations that allowed smoke or flames to emerge from the animal's mouth (it is possible that some pedestal-base vessels may have been used as lamps). Berenguer has suggested that the duality of feline and bird imagery may represent both an opposition between two protagonists in myth and the totems of deep-seated moiety divisions throughout Tiwanaku society (1998). If this is the case, the majority of Omo temple incensarios appear to align with Tiwanaku's feline iconography.

A lesser-known ceramic category associated with temple functions consists of crude miniature plainware vessels. A cache of smashed miniature pots was found in excavations at the base of the Omo temple stairway. Similar miniature vessels have also been reported in association with ceramic incensarios and other offerings in ritual caches on the summit of the Akapana at Tiwanaku (Manzanilla 1992a:70). Elsewhere in Moquegua, miniature vessel fragments have been found concentrated in a small ceremonial structure at the M1 Chen Chen site and in isolated prominences in the hills overlooking the Río Muerto site.

Animal sacrifice was another important ritual activity in Tiwanaku temples. An especially active locus of animal offerings in the Omo temple was a low passageway area between the roofed temple structure and the uphill enclosure wall. This enclosed and secluded area was the site for numerous sacrifices of young and fetal camelids. In one offering left in the southern corner of the Upper Court, a camelid fetus was deposited together with a starfish. Such an offering may be a symbolic representation of the highland and coastal extensions of Tiwanaku civilization. Such a bringing together of the two extremes of Tiwanaku expansion would have consecrated the temple as a seat of both secular and ritual power.

Apart from these deliberate offerings, a number of isolated small fragments of luxury objects of adornment were found in the Omo temple in floor contexts that suggest accidental loss. These include fragments and beads of a variety of materials such as lapis lazuli, malachite, and *Spondylus* shell imported from Ecuador. A Tiwanaku tapestry fragment depicting a staff-bearing "sacrificer" figure with winged eyes, a typical tripartite headdress, and a puma-headed staff was found in a test excavation in the northeastern gallery of the Middle Court (fig. 8:16). Tapestry, by far Tiwanaku's most labor-intensive and iconographically expressive textile medium, was extremely rare in Moquegua Tiwanaku mortuary and domestic contexts and may be considered an elite article. Tiwanaku's stone sculpture indicates that high status individuals wore shirts with similar iconography, and gifts of tapestry tunics were evidently a key element in the acculturation of client chiefs in San Pedro de Atacama (Conklin 1983; Oakland 1992). Among Tiwanaku's general population, however, tapestry was extremely rare, and few fragments have appeared in domestic excavations at Omo (Oakland 1985, pers. comm., 1987). As burial dress, tapestry tunics have been found in only the highest-ranking burial in Moquegua, and it is likely that the right to wear a tapestry tunic was limited to a select few by sumptuary laws, much as it was in Inca times.

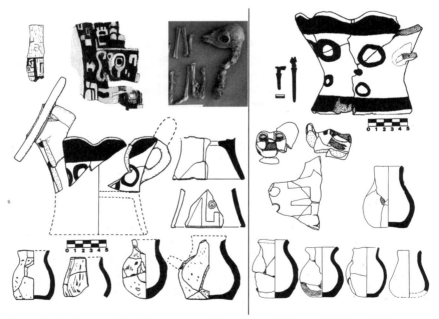

Figure 8.16. Ceremonial artifacts recovered from Omo M10 temple (left) and Chen Chen M1 ceremonial structures 14–1 and 15–1 (right).

The association of tapestry tunics and exotic jewelry with the Middle and Upper courts of the Omo temple implies the presence of elite priestly or administrative specialists. Archaeologists are only beginning to understand Tiwanaku's leaders through the association of these special artifacts with elite residential precincts, burials, and ceremonial structures like the Putuni at Tiwanaku (Kolata 1993), the Akapana at Tiwanaku (Manzanilla 1992; Manzanilla and Woodard 1990), Lukurmata (Bermann 1994), and Omo. Without inscriptions, this effort will never translate into a complete understanding of the palace histories of Tiwanaku's ruling dynasties and priests, as we have for civilizations like the Maya. Nonetheless, the iconography of Tiwanaku's great stone stelae permits us some insight into the leaders who presided over drug-induced rituals and offered sacraments of coca and keros of maize beer to their followers (Berenguer 1998). In the Tiwanaku provinces, images of mustachioed leaders on portrait head drinking vessels remind us that four-pointed knotted polychrome hats, metal earspools, and tapestry tunics were the badges of office for priests and ayllu leaders. This association has been confirmed by the appearance of these emblems in mortuary ensembles discovered in Moquegua. With the Omo temple, we can also associate the activities of Tiwanaku's provincial priests, clan leaders, and political officers with their places of work and residence.

Sacred Landscapes, Ceques, and the Temple Axis

Moore argues that lines of sight are extremely important in governing the human experience of monuments (1996). In the case of the Omo temple, if we assume that the Upper Court was surrounded by a wall 2 m in height, the idol would have been hidden from public view behind its imposing façade. This suggests that access to certain sights and sightlines was a key privilege of those eligible to ascend to the inner temple. The Omo idol itself was aligned with the Upper Court's two axial doorways and must have stared out along the centerline of the temple to the northwest. This all-important sightline along the temple's central axis—from the temple's back building past the idol and across the sunken court, through framing double doorways, to the mundane world below—is identical to what Tiwanaku priests may have seen according to current reconstructions of Tiwanaku's Pumapunku (Vranich 2000). It is perhaps no coincidence that the temple structure in the back of the Upper Court also affords a rare view of the summit of distant Cerro Baúl, to the north.

From the outside, little of this was visible to the uninitiated, and what could be seen must have been carefully and theatrically controlled. The Omo idol would have been obscured from the Omo communities by the angle of elevation and the walls of the Upper Court. Indeed, the idol could have been visible to the public from only one location outside the Upper Court itself. This was the hilltop site of M158, 2 km distant across the valley. This site, named Los Adoradores del Templo (worshipers of the temple) by our 1994 MAS survey team, was mapped as a 2.5-hectare intermittent scatter of Tiwanaku pottery with little evidence of domestic habitation. Instead ceramics at M158 consist of redware keros, fuentes and other serving vessels, incensarios, small plain ollas, and figurines, most of which may be associated with ceremony, feasting, and drinking. Sightings from M158 locate it directly in line with the Omo M10 temple's central axis.

Considering the scarcity of other small Tiwanaku habitation sites, M158's location, and its apparently ceremonial ceramic assemblage, this peak must have been the location of rituals related to the Omo temple. We cannot determine if Omo's priests knowingly organized these rites from the temple or if Los Adoradores arrived to celebrate of their own accord. Small depressions and terraces noted on the surface at M158 may indicate the use of gnomons, beacons, or bonfires on the peak to mark the alignment to viewers from the Upper Court. Conversely, M158 may have offered a tantalizing distant glimpse of the Omo temple idol for anyone willing to make the hike and camp on its peak. This would have been like a view through a gunsight, possible only from a great distance through two framing doorways, and only if both doorways were unobstructed. Yet this may have been the only visual access to the esoterica of the temple for those unable to ascend the stairs and pass through its portals, and priests may have calculated carefully a limited and distant view.

The alignment of the Omo temple axis with stations of worship and festivity is suggestive of the Inca ceque system, with its emphasis on ritual pathways along lines of sight. There is a growing body of evidence that Tiwanaku colonists were concerned with the array of shrine locations on a sacred landscape. While Tiwanaku settlements were almost exclusively limited to the four major town sites, our discovery of isolated *apachetas*—mountain or hill peaks with Tiwanaku ceramic offerings—suggests that Tiwanaku colonists were concerned with creating a sacred landscape in the Moquegua province. Focacci has reported similar finds of Tiwanaku ritual offerings in association with prominent rock outcrops in Azapa that he called *huacas* (pers. comm., 1992). While no consistent spatial pattern can be inferred, these imply a sacralization of the colonized landscape by the Tiwanaku diaspora, perhaps to make new lands comparable to the system of temples, offering sites, and nature shrines they enjoyed in the altiplano (e.g., Bauer and Stanish 2001).

Within-site alignments among smaller ceremonial structures have been identified elsewhere in Moquegua. Excavations at the Chen Chen site in 1995 discovered one such ceremonial complex that was presided over by a small stone building designated Structure 15–1. The entryway of this structure, located along one of Chen Chen's agricultural canals, aligned with a smaller stone booth or gnomon and a series of ring-shaped trench features similar to that of the Omo Lower Court along a northwest-facing axis (fig. 8.17). Because this axis crossed two principal canals that fed the Chen Chen agricultural fields, it is plausible that ritual observances were related to fertility or propitiation. Surface collections and excavated assemblages from both structures were ceremonial in nature, with virtually no domestic debris. The structures' assemblage included numerous incensarios and offerings of bronze *tupus* (brooch pins), a young camelid, a ceramic figurine, seashells, *Spondylus* and greenstone beads, and miniature ceramic vessels. These structures' small size and canalside location suggest a more localized ceremonial practice than that of the Omo M10 temple. One possibility would be an ayllu-specific cult that celebrated the water cycle or controlled irrigation-related ceremonial events. Alternately the offerings of a female figurine and numerous tupus could point to some sodality or gender-specific sect. It appears that many

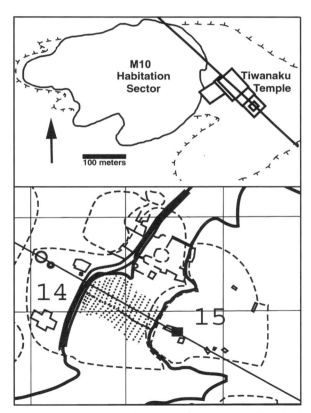

Figure 8.17. Alignment of ceremonial structures in Omo M10 (above) and Chen Chen sectors 14 and 15 (below). See also figure 6.3.

belief systems may have operated within the Tiwanaku diaspora alongside the temple-building state cult.

For both state and corporate cults, the building of nondomestic buildings in alignment with ritual features, mountain peaks, or productive resources like canals suggests a ceremonial aspect to Tiwanaku geography emphasizing ritual paths and sightlines. The alignment of ceremonial sites, apachetas, and hillside geoglyphs throughout the valley show that the Tiwanaku colonists were concerned with marking and celebrating the features of their new valley landscape in ways not unlike the ritual processions along the Inca ceques five hundred years later.

Summary: State and Community Ritual in Moquegua Tiwanaku

We may conclude from a review of Tiwanaku's altiplano monuments that the typical Tiwanaku temple consisted of an artificial mound or landscaped hillside retained in stepped terraces to form tiered platforms. Square or nearly square stone-lined sunken courts were often located in the highest terrace of these temple mounds. Temple structures were generally symmetrical, with access to the sunken court via restrictive entryways and staircases made of overlapping stone slabs. Stone stelae and other sculpture or icons set at the centers of the sunken courts were the pivotal elements of these ritual complexes. There is some evidence that the longitudinal axes of Tiwanaku temple complexes were carefully aligned with other structures and natural features and that these alignments were part of an elaborate design for socially choreographed processions and sightings along straight lines. Unlike the Inca sacred landscapes, which were conceived of as multiple radiating ceques or lines, Tiwanaku temples seem to have only one principal axis. Views and paths to Tiwanaku icons, landmarks, and perhaps celestial events were characteristically pointed out by staircases and framed by elaborate doorways.

Andean provincial ceremonial centers are often smaller, more schematic miniatures of the imperial capitals. If Tiwanaku monumental architecture is considered an amalgam of artificial terraced platforms and rectangular walled and sunken court enclosures, the Omo M10 ceremonial precinct, like the satellite sunken court temples of the altiplano, replicates Tiwanaku ceremonial architecture on a reduced scale. The Omo temple's configuration of stepped temple platforms and sunken courts reflects the physical arrangement of altiplano Tiwanaku's centerpieces: the massive pyramid of Akapana and particularly the platform, sunken court, and temple building of the Pumapunku. On yet another level of sacred miniaturization with resonances in the ethnographic record, the Omo complex was directly represented by an architectural model or maqueta, a practice also known from altiplano Tiwanaku. In imitation of Tiwanaku's major monuments, the Omo complex may have been adorned by facsimiles of Tiwanaku sculpture, including a large stela, placed centrally on the highest tier of the structure. As in the altiplano ceremonial centers, the presence of jewelry and elaborate vestments indicates the day-to-day presence of elite individuals in the Tiwanaku temples. Ritual offerings of young and fetal camelids, zoomorphic ceramic incensarios, and even a starfish support the veneration of the Omo complex as a provincial seat of both secular power and cultic attraction.

Conklin (1991) has described access-controlling gateways and horizontal spanning architraves as the defining elements of a "doorway cult" of Tiwanaku. His analysis of Tiwanaku architectural geometry points to a Tiwanaku public architecture that was designed to impress religious and civic meaning through ritual movement and controlled passage. Gateway architectural elements were the most elaborately worked of all building stones in the Tiwanaku monuments. Tiwanaku architects even celebrated gateways and stairs by replicating them in miniature form in architectural models and in wall decorations of the Tiwanaku monuments themselves (Protzen and Nair 2000). Conklin argues that the iconic motifs chosen for the few surviving monumental doorways with carved figures like the Gateway of the Sun and the Kantatayita lintel all depict supernatural or costumed figures in motion within architectural contexts. This interpretation portrays an altiplano Tiwanaku monumentalism that stressed ritual procession through sacred precincts toward venerated and protected sacred objects.

The way in which movement was controlled in the Omo M10 complex lends support to a similar focus in provincial Tiwanaku monuments. As represented by the Omo maqueta and confirmed by excavation, access to the Upper Court platform was restricted to one central staircase and gateway. Moreover, the Omo temple's alignment with ceremonial activities on the M158 peak across the valley indicates that the doorways connecting the three courts formed a visual and conceptual axis for the structure and, almost certainly, a path of pilgrimage. As the pilgrim progressed toward the Upper Court, the reduction in the courts' size, their increasing decorative and architectural elaboration, and the process of filtering and review implied by the gateways and staircases all suggest a transition from public to increasingly restricted sacred space. The stela that once stood in the center of the Omo temple's sunken court was at the heart of a protective labyrinth. The carefully designed experience of passage up stairs and through temple doors took the faithful to a place beyond the cares of the ordinary world and provided the mystical setting necessary to turn a carved piece of stone or wood into a *huaca*--an oracle object worthy of veneration and sacrifice and a symbolic focus of supernatural power.

If we view Tiwanaku public architecture as a vessel for ritual procession, we can envision channeled movement through the Omo temple, from lower public levels into increasingly restricted precincts presided over by a priestly elite. Perhaps the supplicant was also shunted through administrative offices to take part in more worldly activities of taxation and obeisance. By controlling religious practice, Tiwanaku provincial elites could solidify their position as ritual intermediaries and sole conduits to the political power of the Tiwanaku core region. Similar adobe platform temples with sunken courts have been interpreted as centers for water and labor allocation for agricultural production in Tiwanaku's Pampa Koani hinterland (Kolata 1993:221). It is likely that Omo's temple played an analogous ideologically supportive role in the administration of agricultural production in Moquegua.

The discovery of a Tiwanaku sunken court temple complex at Omo, 300 km southwest of the site of Tiwanaku, is the first confirmation of this characteristic architectural feature outside the Lake Titicaca basin. The temple's social functions of political control and the corporate labor pool required for its construction suggest the existence of a complex and hierarchical administrative structure in the Tiwanaku V colony. In contrast to the household-centered ritual typical of Omo-style colonial communities, the Omo temple's specialized ceremonial complex suggests the transfer of some power from an ayllu-based string of pastoral colonies to an agriculturally based, centrally governed provincial system. On one level, the Omo temple represented Tiwanaku's first monumental materialization of a state ideology in the Tiwanaku diaspora.

Although the construction and public purpose of the Omo temple supports an ideology of state centralization, it should not be implied that other kinds of Tiwanaku religious practices were suppressed in the Tiwanaku diaspora. Indeed, household archaeology confirms that Moquegua Tiwanaku settlers performed most of their ritual feasting and drinking at the level of the household. The copious numbers of keros and other serving vessels in domestic contexts indicate that most ceremonial feasting and chicha drinking took place at home, along with dedicatory offerings of animals and metal and textile artifacts. In contrast, temple rituals emphasized passage through a restricted sacred space marked by awe-inspiring architecture, burning ritual censers, and more elaborate dedicatory offerings but apparently little drinking.

It is tempting to propose a division of ritual labor in which the temple became the focus of a dominant new "state" religion, while a universal Tiwanaku "folk" religion was banished to the household. However, this dichotomy would be an oversimplification. The persistence of a variety of intermediate forms and contexts of worship, like the small ceremonial buildings of Chen Chen and the apachetas that dot the valley landscape, suggests some cults that defy this distinction. These nonstate and nondomestic ritual contexts were associated with diverse corporate cult groups who preserved their spiritual autonomy throughout Tiwanaku's political heyday. Even during the glory days of Tiwanaku state religion when the temples of Omo and Pumapunku were built, state orthodoxy existed only in a dynamic dialectic with household and cult heterodoxy. In the end, Tiwanaku's state ideology may have been less monolithic than its state architecture.

9

Confederation and Pluralism in an Ancient State

The state as a state was not perceived as an administrative or coercive fact, as much as the expression of an idea of unity among many diverse peasant localities, as actualized in ritual linkages between kings and chiefs.

Burton Stein (1985:75)

What kind of state was Tiwanaku? Was it an empire? The answers we choose depend on whether we judge states by their achievements or by the ways in which they achieved them. By most standards, Tiwanaku attained a level of scale and complexity that we usually associate with a powerful state-level society and perhaps even a proto-empire. The people we call the Tiwanaku created the largest and most cosmopolitan city the Andes had yet seen. They built awe-inspiring pyramids, courts, and palaces and developed industries that produced an immense output of utilitarian and sumptuary goods. To feed their capital city the Tiwanaku commanded a vast system of intensified agriculture throughout the altiplano core region. Tiwanaku promulgated a set of spiritual beliefs and a corporate art style shared throughout the south-central Andes that helped it unite diverse peoples under its cultural influence. Finally, a far-flung diaspora of Tiwanaku colonists created a network of new towns and ceremonial centers in distant regions. Despite these achievements, Tiwanaku, like the equally grand Chola and Vijayanagara states of southern India that Burton Stein describes, "cannot be easily incorporated into traditional models of imperial structure" (Sinopoli and Morrison 1995:85).

What Was Tiwanaku?

As I suggested in chapter 1, neoevolutionist theory on the growth of ancient states assumes that increasing complexity and scale must be accompanied by systemic processes of centralization and the imposition of a hierarchical structure on information flow and regulation (Flannery 1972:409; Spencer 1990; Wright 1977; Wright and Johnson 1975).

For neoevolutionists, statehood represents a specific form of centralized control of populations, territories, and resources that extend beyond the normal capacity of chiefdoms. This is not simply a question of scale but a qualitative distinction. Normally, chiefdoms undergo chiefly cycling, "the recurrent process of the emergence, expansion, and fragmentation of complex chiefdoms amid a regional backdrop of simple chiefdoms "(Flannery 1999:5). Successful chiefly polities may briefly come to control neighboring groups but collapse to a limited scale when they surpass the practical limits of resource exploitation. States, by definition, rise above chiefly cycling, achieving stability at a higher level of political scale and centralized authority. Flannery suggests that particularly able chiefs can surpass the limits of chiefly cycling by demanding increased production from their subjects, improving their subjects' production through technology, or finding new subjects to add to the production under chiefly control.

This third option requires territorial expansion, as ambitious leaders attempt to extend their power beyond areas that they can personally oversee. Because a chief can directly control only the area within a day's travel from his residence, territorial expansion forces him to delegate governing authority over distant parts of the new territory to others (Flannery 1999:15). To the neoevolutionists, territorial expansion plays a key role in state formation because it requires a hierarchy of administrators or governors and a specialized form of government that is qualitatively and quantitatively distinct from chiefdoms. Thus, by definition, state political authority is dependent on hierarchy, entailing "a fundamental shift in the regulatory principles and strategies of the central decision-makers" (Spencer 1998:15). States, and above all territorially expansive states, are predatory entities that *must* have highly centralized forms of government.

In social and economic terms, this transformation is marked by the replacement of systems of reciprocity with increasingly asymmetrical relationships that emphasize the power and prestige of elites of the state center. Evolutionary models posit a shift "from ascriptively defined groups of persons to politically organized units based on residence," as hierarchical systems of social classification replace the longitudinal segmentation that characterize "kin-based" societies (Adams 1966:80). Neoevolutionists thus implicitly assume that horizontally distinct corporate social groups like clans or Andean ayllus wither away as their increasingly redundant functions are usurped by the state's hierarchy. Patterns of authority and group identity based on kinship and ethnicity are seen to become socially vestigial, politically impotent, and administratively irrelevant in class-based state societies.

Tiwanaku seems to be one of a small number of ancient states that do not fit this generalization. While aspects of Tiwanaku are statelike, a number of features indicate that a surprising amount of political and economic power remained in the hands of corporate groups that may have been very much like the present-day ayllus of the Andean highlands.

First, unlike the Inca, whose empire grew through military expansion, there is no iconographic, archaeological, or bioarchaeological evidence that Tiwanaku ever expanded through violent conquest. Inca conquest was backed up by enormous investments in roads, fortresses, garrisons, and military stores. Tiwanaku built no such military infrastructure for coercive control after consolidation. If Tiwanaku elites exercised military power, they did it in a remarkably subtle fashion through ideological hegemony rather than physical conquest. Tiwanaku was not a warrior state.

Second, there is only equivocal evidence for kingship and the paramount social classes that would be expected in a fully centralized Tiwanaku social hierarchy. Several buildings at the Tiwanaku site may qualify as residential palaces, but there are not enough data to describe Tiwanaku elites as royalty comparable to the rulers whose palace compounds and monuments mark the "ground plans" of many early state centers (Flannery 1998). Neither are there Tiwanaku burials comparable in wealth and grandeur to the royal tombs of the Moche, Chimu, or other Andean states, let alone the burial cults of the great civilizations of the Old World. Similarly, there is no oral tradition or textual support for Tiwanaku royal genealogies, nor are there surviving myths of separate origins of Tiwanaku kings and commoners, as might be expected under a fully developed ruling-class ideology. Tiwanaku failed to leave us written inscriptions, and it is likely that Tiwanaku's grandest and potentially "royal" tombs were ransacked long ago. However, the individuals in the high status tombs that have been studied have been described as priestly rather than secular elites because of their offerings (Wassen 1972; Money 1991). It seems that if there truly were kings and high lords of Tiwanaku, we would probably know more about them by now.

Iconographic sources also fail to convey images of unitary secular kingship and social hierarchy in Tiwanaku. Tiwanaku art produced few realistic depictions of narrative scenes and action as compared to the identifiable themes that have been so successfully deciphered in Moche art of the northern Andes. Tiwanaku's images are iconic and inscrutable. Nonetheless, it is possible to distinguish "real people" from "gods" or "mythic ancestors" in Middle Horizon iconography, and the distribution of supernatural imagery has been a key tool in assessing the distribution of religious cults. Portraiture in ceramic vessels and stone monuments also depicts specific human individuals, but their positions and titles are unknown and there is no evidence that they represent a unified cult of royalty. Tiwanaku leaders are seldom, if ever, depicted with weapons, and the Tiwanaku art style does not use a convention of relative size to indicate social rank, as was common in many early state art styles. Instead, the symbols of leadership displayed in Tiwanaku's great stelae—hallucinogenic snuff tablets, kero chalices, and vestments decorated with totemic animals and supernatural beings—convey more about leaders' ceremonial responsibilities than their secular power. Even iconographic studies that use the term "king" for Tiwanaku rulers describe a political ideology of pluralism. Berenguer, for example proposes that the oppositional distribution of kero and snuff tablet icons in Tiwanaku art indicates that Tiwanaku kingship was dualistic, with leaders controlling opposed moieties (Berenguer 1998). If nothing else, the diversity of distinct ceremonial objects used as symbolic images of power in different contexts of monumental art suggests that Tiwanaku rulers commanded ritual rather than physical suzerainty.

Finally, Tiwanaku does not display the requisite features of a hierarchically articulated state political economy. Even in the Tiwanaku core region, many features of the administrative infrastructure that are present in other pre-Hispanic Andean states are missing, and there is little evidence that government institutions exercised direct control over food production or tribute extraction (Bermann 1994:36; Isbell 1997:314). The kinds of centrally planned roads, storage depots, and way stations that characterized Inca administration were underdeveloped or absent altogether in Tiwanaku. Administrative devices like Inca *quipus* (string records) or the clay tokens of Protoliterate Mesopotamia that are traditionally associated with state political economies are unknown. Tiwanaku's greatest public buildings had no storerooms or offices for secular economic transactions and were primarily temples designed for worshipful pilgrimage experiences (Conklin 1991; Moore 1996; Protzen and Nair 2000). In terms of urban residential planning, Tiwanaku cannot simply be described as an enormous "company town" of patron elites and dependent attached specialist classes, as Alan Kolata proposes (1997:254). Instead, urban specialist groups may have cohered around shared occupational traditions that were reproduced through descent or ethnic affiliation rather than elite patronage (Janusek 1999). There is mounting evidence from Tiwanaku's urban barrios that groups resembling castes or ethnic business networks retained strong corporate identities. Ayllus were the forces to be reckoned with in the Tiwanaku political economy.

Interpretations suggesting less centralization and more local autonomy are also gaining support in assessment of the surrounding countryside and towns of the Tiwanaku core region (Albarracin-Jordan 1996a,b; Bermann 1997; McAndrews et al. 1997). This stands in contrast to reconstructions of highly centralized state-directed agrarian production (Kolata 1986, 1993). Rural agrarian and household crafts production surely increased under Tiwanaku vertical integration, but these changes may have been a relatively superficial overlay on long-standing local patterns (Bermann 1994). Continued local control over land tenure and irrigation management in the countryside also indicates an enduring segmentary structure of largely autonomous local groups within the Tiwanaku state (Erickson 1999). Certainly Tiwanaku's political economy raised sufficient resources to finance the building projects and lifestyles of its core elites. What is troubling is that Tiwanaku did not develop the permanent and highly centralized tributary institutions shared by most archaic states.

Does this leave us no option but to strip Tiwanaku of its statehood? Hardly. Instead, we should celebrate Tiwanaku as an opportunity to test the limits of evolutionary typology. As in the Chola state of southern India described by Stein, Tiwanaku central authority was a ritual suzerainty that coexisted with the persistent autonomy of corporate groups. Stein and Southall describe these states as segmentary because "the boundaries of political jurisdiction are differently perceived from different points of the system, and a central focus of ritual suzerainty is recognized over a wider area than effective political sovereignty" (Southall 1974:156). Within the Chola state, these competing interest groups included distinct ethnicities, peasant communities, elite lineages, occupational guilds and castes, and even petty kings. Chola kingship depended on a dizzying array of complex cross-cutting alliances with these local factions. Chola kings had to negotiate their political power constantly with other *rajas*, as is evident in their title of *rajadhiraja* (raja of rajas). What we know of Tiwanaku bespeaks a similarly fluid and ambiguous definition of kingship as a negotiated paramountcy. A Tiwanaku king, if indeed there was such a person, may have enjoyed ritual sovereignty but would similarly have had to negotiate constantly with autonomous local lineage or corporate groups over questions of labor, tribute, and ceremonial obligations.

Although Tiwanaku civilization lacked many of the institutions and infrastructures of other archaic states, it nonetheless endured for half a millennium and had an enormous influence on the south-central Andes. Was the Tiwanaku state more a state of mind than a political entity? And if the pluralist elements of this loosely confederated state could somehow expand into new territories, can we call these diasporas the origin of Andean empire?

Formative Antecedents

The long history of highland-lowland interaction in the south-central Andes began in the Formative period with trade and pastoral nomadism. Despite this history, we cannot simply project the conception of an altiplano diaspora or a vertical archipelago to pre-Tiwanaku times. Indigenous agrarian traditions like the Huaracane of Moquegua developed independently from the formative altiplano states. In diet, household traditions and material culture, and skeletal biology, the Huaracane show more common heritage with coastal peoples than with highlanders. Politically, there is no evidence of settlement or household change consistent with foreign domination over Huaracane, nor of the consolidation of a valleywide local chiefdom under foreign patronage. For at least a millennium, the pre-Tiwanaku Moquegua Valley was home to autonomous and culturally conservative agrarian societies. Control over labor, land, and other resources remained in local hands, and the distribution of Huaracane settlements suggests a decentralized village society reliant on simple valley bottom agriculture. The elites of these western valleys traded within the Pukara-dominated north Titicaca exchange sphere, but they also sought exotic textiles from Peru's south coast. Although the polities of Paracas, Nasca, and Pukara may have impressed and inspired political elites of cultures like the Huaracane, these petty local chiefs viewed their exotic connections in a parochial context, parlaying autonomous trade relationships with both altiplano and coast into local prestige.

At the same time in the altiplano, the political cohesion of Tiwanaku in the Formative period is questionable. While it is tempting to suppose that Tiwanaku dominated the southern Titicaca basin much as Pukara dominated the north, the Tiwanaku type site was sparsely populated, with little evidence of political or cultural unification. Late Formative lakeside sites like Lukurmata maintained distinctive local domestic traditions and were probably politically autonomous as well as culturally independent. Neither monumental constructions nor major population centers in the altiplano have yet been correlated with the Tiwanaku I and Tiwanaku III (Qeya) ceramic styles, and systematic survey indicates a limited Formative settlement in the Tiwanaku valley. In contrast to their interest in goods and new ideas coming from the Formative Pukara and Paracas-Nasca states, the peoples of the western slopes of the south-central Andes seem to have had no contact with Tiwanaku culture during the Formative period.

Pioneers and Pastoralists: The Diaspora Begins

Tiwanaku's first expansion into the western valleys of Moquegua and Azapa came about during the middle or later part of Phase IV of the Bolivian Tiwanaku sequence (ca. A.D. 500 to A.D. 725) and is represented by settlements of altiplano people who used Omo-style ceramics. Most likely, the first pioneer Tiwanaku colonists were pastoralists, following on a longer tradition of transhumance by highland camelid herders. Over time, their migrations to lowland valleys increased in distance and duration (Lynch 1983; Nuñez 1996; Nuñez and Dillehay 1979). A pastoral association is plausible for the Omo-style settlements because of their consistent settlement location closer to caravan routes and llama petroglyphs and farther from agricultural areas than other Tiwanaku settlers and in the ephemeral and tentlike nature of their domestic architecture.

Although vanguard Tiwanaku migration preceded the massive El Niño Southern Oscillation (ENSO) event that occurred in approximately cal. A.D. 700, this disaster must have been an important catalyst to the Tiwanaku diaspora. Geomorphological evidence from Moquegua indicates torrential local rainfall, flooding, and remodeling of the floodplain on a scale not seen again until the comparable Miraflores event that occurred six centuries later. Unlike long-term climate change, which might not be perceived by human populations, these short-lived events would have demanded immediate responses to rapid cycles of agricultural instability and competitive dynamics, both in the Moquegua lowland and in the altiplano Tiwanaku homeland. In Moquegua, erosion caused by the far more modest 1998 El Niño caused substantial losses of the richest floodplain lands. The topsoil losses of the severe A.D. 700 event would have been an agrarian disaster to the dense populations of Huaracane agriculturalists. Without alternate agricultural strategies like upland terraces, valleyside canal systems, and desert reclamation, the loss of the midvalley floodplain would have been catastrophic for the indigenous Huaracane farming communities, perhaps forcing some to abandon the valley.

At the same time in the altiplano, a powerful El Niño following a period of demographic growth would have caused a severe short-term drought at Tiwanaku, bringing with it sudden stresses in highland societies. The most mobile populations of highland Tiwanaku would have been the first to react, as herders moved their drought-stricken flocks to lowland regions like Moquegua in unprecedented numbers and for longer periods.

Most long-distance migrations are motivated by a combination of "push" and "pull" factors that create a perception of difference in economic productivity between homelands and frontiers (Anthony 1990:899). In the case of Moquegua, the A.D. 700 event may have accentuated both push and pull. Then, as today, the mobilization of Andean migrants with little to lose may have been motivated by both escape from highland drought and perceived opportunity in the lowlands. Although most of the surface water of the ENSO floods would have dissipated rapidly, the effects of the A.D. 700 event on the Moquegua Valley's crucial subterranean aquifers is not well understood. It is possible that aquifer recharge might have led to the florescence of spring-fed pastures and the creation of new cultivable lands. It is also possible that fluvial modification of landforms by flood erosion could have changed the location of spring outlets, creating new springs in uninhabited locations. Even if these benefits were ephemeral or nonexistent, the A.D. 700 event may have sparked the Tiwanaku diaspora by modifying perceptions about the lowland valleys.

Studies of historical migrations suggest that access to socially communicated information about distant regions is the most significant encouragement to long-distance migration (Anthony 1990:903; 1992:174). Interestingly, this can be equally true even if some of the initial information is false. Access to information about distant places follows kinship linkages with scouting groups and vanguard settlers. Even if the streets are not genuinely paved with gold, these kin-based informational links establish migration streams from particular communities, clans, or ethnicities. These patterns are remarkably persistent because a set of links to earlier migrants both encourages new settlers and advantages them in overcoming obstacles and settling. The results of this positive feedback are apparent in many modern immigrant communities, which tend to maintain segmental solidarity with only a small number of donor communities. Hence it is difficult to speak of "Mexican" or "Ecuadorian" migration to New York today without considering the particular towns in Puebla or Cuenca from which a remarkably disproportionate number of the migrants come.

At Tiwanaku, the most likely to migrate to the lowland valleys would be those in close reciprocal relationships with the vanguard pastoralists. Their reports of lush and vacant lowland valleys in the years following the flood attracted Tiwanaku colonists as farmers. The A.D. 700 ENSO may mark the beginning of permanent Tiwanaku agrarian occupation and the application of new agricultural strategies in the lowland valleys. These colonists brought with them a full array of traditions and lifeways that marked their strong identity with both the Tiwanaku culture and some of its distinct subcultures. Compared to their Chen Chen compatriots, the Omo group's traditions suggest a distinctive subculture or ethnicity within Tiwanaku culture, perhaps with roots in camelid pastoralism. As their settlements became more permanent, the Omo-style colonists brought families and transplanted a Tiwanaku way of life to a foreign region. The settlers brought with them conceptions of appropriate domestic architecture and the stuff of everyday life that identified them with their origin communities within the Tiwanaku core region. Tiwanaku redware and blackware serving vessels of the Omo style were indistinguishable from one style of altiplano pottery of Tiwanaku and may well have been imported. The distribution of these serving vessels was not limited to the occasional burials of local elites, as it was in San Pedro, or to small enclaves of Tiwanaku traders, as it was in Azapa. Instead, Omo-style keros and pitchers appear throughout the ceramic assemblage of ordinary households in large domestic settlement sites at Omo, Los Cerrillos, and Río Muerto. The colonists used a wide range of everyday tools and implements that linked their everyday habitual behaviors to those of their homeland. Even the utilitarian plain pottery that constituted 91 percent of the ceramics at the Moquegua Tiwanaku sites conformed to highland norms. While these utensils may have been locally made, their formal and functional identity with altiplano Tiwanaku prototypes confirms that they were made by Tiwanaku-trained craftspeople for the culinary demands and tastes of Tiwanaku consumers. Tiwanaku domestic life was shaped by a powerfully held adherence to a way of doing things—a Tiwanaku sense of *habitus*. If we accept that cultural identity and social relationships are enacted through the repetitive actions of daily practice, there can be little question that these Tiwanaku colonists were of altiplano origin.

Ayllus in Diaspora: The Tiwanaku Colonies' Segmentary Organization

Some time after the initial Omo-style Tiwanaku colonization of Moquegua, a new set of towns appeared. Their inhabitants shared a distinct subset of Tiwanaku traditions. This distinct migration of Tiwanaku settlers was distinguished by a new style of Tiwanaku material culture known as the Chen Chen style. Astoundingly, this second migration from the altiplano neither replaced nor mingled with the Omo-style colony but established its own independent settlement pattern. Tiwanaku colonization represents not one but two overlapping diasporas.

Who were these dual diasporas? Earlier, I outlined a structural model of south Andean ayllus as corporate groups defined by placing individuals' social identities in a recursive hierarchy of nested segments. At the highest and most inclusive level, maximal ayllus are distinctive ethnic identities shared by large numbers of people (Platt 1986). Kolata, adopting Bouysse-Cassagne's interpretations of ethnic allegiances and identities from ethnohistoric documents, has proposed a complex multiethnic Tiwanaku, in which distinct ethnic and linguistic groups aligned into two great maximal moieties of Urco and Umasuyu opposed along a spatial axis formed by Lake Titicaca (Bouysse-Cassagne 1986:207). Kolata argues that these same dualistic dynamics underlay an earlier Tiwanaku cosmology that also expressed itself in the division of ritual space within Tiwanaku, a site known as Taypicala, or "the stone in the middle of the world" (Cobo 1990 [1653]:100; Kolata 1993:101).

This interpretation of Tiwanaku pluralism cannot yet be linked to specific archaeological populations of the Tiwanaku core region. But in desert Moquegua, we can confirm that at least two Tiwanaku maximal ayllus existed because they established two distinct settlement archipelagos. The results of full coverage survey show that the Omo-style and Chen Chen–style settlement patterns were broadly similar in sharing the fertile midvalley section of Moquegua. Yet settlements of each of these two diaspora communities were symmetrically opposed according to structural norms of social division across space. The Omo-style settlement sectors were consistently situated to the northeast, while the Chen Chen sites were located to the southwest. At each site, ceremonial structures and locations align along a similar axis. Each village's identification with one of the two great diasporas of Tiwanaku settlement may have been encoded in settlement location itself, perhaps an antecedent of the Inca ceque system, which functioned both as a cosmology and a social map of the ayllus of Cusco.

There is not yet enough evidence to connect the binary opposition of Omo and Chen Chen settlement to colonists from any specific location in the altiplano. The Chen Chen and Omo styles' places of origin may someday be understood through careful interregional comparisons of household and mortuary patterns, iconography and material culture, ceramic sourcing, and biological distance. At present, ceramics resembling Moquegua's Chen Chen–style pottery are so ubiquitous throughout the Tiwanaku sphere that they cannot be linked to a particular source. It appears that Omo-style pottery shares the most affinities with Tiwanaku ceramics of the Copacabana peninsula and lake islands.[1] This suggests that Moquegua's first wave of colonists may have originated in Tiwanaku communities on the southwestern shore of Lake Titicaca. Similar vessels also appear in Tiwanaku collections from Cochabamba, perhaps suggesting a mirror colony by the same ethnic group on the eastern slopes. Omo-style pottery is present but uncommon at the Tiwanaku type site, indicating that the style was only one of many used at the cosmopolitan "stone at the center."

A further examination of multiethnic coexistence in Moquegua shows evidence of persistent diversity *within* each of the two Tiwanaku diasporas. Visibly segmentary residential space in the Omo-style sites indicates that Tiwanaku colonial society comprised numerous insular communities, each with its own common ritual space. The Omo-style sites' plaza-centered neighborhoods probably correspond to minimal ayllus within the Omo-style enclave. Possibly, these distinct community segments each corresponded with specific homeland counterparts and maintained their spatial separation in residence and ritual to help maintain these distinct identities. Although community residential plans are not preserved for the Chen Chen–style colonists, similar segmentary principles are suggested by their burial practices, which placed each individual in one of numerous spatially distinct cemetery areas.

Tiwanaku Colonists and Others

More research can also help clarify the initial interaction of the Tiwanaku diaspora with indigenous populations. In Cochabamba, Azapa, and San Pedro, we see that local people accepted Tiwanaku imports and adopted elements of Tiwanaku material culture. Even this moderate degree of cultural interaction implies social and economic relationships between the two populations, perhaps including marriage exchanges to cement alliances. In contrast, in Moquegua we do not find Huaracane people accepting Tiwanaku cultural practices or intermarrying with the new immigrants. Tiwanaku artifacts are never found in Huaracane contexts and no Huaracane artifacts appear in Tiwanaku sites. This discontinuity between the Huaracane domestic tradition and that of the Tiwanaku colonies is borne out by biological distance studies that find little evidence of genetic exchange between the two groups and distinctive practices of cranial deformation (Blom et al. 1998). Putting it together, we can infer that the two populations were not only spatially and culturally distinct but strongly endogamous.

It is possible to interpret the two cultures' lack of interaction in two ways. A globalist scenario might explain the absence of Tiwanaku cultural influences at Huaracane sites by the forced abandonment of the Huaracane villages during the Tiwanaku colonization. A traditional conquest interpretation might assume that the valley's indigenous inhabitants were resettled in new towns where they could be controlled and gradually acculturated as a part of imperial policy. Certainly, this was the case with the Spanish Empire's conquest of much of the Andes, and it is not surprising to see a similar logic applied to settlement changes under the expansion of the great pre-Columbian civilizations (e.g., Bauer 1992; D'Altroy 1992; Schreiber 1992, 1999, 2001). However, without any trace of Huaracane domestic architecture, practices, or artifacts in the Tiwanaku colonies, this seems unlikely. Huaracane villagers might have been put to the sword, forced to flee, or strategically relocated to some unknown region. Alternately, the great floods of the A.D. 700 El Niño could have dealt a crushing blow to valley agriculture, wiping out canals and carrying away crops and fertile floodplain soils. Under either interpretation, Huaracane settlement along the fertile valley edge would have been severely disrupted; yet it is hard to envision this entire population simply vanishing with the arrival of Tiwanaku settlers.

A more likely scenario would ascribe the segregation of late Huaracane and Tiwanaku settlement patterns to the deliberate isolation of an Andean diaspora from a culturally distinct host population. This multiethnic coexistence through conscious segregation was possible in part because the Omo-style colonists occupied a different niche both spatially and occupationally.

Invariably, the archipelago of Tiwanaku colonies was located in areas outside the Huaracane settlement pattern. Entering the valley as pastoralists, the first colonists may have been perceived as noncompetitive by the Huaracane agriculturalists. Whether by cultural preference or by pragmatic design, it is clear that Tiwanaku colonists deliberately avoided the floodplain niche of the Huaracane by clustering their initial settlements near springs and canal-irrigable lands deeper in the desert. The fact that Moquegua Tiwanaku sites were open and unfortified can only be explained by a careful partitioning of valley territory between local populations and Tiwanaku colonists. Further study directed to dating and understanding the late Huaracane sites is the route to confirming exactly how long this remarkable multiethnic coexistence between colonists and natives survived.

Similarly we are left with questions of how Tiwanaku colonists interacted with contemporary Wari communities from southern Peru. The long duration of both settlements points to a complex historical dynamic between Wari and Tiwanaku that has thus far resisted archaeological reconstruction. Only 10 km from Chen Chen and the Moquegua Tiwanaku colonies, the Wari center at Cerro Baúl is a natural shrine and fortress atop a sheer-sided mesa that dominates the upper valley (Feldman 1988; Lumbreras et al. 1982; Moseley et al. 1991; Williams et al. 2001). The defensible location of Cerro Baúl, as opposed to the openness of the Tiwanaku settlements, once suggested a contrast between Wari military occupation and Tiwanaku demographic control. Recently, however, settlement survey has revealed a hinterland of Wari settlements and agricultural fields in the Upper Osmore, suggesting a substantial regional occupation (Owen and Goldstein 2001; Williams et al. 2001). Excavation dates from Cerro Baúl now indicate that this long-term occupation was contemporary with the Tiwanaku colonies only 10 km away in Moquegua (Williams et al. 2001). Even on Tiwanaku turf in the Moquegua Valley, a smaller Wari outpost at Cerro Trapiche and the Moquegua Tiwanaku settlement at Cerro Echenique kept watch on each other from hilltops less than 2 km apart.

Yet despite the proximity of the two cultures' enclaves, their segregation remains their most salient feature. Wari materials are only rarely found in Tiwanaku tombs or household units, and the Tiwanaku materials Williams et al. (2001) describe from Cerro Baúl are curations and derivative imitations at best. Despite the occasional curated obsidian blade or ceramic vessel, there are no significant technology transfers, and each culture maintained its distinctive industries. More important, there is no mutual acculturation evident in the architecture or assemblages of household life of the two colonial systems. The extraordinary segregation of the Wari and Tiwanaku cultural traditions at different sites in Moquegua indicates that the colonists of the two states seldom interacted and generally did not intermarry. Yet without evidence of open warfare, it appears that boundaries on this frontier were more often maintained by rigid cultural rules rather than by outright conflict. There must have been long periods of coexistence among the descendants of indigenous Huaracane farmers and the Tiwanaku and Wari colonists. This was not, however, a warm frontier of rich cultural interaction but a cold coexistence based on segregation, suspicion, and vigilantly guarded cultural identities.

The *Chicha* Economy: From Diaspora to Provincialization

The scale of Tiwanaku settlement represented by the Omo- and Chen Chen–style towns exceeds the hundred or so households that the Garci Diez *visita* describes for the Lupaqa colonies in the Spanish colonial period. With the disappearance of non-Tiwanaku populations from the valley and the unprecedented growth in the size of the colonial settlements, the Moquegua colonies may have begun to test the structural limits of a reciprocity-based vertical archipelago system similar to that of the Lupaqa *mitmaquna* model. As the Tiwanaku colonial settlement grew, it may have arrived at a critical point of economic and social transformation. Textile tools and lithic and lapidary shop debris indicate that most households may have produced finished goods from provided raw materials to meet suprahousehold demands of the state, or of the household's trading partners, or of community leaders at a lower level of hierarchy. The distribution of certain craft activities among community groups suggests an ongoing process of occupational specialization.

Also evident was a visible social differentiation, with some residential groups assuming elite roles by dominating access to imported luxury goods and their associated iconography. We may infer that elite individuals or groups began to control the allocation of local resources as well as the redistribution of imported Tiwanaku goods. This emergence of some ayllu or community segments as colonial elites was accompanied by the specialization of certain households in ritual hospitality.

As the Tiwanaku colonies grew, an increasing appetite for maize encouraged Tiwanaku's ayllus to seek more direct territorial control over lowland provinces. The potential carrying capacity of the altiplano raised field systems make it unlikely that imported foodstuffs contributed to Tiwanaku subsistence in any meaningful sense (Erickson 1987; Kolata 1991, 1993). Moreover, the costs of transporting bulk carbohydrates by llama or human porters in the Andes make subsistence exchange unlikely (D'Altroy 1992). The caloric contribution of the lowland colonies would have been insignificant to subsistence in the altiplano.

However, maize was a vital political resource, essential for the success of the state and its component ayllus. The key to the central role of maize in Tiwanaku political economy is that it fueled Tiwanaku's ritual cycle. In many Andean societies, the acceptance of political leadership mandated the sponsorship of festival drinking bouts. In Aymara communities, the hosting of *ch'alla* (libation) rituals can be critical to economic, social, and political relations. As hosts, leaders are obligated to provide ample quantities of the best drink available. While imported maize had little effect on highland Tiwanaku's subsistence economy, it would have enjoyed a unique importance as the best fermentable grain in the Andes. Maize could be converted to chicha, the single commodity most essential to the ritual economy of the Tiwanaku state. The high sugar content of maize gives it an unparalleled status for chicha beverages. As Cobo reported: "They make chicha from a lot of things. . . . But the best chicha of all, the one that is most generally drunk in this land, and the one that, like a precious wine, takes first place above all the other Indian drinks, is made from maize" (Cobo 1890 [1653]:347).[2]

To guarantee the supply of this precious wine, and their own viability as leaders, Tiwanaku's elites needed to find efficient ways to extract maize from the lowland peripheries. In some lowland valleys like Azapa and Cochabamba that had dense indigenous agrarian populations with well-developed political systems, resource extraction had to be carefully negotiated across a complex political landscape. Small-scale Tiwanaku direct colonization in these regions was balanced by subtle strategies of hegemony over local populations.

Recent macrobotanical research at the Tiwanaku capital confirms the presence of imported lowland maize. Maize found at Tiwanaku represents varieties that cannot grow in the altiplano and that originated in the eastern and western valleys (Wright et al. 2003:393). Additionally, the ratio of maize kernels to cobs suggests that much of the maize found in Tiwanaku had been shelled in the provinces to facilitate bulk shipping and distribution through both centralized and reciprocal kin exchange networks. Future research tracking specific maize varieties promises to shed light on the nature of Tiwanaku's maize exchange.

In Moquegua, the sheer scale of the Tiwanaku presence indicates the mobilization of a large colonial diaspora to establish and run ever larger labor-intensive agricultural systems. In contrast to the more pastoralist traditions of the Omo-style settlers, a new degree of settlement permanence and scale is demonstrated by the large agricultural villages and cemeteries of Chen Chen–style sites. To increase agricultural production, large areas were reclaimed from the desert by laterally extending river-fed canals and by tapping subterranean aquifers through canalizing springs. Cultivating tools and processing and storage facilities indicate that Chen Chen–style households gradually turned to specialized and intensified agricultural production. Beans, gourds, tubers, pumpkins, squashes and peppers, *pacae*, and peanuts were cultivated, eaten, and exported to the Tiwanaku highlands. Cotton became an important industrial cultigen for the Chen Chen–style colonists, who developed a new household crafts industry for Tiwanaku with cotton spinning. But there can be little doubt that the colonists' greatest value to their homeland ayllus and Tiwanaku elites was measured by their surplus production of maize.

These signs of an increasingly specialized agrarian colony contrast with the informal ayllu-organized archipelago of herding and farming communities that I have described. For a parallel situation in the Inca Empire, John Murra has considered how new relations of production could test the limits of folk colonization: "Upon the expansion of the population which it controlled, the growth of the power of the authorities, [and] the increasing difficulty of exercising effective control over rights maintained at the center by the inhabitants settled in the 'islands,' the archipelago changes structurally. Contradictions appear between the interest of the lords and the *mitmaquna*; the relations of reciprocity and redistribution are weakened" (Murra 1985:18).

With this weakening of traditional relations of reciprocity, the Tiwanaku colonies were at a crossroad of historical process and structural change. Somewhere between the initial colonization by herders and pioneer farmers and the growth of the Moquegua colony into a permanently populated province, the Tiwanaku presence began to develop qualitatively different institutions for provincial integration. Moquegua Tiwanaku's transition from colony to province meant conflicts between state agents and ayllu leaders over production and labor, land, and water resources. Growing state authority was represented by state-built ceremonial structures like the Omo temple. For the first time, Tiwanaku colonists constructed corporate architecture that replicated the grandeur of the homeland monuments and provided a stage for public ceremonies that reified and legitimized central power. Increasingly, the actors in these rites saw themselves as citizens of a province rather than as colonists affiliated with a kin group.

The Tiwanaku colonists also expressed their identity in their demand for Tiwanaku-style manufactured goods. The provincial Tiwanaku artifact assemblages of the Omo- and particularly the Chen Chen–style sites were purely Tiwanaku in style, yet surprisingly proletarian when compared to the ceramics, textiles, and utensils of more far-flung Tiwanaku enclaves. Chen Chen–style serving pottery and plainweave woolen blankets and tunics exhibit a uniformity suggesting that many were mass-produced for popular consumption. Most of these Tiwanaku crafts goods, whether imported from the homeland or made in Moquegua by Tiwanaku-trained craftspeople, reinforced Tiwanaku ethnicity and cultural identity. In contrast, "elite" labor-intensive craft items, such as complex zoomorphic vessels, four-pointed hats, tapestry tunics, and carved hallucinogenic snuff tablets and kits were limited in distribution. This contrasts with the Chilean Tiwanaku far periphery, where the few Tiwanaku imports imply the wealth, status, or magico-religious significance of precious gifts sent to indigenous elites. Instead, the Moquegua colonies' vast output of Tiwanaku-style material culture helped reinforce and reproduce the shared identity of Moquegua's diaspora of highlanders by recreating the habitus of everyday altiplano life. Like diasporas everywhere, these colonists in a strange land surrounded themselves with the comfortable clothing, home furnishings, food, music, and games of their homeland.

Imperial Fragmentation: Tiwanaku's Crisis of Faith

Like the collapse of the altiplano Tiwanaku complex and its raised field system, the decentralization that brought Tiwanaku provincial control into decline in the early second millennium A.D. is poorly understood. As new data accrue, debate revolves around whether this decline was triggered by competitive pressure from outside, internal discord, or some sort of ecological stress in the altiplano homeland and sierra valleys.

One model for Tiwanaku collapse has emphasized climate change as the upsetting factor. Tiwanaku's densely populated core region was dependent on complex intensified agricultural systems and on vulnerable overintensified agricultural systems (Kolata 1992, 1996; Kolata et al. 2000). Decreasing rainfall inferred after A.D. 1040 and severe drought from A.D. 1245 to 1310 have been implicated as the determinate cause of the Tiwanaku collapse, both in the homeland and in the Moquegua province (Kolata and Ortloff 1996). We cannot entirely rule out the disruptive effect of long-term drought on Moquegua Tiwanaku's canal-fed agricultural systems. However, neither core region nor provincial Tiwanaku site abandonment coincides with the onset of this drought, and this environmentally determined collapse hypothesis may overestimate social consciousness of long-term climate trends and underestimate Andean peoples' ability to respond to short-term climatic stress (Erickson 1999).

Neither can we discount the possibility of cultural disruption caused by ENSO flood events at the time of the collapse. However, floods on the catastrophic scale of the A.D. 700 and A.D. 1300 events are unknown in the geomorphological record at the time of Tiwanaku abandonment (Magilligan and Goldstein 2001). Moreover, the lessons of the 1998 El Niño in Moquegua suggest that canal systems are easy to rebuild after El Niño events of ordinary magnitude. A more likely scenario might posit social exhaustion after two or more consecutive years of crop failure and futile reconstruction projects. Nonetheless, even if there were such a climatic trigger to collapse, this arguably returns the primary onus for the Tiwanaku collapse to internal social instability rather than climate catastrophe itself (Bermann et al. 1989; Moseley et al. 1991).

For most of its history Tiwanaku unity was rooted in concepts of ritual suzerainty and pluralist confederation, rather than in the centralized infrastructure and institutions of a true state society. At the time of the collapse, Tiwanaku conceptions of political unity were recent, superficial, and probably fragile concepts. I would argue that social tensions inherent in this new project of creating a unified Tiwanaku civic polity are precisely what left it vulnerable to short-term disruptions. In an early review of states as systems, Kent Flannery has defined this phenomenon as "hypercoherence": "The highly centralized but sometimes unstable condition [that] results from the breakdown of whatever autonomy the various small subsystems or institutions in a larger system may have; one by one they are coupled more closely to each other and/or to the central hierarchical control until, like an old-fashioned string of Christmas tree lights set in linear sequence, change in one does in fact affect all the others too directly and rapidly" (Flannery 1972: 420).

For Tiwanaku, the plug was pulled at some time in the tenth century A.D., bringing a pan-Tiwanaku civil collapse. If the centralized aspect of the Tiwanaku state was built on civic ideology, the true cause of Tiwanaku political collapse was a crisis of civic faith. For whatever reason, Tiwanaku civilization no longer provided the spiritual reassurance and perception of a higher living standard that had brought the diverse peoples of the southern Andes together. The citizenry suddenly beheld a state that could no longer guarantee good harvests, access to goods, or intercession with spiritual good. A palpable aura of civic disappointment, even rage, pervades the state's downfall in the peripheries. In iconoclastic frenzy, the Tiwanaku provincials toppled walls, uprooted idols, smashed the finely cut stones of their own temples and systematically sacked elite tombs in Azapa and Moquegua. Even storage and domestic areas were not immune to this fury, and whole Tiwanaku villages were reduced to "rockpiles" by a systematic process of deliberate destruction.

In iconography, it is no accident that icons of Tiwanaku's state ideology such as the front-faced deity and sacrificer figures were resoundingly rejected in the ceramic and textile art of the postcollapse Tiwanaku peoples. Such figures were associated with political unification under "power elites (who) attempted both internal and external integration through a common imagery reflective of relations of dominance" (Cook 1983:179). The rejection of the front-faced god in the Tumilaca Phase was a repudiation of Tiwanaku political authority that stands in sharp contrast to continuities in many other aspects of habitus and cultural identity.

Amazingly, the iconoclasm that leveled Tiwanaku's colonial temples and towns was at the hands of people who continued to use Tiwanaku pottery and observe Tiwanaku burial traditions rather than by any outside agent. Despite evidence of economic and administrative breakdown, a high degree of *cultural* continuity can be traced through the postexpansive period. Tiwanaku's characteristic serving ware assemblage continued to be represented in roughly the same proportions in household and mortuary contexts. The continuing popularity of the kero form demonstrates that ritualized drinking remained an important part of daily household practice and community sociopolitical integration. Continuity in domestic architecture and in most implements and activities of daily practice may also be discerned. With the exception of the front-faced god, postexpansive pottery continued to display local variants of Tiwanaku decorative motifs, such as the step-stair design, suggesting continuity in the artistic vision of the world or cosmos.

In terms of settlement patterns, Tiwanaku's crisis of faith resulted in a major local reorganization and a second period of diaspora for Tiwanaku populations. When security could not be found in the great Tiwanaku towns of Moquegua, their people moved away and settled in isolated smaller communities. Many collapses in antiquity may also be interpreted as the resurgence of patterns of local autonomy that had been suppressed, but never really disappeared, under centralized states. In the Tumilaca Phase, the Tiwanaku colonies returned to many of the segmentary principles that had allowed Tiwanaku to expand in the first place. However, the norms of multiethnic coexistence that had so distinguished the Tiwanaku colonies no longer functioned. This suggests another aspect of the crisis of faith—a political "balkanization" in which fear of internecine hostilities replaced the security provided by state protection. In midvalley Moquegua, the great towns emptied and settlers dispersed to new locations on high hillslopes and peaks or built defensive walls around their villages. Others voted with their feet. Many of what were once considered Tiwanaku colonies on the Pacific Coast and in the steep inaccessible highlands of Moquegua really represent this second diaspora. Refugee populations fleeing Tiwanaku civic collapse in Moquegua settled on the coast, seeking security and new economic niches under older and simpler forms of social and political integration (Owen 1993a). Tumilaca Phase refugees from the Moquegua Valley also recolonized the upper sierra of Moquegua, securing local access to camelid pasturage that had been cut off with the Tiwanaku collapse (Stanish 1992:167).

The political splintering of Tiwanaku was paralleled by the decline of

Tiwanaku's superb regional exchange network. Peoples of the post-Tiwanaku peripheries still sought to secure access to complementary resources and valued craft items, but they now had to do so independently. Without the political unity of Tiwanaku's state and great ayllus to guarantee the safety of long-distance caravans, new networks were vertical archipelagos writ small. Except for a few curated "heirlooms" of an earlier era, imports from altiplano Tiwanaku disappear from the household context. In the absence of altiplano imports, local craft industries developed to meet domestic demand. Ceramics and textiles are found in increasingly diverse and innovative local substyles that bear decreasing resemblance to altiplano prototypes of Tiwanaku.

As trade networks declined, the ayllus of Tiwanaku diaspora returned to diversified and self-sufficient productive strategies. The large-scale community storage and processing facilities seen in the Chen Chen–style sites disappeared, and individual households became increasingly autonomous, each with its own storage units. Without Tiwanaku's chicha-fueled ideology, the love affair with maize also seems to have soured. The refugee Tumilaca Phase settlers in the coastal Osmore site of Loreto Viejo adopted a more diverse diet with a substantial dependence on marine foods and C3 plants as their interest in maize agriculture diminished (Sandness 1992:55).

These localized patterns of production and exchange are consonant with the rise of petty polities from the remnants of Tiwanaku's provinces. New locally defined indicators of rank replace Tiwanaku insignia of power. Increasingly elaborate collared tombs, for example, suggest the emergence of local elites in a competitive milieu (Stanish 1985:144). Cut loose from the orbit of Tiwanaku rule, the descendants of Tiwanaku's diaspora resumed the process of indigenous political development, as local elites vied for control over surplus production and small-scale vertical exchange networks. Out of several competing cultural groups that arose following the Tiwanaku state's collapse in Moquegua, coastal Tumilaca and Chiribaya populations were perhaps the most successful, consolidating into larger polities with distinctive new settlement systems and craft industries. Chiribaya emerged by the end of the eleventh century as an independent chiefdom in the coastal Osmore. Within two centuries, Chiribaya lords controlled a large part of Tiwanaku's former Moquegua province and even established coastal colonies in the upper Osmore. What had been Tiwanaku's periphery became the core of a powerful new ethnic polity.

Igor Kopytoff has proposed a cyclic model of cultural process in which frontier regions and particularly "internal frontiers" are the crucibles of ethnogenesis and political formation. To Kopytoff, frontiers magnetically attract "the ethnic and cultural detritus produced by the routine workings of other societies" (1987:7). Adapting Frederick Jackson Turner's analysis of the role of the American frontier, Kopytoff proposes that most African societies were formed around an initial core group that left a metropole to develop in a local frontier. "In all these instances, displaced Africans have had to face the problem of forging a new social order in the midst of an effective institutional vacuum." Kopytoff further proposes that this political culture led to the continuous reproduction of new frontier polities at the peripheries of mature African societies and a "continuing reorganization of ethnic identities including the formation of new 'colonial tribes'" (Kopytoff 1987:7). He suggests that "large polities—themselves often having risen on the frontiers of declining ones—created new frontiers that in turn nurtured their future rivals. This process of creation of societies and frontiers assured a continuing existence side by side of metropolitan and frontier cultures. And the communication and interplay between them made for the persistence, reproduction and reinvigoration of the frontier pattern in African political culture as a whole" (Kopytoff 1987:30).

A similar political and ethnic genesis came to the south-central Andes as new polities filled the vacuum left by the Tiwanaku collapse. From its coastal core at Chiribaya Alta, the Chiribaya polity, for example, ultimately recolonized the middle Moquegua Valley and the upper Osmore with its own new diaspora. Even in collapse, Tiwanaku's frontier became the fertile soil for the growth of new chiefdoms and the flourishing of new archipelagos.

Tiwanaku Expansion and the Dialectic of Diaspora

The territorial expansion and peripheral integration of early states is one of the pivotal issues in the study of early complex societies. Perhaps because archaeology has grown up alongside European imperialism of the last six centuries, it is not surprising that many interpretations of archaic state expansion take a globalist perspective, focusing on the power strategies of the imperial center as if it were a single unified actor. Globalist perspectives assume that ancient states dominated their peripheries much as did the empires and world systems of the second millennium. Archaic states might incorporate peripheries through hegemonic expansion using systems of clientage and indirect rule. Alternately, state administration might be imposed following military conquest to maximize the exploitation of conquered regions. Globalist perspectives provide a useful framework for discussing indirect and indirect rule under highly centralized expansive states.

Yet globalist models are less satisfactory at explaining expansion by state cores with great internal diversity. Territorial and hegemonic models are particularly problematic for ancient states like Tiwanaku, where strong corporate group identities persisted beneath the veneer of state control. Nor can core-centric globalist models adequately address the complexities of peripheral participation within expanding state systems. As much as the expansion of a civilization transforms its peripheries, it also transforms the homeland, creating outlets for population growth and new paths to economic growth. To address this complexity, agency-oriented scholarship has begun to address states from the points of view of multiple competing factions within state cores and peripheries. These approaches, whether they describe the objects of their research as segmentary states, heterarchy, or corporate strategies, share an interest in studying the survival and continuity of autonomous corporate groups within state societies. As outlined in chapter 1, agency-oriented approaches have been effective at considering state formation but have rarely been invoked in explaining state expansion.

In the final analysis, Tiwanaku civilization was held together by traditions and institutions that ranged from the exchange of precious objects over great distances to the transplantation of entire working cities. Expanding on age-old Andean patterns of transhumance and resource sharing in the Andes, Tiwanaku's ayllus established a demographic presence of pastoralists and agriculturalists in places like Moquegua and Azapa. Later, perhaps schooled by encounters with Wari rivals, Tiwanaku's dominant ayllus formed a state in the altiplano and incorporated colonized regions like Moquegua as dependent provinces. By the ninth century, Tiwanaku's provincial system displayed aspects of the kinds of hierarchical control seen in the provinces of many archaic states, with both religious and secular power focused at provincial centers like Omo and the temples of the Titicaca basin. Nonetheless, the persistent diversity and multiethnic settlement patterns that continued to characterize the Tiwanaku provinces remind us that power never completely passed from the hands of Tiwanaku's component ayllus.

The field investigations described in this book make a case for a pluralistic model of state expansion and an alternate reconstruction of how early Andean empires came to integrate peripheral regions. In describing the later and larger empire of the Inca, Murra (1986) posited that Andean state systems portrayed their political economies as an "Andean reciprocity writ large." Even the most imperialist of Andean state societies claimed to be integrated on principles that were far less coercive and far less hierarchical than might be expected in western models of centralized empire. Was this way of building empire a mere invention of Inca propaganda? Or can we look at the expansion of civilizations like Tiwanaku as a real prototype for consensual confederation in at least some pre-Inca state societies?

The evidence for the expansion of Tiwanaku supports a similar pathway to state growth. Some states, like the Chola state of southern India that Stein describes, were complex hybrids of centralization and pluralism, where distinct corporate segments maintained considerable autonomy both at home and abroad. As was the case with the south Indian states, central power in the Tiwanaku state was rooted in ritual suzerainty, an acknowledgment of paramountcy in matters of worship, and a special relationship with cosmic forces. While ritual suzerainty brings with it many of the trappings of kingship, it does not confer absolute power in the economic and political realms. Like the Chola kings, Tiwanaku leaders constantly negotiated their power with an array of ethnic and political corporate groups founded on segmentary principles.

The importance of Tiwanaku's component corporate groups is reflected in its archipelagos of diasporic colonies. This is the only way to explain provincial Tiwanaku's peculiar peripheral integration—its noncontiguous site distribution, its coexistence with interspersed colonies of other ethnic groups, and its reproduction of the segmentary social structure of the homeland in a colonized landscape. Tiwanaku society retained its pluralistic character, even as it grew into the first empire of the Andes. The structural variability and internal diversity of Tiwanaku's diaspora tells us that early states in the Andes, and probably throughout the ancient world, were far more heterogeneous and far less centralized than has been presumed in neoevolutionist reconstructions. The expansion of Tiwanaku society was organized and articulated through the collective movements of largely autonomous social segments rather than by a single guiding hand. Andean diasporas were held together by enduring identities and ideologies that their people lived in every aspect of daily existence. Even at its zenith, this empire's power remained rooted in ideas and identities more than in force and institutions.

Epilogue
Andean Diasporas Past and Present

I ran into Cecilia Mamani again near the river ford at Trapiche in August of 2002, almost exactly three years after our first encounter. I was going to the Cerro Trapiche archaeological site to prepare a proposal for a future season of fieldwork on its Formative, Wari, and Tiwanaku components—some of the most perplexing examples of archaeological multiethnicity in the Moquegua. Doña Cecilia was commuting to her farm from a new house she is building in one of Moquegua's *pueblos jovenes* (new settlements). I offered a ride to the river crossing, but the river was too high to ford that day. She assured us that the jeep would be fine if we left it at the ford. After all, her family from the highland village of Muylaque now "controlled" the area. As we crossed the fast-moving water on foot, she pointed out the tiny marker stones her people had placed on the submerged stepping stones, and for once, I managed to cross successfully. My colleagues were less fortunate. While the gringos changed their socks, some highland Aymara women in traditional *polleras* (skirts and petticoats) attempted the same crossing. Although she seemed to recognize them, Doña Cecilia did not point out the stepping stones, and the women shared the gringos' soggy fate. Doña Cecilia and I chatted as we watched with amusement from the other side.

The past three years have not been easy for Doña Cecilia and her extended family. The Mamanis had purchased a plot of bottomland at the base of the slope, but the floods of 1998 had stripped it of topsoil and left it strewn with stones. "We can still plant maize or something there, but we just haven't gotten around to clearing it yet," she said. The flood was even worse for others, however, and some of the valley's best lands were lost. "The river was full of potatoes, corn, avocados, animals, even a car!" A new power transmission line tower now stands right behind her tiny original farm plot on the Trapiche slope. I had no doubt that a substantial right-of-way must have been taken by eminent domain, yet I noticed that the base of the tower was green with new alfalfa and Mamani cows were grazing right next to the four steel feet.

Yet overall, the Muylaque colony is thriving. The valley's "indigenous" landholders have grudgingly learned to accept the industry and success of the Muylaqueños and other highland colonists like them. This is made easier by the realization that at least some of the highlanders occupy a different niche by farming marginal lands. Today, Doña Cecilia's pioneering *chacra* is just one of many Mamani family plots on the slopes below the archaeological site. The kinfolk who followed her have taken land that the valley's existing land-holders never would have bothered to farm and have made it verdant with alfalfa, potatoes, and barley. Now she has a small house in town. Her children were doing well, and *gracias a Dios*, there was plenty of water that year and the cows were fat.

As for the "very bad" squatters of Cuchumbaya she had decried three years before, their shanties above the Mamanis' hard-won colony had disappeared as quickly as they had appeared. I did not ask Doña Cecilia why or where they had gone. I already knew that the Instituto Nacional de Cultura had evicted them for building their houses too close to the archaeological site. I also knew that the local INC office had no resources to inspect archaeological sites, and I strongly suspected that Doña Cecilia had blown the whistle on the Cuchumbaya diaspora. Indeed, the Mamanis' own plots on the outskirts of the same archaeological complex had avoided detection.

Wondering if archaeological preservation had a new ally, I shared my latest concern with Doña Cecilia. An enormous 30 m deep trench had mysteriously bisected the Cerro Trapiche archaeological site, literally cutting the mountain in two. I already knew that this was the work of yet another highland Aymara colony, an association of fifty-two immigrant families from the town of Pachas in Omate. Working on weekends and in their spare time, the men of the Pachas group were hand-digging an enormous canal to irrigate deep desert land that neither the Tiwanaku nor the present-day Moqueguanos, nor even the Mamanis of Muylaque, would have thought possible to farm. Remembering her suspicion of the Cuchumbaya squatters three years before, I asked Doña Cecilia about these new "others." Surprisingly, she seemed untroubled by this new invasion; she simply shrugged. "*Son de Pachas, no les conocemos, pues no nos importa*"—They are from Pachas, we don't know them, so they mean nothing to us.

After all that archaeology, I may have learned the most important lesson about Andean diasporas from my conversations with Doña Cecilia. Some combination of personal desperation, family ambitions and loyalty, and simple restlessness still drives pioneers like Doña Cecilia from their highland homes to colonize new territories. Many, perhaps most, of these colonists fail. This seems to be a matter of being in the right place at the right time. But when a pioneer like Doña Cecilia finds a viable niche, it is not hard for her to attract kinfolk to work the claim and solidify the clan's holdings. Like the

Muylaque enclave and the fifty-two people of Pachas, each new colony inevitably comes into contact with colonies of other communities. Multiethnicity has been described as a "language of contention" (Roseberry 1993), and conflict between separate diasporas is not only unavoidable but critical to maintaining each group's sense of identity. More often than not, these multiple diasporas have an uncanny ability to keep to their own and to stay out of one another's way without resorting to the agents of a central state. Only when traditional structures of multiethnic coexistence fail are the Tiwanaku priest kings or the modern bureaucrats called upon to grant titles or oust interlopers. State power plays a role in both colonial diasporas, but that role is complex and historically contingent.

Even under a centralized state in a globalized world, circumstance and history still scatter ayllus across the landscape of the Andes. The Tiwanaku diasporas of A.D. 1000 and the Aymara diasporas of A.D. 2000 differ in many ways. Yet in the ways that they negotiate identity and multiethnicity to make new lands work, they may be surprisingly similar. Perhaps this is Tiwanaku's most enduring legacy.

Notes

Chapter 1. State Expansion

1. Literally "invader," this term has lost its derogatory implication with the legalization of squatter status by title-granting programs in the 1990s. With no trace of embarrassment, Doña Cecilia described her own family as *invasores* in one of their speculative ventures.

2. The Mamani's fields occupy the lower outskirts of the Cerro Trapiche M7 archaeological site. Part of their success in the competitive environment of land claims derives from Doña Cecilia's sense of presence and her negotiating ability with the local INC.

3. Part of the problem is the conflation of Southall's description of political segmentation with Fortes's concept of segmentary lineages developed for the Tallensi (Fortes 1953; Gellner 1995). Because of this, the concept has fallen into disfavor among neoevolutionists, who perceive it as an oxymoron—a model that is neither "segmentary" nor a state (Marcus and Feinman 1998:7). Indeed, many of the societies Southall envisioned in this category, proposed before the publication of Service's evolutionary terminology of tribe, chiefdom, and state (1962), might now be considered "chiefdoms" in comparative terms.

Chapter 2. *Ayllus*, Diasporas, and Archipelagos

1. Isbell (1997) has questioned the universality of the ayllu as a model for ancient Andean social structure, suggesting that Andean studies too often rely on untested homogeneous analogies based on the Inca and other contact period societies. Challenging neoevolutionist assumptions of the ayllu as an Andean cultural essence that was gradually replaced by state-level classes and institutions, Isbell suggests that the ayllu arose as a strategy of resistance to state organization during the Early Intermediate Period (Isbell 1997:311).

2. One discussion of twentieth-century Jewish enclaves in Latin America substituted the term "archipelago" for the traditional term "diaspora." Noting how immigrant enclaves were often prevented from assimilating by their own customs, institutions, and strong sense of identity, the archipelago metaphor describes them as "tight little islands isolated within prevailing national currents" (Elkin 1995: 238).

3. "Este mismo día visitamos . . . en un pueblo que se llama Chinchao 33 yndios que son coca camayos de todas las parcialidades de los chupachos los cuales veinte de estos estan ya visitados en sus mismos pueblos donde son naturales."

4. While a reading of Garci Diez alone suggests that the Lupaqa had the most profound influence in the area (Stanish 1992:101–102), it is possible that Pacajes and Colla colonists were equal in number and influence but had no comparable chronicler to document their claims (Rostworowski 1986).

Chapter 3. The Tiwanaku Core Region

1. "A great stone idol, which they probably worshiped, stands a short distance away in a small recess. It is even said that beside this idol, a quantity of gold was found and around this shrine there were a number of other stones, large and small, dressed and carved like those already mentioned" (Cieza [1553] 1959:284).

2. "Two stone idols of human size and shape, with the features beautifully carved . . . wearing long robes, different from the attire of the natives of these provinces. They seem to have an ornament on their heads" (ibid.).

3. "Close by these stone statues there is another building . . . all one sees is a finely built wall which must have been constructed many ages ago. Some of the stones are very worn and wasted and there are others so large that one wonders how human hands could have brought them to where they stand" (ibid).

4. Kolata asserts that the "two tombs of native lords of this town" that Cieza described as "tall. . ., square cornered towers with their doorways to the rising sun" were the Akapana and Pumapunku ruins (1993:5, 97). The tower description, however, contrasts with Cieza's own depiction of the Akapana as a "man-made hill" and Cobo's characterization of Pumapunku as a mound with no standing walls. Moreover, the principal stairway entrances to the Akapana and Pumapunku face west, not east (Escalante 1994:148, 207, 228; Manzanilla 1992a:41).

5. This argument is at variance with a chronological argument elsewhere in the same volume for the later construction of Pumapunku as a new ethnic earth shrine in reaction to the politicization of Akapana as an elite monument (Kolata 1992:132–134).

6. Few ethnic groups carry a stronger occupational stereotype than the Uru. Quechua and Aymara sources refer to the Uru as primitive fishing specialists who depended on lakeside game and waterfowl and were ignorant of agriculture and herding until the Inca forcibly uprooted them from the lakeside and settled them with the Aymara. These reports must be read in the context of Inca and Aymara informants, however. Wachtel (1986) presents a quantitative study of acculturation the Uru underwent in the sixteenth and seventeenth centuries. Between the Toledan census of 1575 and the La Palata census of 1685, the number of self-described Uru tributaries declined from 16,950 to 1,243. In little more than a century, the proportion of Urus in the indigenous population declined from 24.3 percent to 3.9 percent. This cannot be explained simply by the postconquest demographic catastrophe and represents a systematic Aymarization that began before the Inca conquest.

7. Bandelier notes on file, American Museum of Natural History, 1894: p. 143, August 22, 1894.

8. Although widely distributed, bronze items never replaced stone tools for everyday activities in Tiwanaku.

Chapter 4. The Tiwanaku Periphery

1. Fiber temper is characteristic of some early ceramics of the altiplano and Chiripa, and early features such as "stuccoed" surfaces appear on a few Huaracane Vegetal sherds (Bandy 1995; Cohen et al. 1995; Feldman 1989:216; Ponce Sanginés 1970; Steadman

1995); neckless *ollas* also dominate ceramic plainwares of the far south coast from Arica to Ica (e.g., Bolaños 1987; DeLeonardis 1997; Massey 1991:333; Owen 1993a, 1993b; Rivera Díaz 1976, 1991; Tello 1987).

2. The extensive use of alpaca wool in the textile traditions of Paracas and the south coast, as well as tropical bird feathers, cochineal dye, and spondylus, indicate Paracas exchange relationships that certainly must have included the highlands (Paul 1991:5, 34). The shared practice of seated flexed burials has also been cited as a measure of cultural unity throughout the south-central Andes (Moseley et al. 1991:152), and at least one linguistic analysis suggests that the spread of the Pukina language to lowland regions is a result of Pukara expansion via Tiwanaku (Rostworowski 1986; Torero 1992:183–184).

3. "El mayor río dellos tiene por nombre Viñaque: adonde están vnos grandes y muy antiquíssimos edificios: que cierto según están gastados y ruynados deue auer passado por ellos muchas edades. Preguntando a los indios comarcanos quien hizo aquella antignalla [*sic*], responden que otras gentes barbadas y blancas como nosotros: los cuales muchos tiempos antes que los Ingas reynassen, dizen que vinieron a sestas partes y hizieron allí su morada. Y desto y de otros edificios antiguos que ay en este reyno me parece, que no son la traca dellos como los que los Ingas hizieron o mandaron hazer. Porque este edificio era quadrado: y los de los Ingas largos y angostos. Y también ay fama, que se hallaron ciertas letras en vna losa deste edificio. Lo qual ni lo afirmo, ni de dexo de tener para mí que en los tiempos passados ouiesse llegado aquí alguna genty de tal/juyzio y razón, que hiziesse estas cosas y otras que no vemos" (Cieza 1984 [1553]:249).

4. Uhle was so impressed by the hitherto unknown iconographic parallels that he overlooked the differences in vessel form, paste, slip colors, and surface preparation. He also ascribed the mixture of Tiahuanacoan and non-Tiahuanacoan elements at Pachacamac to the intentional curation of pieces.

5. Lumbreras (1974b) retained the term "Tiahuanacoid," although he preferred "Wari Empire." The "Coastal Tiahuanaco" term also persisted in descriptions of Middle Horizon Wari tapestry textiles, in which design motifs are similar to those of Tiwanaku (Oakland 1986:34–35).

6. Cracked vessels were repaired by drilling, lacing and the application of a mastic, or grinding of broken edges.

7. "Una realidad próxima a un gobierno centralizado . . . como un gran señorío, antesala de un Estado teocrático."

8. "Una sociedad cuya organización social está estrechamente ligada al concepto de linaje (posiblemente clánico) y segmentada de acuerdo a patrones territoriales (Ayllus) con una fuerte connotación dual del manejo territorial y posiblemente vinculada a la institución del liderazgo."

9. The "Late Tiwanaku" or "Regional Development" cultures, such as Maytas/Chiribaya and San Miguel, might best be considered a set of Tiwanaku-derived local styles, as their ceramics have no exact altiplano parallels (Lozada 1998).

10. The small cemetery of Loreto Viejo, in the lower Osmore or Algorrobal Valley near Ilo in the Department of Moquegua, Peru, was adopted as a type site for Tiwanaku influence by Chilean archaeologists after an oral presentation of preliminary reconnaissance there by Gary Vescelius in the early 1960s. As no site or ceramic data from the Loreto Viejo site had been published, there is no clear agreement on the exact definition of the Chilean

Loreto Viejo phase, and subsequent work in Peru questions the site's association with state Tiwanaku settlement (see chapter 5, this volume, and Owen 1993a). Focacci (1983:112) attempted to delineate what he believed to be the first Tiwanaku IV (Classic) context found in Arica from the Loreto Viejo phase. These Classic Tiwanaku objects, from a looted tomb in the AZ-75 cemetery site at San Lorenzo, have been dated to A.D. 560 (Focacci 1983). However, the Loreto Viejo term has come to be a catchall for Tiwanaku-influenced materials, be they Tiwanaku IV, V, or local variants (G. Focacci, I. Muñoz, pers. comm., 1992).

11. "Es claro que la población Tiwanaku inicia la explotación de microzonas anteriormente no utilizadas por los pobladores locales como especialmente las partes medias de los valles."

12. The cemetery at Atoca was first reported by Dauelsberg as AZ-19, though the site may also correspond with AZ-91. Muñoz refers to the site only by the name Atoca-1 (1983b, 1986).

13. By permission of the excavators, I also examined the original Atoca-1 ceramic collections excavated by Iván Muñoz and analyzed by Mariela Santos V.

14. "Cúpula dirigente de las colonias costeras de Tiwanaku."

Chapter 5. Agrarian Settlement in the Middle Moquegua Valley

1. "Excelente clima seco con brillante sol todo el año, tierra fértil, altitud propicia, calor y frío en el momento oportuno para el ciclo vegetativo anual, son condiciones inigualables de este privilegiado valle, con historia documentado y tradición de más de cuatro siglos en el cultivo de la vid."

2. "'El 27 de Noviembre de 1594, Gonzalo de Mazuelo, Hernán Bueno de Arana, Pedro de Guevara, Juan Díaz Ochoa, Hernando Caballero Páez y Jerónima de Miranda (mujer de Alonso de Estrada) dieron poder a Diego Fernández de Córdoba, también residente en Moquegua, para que paraciere ante el corregidor de Arica y compusiera con él las tierras ubicadas en el valle de Omo y Cupina . . . desde el mojón que dibide y parte de las tierras de los yndios Carumas y las jurisdicciones de Moquegua y Arica, que es el principio de dicho valle de Omo, hasta más abajo del angostura de Sillaca y de barranca a barranca río en medio, y pueda hazer las pujas. . .' (Diego Dávila I: 373r–376r). Las partes bajas del valle estaban ya bajo la jurisdicción del puerto de Arica, cosa que se mantuvo a través de la Colonia" (Pease 1984a:166).

The "mojón" may be either Cerro Baúl or Cerro Los Angeles, while "Sillaca" probably refers to the canyon at Yaral/Los Espejos.

3. "Muy buenos membrillos, melocotones, camuesas, higos y otras frutas de España y de la tierra, ingenios y trapiches de azúcar y por el valle abajo muchas chacras y sembrados de maíz, guaranzos frejoles, pallares y otras semillas y mucho ají o pimiento que se coge en este valle y todo tiene mucho valor por la mucha salida que hay de los frutos en carneros [llamas] a la provincia de Chucuito y a toda la tierra arriba, cojense en este valle muy buenos camarones y es todo abastecido y rico y parece un paraíso."

4. Ponce Sanginés's distribution map for the Tiwanaku culture lists only Chen Chen and Loreto Viejo for the Department of Moquegua (Ponce 1972; Portugal Ortiz 1984).

5. Programa Contisuyu convention has assigned site numbers sequentially for each of the principal tributary drainages of the Osmore, with the following prefixes: P for Porobaya, T for Torata, U for Tumilaca, M for middle Moquegua Valley, and C for coastal Osmore Valley.

6. "Oberflachenfunde von Tiahuanaco-Keramik, die mit dem Tiahuanaco der Phase V auf dem bolivianischen Altiplano identisch ist" (Disselhoff 1968:213).

7. Pari mentions eleven sites in the middle Moquegua Valley, five in the Torata area, three in Tumilaca, and one in the lower valley but does not include a map or illustrations of artifacts. Pari reports that several sites have been destroyed since his survey.

8. The sector of the Osmore drainage (400–900 masl) between the lower limit of the Middle Moquegua sector surveyed by MAS and the upper limit of the coastal Osmore Valley was briefly surveyed in 1996. This incised section of the drainage is normally extremely dry, with the river disappearing entirely in most years. The valley was largely devoid of habitation, except for one well-preserved village site at La Capilla at an elevation between 380 and 590 masl, several smaller habitation sites, and one cemetery, all of Chiribaya affiliation. Segments of a trail system indicate that the Chiribaya and possibly earlier occupations of the coastal and middle valley sectors were linked through this region. The presence of lithic remains and pot busts along these routes suggests continual usage of these trails from the Preceramic through the colonial and republican periods. Our travel time suggests that burdened walkers could easily arrive on the coast from the midvalley in well under two days, particularly if way stations were maintained along the trails. Caravan trails over the high pampa were the most efficient route to the coast.

9. Lettered suffixes (without hyphens) were used in all cases except for the M1 Chen Chen site, where letters were used for cemeteries excavated in 1987 by Vargas and numbers (with hyphens) for all sectors identified in 1995 salvage work.

10. The habitation category includes sites with architectural remains and surface sherd scatters. Also registered were four lithic workshops, one ceramic workshop, two isolated projectile points, and two geoglyph sites.

11. Wari structures were built atop a Huaracane cemetery at Cerro Trapiche M7 (Goldstein 2000) and Late Intermediate Estuquiña structures above Tiwanaku buildings at Tumilaca La Chimba (Bawden 1989, 1993).

12. Carbon and nitrogen isotope analysis of samples from Huaracane Phase human skeletons from Omo found them to have highly negative ^{13}C and highly positive ^{15}N values (Sandness 1992). These values closely resemble values from an Early Ceramic period burial reported by Owen from Loreto Viejo in the coastal Osmore and have little in common with later Tiwanaku diet. A dietary simulation using a linear mixing model suggests that both Huaracane and Early Ceramic coastal Osmore diet relied on C3 plant foods, such as legumes, and on animals grazing on C3 vegetation for approximately 50 percent of their diet. Marine resources such as fish, shellfish, and algae comprised 23 percent to 50 percent of the diet. Maize, although represented, made a minimal contribution (3–18 percent) to the Huaracane diets (Sandness 1992:49). Though much of Huaracane subsistence, particularly the importance of highland camelids, will remain a mystery until the excavation of associated habitation sites, these results indicate a substantial reliance on maritime resources by populations located 90 km from the coast. This is being borne out by surface finds of marine shell at most middle Moquegua Valley Huaracane sites (Barrionuevo and Goldstein 1999). The basic subsistence of these midvalley people suggests that their closest affiliations were with closely related coastal specialists and not with the altiplano.

13. Although located adjacent to a large *túmulo* group, the M73 extended burial has not been dated and may predate the Huaracane occupation. Extended burials in Mo-

quegua are usually associated with Preceramic occupations (Torres et al. 1984; Wise et al. 1994).

14. The Trapiche/Pukara ceramic style is typified by well-fired vessels decorated with polychrome designs executed in black, yellow, and cream on a reddish brown background. Prefiring incisions outline the painted motifs, which include typical Pukara side-facing felines, birds, and lozenge-shaped geometric designs. Minuscule fragments of paired warp tapestry, considered a Pukara technique, and of a feathered textile were recovered in test excavations at Cerro Trapiche in 1984 (Feldman 1989).

15. Early dates reported for the coastal Chiribaya culture could suggest continuity from these Early Ceramic populations. Recent examination finds significant biological distance between Chiribaya and the Tumilaca populations, who are presumed to be Tiwanaku descendents (Lozada and Buikstra 2002). Although Chiribaya ceramic style is often considered to be highland-related, there are continuities in some utilitarian forms that suggest the possibility that the Chiribaya descended from Formative populations.

16. The northernmost Chen Chen cemeteries, designated M1 A–G and J–M by Vargas's team in 1987, were obliterated by housing construction before the 1995 salvage project. The numbered cemetery sectors M1–23 through M1–38 were mapped in 1995 by Williams and Owen. These include Vargas's cemeteries H and I, and Ñ through B, although correspondence of the earlier map to aerial photos is inexact (see table 5.3 and figure 5.17 for probable equivalents).

17. Specimen M12=1617, an in-situ wooden wall post removed from domestic structure 2 at Omo site M12, produced a radiocarbon age of 1470 ± 70 B.P. (Beta-36639) cal A.D. 600, 1 sigma range = cal A.D. 538–648.

18. Eroded blackware kero sherds diagnostic for the Omo style appeared in collections from the Inca center at Torata Alta (T5) (E. Torres and M. C. Lozada, pers. comm., 1987). Blackware vessels have also been found in a cemetery near the town of Yacango, at the settlement site of Coplay (P. Burgi, pers. comm., 1989), and at the U2 site on the east bank of the Tumilaca River (R. Feldman, pers. comm., 1986). Pari also considered sherds from several sites in the Tumilaca Valley to be associated with Tiwanaku IV (Pari 1987:73).

19. La Cantera produced three fragments of one Ocros vessel and one possible Chakipampa sherd.

20. After partial salvage excavations directed by Robert Feldman, most of the Los Cerrillos M31 site was destroyed by construction in the late 1980s. The plazas and circles designated M206 were largely obliterated by a modern burial ground known locally as the altiplano cemetery, and only traces could be discerned at the time of the 1995 survey.

21. Materials excavated by Disselhoff at Chen Chen produced uncorrected radiocarbon dates of A.D. 970 ± 75 (Disselhoff 1968:216), A.D. 910 ± 65, and A.D. 1040 ± 65 (Geyh 1967), while material found by Vescelius at Loreto Viejo was dated to A.D. 980 ± 70 (Rivera 1985). However, descriptions of the exact contexts and associated material for these dates are not available.

22. "Tiwanaku" materials found by Vescelius at Loreto Viejo in looted tomb contexts have been the basis for its use as a type site by Chilean archaeologists (Rivera Díaz 1985). Artifacts from Loreto Viejo included a Tiwanaku tapestry with staff-bearing figures (Conklin 1983 and pers. comm., 1987), and a few ceramic vessels, snuff tablets, and other materials, now in private collections, are indeed of Tiwanaku V affiliation (Manuel Pacheco, pers. comm. n.d.). However, examination of Vescelius's notes indicates that the cultural materials he collected were of Tumilaca Phase or Chiribaya style.

Chapter 6. The Diaspora Household

1. My mapping of the Omo M10, M11, and M12 sites in 1986 and 1987 used optical theodolites, plane table, and alidade. The MAS team under my direction completed the mapping of the Chen Chen habitation sectors in 1995 in coordination with a base grid surveyed by Ryan Williams. The Río Muerto and Omo M16 maps were surveyed by the MAS project in 1998 and 1999 using a total station EDM theodolite.

2. Collection methodology varied slightly by site. At most Tiwanaku sites, collection units were 100 m² (10 m × 10 m) located on a systematic grid at every 50 m, for a 4 percent surface coverage. Systematic collections were made in 1986 and 1987 at Omo M10, M11, and M12. Because only diagnostic fragments were collected at Omo, total plainware counts were estimated using a regression of the relationship of number of diagnostic plainware to total number of plainware sherds. Dogleash circular collection units were employed in the 1995 salvage excavations at Chen Chen M1, and units were reduced to 50 m² in areas of extremely high density. In 1998 10 m × 10 m units were collected at Río Muerto (M43, M48, M52, M70) and Omo Alto (M16). Due to the density of ceramics at the Tiwanaku sites, most nondiagnostic sherds and large ground-stone lithics were tallied by ware, recorded, and left in the field. Diagnostic ceramics and all chipped-stone lithics were collected, washed, cataloged, and permanently curated for future analysis at the Museo Contisuyo Moquegua.

3. Household excavations were undertaken in 1986 and 1987 at the Omo M10, M11, and M12. Of sixteen test excavations at Omo, eight—three in M10, two in M11, and three in M12—exposed entire rooms or significant parts of household units. A total area of 1,064 m² was exposed at these three sites. Salvage excavations exposed six habitation units at Chen Chen M1 in 1995 and ten at Omo M16 in 1999. The 1998 MAS excavations at Río Muerto opened six test units at M70 and two at M43, totaling 243 m².

4. Soil samples for flotation and fine screening were collected from all floors, features, and subfloor deposits.

5. A total of 48,278 sherds and 44.9 kg of faunal remains was recovered in the 1986–87 Omo project domestic excavations.

6. Wooden posts were best preserved at Omo M12 and Río Muerto M70 and provide the majority of dated samples.

7. *Tupus* from Tiwanaku with similar flat disk heads are illustrated in Posnansky (1957: vols. 3–4, plates 84–86) and on display at the Museo de Metales Preciosos Precolombinos, La Paz.

8. One such quarry site, a 2km² area on a ridgetop downvalley from Río Muerto, was noted to include extensive evidence of primary exploitation of chert nodules and isolated ceramic fragments from all periods.

9. M12=1827, M12 Structure 1 H1 S12E2, from Chivay source in Colca Valley.

10. Samples M10=1685, M10 Structure 13, from Andahuaylas A source. Sample M10–383, M10 surface, from Quispisisa source in Huancavelica.

11. For example, of twenty-six surface finds of modeled portrait head vessel fragments, twenty-five were collected in the South Community.

12. These are the blackware portrait vessels found southeast of Structure 2; keros with rectangularized front-faced or gateway god figures found in and around the four-room longhouse in surface collection, Unit L5; skull-shaped "trophy head" drinking vessels found in a three-room longhouse in Unit L6; duck-shaped zoomorphic vessels concentrated

northeast of the south plaza; and a type of redware portrait head vessel with horizontally pierced nose, concentrated in Units K7 and K8.

13. The Omo M12 blackware vessels are stylistically similar to blackware portrait vessels from the altiplano, although perhaps not by the same hand. Comparata would include vessels excavated by Bandelier at Island of the Sun (AMNH B/1903 and B/2144 from Titin Uayani) and in the Museo Nacional de Antropología, La Paz, from Ingavi (MNA 2641, http://www.bolivian.com/arqueologia/ryr-3.html). This portrait style in blackware appears most frequently at the lakeside sites of the Tiwanaku core region.

14. The sitewide density of plainware sherds in M10 excavation units that were excavated to sterile (2357.8 grams/m²) is over three times the density in M12 excavations.

15. Structures 15–1 and 14–1.

16. Additionally, pottery grave goods at Chen Chen M1 and in two cemeteries at Omo M10 suggests that some burials are associated with the Tumilaca Phase. This indicates continued use after the intentional destruction of the sites.

17. These included several fragments of Omo-style blackware, a redware everted bowl, and hooves from an unusually fine llama vessel. Only sixty-six blackware sherds, considered a marker for the Omo style, were found sitewide at M10, mostly in lower excavation levels.

18. Feature R13, specimen M10=1479.

19. Specimen M10=1515.

20. Camelids can conceive twins but usually support only one live birth.

21. Edible bivalve species from a sandy beach ecosystem, particularly *Choromytilus chorus* (known as *choro zapato*) and *Protothaca thaca* (*almeja*), overwhelmingly dominate. Rocky littoral species such as *Tegula atra* and *Prisogaster niger* (*caracoles turbantes*), at least one limpet species (possibly *Acmaea*), and marine and riverine crustaceans are also represented (Barrionuevo and Goldstein, 1999; Sandweiss, pers. comm., 1987). *Oliva peruvianus* (*oliva*) continued to be worked for ornamental use. Even heavy coral-like marine exoskeletons were imported for use as abraders or polishers.

22. Examination of M10's proletarian textile inventory from domestic contexts points out the bias in the traditional artifact-oriented approach to mapping Tiwanaku peripheral expansion. Most considerations of Tiwanaku textile style focus on the few textile media that can convey polychrome iconographic images, notably interlocked weft-face tapestry and knotted hats. These are rare in domestic contexts.

23. Unwalled exterior spaces were largely devoid of features and have low densities of ceramics and large mammal remains, suggesting that little domestic activity took place there.

24. The average weight per fragment of mammal bone was 2.88 grams, as compared to 1.2 grams per fragment for bone from the roofed core.

25. An entirely cane-walled feature in Structure 1 may have fulfilled an analogous role.

26. Another possible explanation for the change in infrastructure is a shift from corn meal grinding for *chicha* production to other forms of maize consumption, such as roasting or parching, which became dominant in the Late Intermediate Estuquiña Phase (Lozada 1987). Roasted maize is not as easily transported in bulk as corn meal and might be more suited to local storage and household consumption.

27. The proportion of Tumilaca Phase redware in the household increased markedly at M11. The percentage of redware in the M11 excavated ceramic inventory (19 percent by

sherd count; 10.7 percent by weight) is greater than the combined percentage of redware and blackware in the M10 and M12 excavations. This may be due to increased availability of these locally produced redwares.

28. M11=1515.

29. Specimens M11=1513, 1514, and 1515.

Chapter 7. Death in a Faraway Land

1. Six of the M10 cemeteries (B, M, P, R, S, and T) can be associated with the Chen Chen style by excavated grave offerings, while nine are affiliated based on surface sherds. The number of tomb depressions visible on the surface in these cemeteries ranged from 20 (M10L) to 120 (M10H). Only one cemetery, M10Y (the Huaracane "boot tombs" discussed in chapter 5), predates the Tiwanaku occupation. Three cemeteries (M10 N, A, and Q) appear to be intrusive, dating to the subsequent Tumilaca Phase. Pottery and tomb type in the N cemetery are identical to those of the Omo M11 cemetery. Excavations in M10 cemeteries A and Q have not produced pottery offerings, but their superior preservation, intrusive locations, and textiles of variant techniques suggest that they also date to relatively late in the Tiwanaku sequence.

2. Moquegua Tiwanaku's distinct cemeteries also contrast with the below-floor burials at Late Intermediate Period sites such as Chiribaya and Estuquiña (Lozada 1998; Williams 1990).

3. Few tombs at either Omo or Chen Chen were found with capstones in place; most of the capstones were found on the surface of the M10 cemeteries or had fallen into opened tombs. The only exceptions are some of the tombs of M10 cemeteries K and L, which are located in the quebrada between M10 and M11. These were buried under up to a meter of overburden and exposed to looting from the side by the road cut.

4. The braided technique of these ropes differs from the twisted vegetable fiber ropes of the Estuquiña Phase.

5. For a contrasting reading of this passage as a reference to the Akapana and Pumapunku, see Kolata 1993:98.

6. The following description is based primarily on analysis of 138 tombs that have been examined at the Omo cemeteries. Some 104 disturbed Tiwanaku tombs in nine of the M10 cemeteries were examined by Marc Bermann, the author, and members of Programa Contisuyu in 1984 or by the Omo project in 1987. Sixty-seven of these tombs were reexcavated and found to be at least partially intact. A total of thirty-four tombs at cemeteries M16D and M16E was excavated in 1999 salvage operations at the Omo-style site M16.

A larger sample of 334 intact tombs and hundreds of recently looted tombs was excavated in cemeteries A–L of the Chen Chen site by Instituto Nacional de Cultura rescue excavations at Chen Chen M1 in 1987 (Blom 1999, Blom et al. 1998; Buikstra 1995; Vargas 1988, 1994). A smaller-scale salvage project in 1995 excavated approximately sixty additional tombs in cemeteries not excavated by Vargas (Owen and Goldstein 2001). The Omo M10 and Chen Chen M1 burials are similar in most aspects of tomb construction and offerings.

7. *Cistas* comprised between 27 percent and 86 percent of tombs in the cemeteries examined by Vargas.

8. Twenty-two tombs of this type (37 percent) were identified in the Omo M10 sample.

9. The Omo examples range from 4 to 6 cm in diameter. Vargas (1994) suggests that these posts may be the remains of roofing material, but tombs seldom have more than one post and no smaller branches, cane, or impressed mud are found in standard tombs.

10. This object (M10M-7=10), excavated in 1984, was so well hidden that it was not detected until Oakland's textile analysis in 1986.

11. Cieza describes the importance of camelid sacrifices in high status Colla Aymara burial ceremonies: "If it was a headman, the body was accompanied by most of the people of the village, and beside it they burned ten llamas, or twenty, or more or less, depending on who the deceased was" ([1553] 1959:275). In Moquegua, offerings of llama hooves are common in Late Intermediate burials of the Estuquiña Phase (Williams 1990). In cemeteries of the post-Tiwanaku Chiribaya chiefdoms, llama heads and sometimes entire animals would be placed in the most elaborate and best furnished elite tombs (Lozada 1998; Owen 1993a).

12. The collection of Father Francis Fahlman, consisting primarily of vessels purchased from local children who found them at the Chen Chen site, was examined by the author in 1984 (Goldstein 1985). The collection included 135 keros, 111 tazones, and 87 pitchers. The relatively high number of pitchers and the fact that only six plainware ollas were represented in the Chen Chen sample may be due to looters' bias.

13. Of nineteen spoons collected in M10 Tiwanaku tombs, all but two were of the flat-handled variety. Of these, one was plain, five had notched edges, two were decorated with incised crosshatched designs, four had llama-shaped silhouettes on the tip of the handle, and two had scalloped edges.

14. Blom had conflicting results with the larger Chen Chen sample, finding that cranial modification techniques crosscut spatial boundaries (1999:163).

15. The 2 sigma calibrated date is based on radiocarbon age of 1290 ± 70 B.P. This date for the original interment is consistent with the Omo-style occupation of the adjacent M16 domestic areas. Stratigraphy indicates that tomb 15 was opened and severely disturbed considerably before the A.D. 1600 eruption of Huayna Putina.

16. The cemetery at Atoca was first reported by Dauelsberg as AZ-19, though the site may also correspond with AZ-91. Muñoz refers to the site only by the name Atoca 1 (1983b, 1986).

17. I also examined the original Atoca 1 ceramic collections excavated by Iván Muñoz and analyzed by Mariela Santos.

Chapter 8. Provincial Tiwanaku Temples and Sacred Landscapes

1. The principal stair accesses to the Akapana and Pumapunku faced west, however, perhaps differentiating ceremonial processions from mortuary practices, in which interred individuals faced east (Protzen and Nair 2000:359).

2. Manzanilla (1992a) reconstructs the Akapana with seven terraces and a dual stair-case on the west side. Protzen and Nair (2000:359) note that the exposed terraces are not symmetrical around the structure and that their exact configuration and number are not clear.

3. These vessels were most likely used for the burning of llama fat to produce smoke, rather than for incense. Although the term *sahumario* (censer) is probably more accurate, the more commonly used term *incensario* is used henceforth.

4. Only the bottom step was discovered in situ in the Middle Court, but plaster and

mortar impressions indicate an overlapping series of large stone slabs. This overlapping slab technique is similar to the staircase of the Templete Semisubterráneo and other altiplano Tiwanaku monuments.

5. Posnansky (1945) posited swinging doors for the Gateway of the Sun. However, the conical holes he referred to may instead have housed anchors that secured jambs and lintels in the great lithic gateways of Tiwanaku (Protzen and Nair 2002:204).

6. The stela head (M10=137) was found in the domestic area, adjacent to a storage cist.

Chapter 9. Confederation and Pluralism in an Ancient State

1. Notable are the prevalence of polished blackware, the Omo-style kero shape, and the continuous volute motif.

2. "Hácese la Chicha de muchas cosas. . . . Pero la mejor Chicha de todas y que más generalmente se bebe en esta tierra, la cual, como vino precioso, tiene el primer lugar entre todas las demás bebidas de los indios es la que se hace de Maíz."

Bibliography

Abercrombie, T.
1986   The Politics of Sacrifice: An Aymara Cosmology in Action. Unpublished Ph.D. dissertation, Department of Anthropology, University of Chicago.
1998   *Pathways of Memory and Power: Ethnography and History among an Andean People.* University of Wisconsin, Madison.

Abu-Lughod, J. L.
1989   *Before European Hegemony: The World System* A.D. *1250–1350.* Oxford University Press, New York.

Adams, R. M.
1966   *The Evolution of Urban Society.* Aldine, Chicago.
1974   Anthropological Perspectives on Ancient Trade. *Current Anthropology* 15:239–258.
1978   Strategies of Maximization, Stability and Resilience in Mesopotamian Society, Settlement and Agriculture. *Proceedings of the American Philosophical Society* 122(5):329–335.
1988   Context of Civilization Collapse: A Mesopotamian View. In *The Collapse of Ancient States and Civilizations*, edited by N. Yoffee and G. Cowgill, pp. 20–43. University of Arizona Press, Tucson.

Albarracin-Jordan, J.
1996a   Tiwanaku Settlement Systems: The Integration of Nested Hierarchies in the Lower Tiwanaku Valley. *Latin American Antiquity* 3(3):183–210.
1996b   *Tiwanaku: Arqueología regional y dinámica segmentaria.* Editores Plural, La Paz.

Albarracin-Jordan, J., and J. E. Mathews
1990   *Asentamientos prehispánicos del Valle de Tiwanaku.* Producciones CIMA, La Paz.

Alconini Mujica, S.
1993   *La cerámica de la Pirámide Akapana y su contexto social en el estado de Tiwanaku*, La Paz.
1995   *Rito, símbolo e historia en la Pirámide de Akapana, Tiwanaku: Un análisis de cerámica ceremonial prehispánica.* Editorial Acción, La Paz.

Aldenderfer, M. S. (editor)
1993a   *Domestic Architecture, Ethnicity, and Complementarity in the South-Central Andes.* University of Iowa Press, Iowa City.
1993b   Domestic Space, Mobility, and Ecological Complementarity: The View from Asana. In *Domestic Architecture, Ethnicity, and Complementarity in the South-Central Andes*, edited by M. S. Aldenderfer, pp. 13–24. University of Iowa Press, Iowa City.
1998   *Montane Foragers: Asana and the South-Central Andean Archaic.* University of Iowa Press, Iowa City.

Alexander, H. B.

1948   *The Mythology of all Races: Latin American* Volume XI. MacMillan Company,
        New York.

Algaze, G.

1989   Uruk Expansion: Cross-cultural Exchange in Early Mesopotamian Civilization.
        Current Anthropology 30(5):571–608.

1993a   Expansionary Dynamics of Some Early Pristine Sites. *American Anthropologist*
        95(2):304–333.

1993b   *The Uruk World System: The Dynamics of Early Mesopotamian Civilization.* Uni-
        versity of Chicago Press, Chicago.

Allen, C.

1988   *The Hold Life Has: Coca and Cultural Identity in an Andean Community.* Smith-
        sonian Institution Press, Washington, D.C.

Anderson, B.

1987   *Imagined Communities.* Verso, London.

Anderson, K.

1997   *Omereque: A Middle Horizon Ceramic Style of Central Bolivia.* Unpublished
        Master's thesis, University of California at Santa Barbara.

Anderson, K., R. Céspedes, and R. Sanzetenea

1998   Tiwanaku and the Local Effects of Contact: The Late Formative to Middle Hori-
        zon Transition in Cochabamba, Bolivia. Paper presented at the 63rd Annual Meet-
        ing of the Society of American Archaeology, Seattle.

Anthony, D. W.

1990   Migration in Archaeology: The Baby and the Bathwater. *American Anthropologist*
        92(3):895–914.

1992   The Bath Refilled: Migration in Archaeology Again. *American Anthropologist*
        94:174–176.

Arriaga, P. J.

1968   [1621] *The Extirpation of Idolatry in Peru.* Translated by L. Clark Keating. Univer-
        sity of Kentucky Press, Lexington.

Astvaldsson, A.

2000   The Dynamics of Aymara Duality: Change and Continuity in Sociopolitical Struc-
        tures in the Bolivian Andes. *Journal of Latin American Studies* 32(1):145–174.

Baines, J., and N. Yoffee

1998   Order, Legitimacy, and Wealth in Ancient Egypt and Mesopotamia. In *Archaic
        States*, edited by G. M. Feinman and J. Marcus, pp. 199–260. School of American
        Research, Santa Fe.

Balkansky, A.

1998   Origin and Collapse of Complex Societies in Oaxaca (Mexico): Evaluating the era
        from 1965 to the Present. *Journal of World Prehistory* 12(4):451–493.

Bandelier, A. F.

1894   Unpublished Field Notes of A. F. Bandelier. American Museum of Natural History,
        New York.

1910   *The Islands of Titicaca and Koati.* Hispanic Society of America, New York.

1911   The Ruins at Tiahuanaco. *Proceedings of the American Antiquarian Society* 21:
        218–265.

Bandy, M.
1995   The Early Ceramic Periods of Moquegua: A Reappraisal. Paper presented at the Society for American Archaeology 60th annual meeting, Minneapolis.

Bandy, M., A. Cohen, A. Cardona, A. Oquiche, and P. S. Goldstein
1996   The Tiwanaku Occupation of Chen Chen (M1), Report on the 1995 Salvage Excavations. Paper presented at the Society for American Archaeology 61st Annual Meeting, New Orleans.

Barnett, W.
1991   Ceramic Production In The Socio-Economic Organization Of The Tiwanaku Periphery. Paper presented at the Society for American Archaeology 56th Annual Meeting, New Orleans.

Barrionuevo A., M. and P. Goldstein
1999   Different Worlds?: Tiwanaku Provincial Political Economy, and the People who Would not Join. Paper presented at the Society for American Archaeology 64th Annual Meeting, Chicago.

Bastien, J.
1978   *Mountain of the Condor: Metaphor and Ritual in an Andean Ayllu*. West Publishing, New York.

Bauer, B. S.
1992   *The Development of the Inca State*. University of Texas Press, Austin.
1998   *Sacred Landscape of the Inca: The Cusco Ceque System*. University of Texas Press, Austin.
1999   *Early Ceramics of the Inca Heartland*. Fieldiana Anthropology. New Series 31. Field Museum of Natural History, Chicago.

Bauer, B. S., and C. Stanish
2001   *Ritual and Pilgrimage in the Ancient Andes: The Islands of the Sun and the Moon*. University of Texas, Austin.

Bawden, G.
1989   The Tumilaca Site and Post-Tiahuanaco Occupational Stratigraphy in the Moquegua Drainage. In *Settlement, History and Ecology in the Osmore Drainage, Southern Peru*, edited by D. S. Rice, C. Stanish, and P. Scarr, pp. 287–302. BAR International Series 545 part 2. British Archaeological Reports, Oxford.
1993   An Archaeological Study of Social Structure and Ethnic Replacement in Residential Architecture of the Tumilaca Valley. In *Domestic Architecture, Ethnicity, and Complementarity in the South-Central Andes*, edited by M. Aldenderfer, pp. 42–54. University of Iowa Press, Iowa City.

Benavente, M. A., C. Massone, and C. T. Winter
1986   Larrache, evidencias atipicas, Tiwanaku en San Pedro de Atacama? *Chungará* 16–17:67–73.

Bennett, W. C.
1934   Excavations at Tiahuanaco. *Anthropological Papers of the American Museum of Natural History* 34(3):361–493.
1936   Excavations in Bolivia. *Anthropological Papers of the American Museum of Natural History* 35(4):329–508.
1948   A Revised Sequence for the South Titicaca Basin. *Memoirs of the Society for American Archaeology* 4:90–93.

1953   Excavations at Wari, Ayacucho, Peru. *Yale University Publications in Anthropology* 49–50.

Bennett, W. C., and J. B. Bird

1960   *Andean Culture History.* American Museum of Natural History, New York.

Berberian, E. E.

1977   El problema de la expansion de la cultura de Tiwanaku en el Noroeste Argentino. *Arqueología en Bolivia y Peru* 2.

Berenguer, J. R.

1978   La problemática Tiwanaku en Chile: Visión retrospectiva. *Revista Chilena de Antropología* 1:17–40.

1985   Evidencias de inhalación de alucinógenos en esculturas Tiwanaku. *Chungará* 14: 61–70.

1986   Relaciónes iconográficas de larga distancia en los Andes: Nuevos ejemplos para un viejo problema. *Boletín del Museo Chileno de Arte Precolombino* 1:55–78.

1998   La iconografía del poder en Tiwanaku y su rol en la integración de zonas de frontera. *Boletín del Museo Chileno de Arte Precolombino* 7:19–38

Berenguer, J. R., and P. Dauelsberg H.

1989   El Norte Grande en la órbita de Tiwanaku (400 a 1,200 d.C). In *Culturas de Chile, Prehistoria desde sus orígenes hasta los albores de la Conquista,* edited by J. Hidalgo L., V. Schiappacasse F., H. Niemeyer F., C. Aldunate, and I. Solimano R., pp. 129–180. Editorial Andrés Bello, Santiago de Chile.

Bermann, M. P.

1994   *Lukurmata: Household Archaeology in Prehispanic Bolivia.* Princeton University Press, Princeton.

1997   Domestic Life and Vertical Integration in the Tiwanaku Heartland. *Latin American Antiquity* 8(2):93–112.

Bermann, M. P., and J. Estevez C.

1993   Jachakala: A New Archaeological Complex of the Department of Oruro Bolivia. *Annals of Carnegie Museum* 62(4):311–340.

Bermann, M. P., P. Goldstein, C. Stanish, and L. Watanabe M.

1989   The Collapse of the Tiwanaku State: A View from the Osmore Drainage. In *Settlement, History and Ecology in the Osmore Drainage, Southern Peru,* edited by D. S. Rice, C. Stanish, and P. Scarr, pp. 269–286. BAR International Series 545(2). British Archaeological Reports, Oxford.

Billman, B. R., and G. M. Feinman (editors)

1999   *Settlement Pattern Studies in the Americas.* Smithsonian Institution Press., Washington, D.C.

Binford, L. R.

1971   Mortuary Practices: Their Study and Their Potential. In *Approaches to the Social Dimensions of Mortuary Practices,* edited by J. A. Brown, pp. 1–112. Society for American Archaeology, American Anthropological Association, Washington.

Binford, M. W., A. L. Kolata, M. Brenner, J. W. Janusek, M. T. Seddon, M. Abbott, and J. H. Curtis

1997   Climate Variation and the Rise and Fall of an Andean Civilization. *Quaternary Research* 47(2):235–248.

Bird, J.

1943   Excavations in Northern Chile. *Anthropological Papers of the American Museum of Natural History* 38(4):173–318.

1979   The "Copper Man": A Prehistoric Miner and His Tools from Northern Chile. In *Pre-Columbian Metallurgy of South America*, edited by E. P. Benson, pp. 105–132. Dumbarton Oaks Conference on Pre-Columbian Metallurgy of South America. Dumbarton Oaks, Washington, D.C.

Bittman, B., G. LePaige, and L. Nuñez
1978   *Cultura Atacameña*. Extensión Cultural, Ministerio de Educación, Santiago.

Blanton, R. E.
1983   The Ecological Perspective in Highland Mesoamerican Archaeology. In *Archaeological Hammers and Theories*, edited by J. Moore and A. Keene, pp. 221–231. Academic Press, New York.
1998   Beyond Centralization: Steps toward a Theory of Egalitarian Behavior in Archaic States. In *Archaic States*, edited by G. M. Feinman and J. Marcus, pp. 135–172. School of American Research, Santa Fe.

Blanton, R., and G. Feinman
1984   The Mesoamerican World System. *American Anthropologist* 86:673–682.

Blanton, R., G. Feinman, S. Kowaleski, and P. Peregrine
1996   Agency, Ideology and Power in Archaeological Theory: A Dual Processual Theory of the Evolution of Mesoamerican Civilization. *Current Anthropolology* 37(1):1–14.

Blom, D.
1999   Tiwanaku and the Moquegua Settlements: A Bioarchaeological Approach. Unpublished Ph.D. dissertation, Department of Anthropology, University of Chicago.

Blom, D., B. Hallgrímsson, L. Keng, M. C. Lozada C., and J. E. Buikstra
1998   Tiwanaku State Colonization: Bioarchaeological Evidence of Migration in the Moquegua Valley, Perú. *World Archaeology* 30(2):238–261.

Bolaños B., A.
1987   Carrizal: Nueva fase temprana en el valle de Ilo. *Gaceta Arqueológica Andina* 14:18–22.

Boone, J. L.
1986   Parental Investment and Elite Family Structure in Preindustrial States: A Case Study of Late Medieval-Early Modern Portuguese Genealogies. *American Anthropologist* 88(4):859–878.

Bourdieu, P.
1977   *Outline of a Theory of Practice*. Cambridge University Press, Cambridge.
1990   *The Logic of Practice*. Stanford University Press, Stanford.

Bouysse-Cassagne, T.
1986   Urco and Uma: Aymara Concepts of Space. In *Anthropological History of Andean Polities*, edited by J. V. Murra, N. Wachtel, and J. Revel, pp. 201–27. Cambridge University Press, Cambridge.

Brooks, S., M. D. Glascock, and M. Giesso
1997   Source of volcanic glass for ancient Andean tools. *Nature* 386(3):449–450.

Browman, D. L.
1974   Pastoral Nomadism in the Andes. *Current Anthropology* 15:188–196.
1978a   The Temple of Chiripa, Lake Titicaca, Bolivia. Paper presented at the 3rd Congreso Peruano, el Hombre y la Cultura Andina, Lima.
1978b   Toward the Development of the Tiahuanaco (Tiwanaku) State. In *Advances in Andean Archaeology*, edited by D. Browman, pp. 327–349. Mouton, the Hague.
1980a   New Light on Andean Tiwanaku. *American Scientist* 69:408–419.

1980b   Tiwanaku Expansion and Altiplano Economic Patterns. *Estudios Arqueológicos* 5:107–120.

1984a   Prehistoric Aymara Expansion, the Southern Altiplano and San Pedro de Atacama. *Estudios Atacameños* 7:236–252.

1984b   Tiwanaku: Development of Interzonal Trade and Economic Expansion in the Altiplano. In *Social and Economic Organization in the Prehispanic Andes*, edited by D. Browman, R. Burger, and M. Rivera, pp. 117–142. BAR International Series 194. British Archaeological Reports, Oxford.

1985   Cultural Primacy of Tiwanaku in the Development of Later Peruvian States. *Diálogo Andino* 4 (La problemática Tiwanaku Huari en el contexto panandino del desarollo cultural, edited by M. Rivera, pp. 59–72). Universidad de Tarapacá, Arica, Chile.

1997   Political Institutional Factors Contributing to the Integration of the Tiwanaku State. In *Emergence and Change in Early Urban Societies*, edited by L. Manzanilla, pp. 229–243. Plenum, New York.

Brown, J. A.

1985   The Search for Rank in Prehistoric Burials. In *The Archaeology of Death*, edited by R. Chapman, I. Kinne, and K. Randsborg, pp. 25–37. Cambridge University Press, Cambridge.

1995   Andean Mortuary Practices in Perspective. In *Tombs for the Living: Andean Mortuary Practices*, edited by T. D. Dillehay, pp. 391–403. Dumbarton Oaks, Washington, D.C.

Brumfiel, E.

1992   Breaking and Entering the Ecosystem: Gender, Class, and Faction Steal the Show. *American Anthropologist* 94:551–567.

1994   Introduction. In *Factional Competition and Political Development in the New World*, edited by E. Brumfiel and J. Fox, pp. 3–13. Cambridge University Press, Cambridge.

Brumfiel, E., and T. Earle (editors)

1987   *Specialization, Exchange, and Complex Societies*. Cambridge University Press, Cambridge.

Brush, S.

1977   *Mountain, Field and Family: The Economy and Human Ecology of an Andean Valley*. University of Pennsylvania, Philadelphia.

Buechler, H., and J. M. Buechler

1971   *The Bolivian Aymara*. Holt Rinehart and Winston, New York.

Buikstra, J. E.

1995   Tombs for the Living . . . or . . . for the Dead: The Osmore Ancestors. In *Tombs for the Living: Andean Mortuary Practices*, edited by T. D. Dillehay, pp. 229–280. Dumbarton Oaks, Washington, D.C.

Buikstra, J. E., M. Lozada C., P. Goldstein, A. Poznanski, and L. Leuschner

1990   A Case of Juvenile Rheumatoid Arthritis from Pre-Columbian Peru. In *A Life in Science: Papers in Honor of J. Lawrence Angel*, edited by J. Buikstra, pp. 99–137. Center for American Archeology, Scientific Papers, vol. 6. Kampsville, Ill.

Burger, R. L.

1992   *Chavin and the Origins of Andean Civilization*. Thames and Hudson, London.

Burger, R. L., K. L. Mohr Chávez, and S. J. Chávez
2000   Through the glass darkly: Prehispanic obsidian procurement and exchange in southern Peru and northern Bolivia. *Journal of World Prehistory* 14(3):267–362.

Burkholder, J.
2001   The Ceramics of Tiwanaku: What does the Variability Mean? *Boletín de Arqueología, Pontificia Universidad Católica del Perú* 5: Huari y Tiwanaku: Modelos vs. Evidencias:217–250.

Byrne de Caballero, G.
1984   El Tiwanaku en Cochabamba. *Arqueología Boliviana* 1:67–72.

Caldwell, J. A.
1964   Interaction Spheres in Prehistory. In *Hopewellian Studies*, edited by J. A. Caldwell and R. L. Hall, pp. 133–43. Vol. 12. Illinois State Museum Papers.

Carney, H. J., M. W. Binford, A. L. Kolata, R. R. Marin, and C. R. Goldman
1993   Nutrient and Sediment Retention in Andean Raised-Field Agriculture. *Nature* 364:131–133.

Casanova, E.
1937   Investigaciones arqueológicas en el altiplano Boliviano. *Relaciones de la Sociedad Argentina de Antropología* 1:167–175.
1942   Dos yacimientos arqueológicos en la península de Copacabana (Bolivia). *Anales del Museo Argentino de Ciencias Naturales* 40:333–339.

Caviedes, C.
2001   *El Niño in History: Storming through the Ages.* University Press of Florida, Gainesville.

Céspedes Paz, R.
1982   Mapa Arqueológico de Cochabamba. Instituto de Investigaciones Antropológicas, Universidad Mayor de San Simón–Banco Boliviano Americano, Cochabamba.
1993   Tiwanaku y los Valles Subtropicales de los Andes. *Análisis Cultural, Revista de la Sociedad de Geografía, História y Estudios Geopolíticos de Cochabamba* 2:63–66.

Chapman, A.
1957   Port of trade enclaves in Aztec and Maya civilization. In *Trade and Market in Early Empires*, edited by K. Polanyi, C. Arensberg, and H. Pearson. Free Press, Glencoe, Ill.

Chase-Dunn, C., and H. M. Mann
1998   *The Wintu and their Neighbors: A Very Small World-System in Northern California.* University of Arizona Press, Tucson.

Chávez, S. J.
1976   The Arapa Thunderbolt Stelae: A Case of Stylistic Identity with Implications for Pucara Influences in the Area of Tiahuanaco. *Nawpa Pacha* 13:3–25.
1981   Notes on Some Stone Sculpture from the Northern Lake Titicaca Basin. *Nawpa Pacha* 19:79–92.
1992   The Conventionalized Rules in Pucara Pottery Technology and Iconography: Implications for Socio-Political Developments in the Northern Lake Titicaca Basin. Unpublished Ph.D. dissertation, Department of Anthropology, Michigan State University.

Chávez, S. J., and K. Mohr Chávez
1976   A Carved Stela from Taraco, Puno, Peru and the Definition of an Early Style of Stone Sculpture from the Altiplano of Peru and Bolivia. *Nawpa Pacha* 13:45–85.

Cieza de León, P.
1959   [1553] *The Incas of Pedro de Cieza de Leon*. Translated by Harriet de Onis. University of Oklahoma, Norman.
1984   [1553] *Crónica del Perú, Primera Parte*. Colección Clásicos Peruanos. Pontificia Universidad Católica del Perú, Lima.

Clark, J., and M. Blake
1994   The Power of Prestige: Competitive Generosity and the Emergence of Rank Societies in Lowland Mesoamerica. In *Factional Competition and Political Development in the New World*, edited by E. Brumfiel and J. Fox, pp. 17–30. Cambridge University Press, Cambridge.

Clark, N. R.
1993   *The Estuquiña Textile Tradition: Cultural Patterning In Late Prehistoric Fabrics, Moquegua, Far Southern Peru*. Unpublished Doctoral dissertation, Department of Anthropology, Washington University.

Clifford, J.
1994   Diasporas. *Cultural Anthropology* 9(3):302–338.

Cobo, B.
1890   [1653] *Historia del Nuevo Mundo*. Sociedad de Bibliófilos Andaluces, Seville.
1984   [1653] *History of the Inca Empire: An Account of the Indian's Customs and Their Origin Together with a Treatise on Inca Legends, History and Social Institutions*. Translated by Roland Hamilton. University of Texas Press, Austin.
1990   [1653] *Inca Religion and Customs*. Translated by Roland Hamilton. University of Texas Press, Austin.

Cohen, A.
1969   *Custom and Politics in Urban Africa: A Study of Hausa Migrants in Yoruba Towns*. University of California Press, Berkeley.
1971   The development of indigenous trade and markets in West Africa: Studies presented and discussed at the Tenth International African Seminar at Fourah Bay College, Freetown, December 1969. In *Cultural Strategies in the Organization of Trading Diasporas*, edited by C. Meillassoux, pp. 266–281. Evolution du commerce africain depuis le XIXe siecle en Afrique de l'ouest. Oxford University Press, London.
1974   *Urban Ethnicity*. Tavistock, London.

Cohen, A., M. Bandy, and P. S. Goldstein
1995   How Archaic Is That Archipelago? The Huaracane Tradition and the Antiquity of Vertical Control in the South Andes. Paper presented at the 35th Annual Meeting, Institute of Andean Studies, Berkeley.

Cohen, A. P. (editor)
2000   *Signifying Identities: Anthropological Perspectives on Boundaries and Contested Values*. Routledge, London.

Conklin, W.
1983   Pucara and Tiahuanaco Tapestry: Time and Style in a Sierra Weaving Tradition. *Nawpa Pacha* 21:1–44.

1991   Tiwanaku and Huari: Architectural Comparisons and Interpretations. In *Huari Administrative Structure: Prehistoric Monumental Architecture and State Government*, edited by W. Isbell and G. McEwan, pp. 281–292. Dumbarton Oaks, Washington, D.C.

Conrad, G. W.

1993   Domestic Architecture of the Estuquiña Phase: Estuquiña and San Antonio. In *Domestic Architecture, Ethnicity, and Complementarity in the South-Central Andes*, edited by M. Aldenderfer, pp. 55–65. University of Iowa Press, Iowa City.

Cook, A. G.

1983   Aspects of State Ideology in Huari and Tiwanaku Iconography: The Central Deity and the Sacrificer. In *Investigations of the Andean Past*, edited by D. Sandweiss, pp. 161–185. Vol. 1, A. Past, general editor. Cornell University, Ithaca.

1985   The Politico-Religious Implications of the Huari Offering Traditions. *Diálogo Andino* 4 (La problemática Tiwanaku Huari en el contexto panandino del desarollo cultural), edited by M. Rivera, pp. 203–222. Universidad de Tarapacá, Arica, Chile.

1992   The Stone Ancestors: Idioms of Imperial Attire and Rank among Huari Figurines. *Latin American Antiquity* 3(4):341–364.

Costin, C. L.

1991   Craft Specialization: Issues in Defining, Documenting and Explaining the Organization of Production. *Archaeological Method and Theory* 3:1–56.

Costin, C. L., and T. Earle

1989   Status distinction and legitimation of power as reflected in changing patterns of consumption in late Prehispanic Peru. *American Antiquity* 54(4):691–714.

Courty, G., and G. de Crequi-Montfort

1906   Fouilles de la Mission Scientifique Française à Tiahuanaco. Paper presented at the Internationaler Americanisten Kongress, Vierzehnte Tagung, Stuttgart.

Crumley, C. L.

1976   Toward a Locational Definition of State Systems of Settlement. *American Anthropologist* 78:59–73.

1987   Dialectical Critique of Hierarchy. In *Power Relations and State Formation*, edited by T. C. Patterson and C. W. Gailey. American Anthropological Association, Washington, D.C.

1995   Heterarchy and the Analysis of Complex Societies. In *Heterarchy and the Analysis of Complex Societies*, edited by R. M. Ehrenreich, C. L. Crumley, and J. E. Levy. Archeological Papers of the American Anthropological Association no. 6. Washington, D.C.

Curtin, P. D.

1984   *Cross-Cultural Trade in World History*. Cambridge University Press, New York.

D'Altroy, T. N.

1981   Empire Growth and Consolidation: The Xauxa region of Peru under the Incas. Ph.D. dissertation, University of California, Los Angeles.

1992   *Provincial Power in the Inka Empire*. Smithsonian Institution Press, Washington D.C.

2001   Politics, Resources and Blood in the Inka Empire. In *Empires: Perspectives from Archaeology and History*, edited by S. E. Alcock, T. N. D'Altroy, K. D. Morrison and C. M. Sinopoli, pp. 201–226. Cambridge University Press, Cambridge.

D'Altroy, T., and T. Earle
1985   Staple Finance, Wealth Finance, and Storage in the Inca Political Economy. *Current Anthropology* 26:187–206.
Dauelsberg, P.
1961   Algunos problemas sobre la cerámica de Arica. In *Boletín del Museo Regional de Arica*, pp. 7–17. vol. 5.
1972a   [1960] Contribución al estudio de la arqueología del Valle de Azapa. In *Antiguo Peru: espacio y tiempo*, edited by Semana de Arqueologia Peruana. Lima, Librería-Editorial J. Mejia Baca, 273–297.
1972b   La cerámica de Arica y su situacion cronologica. *Chungará* 1:15–25.
1985   Desarollo regional en los valles costeros del norte de Chile. *Diálogo Andino* 4 (La problematica Tiwanaku Huari en el contexto panandino del desarrollo cultural), edited by M. Rivera, pp. 277–287. Universidad de Tarapacá, Arica, Chile.
DeBenedetti, S.
1912   Influencias de la cultura de Tiahuanaco en la región del Noroeste Argentino. *Revista de la Universidad de Buenos Aires* 17:326–348.
DeLeonardis, L.
1997   Paracas Settlement in Callango, Lower Ica Valley, 1st Millenium B.C., Peru. Unpublished Ph.D. dissertation, Catholic University, Washington, D.C.
Demarest, A. A.
1981   *Viracocha: The Nature and Antiquity of the Andean High God.* Peabody Museum Monographs, Cambridge.
DeMarrais, E., L. J. Castillo, and T. Earle
1996   Ideology, materialization, and power strategies. *Current Anthropology* 37:15–31.
DeMontmillon, O.
1989   *The Archaeology of Political Structure.* Cambridge University Press, Cambridge.
Denevan, W.
1970   Aboriginal Drained Field Cultivation in the Americas. *Science* 169:647–654.
1980   Latin America. In *World Systems of Traditional Resource Management*, edited by G. Klee, pp. 217–244. Hasted Press, New York.
2001   *Cultivated landscapes of Native Amazonia and the Andes.* Oxford University Press, New York.
Dietler, M., and I. Herbich
1998   Habitus, Techniques, Style: An Integrated Approach to the Social Understanding of Material Culture and Boundaries. In *The Archaeology of Social Boundary*, edited by M. T. Stark. Smithsonian Institution Press, Washington, D.C.
Diez de San Miguel, G.
1964   [1567] Visita hecha a la Provincia de Chucuito por Garci Diez de San Miguel en el año 1567. In *Documentos Regionales para la Etnología y Etnohistoria Andinas*, vol. 1, pp. 1–287. Casa de la Cultura del Peru, Lima.
Dillehay, T. D.
1977   Tawantinsuyu Integration of the Chillon Valley, Peru: A Case of Inca Geo-political Mastery. *Journal of Field Archaeology* 4:397–405.
1995   *Tombs for the Living: Andean Mortuary Practices.* Dumbarton Oaks, Washington, D.C.
Disselhoff, H. D.
1968   Huari und Tiahuanaco: Grabungen und Funde in Sud-Peru. *Zeitschrift fur Ethnologie* 93:207–216.

Dittmar, K.
2000   Evaluation of Ectoparasites on the guinea pig mummies of El Yaral and Moquegua Valley, in Southern Peru. *Chungará* 32(1):123–125.
Dittmar, M.
1994   *Mikroevolution der Aymara-Bevölkerung Südamerikas: Eine Univariate und Multivariate Statistche Analyse von Morphometrischen, Dermatoglyphischen und Serologischen Merkmalen unter Besondere Berücksichtigung der Beziehung der Aymaravorfahren zur Prähistorischen Tiwanaku-Bevölkerung.* Deutsche Hochschulshriften 553. Hänsel-Hohenhausen, Egelsbach, Frankfurt.
1996   Aymaras prehispánicos y actuales: Etnogénesis, microdiferenciación y su relación con la población Tiwanaku de América del Sur. *Revista Española de Antropología Americana* 26:231–248.
Donnan, C. B.
1978   *Moche art of Peru: Pre-Columbian Symbolic Communication.* Fowler Museum, UCLA, Los Angeles.
1995   Moche Funerary Practice. In *Tombs for the Living: Andean Mortuary Practices*, edited by T. D. Dillehay, pp. 111–159. Dumbarton Oaks, Washington, D.C.
Doyle, M. W.
1986   *Empires.* Cornell University Press, Ithaca, N.Y.
Earle, T.
1987   Chiefdoms in Archaeological and Ethnohistorical Perspective. *Annual Review of Anthropology* 16:279–308.
1994   Wealth Finance in the Inka Empire: Evidence from the Calchaqui Valley, Argentina. *American Antiquity* 59:433–60.
1997   *How Chiefs Come to Power: The Political Economy in Prehistory.* Stanford University Press, Stanford.
Earle, T., T. D'Altroy, C. Hastorf, C. Scott, C. Costin, G. Russell, and E. Sandefur
1987   Archaeological Field Research in the Upper Mantaro, Peru, 1982–1983: Investigations of Inka Expansion and Exchange. *Monograph* 28.
Eisenstadt, S. N. (editor)
1968   *Comparative perspectives on social change.* Little, Brown, Boston.
Eisleb, D., and R. Strelow
1980   *Altperuanische Kulturen III: Tiahuanaco.* Museum fur Volkerkunde, Berlin.
Elkin, J. L.
1995   Exploring the Jewish Archipelago in Latin America. *Latin American Research Review* 30(3):224–238.
Emberling, G.
1997   Ethnicity in Complex Societies: Archaeological Perspectives. *Journal of Archaeological Research* 15(4):295–344.
Erickson, C. L.
1984   Waru Waru: Una tecnología agrícola del Altiplano pre-hispánico. *Boletín del Instituto de Estudios Aymaras* 2(18):4–37.
1985   Applications of Prehistoric Andean Technology: Experiments in Raised Field Agriculture. In *Prehistoric Intensive Agriculture in the Tropics*, edited by I. Farrington, pp. 209–232. BAR International Series. British Archaeological Reports, Oxford.
1987   The Dating of Raised-Field Agriculture in the Lake Titicaca Basin, Peru. In *Pre-Hispanic Agricultural Fields in the Andean Region*, Part 2, edited by W. Denevan,

K. Mathewson, and G. Knapp, pp. 373–384. BAR International Series 359. British Archaeological Reports, Oxford.

1988   Raised Field Agriculture in the Lake Titicaca Basin: Putting Ancient Andean Agriculture Back to Work. *Expedition* 30(3):8–16.

1999   Neo-Environmental Determinism and Agrarian 'Collapse' in Andean Prehistory. *Antiquity* 73:634–642.

Escalante Moscoso, J.

1994   *Arquitectura Prehispánica en los Andes Bolivianos.* Producciones CIMA, La Paz.

Espouyes, O.

1976   Tipificación de Kercs de Madera de Arica. *Chungará* 4:39–54.

Feinman, G. M.

1998   *Scale and Social Organization: Perspectives on the Archaic State,* pp. 95–134. School of American Research, Santa Fe.

1999   The Changing Structure of Macroregional Mesoamerica: The Classic-Postclassic Transition in the Valley of Oaxaca. In *World-Systems Theory in Practice: Leadership, Production, and Exchange,* edited by P. N. Kardulias, pp. 53–62. Rowman and Littlefield, Lanham.

Feinman, G. M., and J. Marcus (editors)

1998   *Archaic States.* School of American Research, Santa Fe.

Feinman, G. M., and L. M. Nicholas

1992   Pre-Hispanic Interregional Interaction in Southern Mexico: The Valley of Oaxaca and the Ejutla Valley. In *Resources, Power and Interregional Interaction,* edited by E. M. Schortman and P. A. Urban, pp. 75–114. Plenum Press, New York.

Feldman, R. A.

1987   *Imperial Expansion in the Andes: Wari Settlements in Moquegua.* Field Museum of Natural History. Submitted to Proposal to the National Science Foundation.

1988   A Speculative Hypothesis of Wari Southern Expansion. Paper presented at the International Congress of Americanists, Amsterdam.

1989   The Early Ceramic Periods of Moquegua. In *Ecology, Settlement and History in the Osmore Drainage, Peru,* edited by D. S. Rice, C. Stanish, and P. Scarr, pp. 207–217. BAR International Series 545(2). British Archaeological Reports, Oxford.

Flannery, K. V.

1972   The Cultural Evolution of Civilizations. *Annual Review of Ecology and Systematics* 3:399–426.

1998   The Ground Plans of Archaic States. In *Archaic States,* edited by G. M. Feinman and J. Marcus, pp. 15–58. School of American Research, Santa Fe.

1999   Process and Agency in Early State Formation. *Cambridge Archaeological Journal* 9(1):3–21.

Flores Espinoza, I.

1969   Informe preliminar sobre las investigaciones arqueológicas de Tacna. Paper presented at the Mesa Redonda de Ciencias Prehistoricas y Antropológicas, Lima.

Flores Ochoa, J.

1972   El Reino Lupaca y el actual control vertical de la ecologia. *Historia y Cultura* 6:195–201.

Focacci Aste, G.

1969   Arqueología de Arica: Sequencia cultural del Período Agroalfarero, Horizante Tiahuanacoide. Paper presented at the Actas del 5 Congreso Nacional de Arqueología, La Serena.

1981   Nuevos fechados para la época del Tiahuanaco en la arqueología del norte de Chile. *Chungará* 8:63–77.

1983   El Tiwanaku Clásico en el valle de Azapa. In *Asentamientos aldeanos en los valles costeros de Arica*. Documentos de Trabajo, vol. 3. Instituto de Antropología y Arqueología, Universidad de Tarapacá, Arica.

1993   Excavaciones arqueológicas en el cementerio AZ-6, Valle de Azapa. *Chungará* 24–25:69–124.

Focacci Aste, G., and S. Erices

1971   Excavaciones en los túmulos de San Miguel de Azapa (Arica, Chile). In *Actas del 6 Congreso Nacional de Arqueología Chilena*, pp. 47–62. Santiago.

Fonseca Martel, C.

1972   La economía vertical y la economía del mercado en las comunidades campesinas del Perú. In *Visita a la Provincia León de Huánuco, 1562, Iñigo Ortiz de Zúñiga*. Universidad Nacional Hermilio Valdizán, Huánuco.

Fortes, M.

1953   The Structure of Unilineal Descent Groups. *American Anthropologist* 55:17–41.

Fox, J. W., G. W. Cook, A. F. Chase, and D. Z. Chase

1996   Questions of Political and Economic Integration: Segmentary versus Centralized States among the Ancient Maya. In special section, The Maya State: Centralized or Segmentary? *Current Anthropology* 37(5):795–801.

Frame, M.

1990   Andean Four-Cornered Hats: Ancient Volumes. In *Exhibit from the Collection of Arthur Bullowa, Organized by Julie Jones*. Metropolitan Museum of Art, New York.

Frank, A. G.

1993   Bronze Age World System Cycles. *Current Anthropology* 34(4):383–430.

Franquemont, E. M.

1986   The Ancient Pottery from Pucara, Peru. *Nawpa Pacha* 24:1–30.

Fritz, J.

1986   Vijayanagara: Authority and Meaning in a South Indian Imperial Capital. *American Anthropologist* 88:44–55.

Fujii, T.

1980   Prehispanic Cultures of the Western Slope of the Southern Peruvian Andes. *Bulletin of the National Museum of Ethnology* 5:83–120.

García Marquez, M.

1989   Yaral, un Asentamiento Chiribaya en Moquegua. Unpublished Bachelor's thesis, Universidad Católica de Santa María, Arequipa.

1990   *Excavación en el cementerio de Chen Chen, Moquegua, una interacción de contextos funerarios Tiwanaku / Wari*. Unpublished Thesis, Titulo Profesional de Licenciado en Arqueología, Universidad Católica de Santa María, Arequipa.

Gasparini, G., and L. Margolies

1977   *Arquitectura Inka*. Centro de Investigaciónes Históricas y Estéticas, Facultad de Arquitectura y Urbanismo, Universidad Central de Venezuela, Caracas.

Geertz, C.

1980   *Negara: the Theatre State in Nineteenth-century Bali*. Princeton University Press, Princeton.

Gellner, E.

1995   Segmentation: Reality or Myth? *Journal of the Royal Anthropological Institute* 1(4):821–829.

Geyh, M. A.
1967   Hannover Radiocarbon Measurements IV. *Radiocarbon* 9:198–217.
Giddens, A.
1984   *The Constitution of Society: Outline of the Theory of Structuration.* University of California Press, Berkeley.
Giesso, M.
2000   *Stone Tool Production in the Tiwanaku Heartland: The Impact of State Emergence and Expansion on Local Households,* University of Chicago.
2003   Stone tool production in the Tiwanaku heartland. In *Tiwanaku and its Hinterland : Archaeology and Paleoecology of an Andean Civilization:,* edited by A. L. Kolata, pp. 363–383. vol. 2: Urban and Rural Archaeology. Smithsonian Institution Press, Washington, D.C.
Gillespie, S. D.
2000   Rethinking Ancient Maya Social Organization: Replacing "Lineage" with "House." *American Anthropologist* 102(3).
Girault, L.
1987   *Kallawaya, curanderos itinerantes de los Andes: Investigación sobre prácticas medicinales y mágicas.* UNICEF, Impresores Quipus, La Paz.
1990   *La cerámica del Templete Semisubterráneo de Tiwanaku.* Centro de Estudios de la Realidad Económica y Social, La Paz.
Goldstein, M. C., and D. A. Messerschmidt
1980   The Significance of Latitudinality in Himalayan Mountain Ecosystems. *Human Ecology* 8(2):117–134.
Goldstein, P. S.
1985   Tiwanaku Ceramics of the Moquegua Valley, Peru. Unpublished Master's thesis, University of Chicago.
1989a   Omo, A Tiwanaku Provincial Center in Moquegua, Peru. Unpublished Ph.D. dissertation, Department of Anthropology, University of Chicago.
1989b   The Tiwanaku Occupation of Moquegua. In *Ecology, Settlement and History in the Osmore Drainage, Peru,* edited by D. S. Rice, C. Stanish, and P. Scarr, pp. 219–256. BAR International Series 545(2). British Archaeological Reports, Oxford.
1990a   La Cultura Tiwanaku y la relación de sus fases cerámicas en Moquegua. In *Trabajos arqueológicos en Moquegua, Perú,* edited by L. K. Watanabe, M. E. Moseley, and F. Cabieses, pp. 31–58. Editorial Escuela Nueva, Lima.
1990b   La Ocupación Tiwanaku en Moquegua. *Gaceta Arqueológica Andina* 18–19:75–104.
1993a   House, Community and State in the Earliest Tiwanaku Colony: Domestic Patterns and State Integration at Omo M12, Moquegua. In *Domestic Architecture, Ethnicity, and Complementarity in the South-Central Andes,* edited by M. Aldenderfer, pp. 25–41. University of Iowa Press, Iowa City.
1993b   Tiwanaku Temples and State Expansion: A Tiwanaku Sunken Court Temple in Moquegua, Peru. *Latin American Antiquity* 4(3):22–47.
1994   Formative and Tiwanaku-Contemporary Settlement Patterns in the Moquegua Valley, Peru: Report of the Moquegua Archaeological Survey, 1993 Season. Paper presented at the Society for American Archaeology 59th Annual Meeting, Anaheim.

1995   Informe de Campo, Rescate Chen Chen 1995: Investigaciones de los Sectores Habitacionales. Report on file, Instituto Nacional de Cultura, Lima.
1996   Tiwanaku Settlement Patterns of the Azapa Valley, Chile: New Data, and the Legacy of Percy Dauelsberg. *Diálogo Andino* 14–15 (Prehistoria del norte de Chile y del desierto de Atacama: Simposio homenaje a Percy Dauelsberg Hahmann, pp. 57–73). Universidad de Tarapacá, Arica, Chile.
2000a   Communities without Borders: The Vertical Archipelago, and Diaspora Communities in the Southern Andes. In *The Archaeology of Communities: A New World Perspective*, edited by Jason Yaeger and Marcello Canuto, pp. 182–209. Routledge Press, New York.
2000b   Exotic Goods and Everyday Chiefs: Pukara, Paracas-Nasca and Indigenous Sociopolitical Development in the South Andes. *Latin American Antiquity* 11(4):1–27.

Goldstein, P. S., and R. A. Feldman
1986   Tiwanaku and Its Antecedents in Moquegua. Paper presented at the Society for American Archaeology 51st annual meeting, New Orleans.

Goldstein, P. S., and B. D. Owen
2001   Tiwanaku en Moquegua: Las colonias altiplánicas. *Boletín de Arqueología, Pontificia Universidad Católica del Perú* 5: Huari y Tiwanaku: Modelos vs. Evidencias:139–168.

Gose, P.
1993   Segmentary State Formation and the Ritual Control of Water under the Incas. *Comparative Studies in Society and History* 35:480–514.

Graffam, G. C.
1988   Back across the Great Divide: The Pakaq Senorio and Raised Field Agriculture. In *Multidisciplinary Studies in Andean Anthropology*, edited by V. J. Vitzthum. Michigan Discussions in Anthropology, Ann Arbor.
1992   Beyond State Collapse: Rural History, Raised Fields and Pastoralism in the South Andes. *American Anthropologist* 94(4):882–904.

Graffam, G. C., M. Rivera, and A. Carevic
1996   Ancient Metallurgy in the Atacama: Evidence for Copper Smelting during Chile's Early Ceramic Period. *Latin American Antiquity* 7(2):101–113.

Hall, S.
1990   Cultural Identity and Diaspora. In *Identity Community, Culture, Difference*, edited by J. Rutherford, pp. 222–237. Lawrence and Wishart, London.

Harris, O.
1986   From Asymmetry to Triangle: Symbolic Transformations in Northern Potosi. In *Anthropological History of Andean Polities*, edited by J. Murra, N. Wachtel, and J. Revel, pp. 260–280. Cambridge University Press, Cambridge.

Hassig, R.
1988   *Aztec Warfare: Imperial Expansion and Political Control*. University of Oklahoma Press, Norman.

Hastorf, C. A.
1990   Effect of the Inka state on Sausa agricultural production and crop consumption. *American Antiquity* 55(2):262–290.
1991   Gender, Space, and Food in Prehistory. In *Engendering Archaeology: Women and Prehistory*, pp. 132–159. Basil Blackwell, Oxford.

Helms, M.
1979   *Ancient Panama: Chiefs in Search of Power*. University of Texas Press, Austin.
1993   *Craft and the Kingly Ideal: Art Trade and Power*. University of Texas Press, Austin.
Henrickson, E. F.
1994   The Outer Limits: Settlement and Economic Strategies in the Central Zagros High-
        lands during the Uruk Era. In *Chiefdoms and Early States in the Near East: The
        Organizational Dynamics of Complexity*, edited by G. Stein and M. Rothman, pp.
        85–102. Monographs in World Archaeology, vol. 18. Prehistory Press, Madison.
Hidalgo Lehuedé, J.
1996   Relaciones protohistóricas interétnicas entre las poblaciones locales y altiplánicas
        en Arica. In *La integración surandina cinco siglos después*, edited by X. Albó, M.
        Arratia, J. Hidalgo, L. Nuñez, A. Llagostera, M. Remy and B. Revesz, pp. 161–
        174. Centro de Estudios Regionales Andinos Bartolomé de Las Casas, and Uni-
        versidad Católica del Norte, Cusco and Antofagasta.
Hidalgo Lehuedé, J. and G. Focacci Aste
1986   Multietnicidad en Arica S. XVI: Evidencias etnohistóricas y arqueológicas. *Chun-
        gara, Revista de Antropologia Chilena* 16–17:137–147.
Higueras, A.
1996   Prehispanic Settlement and Land Use in Cochabamba, Bolivia. Unpublished Ph.D.
        dissertation, University of Pittsburgh.
Hoshower, L. M., J. E. Buikstra, P. S. Goldstein, and A. D. Webster
1995   Artificial Cranial Deformation at the Omo M10 Site: A Tiwanaku Complex from
        the Moquegua valley, Peru. *Latin American Antiquity* 6(2):145–164.
Houston, S. D.
1993   *Hieroglyphs and History at Dos Pilas: Dynastic Politics of the Classic Maya*. Uni-
        versity of Texas Press, Austin.
Hyslop, J.
1976   An Archaeological Investigation of the Lupaqa Kingdom and Its Origins. Unpub-
        lished Ph.D. dissertation, Department of Anthropology, Columbia University.
1990   *Inka Settlement Planning*. University of Texas Press, Austin.
Ibarra Grasso, D. E., and R. Querejazu Lewis
1986   *30,000 Años de Prehistoria en Bolivia*. Los Amigos del Libro, La Paz.
Isbell, W. H.
1977   *The Rural Foundations for Urbanism: Economic and Stylistic Interaction between
        Rural and Urban Communities in Eighth-Century Peru*. Illinois Studies in Anthro-
        pology 10. University of Illinois Press, Urbana.
1983   Shared Ideology and Parallel Political Development: Huari and Tiwanaku. In *In-
        vestigations of the Andean Past*, edited by D. Sandweiss, pp. 186–208. Cornell
        University, Ithaca.
1987   State Origins in the Ayacucho Valley, Central Highlands, Peru. In *The Origins and
        Development of the Andean State*, edited by J. Haas, S. Pozorski, and T. Pozorski,
        pp. 83–90. Cambridge University Press, Cambridge.
1991   Huari Administration and the Orthogonal Cellular Architecture Horizon. In *Huari
        Administrative Structure: Prehistoric Monumental Architecture and State Govern-
        ment*, edited by W. Isbell and G. McEwan, pp. 293–316. Dumbarton Oaks, Wash-
        ington, D.C.

1997   *Mummies and Mortuary Monuments: A Postprocessual Prehistory of Central Andean Social Organization.* University of Texas, Austin.

Isbell, W., C. Brewster-Wray, and L. Spickard

1991   Architecture and Spatial Organization at Huari. In *Huari Administrative Structure: Prehistoric Monumental Architecture and State Government*, edited by W. Isbell and G. McEwan, pp. 19–54. Dumbarton Oaks, Washington, D.C.

Isbell, W. H., and A. G. Cook

2002   A New Perspective on Conchopata and the Andean Middle Horizon. In *Andean Archaeology*, edited by W. H. Isbell and H. Silverman, pp. 249–305. vol. 2. 2 vols. Kluwer Academic/Plenum Publishers, New York.

Isbell, W. H., and K. J. Schreiber

1978   Was Huari a State? *American Antiquity* 43:372–389.

Ishida, E.

1960   *Andes: The Report of the University of Tokyo Scientific Expedition to the Andes.* University of Tokyo Press, Tokyo.

Janusek, J. W.

1993   Nuevos datos sobre el significativo de la producción y uso de instrumentos musicales en el Estado de Tiwanaku. *Pumapunku* 2(4):9–47.

1994   State and Local Power in a Prehispanic Andean Polity: Changing Patterns of Urban Residence in Tiwanaku and Lukurmata. Unpublished Ph.D. dissertation, Department of Anthropology, University of Chicago.

1999   Craft and Local Power: Embedded Specialization in Tiwanaku Cities. *Latin American Antiquity* 10(2):107–131.

2002   Out of Many, One: Style and Social Boundaries in Tiwanaku. *Latin American Antiquity* 13(1):35–61.

2003   Vessels, Time and Society: Toward a Ceramic Chronology in the Tiwanaku Heartland. In *Tiwanaku and its Hinterland: Archaeology and Paleoecology of an Andean Civilization*, edited by A. L. Kolata, pp. 30–91. vol. 2: Urban and Rural Archaeology. Smithsonian Institution Press, Washington, D.C.

Jennings, J., and W. Yepez

2001   Collota, Netahaha and the Development of the Wari Power in the Cotahuasi Valley, Arequipa, Peru. *Boletín de Arqueología, Pontificia Universidad Católica del Perú 5*: Huari y Tiwanaku: Modelos vs, Evidencias:13–30.

Johnson, G., and T. Earle

1987   *The Evolution of Human Societies.* Stanford University Press, Stanford.

Joyce, A. A.

1991   Formative Period Social Change in the Lower Rio Verde Valley, Oaxaca, Mexico. *Latin American Antiquity* 2(2):126–150.

Joyce, A. A., and M. Winter

1996   Ideology, Power, and Urban Society in Pre-Hispanic Oaxaca. *Current Anthropology* 37:33–47.

Joyce, R., and S. D. Gillespie

2000   *Beyond Kinship : Social and Material Reproduction in House Societies.* University of Pennsylvania Press, Philadelphia.

Julien, C.

1982   Inca Decimal Administration in the Lake Titicaca Region. In *The Inca and Aztec*

States, 1400–1800, edited by G. Collier, R. Rosaldo, and J. Wirth, pp. 119–152. Academic Press, New York.

1985 Guano and Resource Control in Sixteenth-Century Arequipa. In *Andean Ecology and Civilization*, edited by S. Masuda, I. Shimada, and C. Morris, pp. 185–232. University of Tokyo Press.

Julien, C. J.
1993 Finding a Fit: Archaeology and Ethnohistory of the Incas. In *Provincial Inca: Archaeological and Ethnohhistorical Assesment of the Impact of the Inca State*, edited by M. Malpass. pp. 177–233. University of Iowa Press, Iowa City.

Kardulias, P. N. (editor)
1999 *World-Systems Theory in Practice: Leadership, Production, and Exchange*. Rowman and Littlefield, Lanham.

Keatinge, W., and G. Conrad
1983 Imperialist expansion in Peruvian prehistory: Chimu Administration of a Conquered Territory. *Journal of Field Archaeology* 10:255–283.

Kidder, A. I.
1943 Some Early Sites in the Northern Lake Titicaca Basin. In *Papers of the Peabody Museum of American Archaeology and Ethnology, Harvard University*, vol. 27. Cambridge.
1956 Digging in the Lake Titicaca Basin. *University Museum Bulletin* 20(3):16–29.

Klymshyn, A. M. U.
1987 The development of Chimu administration in Chan Chan. In *The Origins and Development of the Andean State*, edited by J. Haas, S. Pozorski and T. Pozorski. Cambridge University Press, Cambridge.

Knobloch, P. J.
2000 Wari ritual power at Conchopata: An interpretation of Anadenanthera colubrina iconography. *Latin American Antiquity* 11(4):387–402.

Kohl, P. L.
1987 The Use and Abuse of World Systems Theory: The Case of the Pristine West Asian State. *Advances in Archaeological Method and Theory* 11:1–35.

Kolata, A. L.
1982 Tiwanaku: Portrait of an Andean Civilization. *Field Museum of Natural History Bulletin* 53(8):13–18, 23–28.
1983 The South Andes. In *Ancient South Americans*, edited by J. Jennings, pp. 241–285. W. H. Freeman and Company, San Francisco.
1985 El papel de la agricultura intensiva en la economia politica del estado Tiwanaku. In *La problematica Tiwanaku Huari en el contexto panandino del desarrollo cultural*, edited by M. Rivera, pp. 11–38. Diálogo Andino 4. Universidad de Tarapacá, Arica, Chile.
1986 The Agricultural Foundations of the Tiwanaku State: A View from the Heartland. *American Antiquity* 51:748–762.
1991 Sacred Mountain, Urban Enceinte: Cosmogony and the Reproduction of Tiwanaku Urban Form. Paper presented at the Society for American Archaeology 56th annual meeting, New Orleans.
1992 Economy, Ideology and Imperialism in the South-Central Andes. In *Ideology and Pre-Columbian Civilizations*, edited by A. A. Demarest and G. W. Conrad, pp. 65–87. School of American Research, Santa Fe.

1993   *Tiwanaku: Portrait of an Andean Civilization.* Blackwell Publishers, Cambridge, Mass.

1996a   *Tiwanaku and its Hinterland: Archaeology and Paleoecology of an Andean Civilization.* 1: Agroecology. Smithsonian Institution Press, Washington, D.C.

1996b   Mimesis and Monumentalism in Native Andean Cities. *Res* 29–30: p. 223–236.

1997   Of Kings and Capitals: Principles of Authority and the Nature of Cities in the Native Andean State. In *The Archaeology of City States: Cross-Cultural Approaches*, edited by D. L. Nichols and T. H. Charlton, pp. 245–254. Smithsonian Institution Press, Washington, D.C.

2003a   The Social Production of Tiwanaku: Political Economy and Authority in a Native Andean State. In *Tiwanaku and its Hinterland : Archaeology and Paleoecology of an Andean Civilization:*, edited by A. L. Kolata, pp. 449–472. vol. 2: Urban and Rural Archaeology. Smithsonian Institution Press, Washington, D.C.

2003b   *Tiwanaku and Its Hinterland: Archaeology and Paleoecology of an Andean Civilization.* 2: Urban and Rural Archaeology. Smithsonian Institution Press, Washington, D.C.

Kolata, A. L. (editor)

1989   *Arqueología de Lukurmata.* Vol. 2. Instituto Nacional de Arqueología, La Paz.

1996   *Tiwanaku and Its Hinterland: Archaeology and Paleoecology of an Andean Civilization.* Smithsonian Institution Press, Washington, D.C.

Kolata, A. L., M. W. Binford and M. Brenner

2000   Environmental thresholds and the empirical reality of state collapse: a response to Erickson (1999). *Antiquity* 74:424–426.

Kolata, A. L., and C. Ortloff

1989   Thermal Analysis of Tiwanaku Raised Field Systems in the Lake Titicaca Basin of Bolivia. *Journal of Archaeological Science* 16(3):233–263.

1996   Agroecological Perspectives on the Decline of the Tiwanaku State. In *Tiwanaku and Its Hinterland: Archaeology and Paleoecology of an Andean Civilization*, edited by A. L. Kolata, pp. 181–202. Smithsonian Institution Press, Washington, D.C.

Kolata, A. L., C. Stanish, and O. Rivera S.

1987   *The Technology and Organization of Agricultural Production in the Tiwanaku State: First Preliminary Report of Proyecto Wila Jawira.* University of Chicago.

Kopytoff, I.

1987   *The African Frontier: The Reproduction of Traditional African Societies.* Indiana University Press, Bloomington.

Kowalewski, S. A.

1990   The Evolution of Complexity in the Valley of Oaxaca. *Annual Review of Anthropology* 19:39–58.

Kroeber, A. L.

1944   *Peruvian Archaeology in 1942.* Viking Fund Publications in Anthropology, New York.

Kuon Cabello, L. E.

1981   *Retazos de la historia de Moquegua.* Editores Abril, Lima.

Kuznar, L.

1990   Pastoralismo temprano en la sierra alta del Departamento de Moquegua, Perú. *Chungará* 24–25:53–68.

LaBarre, W.
1941   The Uru of Lake Titicaca. *American Anthropologist* 43:493–522.
Lange, C. H. and C. L. Riley
1996   *Bandelier: The Life and Adventures of Adolph Bandelier.* University of Utah Press, Salt Lake City.
Lansing, S.
1991   *Priests and Programmers: Technologies of Power in the Engineered Landscape of Bali.* Princeton University Press, Princeton, N.J.
Latcham, R. E.
1938   *Arqueología de la región atacameña.* Universidad de Chile, Santiago.
Lechtman, H.
1997   El Bronce arsenical y el Horizonte Medio. In *Arqueología, antropología e história en los Andes: Homenaje a María Rostworowski,* edited by R. Varón G. and J. Flores E., pp. 153–186. Instituto de Estudios Peruanos, Banco Central de Reserva del Perú, Lima.
2000   Middle Horizon Bronze: Centers and Outliers. In *Patterns and Process: A Festschrift in Honor of Edward V. Sayre,* edited by L. van Zelst. Smithsonian Center for Materials Research and Education, Washington, D.C.
Lennon, T. J.
1982   Raised Fields of Lake Titicaca, Peru: A Pre-Hispanic Water Management System. Unpublished Ph.D. dissertation, Department of Anthropology, University of Colorado.
LePaige, G.
1964   El Precerámico en la cordillera Atacameña y los cementerios del período agroalfarero de San Pedro de Atacama. *Anales de la Universidad del Norte 3.*
1965   San Pedro de Atacama y su zona. *Anales de la Universidad del Norte 4.*
1977   Recientes descubrimientos arqueológicos en la zona de San Pedro de Atacama. *Estudios Atacameños* 6:109–124.
Llagostera, A.
1996   San Pedro de Atacama: Nodo de complementariedad reticular. In *La Integración Surandina Cinco Siglos Después,* edited by X. Albó, M. Arratia, J. Hidalgo, L. Nuñez, A. Llagostera, M. Remy, and B. Revesz, pp. 17–42. Centro de Estudios Regionales Andinos Bartolomé de Las Casas and Universidad Católica del Norte, Cusco and Antofagasta.
Llagostera, A., M. Constantino Torres, and M. A. Costa
1988   El complejo psicotrópico en Solcor-3 (San Pedro de Atacama). *Estudios Atacameños* 9:61–98.
Lozada Cerna, M. C.
1987   La cerámica del componente mortuorio de Estuquiña, Moquegua. Unpublished Bachelor's thesis, Universidad Católica de Santa María, Arequipa.
1998   The Señorio of Chiribaya: A Bio-Archaeological Study in the Osmore Drainage of Southern Peru. Unpublished Ph.D. dissertation, Department of Anthropology, University of Chicago.
Lumbreras, L.
1974a   Los reinos post Tiwanaku en el area altiplánico. *Revista del Museo Nacional* 40: 55–85.
1974b   *The Peoples and Cultures of Ancient Peru.* Smithsonian Institution Press, Washington D.C.

Lumbreras, L., E. Mujica, and R. Vera
1982   Cerro Baul: un enclave Wari en territorio Tiwanaku. *Gaceta Arqueológica Andina* 1:4–5.

Luttwak, E.
1976   *The Grand Strategy of the Roman Empire from the First Century A.D. to the Third.* Johns Hopkins University Press, Baltimore.

Lynch, T. F.
1983   Camelid Pastoralism and the Emergence of Tiwanaku Civilization in the South-Central Andes. *World Archaeology* 15:1–14.

Mackey, C. J.
1987   Chimu Administration in the Provinces. In *The Origins and Development of the Andean State*, edited by J. Haas, S. Pozorski, and T. Pozorski, pp. 91–96. Cambridge University Press, Cambridge.

Magilligan, Francis J., and Paul S. Goldstein
2001   El Niño Floods and Culture Change: A Late Holocene Flood History for the Rio Moquegua, Southern Peru. *Geology* 29(5):431–434.

Malpass, M.
2001   Sonay: A Wari Orthogonal Center in the Camana Valley, Peru. *Boletín de Arqueología, Pontificia Universidad Católica del Perú 5*: Huari y Tiwanaku: Modelos vs. Evidencias:51–68.

Manzanilla, L.
1992a   *Akapana: Una Pirámide en el Centro del Mundo.* Universidad Nacional Autónoma de México, Instituto de Investigaciones Antropológicas, Mexico City.
1992b   The Economic Organization of the Teotihuacan Priesthood. In *Art, Ideology, and the City of Teotihuacan*, edited by J. C. Berlo, pp. 321–338. Dumbarton Oaks, Washington, D.C.

Manzanilla, L., and E. Woodard
1990   Restos humanos asociados a la pirámide de Akapana (Tiwanaku, Bolivia). *Latin American Antiquity* 1:133–149.

Marchbanks, M.
1991   Trace Element Analysis of Ceramics from Tiwanaku. Paper presented at the 19th Annual Midwest Conference on Andean and Amazonian Archaeology, Bloomington, Ind.

Marcus, J.
1993   Ancient Maya Political Organization. In *Lowland Maya Civilization in the Eighth Century A.D.*, edited by J. A. Sabloff and J. S. Henderson, pp. 111–183. Dumbarton Oaks, Washington, D.C.
1998   The peaks and valleys of ancient states: An extension of the Dynamic Model. In *Archaic States*, edited by G. M. Feinman and J. Marcus, pp. 59–94. School of American Research, Santa Fe.

Marcus, J., and G. M. Feinman
1998   Introduction. In *Archaic States*, edited by G. M. Feinman and J. Marcus, pp. 3–14. School of American Research, Santa Fe.

Marcus, J. and K. V. Flannery
1996   *Zapotec Civilization : How Urban Society Evolved in Mexico's Oaxaca Valley.* Thames and Hudson, New York.

Massey, S. A.
1991   Social and Political Leadership in the Lower Ica Valley, Ocucaje Phases 8 and 9. In

Paracas Art and Architecture, edited by A. Paul, pp. 313–348. University of Iowa Press, Iowa City.

Mathews, J.
1989   Preliminary Investigations of Prehistoric Raised Fields in the Tiwanaku Mid-Valley, Tiwanaku, Bolivia. Paper presented at the 17th Annual Midwest Conference on Andean and Amazonian Archaeology and Ethnohistory, Mt. Pleasant, Michigan.
1997   Populations and Agriculture in the Emergence of Complex Society in the Bolivian *Altiplano*: The Case of Tiwanaku. In *Emergence and Change in Early Urban Societies*, edited by L. Manzanilla, pp. 245–274. Plenum, New York.

McAnany, P.
1995   *Living with the Ancestors: Kinship and Kingship in Ancient Maya Society*. University of Texas Press, Austin.

McAndrews, T., J. Albarracin-Jordan, and M. P. Bermann
1997   Regional Settlement Patterns of the Tiwanaku Valley of Bolivia. *Journal of Field Archaeology* 24:67–83.

McGuire, R.
1989   The Greater Southwest as a Periphery of Mesoamerica. In *Centre and Periphery: Comparative Studies in Archeology*, edited by T. Champion, pp. 40–66. Unwin, London.

McIntosh, S. K. (editor)
1999   *Beyond Chiefdoms: Pathways to Complexity in Africa*. Cambridge University Press, New York.

Meisch, L. A. (editor)
1997   *Traditional Textiles of the Andes: Life and Cloth in the Highlands: The Jeffrey Appleby Collection of Andean Textiles*. Thames and Hudson, New York.

Menzel, D.
1964   Style and Time in the Middle Horizon. *Ñawpa Pacha* 2:1–105.

Menzel, D., J. Rowe, and L. Dawson.
1964   *The Paracas Pottery of Ica: A Study in Style and Time*. University of California Publications in American Archaeology and Ethnology 50. University of California Press, Berkeley.

Metraux, A.
1945   People of the Past. *Natural History* 54:425–431.

Miller, G.
1977   Sacrificio y beneficio de camélidos en el Sur del Perú. In *Pastores de Puna, Uywamichiq Punarunakuna*, edited by J. Flores Ochoa, pp. 193–211. Instituto de Estudios Peruanos, Lima.

Miller, G. R., and R. L. Burger
1995   Our Father the Cayman, our Dinner the Llama: Animal Utilization at Chavin de Huantar, Peru. *American Antiquity* 60:421–458.

Millón, R.
1988   The Last Years of Teotihuacan Dominance. In *The Collapse of Ancient States and Civilizations*, edited by N. Yoffee and G. L. Cowgill, pp. 102–164. University of Arizona Press, Tucson.
1992   Teotihuacan Studies: From 1950 to 1990 and Beyond. In *Art, Ideology, and the City of Teotihuacan*, edited by J. C. Berlo, pp. 339–430. Dumbarton Oaks, Washington, D.C.

Mohr Chávez, K.
1985   Early Tiahuanaco-Related Ceremonial Burners from Cuzco, Peru. In *La prob-*

lemática Tiwanaku Huari en el contexto panandino del desarrollo cultural, edited by M. Rivera, pp. 137–178. Diálogo Andino 4. Universidad de Tarapacá, Arica, Chile.

1988   The Significance of Chiripa in Lake Titicaca Basin Developments. *Expedition* 30(3):17–26.

Molina, Y., T. Torres, E. Belmonte, and C. Santoro

1989   Uso y posible cultivo de coca (*erythroxylum spp.)* en Epocas Prehispánicas en los Valles de Arica. *Chungará* 23:37–49.

Money, M.

1991   El tesoro de San Sebastián: Una tumba importante de la cultura Tiwanaku. *Beitrage zur allgemeinen und vergleichenden Archaeologie* 11:189–198.

Moore, J. D.

1989   Pre-Hispanic Beer in Coastal Peru: Technology and Social Context of Prehistoric Production. *American Anthropologist* 91:682–695.

1996   *Architecture and Power in the Ancient Andes: The Architecture of Public Buildings*. Cambridge University Press, Cambridge.

Morris, C.

1982   The Infrastructure of Inka Control in the Peruvian Central Highlands. In *The Inca and Aztec States, 1400–1800*, edited by G. Collier, R. Rosaldo, and J. Wirth, pp. 153–172. Academic Press, New York.

1986   Storage, Supply, and Redistribution in the Economy of the Inka State. In *Anthropological History of Andean Polities*, edited by J. Murra, N. Wachtel and J. Revel, pp. 59–68. Cambridge University Press, Cambridge.

Morris, C., and D. Thompson

1985   *Huanaco Pampa: An Inca City and Its Hinterland*. Thames and Hudson, London.

Moseley, M. E.

1992   *The Incas and Their Ancestors: The Archaeology of Peru*. Thames and Hudson, New York.

Moseley, M. E., R. A. Feldman, P. S. Goldstein, and L. Watanabe M.

1991   Colonies and Conquest: Tiahuanaco and Huari in Moquegua. In *Huari Administrative Structure: Prehistoric Monumental Architecture and State Government*, edited by W. Isbell and G. McEwan, pp. 91–103. Dumbarton Oaks, Washington, D.C.

Mujica B., E.

1978a   *Estudio de la colección Bandelier procedente de Kea Kollu Chico, Isla Titicaca, que se encuentra en el AMNH: Objetivo, metodología e informe preliminar*. Department of Anthropology, American Museum of Natural History.

1978b   Nueva hipótesis sobre el desarrollo temprano del altiplano del Titicaca y de sus areas de interaction. *Arte y Arqueología* 5–6:285–308.

1985   Altiplano-Coast Relationships in the South Central Andes: From Indirect to Direct Complementarity. In *Andean Ecology and Civilization*, edited by S. Masuda, I. Shimada, and C. Morris, pp. 103–140. University of Tokyo Press, Tokyo.

1990   Pukara: Une societe complexe ancienne du bassin septentrional du Titicaca. In *Inca Peru: 3000 ans d'histoire*, edited by S. Purin, pp. 156–177. Musées Royaux d'Art et d'Histoire, Brussels.

1996   La integración surandina durante el periódo Tiwanaku. In *La integración surandina cinco siglos después*, edited by X. Albó, M. Arratia, J. Hidalgo, L. Nuñez, A. Llagostera, M. Remy, and B. Revesz, pp. 81–116. Centro de Estudios Regionales

Andinos Bartolomé de Las Casas, and Universidad Católica del Norte, Cusco and Antofagasta.

Mujica B., E., M. Rivera, and T. Lynch

1983   Proyecto de estudio sobre la complementaridad económica Tiwanaku en los valles occidentales del centro-sur Andino. *Chungará* 11:85–109.

Muñoz Ovalle, I.

1983a   El poblamiento aldeano en el valle de Azapa y su vinculación con Tiwanaku (Arica, Chile). In *Asentamientos aldeanos en los valles costeros de Arica*. Documentos de Trabajo vol. 3. Instituto de Antropología y Arqueología, Universidad de Tarapacá, Arica.

1983b   La fase Alto Ramírez en los valles del extremo norte de Chile. In *Asentamientos aldeanos en los valles costeros de Arica*, pp. 3–42. Documentos de Trabajo vol. 3. Instituto de Antropología y Arqueología, Universidad de Tarapacá, Arica.

1986   Aportes a la reconstrucción histórica del poblamiento aldeano en el valle de Azapa (Arica, Chile). *Chungará* 16–17:307–322.

1987   Enterramientos en túmulos en el valle de Azapa: Nuevas evidencias para definir la fase Alto Ramírez en el extremo norte de Chile. *Chungará* 19:93–128.

1996a   Integración y complementaridad en las sociedades prehispánicas en el extremo norte de chile: Hipótesis de trabajo. In *La integración surandina cinco siglos después*, edited by X. Albó, M. Arratia, J. Hidalgo, L. Nuñez, A. Llagostera, M. Remy, and B. Revesz, pp. 117–134. Centro de Estudios Regionales Andinos Bartolomé de Las Casas and Universidad Católica del Norte, Cusco and Antofagasta.

1996b   Poblamiento humano y relaciones interculturales en el valle de Azapa: Nuevos hallazgos en torno al período Formativo y Tiwanaku. In special issue, *Prehistoria del norte de Chile y del desierto de Atacama: Simposio homenaje a Percy Dauelsberg Hahmann*, pp. 241–278. Diálogo Andino 14–15. Universidad de Tarapacá, Arica, Chile.

Muñoz Ovalle, I., and G. Focacci

1985   San Lorenzo: Testimonio de una comunidad de agricultores y pescadores Postiwanaku en el valle de Azapa (Arica, Chile). *Chungará* 15:7–30.

Murra, J. V.

1962   Cloth and its Functions in the Inka State. *American Anthropologist* 64:710–728.

1964   Una Apreciacion Etnológica de la Visita. In *Visita Hecha a la Provincia de Chucuito*, edited by J. V. Murra, pp. 419–442. Casa de la Cultura del Perú, Lima.

1968   An Aymara Kingdom in 1567. *Ethnohistory* 15:115–51.

1972   El "control vertical" de un máximo de pisos ecológicos en la economía de las sociedades andinas. In *Visita de la Provincia de León de Huánuco en 1562 por Iñigo Ortiz de Zuñiga*, edited by J. V. Murra, pp. 427–476. Documentos para la historia y etnología de Huánuco y la selva central, vol. 2. Universidad Nacional Hermilio Valdizan, Huánuco.

1980   [1955] *The Economic Organization of the Inka State*. JAI Press, Greenwich, Connecticut.

1982   The mit'a obligations of ethnic groups to the Inka State. In *The Inca and Aztec States, 1400–1800*, edited by G. Collier, R. Rosaldo and J. Wirth, pp. 237–264. Academic Press, New York.

1985   "El Archipiélago Vertical" Revisited: Limits and Limitations of the "Vertical Archipelago" in the Andes. In *Andean Ecology and Civilization*, edited by S. Masuda, I. Shimada, and C. Morris, pp. 3–20. University of Tokyo Press, Tokyo.

1989   Cloth and its function in the Inka state. In *Cloth and Human Experience*, edited by J. Schneider and A. B. Weiner, pp. 275–302. Smithsonian Institution Pres, Washington, D.C.

Nelson, B. A.

1994   Outposts of Mesoamerican Empire and Architectural Patterning at La Quemada, Zacatecas. In *Culture and Contact*, edited by A. I. Wooseley and J. C. Ravesloot, pp. 173–190. University of New Mexico Press, Albuquerque.

2000   Aggregation, warfare, and the spread of the Mesoamerican tradition. In *The archaeology of regional interaction: religion, warfare, and exchange across the American Southwest and beyond: Proceedings of the 1996 Southwest Symposium*, edited by M. Hegmon, pp. 317–337. vol. 5. University Press of Colorado, Boulder.

Nelson, B. A., J. A. Darling, and D. A. Kice

1992   Mortuary practices and the social order at La Quemada, Zacatecas, Mexico. *Latin American Antiquity* 3(4):298–315.

Nichols, D. L., and T. H. Charlton (editors)

1997   *The Archaeology of City States: Cross-Cultural Approaches*. Smithsonian Institution Press, Washington, D.C.

Nuñez Atencio, L.

1972   Sobre el comienzo de la agricultura prehistórica en el norte de Chile. *Pumapunku* 4:25–48.

Nuñez Atencio, L., and T. Dillehay

1979   Movilidad giratoria, armonia y desarrollo en los Andes Meridionales, patrones de trafico e interacción economica. In *Direccion General de Investigaciones cientificas y technologicas*. Universidad del Norte, Antofagasta.

Oakland, A.

1986   *Tiwanaku Textile Style from the South Central Andes*. Unpublished Ph.D. dissertation, Department of Art, University of Texas, Austin.

1992   Textiles and Ethnicity: Tiwanaku in San Pedro de Atacama, North Chile. *Latin American Antiquity* 3(4):316–340.

Oficina Nacional de Evaluación de Recursos Naturales (ONERN)

1976   *Inventario, evaluación y uso racional de los recursos naturales de la costa: Cuencas de los ríos Moquegua-Locumba-Sama y Caplina*. Oficina Nacional de Evaluación de Recursos Naturales, Lima.

Orellana R., M.

1984   Influencias altiplánicas en San Pedro de Atacama. *Estudios Atacameños* 7:197–208.

1985   Relaciónes culturales entre Tiwanaku y San Pedro de Atacama. *Diálogo Andino* 4 (La problemática Tiwanaku Huari en el contexto panandino del desarrollo cultural, edited by M. Rivera):247–258. Universidad de Tarapacá, Arica, Chile.

Ortloff, C. and A. Kolata

1989   Hydraulics innovations of the Tiwanaku state. Paper presented at the 29th Annual Meeting of the Institute of Andean Studies, Berkeley.

Owen, B. D.
1993a   Early Ceramic Settlement in the Coastal Osmore Valley: Preliminary Report. Paper presented at the Institute of Andean Studies Annual Meeting, Berkeley.
1993b   *A Model of Multiethnicity: State Collapse, Competition, and Social Complexity from Tiwanaku to Chiribaya in the Osmore Valley, Perú.* Unpublished Ph.D. dissertation, Department of Anthropology, University of California, Los Angeles.
1994   Were Wari and Tiwanaku in Conflict, Competition, or Complementary Coexistence? Survey Evidence from the Upper Osmore Drainage, Peru. Paper presented at the Society for American Archaeology 59th annual meeting.
1995   Warfare and Engineering, Ostentation and Social Status in the Late Intermediate Period Osmore Drainage. Paper presented at the Society for American Archaeology 60th annual meeting, Minneapolis.
1997   *Informe de Excavaciones en los Sectores Mortuorios de Chen Chen, Parte del Proyecto Rescate de Chen Chen, Temporada de 1995.* Report submitted to the Instituto Nacional de Cultura.
Owen, B. D. and P. S. Goldstein
2001   Tiwanaku en Moquegua: interacciones regionales y colapso. *Boletín de Arqueología, Pontificia Universidad Católica del Perú* 5: Huari y Tiwanaku: Modelos vs, Evidencias:169–188.
Palacios Rios, F.
1982   El simbolismo Aymara de la casa. In *Boletín del Instituto de Estudios Aymaras* (Puno) 2:37–57.
Pari F., R.
1987   El proceso historico social de los Tiwanaku y su implicancia en el Valle de Moquegua. Unpublished Licenciado thesis, Universidad Católica Santa María, Arequipa.
Parsons, J. R.
1968 An Estimate of Size and Population for Middle Horizon Tiahuanaco, Bolivia. *American Antiquity* 33:243–245.
Parssinen, M.
1997   Inka-style ceramics and their chronological relationship to the Inka expansion in the southern Lake Titicaca area (Bolivia). *Latin American Antiquity* 8(3):255–71.
2001   Tiwanaku IV en Nazacara, Bolivia: Apuntes para una cronologia cultural. *Boletín de arqueología PUCP* 5(3):605–624.
Patterson, T., and C. W. Gailey
1987   Power Relations and State Formation. In *Power Relations and State Formation*, edited by T. Patterson and C. Gailey, pp. 1–27. American Anthropological Association, Washington D.C.
Paul, A. (editor)
1991   *Paracas Art and Architecture.* University of Iowa Press, Iowa City.
Paulsen, A.
1976   Environment and Empire: Climatic Factors in Prehistoric Andean Culture Change. *World Archaeology* 8:121–132.
Paynter, R.
1989   The Archaeology of Equality and Inequality. *Annual Review of Anthropology* 18:369–399.

Pearson, M.
1999   *The Archaeology of Death and Burial.* Texas A&M University Press., College Station.

Pease G.Y., F.
1980   Las relaciones entre las tierras altas y la costa del Sur del Perú: Fuentes documentales. *Bulletin of the National Museum of Ethnology* 5(1).
1984a   Indices notariales de Moquegua, siglo 16: Una introducción. In *Contribuciones a los estudios de los Andes centrales*, edited by S. Masuda, pp. 151–383. University of Tokyo Press, Tokyo.
1984b   Introducción. In *Crónica del Perú*, Part 1, edited by P. Cieza de Leon, pp. xi–liv. Pontificia Universidad Católica del Perú, Lima.

Peregrine, P. N. and G. M. Feinman (editors)
1996   *Pre-Columbian World-Systems.* Prehistory Press, Madison.

Piazza K., F.
1981   Analisis descriptivo de una aldea incaica en el sector del Pampa Alto Ramírez. *Chungará* 7:172–211.

Platt, T.
1980   Espejos y maíz: El concepto de Yanantin entre los Macha de Bolivia. In *Parentezco y matrimonio en los Andes*, edited by E. Mayer and R. Bolton, pp. 139–182. Pontificia Universidad Católica del Perú, Lima.
1986   Mirrors and Maize: The Concept of Yanantin among the Macha of Bolivia. In *Anthropological History of Andean Polities*, edited by J. Murra, N. Wachtel, and J. Reve, pp. 228–259. Cambridge University Press, Cambridge.

Polanyi, K.
1963   Ports of Trade in Early Societies. *Journal of Economic History* 23:30–45.

Polanyi, K., C. Arensburg, and H. Pearson (editors)
1957   *Trade and Market in Early Empires.* Free Press, Glencoe, Ill.

Ponce Sanginés, C.
1947   Cerámica Tiwanacota. *Revista Geográfica Americana* 28:204–214.
1948   *Cerámica Tiwanacota, Vasos con Decoración Prosopomorfa.* Imprenta López, Buenos Aires.
1969   *Tiwanaku: Descripción sumaria del templete semisubterráneo.* Academia Nacional de Ciencias de Bolivia, La Paz.
1970   *Las culturas Wankarani y Chiripa y su relación con Tiwanaku.* Publicación del Instituto Nacional de Arqueología 25. Editorial Universo, La Paz.
1972   *Tiwanaku: Espacio Tiempo y Cultura.* Academia Nacional de Ciencias de Bolivia, La Paz.
1976   *La cerámica de la época I de Tiwanaku.* Publicación del Instituto Nacional de Arqueología 18. Editorial Universo, La Paz.
1989   *Arqueología de Lukurmata*, vol. 1. Instituto Nacional de Arqueología, La Paz.

Ponce Sanginés, C., and G. Mogrovejo Terrazas
1970   *Acerca de la procedencia del material lítico de los monumentos de Tiwanaku.* Instituto Nacional de Arqueología, La Paz.

Portugal Ortíz, M.
1984   Testimonios arqueológicos para la historia de la expansión cultural altiplánica sobre los valles y costas del Pacífico. *Arqueología Boliviana* 1:115–122.

Portugal Zamora, M.
1941   Las Ruinas de Jesús de Machaca. *Revista Geográfica Americana* 16:291–300.
Portugal Zamora, M., and M. Portugal Ortiz
1977   Investigaciones arqueológicas en el Valle de Tiwanaku. In *Arqueología en Bolivia y Perú*, vol. 2, La Paz.
Posnansky, A.
1934   Los Urus o Uchumi. Paper presented at the Actas y Trabajos Cientificos del 25 Congreso Internacional de Americanistas, La Plata.
1945   *Tihuanaco: The Cradle of American Man*, vols. 1, 2. American Museum, New York.
1957   *Tihuanaco: The Cradle of American Man*, vols, 3, 4. Ministerio de Educación, La Paz.
Possehl, G. L.
1998   Sociocultural Complexity without the State: The Indus Civilization. In *Archaic States*, edited by G. M. Feinman and J. Marcus, pp. 261–292. School of American Research, Santa Fe.
Potter, D. R., and E. M. King
1995   A Heterarchical Approach to Lowland Maya Socioeconomics. In *Heterarchy and the Analysis of Complex Societies*, edited by R. M. Ehrenreich, C. L. Crumley, and J. E. Levy, pp. 17–32. Archeological Papers of the American Anthropological Association no. 6. Washington, D.C.
Protzen, J.-P.
1993   *Inca Architecture and Construction at Ollantaytambo*. Oxford University Press, New York.
Protzen, J.-P., and S. E. Nair
1997   Who Taught the Inca Stonemasons Their Skills? A Comparison of Tiahuanaco and Inca Cut-Stone Masonry. *Journal of the Society of Architectural Historians* 56(2):146–167.
2000   On Reconstructing Tiwanaku Architecture. *Journal of the Society of Architectural Historians* 59(3):358–371.
2002   The Gateways of Tiwanaku: Symbols or Passages. In *Andean Archaeology*, edited by W. H. Isbell and H. Silverman, pp. 189–223. vol. 2. 2 vols. Kluwer Academic/Plenum Publishers, New York.
Quilter, J.
1997   The Narrative Approach to Moche Iconography. *Latin American Antiquity* 8(2): 113–133.
Rattray, E. C.
1989   Barrio de los comerciantes y el conjunto de Tlamimilolpa: Un estudio comparativo. *Arqueología* 5:105–129.
1990   New Findings on the Origins of Thin Orange Ceramics. *Ancient Mesoamerica* 1(2):181–195.
Redmond, E. M.
1983   *A Fuego y Sangre: Early Zapotec Imperialism in the Cuicatlán Cañada, Oaxaca.* University of Michigan, Museum of Anthropology, Ann Arbor.
Reinhard, J.
1985   Chavín and Tiahuanaco: A New Look at Two Andean Ceremonial Centers. *National Geographic Research* 1:395–422.

1990   Tiahuanaco, Sacred Center of the Andes. In *The Cultural Guide of Bolivia*, edited by P. McFarren, pp. 151–181. Fundación Quipus, La Paz.

Renfrew, C.

1975   Trade as Action at a Distance. In *Ancient Civilization and Trade*, edited by J. Sabloff and C. C. Lamberg Karlovsky, pp. 1–60. School of American Research, Santa Fe.

1996   Peer Polity Interaction and Socio-Political Change. In *Contemporary Archaeology in Theory: A Reader*, edited by R. Preucel and I. Hodder, pp. 114–142. Blackwell, Cambridge, Mass.

Rice, D. S.

1985   *Late Prehistoric Economic Complementarity in the Osmore Drainage, Peru*. National Science Foundation.

1993   Late Intermediate Period Domestic Architecture and Residential Organization at La Yaral. In *Domestic Architecture, Ethnicity, and Complementarity in the South-Central Andes*, edited by M. Aldenderfer, pp. 66–82. University of Iowa Press, Iowa City.

Rice, D. S., C. Stanish, and P. R. Scarr

1989   *Ecology, Settlement and History in the Osmore Drainage, Peru*. BAR International Series 545(1,2). British Archaeological Reports, Oxford.

Rice, P. M.

1987   The Moquegua Bodegas Survey. *National Geographic Research* 3(2):136–38.

Rice, P. M., and G. C. Smith

1989   The Spanish Colonial Wineries of Moquegua, Peru. *Journal of the Society for Historical Archaeology* 23(2):41–49.

Rivera Casanovas, C. S.

1994   *Evidencias sobre la producción de cerámica en Tiwanaku*. Tesis de Licenciatura, Universidad Mayor de San Andres.

Rivera Díaz, M. A.

1976   Nuevos aportes sobre el desarrollo cultural altiplánico en los valles bajos del extremo norte de Chile, durante el período Intermedio Temprano. *Anales de la Universidad del Norte* 10:71–82.

1985   Alto Ramírez y Tiwanaku: Un caso de interpretación simbólica a través de datos arqueológicos en el área de los valles occidentales, Sur del Perú y Norte de Chile. *Diálogo Andino* 4 (La problemática Tiwanaku Huari en el contexto panandino del desarrollo cultural), edited by M. Rivera, pp. 39–58. Universidad de Tarapacá, Arica, Chile.

1987   Tres fechados radiométricos de Pampa Alto de Ramírez, norte de Chile. *Chungará* 18:7–14.

1991   The Prehistory of Northern Chile: A Synthesis. *Journal of World Prehistory* 5(1): 1–48.

1995   Hacia la complejidad social y política: El desarrollo Alto Ramirez del norte de Chile. *Diálogo Andino* 13:9–38.

1999   Prehistory of the Southern Cone. In *The Cambridge History of the Native Peoples of the Americas, South America*, edited by F. Salomon and S. Schwartz, vol. 3, pp. 734–768.

2002   *Historias del Desierto. Arqueología del Norte de Chile*. Editorial del Norte, La Serena.

Rivera Díaz, M. A., and A. C. Aufderheide
1998   Camarones y Pisagua, dos casos de adaptación al medio marítimo y su coexis-
        tencia con pueblos de estracción altiplánica (1500–500 AC). In *50 Años de Estu-
        dios Americanistas en la Universidad de Bonn Nuevas contribuciónes a la arque-
        ología, etnohistoria, etnolingüística y etnogafía de las Americas*, edited by S.
        Dedenbach-Salazar Sáenz, C. Arellano Hoffman, E. König and H. Prümers, vol.
        30, pp. 259–289. Bonner Amerikanistische Studien, verlan Anton Saurwein.

Rivera Sundt, O.
1989   Resultados de la excavación en el centro ceremonial de Lukurmata. In *Arqueología
        de Lukurmata*, vol. 2, edited by A. L. Kolata, pp. 59–89. Instituto Nacional de
        Arqueología, La Paz.

Roseberry, W.
1993   Hegemony and the Language of Contention. In *Everyday Forms of State Forma-
        tion*, edited by G. Joseph and D. Nugent, pp. 355–366. Duke University Press.

Rostworowski de Diez Canseco, M.
1986   La Región del Colesuyu. *Chungara* 16–17:127–135.
1988   *Historia del Tahuantinsuyu*. Instituto de Estudios Peruanos, Lima.

Rothhammer, F., J. Cocilovo, E. Llop, and S. Quevedo
1989   Orígenes y microevolución de la población chilena. In *Culturas de Chile, pre-
        historia desde sus orígenes hasta los albores de la Conquista*, edited by J. Hidalgo
        L., V. Schiappacasse F., H. Niemeyer F., C. Aldunate and I. Solimano R., pp. 403–
        413. Editorial Andrés Bello, Santiago de Chile.

Rothhammer, F., and C. Santoro
2001   El desarrollo cultural en el Valle de Azapa, Extremo Norte de Chile y su vincu-
        lación con los desplazamientos poblacionales altiplánicos. *Latin American Antiq-
        uity* 12(1):59–66.

Rowe, J. H.
1946   Inca Culture at the Time of the Spanish Conquest. In *Handbook of South Ameri-
        can Indians*, vol. 2: *The Andean Civilizations*, edited by J. H. Steward, pp. 183–
        330. Bureau of American Ethnology 143. Washington, D.C.
1982   Inca Policies and Institutions Relating to the Cultural Unification of the Empire. In
        The Inca and Aztec States, 1400–1800, edited by G. Collier, R. Rosaldo, and J.
        Wirth, pp. 93–118. Academic Press, New York.
1995   Behavior and Belief in Ancient Peruvian Mortuary Practice. In *Tombs for the Liv-
        ing: Andean Mortuary Practices*, edited by T. D. Dillehay, pp. 27–41. Dumbarton
        Oaks, Washington, D.C.

Rowe, J. H., D. Collier, and G. Willey
1950   Reconnaissance notes on the site of Huari, near Ayacucho, Peru. *American Antiq-
        uity* 16(2):120–137.

Rowe, J. H., and J. Donahue
1975   The Donahue Discovery: An Ancient Stela Found Near Ilave, Puno, Peru. *Nawpa
        Pacha* 13:35–44.

Rowlands, M., M. Larsen, and K. Kristiansen (editors)
1987   *Centre and Periphery in the Ancient World*. Cambridge University Press, Cam-
        bridge.

Rydén, S.
1947   *Archaeological Researches in the Highlands of Bolivia*. Elanders Boktryckeri
        Aktiebolag, Goteborg, Sweden.

1957   *Andean Excavations*, vol. 1. Etnographical Museum of Sweden, Stockholm.
1959   *Andean Excavations*, vol. 2. Etnographical Museum of Sweden, Stockholm.
Saignes, T.
1986   The Ethnic Groups in the Valley of Larecaja: From Descent to Residence. In *Anthropological History of Andean Polities*, edited by J. Murra, N. Wachtel, and J. Revel, pp. 311–341. Cambridge University Press, Cambridge.
Salomon, F.
1986   Vertical politics on the Inka frontier. In *Anthropological History of Andean Polities*, edited by J. Murra, N. Wachtel and J. Revel, pp. 89–117. Cambridge University Press, Cambridge.
1991   Introductory Essay: The Huarochirí Manuscript. In *The Huarochirí Manuscript*, edited by F. Salomon and G. L. Urioste, pp. 1–38. University of Texas Press, Austin.
1995   The Beautiful Grandparents: Andean Ancestor Shrines and Mortuary Ritual as Seen through Colonial Records. In *Tombs for the Living: Andean Mortuary Practices*, edited by T. D. Dillehay, pp. 315–353. Dumbarton Oaks, Washington, D.C.
Sanders, W. T., and J. Michels (editors)
1977   *Teotihuacan and Kaminaljuyu*. Pennsylvania State University Press, University Park.
Sandness, K.
1992   Temporal and Spatial Dietary Variability in the Osmore Drainage, Southern Peru: The Isotope Evidence. Unpublished Master's thesis, Department of Anthropology, University of Nebraska.
Santley, R. S., and R. T. Alexander
1992   The Political Economy of Core-Periphery Systems. In *Resources, Power and Interregional Interaction*, edited by E. M. Schortman and P. A. Urban, pp. 23–50. Plenum Press, New York.
Santley, R. S., C. Yarborough, and B. Hall
1987   Enclaves, Ethnicity and the Archaeological Record at Matacapan. In *Ethnicity and Culture*, edited by R. Auger, M. Glass, S. MacEachern, and P. McCartney, pp. 85–100. University of Calgary, Calgary.
Santoro, C.
1980   Estratigrafía y secuencia cultural funeraria: Fase Azapa, Alto Ramírez y Tiwanaku. *Chungará* 6.
Sarmiento de Gamboa, P.
1908 [1571]   *History of the Incas. Translated and Edited by Sir Clements Markham.* The Hakluyt Society, London.
Schiappacasse F., V., A. Román, I. Muñoz, A. Deza, and G. Focacci
1991   Cronología por termoluminiscencia de la cerámica del extremo norte de Chile: Primera parte. In *Actas del 11 Congreso Nacional de Arqueología Chilena*, pp. 43–60. Museo Nacional de História Natural, Santiago.
Schiffer, M. B.
1987   *Formation Processes of the Archaeological Record.* University of New Mexico Press, Albuquerque.
Schildkraut, E.
1978 *People of the Zongo: The Transformation of Ethnic Identities in Ghana.* Cambridge University Press, New York.
1987   *The Golden Stool: Studies of the Asante Center and Periphery* 65. Anthropological Papers of the American Museum of Natural History, New York.

Schneider, J.
1977   Was There a Pre-Capitalist World System? *Peasant Studies* 6(1):20–29.
Schortman, E. M.
1989   Interregional Interaction in Prehistory. *American Antiquity* 54:52–65.
Schortman, E. M., and P. A. Urban
1994   Living on the Edge: Core-Periphery Relations in Ancient Southeastern Mesoamerica. *Current Anthropology* 35:401–430.
Schortman, E. M., and P. A. Urban (editors)
1992   *Resources, Power and Interregional Interaction.* Plenum Press, New York.
Schreiber, K. J.
1992   *Wari Imperialism in Middle Horizon Peru.* Anthropological Papers 87. Museum of Anthropology, University of Michigan, Ann Arbor.
1993   The Inca Occupation of the Province of Andamarca Lucanas. In *Provincial Inca: Archaeological and Ethnohhistorical Assesment of the Impact of the Inca State,* edited by M. Malpass, pp. 77–116. University of Iowa, Iowa City.
1999   Regional Approaches to the Study of Prehistoric Empires: Examples from Ayacucho and Nasca, Peru. In *Settlement Pattern Studies in the Americas,* edited by B. R. Billman and G. M. Feinman, pp. 160–171. Smithsonian Institution Press, Washington, D.C.
2001   The Wari Empire of Middle Horizon Peru: The Epistomological Challenge of documenting an Empire without Documentary Evidence. In *Empires: Perspectives from Archaeology and History,* edited by S. E. Alcock, T. N. D'Altroy, K. D. Morrison and C. M. Sinopoli, pp. 70–92. Cambridge University Press, Cambridge.
Seddon, M.
1998   *Ritual, Power and the Development of a Complex Society: The Island of the Sun and the Tiwanaku State.* Unpublished Ph.D. dissertation, University of Chicago.
Shennan, S. (editor)
1989   *Archaeological approaches to cultural identity.* Unwin Hyman, One world archaeology, London.
Sherbondy, J.
1982   The Canal Systems of Hanan Cuzco. Ph.D. dissertation, University of Illinois, Urbana.
Silverman, H.
1996   The Formative Period on the South Coast of Peru: A Critical Review. *Journal of World Prehistory* 10(2):95–146.
Sinopoli, C. M.
1991   *Approaches to Archaeological Ceramics.* Plenum Press, New York.
1994   Archaeology of Empire. *Annual Review of Anthropology* 23:159–180.
2001   On the Edge of Empire: Form and Substance in the Satavahana Dynasty. In *Empires: Perspectives from Archaeology and History,* edited by S. E. Alcock, T. N. D'Altroy, K. D. Morrison and C. M. Sinopoli, pp. 155–200. Cambridge University Press, Cambridge.
Sinopoli, C. M., and K. D. Morrison
1995   Dimensions of Imperial Control: The Vijayanagara Capital. *American Anthropologist* 97(1):83–96.
Smith, M. E.
1987   The Expansion of the Aztec Empire: A Case Study in the Correlation of Diachronic Archaeological and Ethnohistorical Data. *American Antiquity* 52:37–54.

Smith, M. E., and F. F. Berdan
1992   Archaeology and the Aztec Empire. *World Archaeology* :353–367.
Southall, A.
1974   State Formation in Africa. *Annual Review of Anthropology* 3:153–165.
1988   The Segmentary State in Africa and Asia. *Comparative Studies in Society and History* :52–82.
1999   The Segmentary State and the Ritual Phase in Political Economy. In *Beyond Chiefdoms: Pathways to Complexity in Africa*, edited by S. K. McIntosh, pp. 32–38. Cambridge University Press, Cambridge.
Spector, J. D.
1996   What This Awl Means: Toward a Feminist Archaeology. In *Contemporary Archaeology in Theory*, edited by R. W. Preucel and I. Hodder, pp. 485–500. Blackwell, Cambridge, Mass.
Spence, M. W.
1992   Tlailotlacan: A Zapotec Enclave in Teotihuacan. In *Art, Ideology, and the City of Teotihuacan*, edited by J. C. Berlo, pp. 59–88. Dumbarton Oaks, Washington, D.C.
Spencer, C. S.
1982   *The Cuicatlán Cañada and Monte Albán: A Study of Primary State Formation.* Academic Press, New York.
1990   On the Tempo and Mode of State Formation: Neoevolutionism Reconsidered. *Journal of Anthropological Archaeology* 9:1–30.
1998   A mathematical model of primary state formation. *Cultural Dynamics* 10(1):5–20.
2001   Multilevel Selection and Political Evolution in the Valley of Oaxaca, 500–100 B.C. *Journal of Anthropological Archaeology* 20(2):195–229.
Spencer, C. S., and E. M. Redmond
1997   *Archaeology of the Cañada de Cuicatlán, Oaxaca.* American Museum of Natural History, New York, N.Y.
2001   The Chronology of Conquest: Implications of new Radiocarbon Analyses from the Canada de Cuicatlán, Oaxaca. *Latin American Antiquity* 12(2):182–202.
Squier, E.
1877   *Peru: Incidents of Travel and Exploration in the Land of the Incas.* Macmillan, London.
Stahl, A. B.
1999   Perceiving Variability in Time and Space: The Evolutionary Mapping of African Societies. In *Beyond Chiefdoms: Pathways to Complexity in Africa*, edited by S. K. McIntosh, pp. 39–55. Cambridge University Press, New York.
Stanish, C.
1985   Post Tiwanaku Regional Economics in the Otora Valley, Southern Peru. Unpublished Ph.D. dissertation, Department of Anthropology, University of Chicago.
1989   Household Archeology: Testing Models of Zonal Complementarity in the South Central Andes. *American Anthropologist* 91:7–24.
1992   *Ancient Andean Political Economy.* University of Texas Press, Austin.
1999   Settlement Pattern Shifts and Political Ranking in the Lake Titicaca Basin, Peru. In *Settlement Pattern Studies in the Americas: Fifty Years since Virú*, edited by B. R. Billman and G. M. Feinman, pp. 116–130. Smithsonian Institution Press., Washington, D.C.

2003   *Ancient Titicaca: The evolution of complex society in southern Peru and northern Bolivia*. University of California Press.

Stanish, C., E. De La Vega M., L. Steadman, C. Chavez J., K. Frye, L. Onofre M., M. Seddon, and P. Calisaya Ch.

1996   Archaeological Survey in the Southwestern Lake Titicaca Basin. *Diálogo Andino* 14/15:97–143.

Stanish, C., and L. Steadman

1994   *Archaeological Research at Tumatumani, Juli, Peru*. Fieldiana Anthropology, new series 23. Field Museum of Natural History, Chicago.

Steadman, L. H.

1995   Excavations at Camata: An Early Ceramic Chronology for the Western Titicaca Basin, Peru. Unpublished Ph.D. dissertation, Department of Anthropology. University of California, Berkeley.

Stein, B.

1980   *Peasant, State and Society in Medieval South India*. Oxford University Press, Oxford.

1985   Politics, Peasants and the Deconstruction of Feudalism in Medieval India. *Journal of Peasant Studies* 12:54–86.

Stein, G. J.

1998   World Systems Theory and Alternative Modes of Interaction in the Archaeology of Culture Contact. In *Studies in Culture Contact: Interaction, Culture Change, and Archaeology*, edited by J. Cusick, pp. 220–255. Occasional Paper 25, Center for Archaeological Investigations. Southern Illinois University Press, Carbondale.

1999a   Material Culture and Social Identity: The Evidence for a 4th Millennium B.C. Uruk Mesopotamian Colony at Hacinebi, Turkey. *Paléorient* 25:11–22.

1999b   *Rethinking World Systems: Diasporas, Colonies, and Interaction in Uruk Mesopotamia*. University of Arizona Press, Tucson.

Stein, G. J., R. Bernbeck, C. Coursey, A. McMahon, N. F. Miller, A. Misir, J. Nicola, H. Pittman, S. Pollock, and H. Wright

1996   Uruk Colonies and Anatolian Communities: An Interim Report on the 1992–1993 Excavations at Hacinebi, Turkey. *American Journal of Archaeology* 100(2):205–260.

Steiner, C. B.

1994   *African Art in Transit*. Cambridge University Press, Cambridge.

Stern, S. J.

1988   Confronting Historical Paradigms: Peasants, Labor, and the Capitalist World System in Africa and Latin America. *American Historical Review* 93(4):829–72.

Stovel, E.

1997   Tiwanaku Expansion and Coyo Aldea, San Pedro de Atacama, Northern Chile. Paper presented at the Society for American Archaeology 62nd annual meeting, Nashville.

Stubel, A., and M. Uhle

1892   *Die Ruinenstatte von Tiahuanaco im Hochlande des Alten Peru*, Leipzig.

Sutter, R. C.

1996   A Bioarchaeological Perspective on Verticality in the Middle and Lower Moquegua Valley, Perú, During the Late Intermediate Period. Paper presented at the Society for American Archaeology 61st annual meeting.

2000   Prehistoric Genetic and Culture Change: A Bioarchaeological Search for Pre-Inka Altiplano Colonies in the Coastal Valleys of Moquegua Valley, Perú, and Azapa, Chile. *Latin American Antiquity* 11(1):43–70.

Tainter, J. A.

1975   Social Inference and Mortuary Practices: An Experiment in Numerical Classification. *World Archaeology* 7(1).

1977   Modeling Change in Prehistoric Social Systems. In *For theory building in archaeology: Essays on faunal remains, aquatic resources, spatial analysis, and systemic modeling*, edited by L. R. Binford, pp. 327–351. Academic Press, New York.

1978   Mortuary practices and the study of prehistoric social systems. *Advances in Archaeological Method and Theory* 1:105–141.

1980   Behavior and status in a Middle Woodland mortuary population from the Illinois Valley. *American Antiquity* 45:308–313.

Tambiah, S. J.

1977   The Galactic Polity: The Structure of Traditional Kingdoms in Southeast Asia. *Annals of the New York Academy of Science* 293:69–97.

2000   Transnational Movements, Diaspora, and Multiple Modernities. *Daedalus* 129(1):163–194.

Tarrago, M. N.

1976   Alfarería típica de San Pedro de Atacama. *Estudios Atacameños* 4:37–64.

1977   Relaciones prehispánicas entre San Pedro de Atacama (Norte de Chile) y regiones aledañas: La quebrada de Humahuaca. *Estudios Atacameños* 5:50–63.

1984   La historia de los pueblos circumpuneños en relación con el atltiplano y los Andes Meridionales. *Estudios Atacameños* 7:116–132.

Tello, J. C.

1987   Pocoma: Cerámica de la fase Carizal? *Gaceta Arqueólogica Andina* 15:21–25.

Thapar, R.

1984   *From Lineage to State: Social Formations in the Mid-First Millennium* B.C. *in the Ganga Valley*. Oxford University Press, Bombay.

Thomas, C., M. Benavente, and C. Massone

1985   Algunos efectos de Tiwanaku en la cultura de San Pedro de Atacama. *Diálogo Andino* 4 (La problematica Tiwanaku Huari en el contexto panandino del desarrollo cultural), edited by M. Rivera, pp. 259–276. Diálogo Andino 4. Universidad de Tarapacá, Arica, Chile.

Torero, A.

1992   Acerca de la familia linguística Uruquilla (Uru-Chipaya). *Revista Andina* 10(1): 171–192.

Torres, C. M.

1984   Tabletas para alucinogenos de San Pedro de Atacama: Estilo e iconografía. In *Tesoros de San Pedro de Atacama*, pp. 23–36. Museo Chileno de Arte Precolombino, Banco O'Higgins, Santiago.

1985   Estilo y iconografía Tiwanaku en la cultura de San Pedro de Atacama. In *La problematica Tiwanaku Huari en el contexto panandino del desarrollo cultural*, edited by M. Rivera, pp. 247–259. Diálogo Andino 4. Universidad de Tarapacá, Arica, Chile.

1987   The Iconography of Prehispanic Snuff trays From San Pedro de Atacama. *Andean Past* 1:191–245.

2001   Iconografía Tiwanaku en la parafernalia inhalatoria de los Andes centro-sur. *Boletín de Arquieclogía PUCP 5*, Huari y Tiwanaku: Modelos vs. Evidencias, segunda parte:427–454.

Torres, E., C. Clement, N. R. Clark, and J. C. Tello
1984   Entierro precerámico doble en Ilo, Perú: Reporte preliminar. In *Trabajos Arqueológicos en Moquegua, Peru*, vol. 1, edited by L. K. Watanabe, M. E. Moseley, and F. Cabieses. Museo Peruano de Ciencias de la Salud, Southern Peru Copper Corporation, Lima.

Towles, M.
1961   *The Ethnobotany cf Ancient Peru.* University of Chicago Press, Chicago.

Townsend, R.
1982   Pyramid and Sacred Mountain. In *Ethnoastronomy and Archaeoastronomy in the American Tropics*, edited by A. Aveni and G. Urton, pp. 37–62. Annals of the New York Academy of Sciences, vol. 385. New York Academy of Sciences, New York.

Trigger, B.
1993   *Early Civilizations: Ancient Egypt in Context.* American University in Cairo Press, Cairo.

Trimborn, H.
1973   Investigaciones arqueológicas en el Departamento de Tacna. In *Atti del 40 Congreso Internazionale degle Americanisti*, vol. 1, pp. 333–335. Genoa.

Tschopik, M.
1946   *Some Notes on the Archaeology of the Department of Puno, Peru.* American Archaeology and Ethnology 27. Peabody Museum, Harvard University, Cambridge.

Turner, M. H.
1992   Style in Lapidary Technology: Identifying the Teotihuacan Lapidary Industry. In *Art, Ideology, and the City of Teotihuacan*, edited by J. C. Berlo, pp. 89–112. Dumbarton Oaks, Washington, D.C.

Ucko, P. J.
1969   Ethnography and archaeological interpretation of funerary remains. *World archaeology* 1(2):262–280.

Uhle, M.
1903   *Pachacamac: Report of the William Pepper Peruvian Expedition of 1896.* Department of Archaeology, University of Pennsylvania.
1912   Los orígenes de los Incas. Paper presented at the Actas del 17 Congreso Internacional de Americanistas, Buenos Aires.
1918   Los aborígenes de Arica. *Revista Histórica* 6(1):5–26.
1919   La arqueología de Arica y Tacna. *Boletín de la Sociedad Ecuatoriana de Estudios Históricos Americanos* 3:1–48.

Ulloa, L.
1982   Estilos decorativos y formas textiles de poblaciones agromarítimas en el extremo norte de Chile. *Chungará* 8:109–136.

Ulloa Mogollón, J.
1965 [1586]   Relación de la provincia de los collaguas para la discrepción de las Indias que su magestad manda hacer. *Relaciones geográficas de Indias*:326–333.

Urton, G.
1990   *The History of a Myth : Pacariqtambo and the Origin of the Inkas.* University of Texas Press, Austin.

1993   Moieties and Ceremonialism in the Andes: The Ritual Battles of the Carnival Season in Southern Peru. In *El Mundo Ceremonial Andino*, edited by L. Millones and Y. Onuki, pp. 117–142. Senri Ethnological Studies vol. 37. National Museum of Ethnology, Osaka.

Valcárcel, L.
1935   Los trabajos arqueológicos en el Departamento de Cuzco. *Revista del Museo Nacional* 4(2):163–208.

Van Buren, M.
1996   Rethinking the Vertical Archipelago. *American Anthropologist* 98(2):338–351.

Vargas V., B.
1988   *Informe final del proyecto: "Rescate arqueológico del cementerio de Chen Chen."* Instituto Nacional de Cultura, Sucursal Departamental Moquegua.
1994   *Informe sobre tumbas intactas (334) excavadas durante el proyecto: "Rescate arqueológico en el cementerio de Chen Chen, Moquegua."* Instituto Nacional de Cultura.

Vásquez de Espinosa, A.
[1619] 1948 *Compendio y descripción de las Indias Occidentales*. Smithsonian Institution Press, Washington D.C.

Vela Velarde, C.
1992   Tiwanaku en el Valle de Caplina (Tacna). *Pumapunku* new series 1(3):31–45.

Vescelius, G.
1960   Notes on file. American Museum of Natural History, Department of Anthropology.

von Hagen, A., and C. Morris
1998   *The cities of the ancient Andes*. Thames and Hudson, New York.

Voorhies, B.
1989   *Ancient Trade and Tribute, Economies of the Soconusco Region of Mesoamerica*. University of Utah Press, Salt Lake City.

Vranich, A.
1997   Investigations at the temple of Pumapunku. Paper presented at the 16th Annual Northeast Conference on Andean Archaeology and Ethnohistory, University of Maine, Orono.
2000   The Creation and Recreation of Sacred Space in Tiwanaku. Paper presented at the Society for American Archaeology 65th annual meeting, Chicago.
2001   The Akapana Pyramid: Reconsidering Tiwanaku's Monumental Center. *Boletín de Arqueología, Pontificia Universidad Católica del Perú* 5: Huari y Tiwanaku: Modelos vs. Evidencias:295–308.

Wachtel, N.
1982   The Mitimas of the Cochabamba Valley: The Colonization Policy of Huayna Capac. In *The Inca and Aztec States, 1400–1800*, edited by G. Collier, R. Rosaldo, and J. Wirth, pp. 199–236. Academic Press, New York.
1986   Men of the water: The Uru problem (sixteenth and seventeenth centuries). In *Anthropological History of Andean Polities*, edited by J. V. Murra, pp. 283–310. Cambridge University Press, Cambridge.
1997   Nota sobre el problema de las identidades colectivas en los Andes Meridionales. In *Arqueología, antropología e historia en los Andes: Homenaje a María Rostworowski*, edited by R. Varón Gabai and J. F. Espinoza. Instituto de Estudios Peruanos, Banco Central de Reserva del Peru, Lima.

Wallace, D.
1957   The Tiahuanaco Horizon Styles in the Peruvian and Bolivian Highlands. Unpublished Ph.D. dissertation, Department of Anthropology, University of California.

Wallerstein, I.
1974   *The Modern World System.* Academic Press, New York.

Wassen, S. H.
1972   A Medicine-Man's Implements and Plants in a Tiahuanacoid Tomb in Highland Bolivia. *Etnologiska Studier* 32.

Watanabe M., L.
1990   Cerro Baúl: Un santuario de filiación Wari en Moquegua. In *Trabajos Arqueológicos en Moquegua, Perú*, edited by L. Watanabe M, M. E. Moseley, and F. Cabieses. Programa Constisuyo del Museo Peruano de Ciencias de la Salud y Southern Peru Copper Corporation, Lima.

Waylen, P. R., and C. N. Caviedes
1987   El Niño and annual floods in coastal Peru. In *Catastrophic Flooding*, edited by L. Mayer and D. Nash, pp. 57–87. John Wiley and Sons, New York.

Weberbauer, A.
1936   *Phytogeography of the Peruvian Andes.* Field Museum of Natural History Botanical Series, no. 351.

Webster, A. D.
1989   Preliminary Analysis of the Faunal Remains of Tiwanaku. Paper presented at the 17th Annual Midwest Conference on Andean and Amazonian Archaeology and Ethnohistory, Mt. Pleasant, Michigan.
1993   The Role of the South American Camelid in the Development of the Tiwanaku State. Unpublished Ph.D. dissertation, University of Chicago.

Webster, A. D., and J. W. Janusek
2003   Tiwanaku Camelids: Subsistence, Sacrifice and Social Reproduction. In *Tiwanaku and its Hinterland: Archaeology and Paleoecology of an Andean Civilization*, edited by A. L. Kolata, pp. 343–362. Vol. 2: *Urban and Rural Archaeology*. Smithsonian Institution Press, Washington, D.C.

Webster, D.
1998   Warfare and Status Rivalry: Lowland Maya and Polynesian Comparisons. In *Archaic States*, edited by G. M. Feinman and J. Marcus, pp. 311–352. School of American Research, Santa Fe.

Weiss, H., and T. C. Young
1975   The Merchants of Susa. *Journal of Persian Studies* 13:1–17.

Wheatley, P.
1971   *The Pivot of the Four Quarters.* Aldine, Chicago.

Wheatley, P., and T. See
1978   *From Court to Capital.* Aldine, Chicago.

Whitecotton, J. W.
1992   Culture and Exchange in Postclassic Oaxaca: A World-System Perspective. In *Resources, Power and Interregional Interaction*, edited by E. M. Schortman and P. A. Urban, pp. 51–74. Plenum Press, New York.

Wilcox, D. R.
1999   A Peregrine View of Macroregional Systems in the North American Southwest, A.D. 750–1250. In *Great Towns and Regional Polities: In the Prehistoric American*

Southwest and Southeast, edited by J. E. Neitzel, pp. 115–142. University of New Mexico, Albuquerque.

Williams, P. R.

1997   The Role of Disaster in the Development of Agriculture and the Evolution of Social Complexity in the South-Central Andean Sierra. Unpublished Ph.D. dissertation, Department of Anthropology, University of Florida.

2002   Rethinking Disaster-Induced Collapse in the Demise of the Andean Highland States: Wari and Tiwanaku. *World Archaeology* 33(3):361–374.

Williams, P. R., J. Isla C., and D. J. Nash

2001   Cerro Baúl: Un enclave Wari en interacción con Tiwanaku. *Boletín de Arqueología, Pontificia Universidad Católica del Perú* 5: Huari y Tiwanaku: Modelos vs. Evidencias:69–88.

Williams, P. R., M. E. Moseley, and D. J. Nash

2000   Empires of the Andes: A Majestic Frontier Outpost Chose Cooperation Over War. *Discovering Archaeology* 8.

Williams, S.

1990   *The Skeletal Biology of Estuquiña: A Late Intermediate Period Site in Southern Perú*. Northwestern University, Evanston, Ill.

Wilson, D. J.

1988   *Prehispanic Settlement Patterns in the Lower Santa Valley, Peru*. Smithsonian Institution Press, Washington, D.C.

Wise, K., N. R. Clark, and S. R. Williams

1994   Late Archaic Period Burial from the South-Central Andean Coast. *Latin American Antiquity* 5(3):212–227.

Wolf, E.

1982   *Europe and the People without History*. University of California Press, Berkeley.

Wright, H. T.

1977   Recent Research on the Origin of the State. *Annual Review of Anthropology* 6:379–397.

1994   Prestate Political Formations. In *Chiefdoms and Early States in the Near East: The Organizational Dynamics of Complexity*, edited by G. Stein and M. Rothman, pp. 67–84. Monographs in World Archaeology 18. Prehistory Press, Madison.

Wright, H. T., and G. A. Johnson

1975   Population, Exchange and Early State Formation in Southwestern Iran. *American Anthropologist* 77:267–289.

Wright, M. F., C. A. Hastorf, and H. A. Lennstrom

2003   Pre-Hispanic Agriculture and Plant Use at Tiwanaku: Social and Political Implications. In *Tiwanaku and its Hinterland: Archaeology and Paleoecology of an Andean Civilization*, edited by A. L. Kolata, pp. 384–402. Vol. 2: *Urban and Rural Archaeology*. Smithsonian Institution Press, Washington, D.C.

Yaeger, J., and M. Canuto (editors)

2000   *The Archaeology of Communities: A New World Perspective*. Routledge Press, London.

Yoffee, N.

1988   The Collapse of Ancient Mesopotamian States and Civilizations. In *The Collapse of Ancient States and Civilizations*, edited by N. Yoffee and G. L. Cowgill, pp. 44–68. University of Arizona Press, Tucson.

Zagarell, A.
1995   Hierarchy and Heterarchy: The Unity of Opposites. In *Heterarchy and the Analysis of Complex Societies*, edited by R. M. Ehrenreich, C. L. Crumley, and J. E. Levy, pp. 87–100. Archeological Papers of the American Anthropological Association no. 6. Washington, D.C.

Zeitlin, R. N., and A. A. Joyce
1999   The Zapotec-Imperialism Argument: Insights from the Oaxaca coast. *Current Anthropology* 40, no. 3 (June 1999): 383–92.

Zuidema, R. T.
1964   *The ceque system of Cuzco: the social organization of the capital of the Inca.* E. J. Brill, Leiden.

Index

Ritual—*continued*
  tality, 206–10, 230, 254, 296, 300, 304;
  and household artifacts, 198; and minia-
  tures, 296; and sovereignty, 19, procession,
  304; sponsorship and rank, 31, 208–9;
  state, 302–5; suzerainty, 20–21, 306–9,
  327. *See also* Aymara; Burials; Grave
  goods; Offerings
Rivera, M., xviii
Rocha, R., xvii
Rockpiles, 159, 211, 225–26
Rogers, D., xvii
Roman empire, 12
Rostworowski, M., 38, 164
Rowe, J., 69, 73
Rydén, S., 67, 72, 200

Sacaba valley, 99
Sacred landscapes and axes: and ayllus, 31;
  at Chen Chen site, 300, 301; at Chen
  Chen–style settlements, 160–61, 163;
  Inca, 271; Omo M10 temple, 299–301f.
  See also Ceques; Huacas
Sahumarios, 280. *See also* Incensarios
Saignes, T., 48
Salomon, F., 38, 46
Salta, 92
Sama valley, 46, 104, 176
Samegua, 178
Sandness, K., xix
San Lorenzo (AZ-75), 109, 215
San Miguel-Gentilar, 235
San Pedro de Atacama, 91–98, 241, 249,
  253, 266. *See also* Ayllus; Burials; Gold;
  Snuff tablets; Textiles
San Pedro negra pulida blackware, 95f, 96.
  See also Omo-style ceramics: Island of the
  Sun; Tiwanaku ceramics
Santa Valley, 120
Santiago de Machaca, 279
Santivañez Valley, 99
Santoro, C., xviii
Sarmiento de Gamboa, P., 58–59
Saucache, 107
Sausa, 185
Schneider, J., 16
Schreiber, K. J., 12
Sea mammals, 164

Segmentary social structure, 16, 19; in
  ayllus, 44–45; and community archaeology, 200; in ethnic barrios at Tiwanaku,
  188; and sacred landscapes, 163; San
  Pedro de Atacama, 98; Tiwanaku colonies, 179, 235; Tiwanaku core region, 77,
  82–83; and settlement pattern, 163. *See
  also* Social organization
Segmentary states, 20–22: African, 20; as
  agency models, 18; Maya, 20; South
  Asian, 21–22, 26; Tiwanaku as, 82–83,
  307–10, 327. *See also* Ritual: suzerainty
Segregation: in ancient states, 7; of
  Huaracane and Tiwanaku settlements,
  132, 316; of Omo and Chen Chen settlements, 190–93, 236
Semiprecious stones, 92, 108
Semisubterranean Temple (templete semi-
  subterraneo), 53f; as archetype, 277, 281;
  ashlar masonry, 273, 287; ceramic fragments, 71; colonial description, 52; construction date, 71, 277, 280; as cosmological map: 278; excavations, 64, 67;
  and huaca capture, 278; sculpture in,
  277–78, 292
Settlement patterns: Azapa Valley, 107–8;
  Chen Chen, 158–61, 163; Cochabamba,
  102; hierarchy and statehood, 8, 17;
  Huaracane, 123–25f; Moquegua
  Tiwanaku, 123t, 134–80 passim; Omo,
  199–200; survey methods, xviii, 119–20;
  San Pedro de Atacama, 97; Tiwanaku
  core region, 80–83; Tiwanaku site, 67;
  See also Chen Chen; Huaracane; Omo;
  States; Tumilaca; Wari
Shellfish. *See* Maritime resources
Sherd polisher, 199f, 201
Shining Path, 2
Shrines, 31, 161, 300. *See also* Apachetas;
  Ceques; Huacas; Sacred landscapes and
  axes
Sikuy kollu, 279
Sillumocco style, 86
Silver, 76–77, 117, 252; at Lukurmata, 281
Silverman, H., xix
Simillake, 280
Sinopoli, C., 10–12
Sinu artifacts, 24

Site destruction. *See* Burials; Rockpiles

Site formation processes: and preservation, 282, 289; and climate, 120–21; and sherd weights, 226

Skxala. *See* Raised fields

Smith, M. E., 12

Snuff tablets: Azapa, 105; Cochabamba, 102–3; San Pedro de Atacama, 92, 93f; 94; in stone sculpture, 75f, 76, 94. *See also* Grave goods

Social organization, 30; complexity, 241; endogamy, 44, 256, 316; and dress, 248–50, 255; and feasting, 208–9; rank and status, 91, 209, 238–42, 247, 259–66. *See also* Ayllus; Empires; Ethnicity; Identity; Multiethnicity; Segmentary states

Soil development, 120–21

Solcor ayllu, 98

Solidarity, 30

South Asia, 21–22, 310

Southall, A., 1, 20, 310

South-central Andes, 85f

Southern Peru Copper Corporation, xvii

Southwestern United States, 15

Sovereignty: nested, 19; ritual, 20

Spanish colonial period, 30, 113; chroniclers, 52; Moquegua agriculture, 178; Moquegua land claims, 114

Specialization. *See* Agriculture; Craft production

Spence, M., 29, 182

Spencer, Charles, xvii

Spindles and whorls: Chen Chen style, 222; Inca, 185; Omo style, 199f, 200

Spondylus, 38, 94; in Chen Chen Structure 14-1, 301; in Omo M10 temple, 298

Springs: Azapa Tiwanaku site location, 107; Omo M12, 154–55; recharge, 312; Río Muerto, 149. *See also* Agriculture; Floods; Settlement patterns; Water

Squier, E.G., 62–64

Staff god, 95. *See also* Gateway of the Sun

Stahl, P., 18

Stair-step motif, 277

Standardization. *See* Craft production

Stanish, Charles, xvii, xix, 171, 176, 177, 186

State expansion: Andean, 2; dynamics of, 6, 307, 325–26; diasporic model of, 6, 34, 310; ethnic groups and, 29, 307; evolutionary models, 306–7, 310; hegemonic and territorial strategies, 11–14, 27; and heterarchy, 22, 326; ideology of, 14; in mortuary record, 267–68; top-down interpretations, 8

States: and agency models, 18; and ayllu, 32, 307; definitions of, 19, 306–7; formation, xiii; and heterarchy, 22–23, 26, 44, 236, 256, 316; and hierarchy, 7, 12, 30–32, 83, 179, 239–44, 270, 276, 304; systemic models, 322; Maya, 19; segmentary, 20–22, 82–83, 307–10, 327. *See also* Agency models; Empires; Globalist models; Tiwanaku; World systems approaches

Stein, B., 306, 310, 326

Stein, G., 34, 36–37

Storage bins: Tumilaca, 227f, 230f, 231–32

Storage cists: Arani, 102; Chen Chen site M1, 217f–18f; Omo M10, 213f, 227f

Stratigraphy, 121

Structural reproduction, 44

Structuration, 182

Student assistants, xviii

Style. *See* Tiwanaku corporate style

Subsistence patterns: altiplano, 77–80; Chen Chen style, 216–21. *See also* Agriculture

Sumerian state, 9, 35. *See also* Mesopotamia; Uruk

Sumptuary goods, 13, 298. *See also* Elites, Exotic goods; Prestige goods exchange

Surface collections, 189, 190t

Susa, 35

Suzerainty, ritual, 20

Syria, 35

Tainter, J. A., 240

Tambiah, S., 20, 33

Tambos, 13, 178

Taraco, 86

Tattoos, 259. *See also* Face painting

Taypicala, 55, 315

Tazones: Chen Chen, 158, 159f, 223, 251–52f; San Pedro de Atacama, 93f, 94; Tiwanaku V, 74; Tumilaca style, 174, 175f

Technological style, 36

Paul S. Goldstein is associate professor of anthropology at the University of California, San Diego. He has published articles on the pre-Columbian archaeology of the Andes in journals including *Latin American Antiquity* and *Diálogo Andino*.